Creating an
Ethical Jewish Life

D0207807

Creating an Ethical Jewish Life

A Practical Introduction to Classic Teachings on How to Be a Jew

Byron L. Sherwin
Seymour J. Cohen

JEWISH LIGHTS Publishing
Woodstock, Vermont

Pages 293 and 294 constitute a continuation of this copyright information.

Creating an Ethical Jewish Life: A Practical Introduction to Classic Teachings on How to Be a Jew

© 2001 by Byron L. Sherwin and Seymour J. Cohen

All rights reserved. No part of this book may be reproduced or transmitted in any form or by any means, electronic or mechanical, including photocopying, recording, or by any information storage and retrieval system, without permission in writing from the publisher.

For information regarding permission to reprint material from this book, please mail or fax your request in writing to Jewish Lights Publishing, Permissions Department, at the address / fax number listed below.

Library of Congress Cataloging-in-Publication Data

Sherwin, Byron L.
[How to be a Jew]
Creating an ethical Jewish life : a practical introduction to classic teachings on how to be a Jew / Byron L. Sherwin, Seymour J. Cohen.
       p. cm.
Originally published: How to be a Jew. Northvale, N.J. : J. Aronson, c1992.
Includes bibliographical references and index.
ISBN 1-58023-114-4 (pbk.)
1. Ethics, Jewish—History—Sources. 2. Jewish literature—History and criticism. 3. Jewish literature. I. Cohen, Seymour J. II. Title.
BJ1280 .S47 2001
296.3'6—dc21

00-069008

10   9   8   7   6   5   4   3   2   1

Manufactured in the United States of America

Published by Jewish Lights Publishing
A Division of LongHill Partners, Inc.
Sunset Farm Offices, Route 4, P.O. Box 237
Woodstock, VT 05091
Tel: (802) 457-4000   Fax: (802) 457-4004
www.jewishlights.com

For
Naomi Greenberg Cohen
and
Judith Schwartz Sherwin
Loving Partners and Devoted Friends

Contents

Preface   ix

Introduction: Life as Art Form—An Invitation to
Jewish Ethical Values and Literature   xi

Part I
GOD

1. How to Believe in God   3
2. How to Thank God   15
3. How to Love God   29
4. How to Study the Torah   45
5. How to Repent   59

Part II
THE SELF

6. How to Deal with the Ego   81
7. How to Be Wise   97

8. How to Be Healthy   107

9. How to Employ Wealth   123

10. How to Die   135

Part III
THE SELF AND OTHERS

11. How to Behave Sexually   153

12. How to Treat One's Parents   163

13. How to Parent   177

14. How to Speak about Another   193

15. How to Be Philanthropic   211

Endnotes   237

References   275

Acknowledgments   293

Index   295

About Jewish Lights   303

Preface

This book has two goals: to introduce the major works and genre of Jewish ethical literature and to present some of that literature's fundamental concerns. While the texts cited and the ideas discussed in the following pages are of historical and conceptual interest, they were neither composed, nor were they formulated, for the intellectually curious. Rather, their intention is to offer a road map for the individual committed to the creation of the supreme art form—one's own life.

As this work has two goals, it also has two authors/editors: Byron L. Sherwin and Seymour J. Cohen. The conceptual organization of this volume was conceived by Seymour J. Cohen, who over many years has been engaged in the translation of classical works of Jewish ethical literature into English. Cohen's intention has been to provide the English reader access to the treasure-trove of Jewish ethical literature (i.e., to its most significant works and to its most compelling ideas). Besides giving form and direction to this volume, Cohen also contributed to Chapters 3, 9, 11, and 14. The balance of this work has been written and edited by me, except, of course, the excerpts from classical Jewish ethical literature that accompany each chapter. These excerpts were carefully chosen to introduce the reader to the breadth, depth, and variety of literary genre that characterize Jewish ethical literature. Additional discussion regarding the structure of this book is found at the end of the introduction.

One of the prominent teachings of Jewish ethics is the obligation of gratitude. Seymour Cohen and I would be remiss were we not to express gratitude to a number of individuals and organizations.

Profound thanks are due to the late David S. Malkov for helping to fund some of the research and writing costs related to the preparation of this work for publication. Deep thanks are also due to Rosaline Cohn and to the Cohn Scholars Fund of Spertus College of Judaica for their financial support for research-related costs.

My proficient and conscientious secretary, Pam Spitzner, and Seymour Cohen's steadfast and thorough secretary, Ingrid Hernandez, worked diligently and felicitously to prepare this manuscript for publication. Our families, especially our wives, Naomi Cohen and Judith Sherwin, deserve our immense gratitude for their forbearance and for their encouragement in the composition of this work. Seymour Cohen and I acknowledge and are grateful for permission to reprint excerpts from previously published materials.

I would be remiss were I not also to express my profound gratitude to my partner in this work, Seymour J. Cohen. Since my arrival in Chicago in 1970, he has been a faithful friend, colleague, and advisor. He introduced me to my wife Judith, and he has continuously been preoccupied with our well-being. During times of despair and professional difficulties, he has been a source of encouragement and help.

Finally, some technical points require elucidation. In a number of excerpted works, I have taken the liberty of altering the English style to make it more consonant with contemporary English usage. To avoid confusion, citations in excerpted texts from biblical and rabbinic sources have been standardized. Similarly, transliterations from those texts have also been standardized. The form of transliteration used is my own and should be of help both to the Hebrew and the non-Hebrew reader. A bibliography is provided at the end of the book to record works cited in its pages.

Byron L. Sherwin
Chicago, Illinois

Introduction

Life as Art Form – An Invitation to Jewish Ethical Values and Literature

The works that comprise Jewish ethical literature are self-help manuals in the art form of life. Their primary goal is not to inform, but to transform their readers. Their agenda addresses the most ultimate and the most intimate problems of human experience. They deal with the nature and expression of basic human emotions such as joy and love, anger and envy. They circumscribe and prescribe fundamental humane values such as humility and compassion. They address visceral human drives such as acquisitiveness and lust. They discuss and analyze social issues such as interpersonal communication and the employment of wealth. They confront perennially omnipresent human problems such as how to maintain integrity and how to retain dignity. They struggle to discern the purpose and meaning of human existence and to draw road maps toward their attainment. No human emotion, no human conflict, no moral problem eludes their grasp.

Rather than demonstrating how to accumulate wealth for oneself, Jewish ethical literature deals with how wealth may be employed for the benefit of others. Rather than offering strategies on how to manipulate others to do one's will, it focuses on how best to live a life correlative with the divine will. Rather than teaching one how to deliver a speech, it is preoccupied with how to speak without harming others by one's speech. Rather than offering ways of improving sexual technique, it formulates ways of enhancing love.

While old, the texts that comprise Jewish ethical literature are not obsolete. The questions they pose, the wisdom they impart, and the traditions they evoke often surprise their readers with unanticipated contemporaneity. While conditions of daily human life have changed since the time of their composition, the human condition has not substantially changed. The problems that vexed and challenged their authors continue to vex and to perplex us today.

For the authors of the classics of Jewish ethical literature, human existence is too precarious, life is too fragile, not to be taken with the utmost seriousness. In painting the portrait that is one's own life, a single reckless stroke can mar the entire work. Commenting on the verse in Ecclesiastes (9:8), "Let your garments be always white; let not oil be lacking on your head," a hasidic master observed, "A person should view himself as being dressed in white silken garments with a pitcher of oil on his head, walking a tightrope. A single wrong small step and he becomes soiled; a single irretrievable step and he falls into the abyss below."[1]

In his famous treatise, *Common Sense*, Thomas Paine wrote, "When we are planning for posterity, we ought to remember that virtue is not hereditary." An identical statement might have been penned by any of the authors of any one of the works of Jewish ethical literature. Like Thomas Paine, they knew that building one's life as a work of art is the product of continuous, deliberate choice and unstinting personal effort. In this regard, Israel Salanter, founder of the nineteenth-century *Musar* movement, compared continuous moral development to the flight of a bird. Once a bird stops exerting effort to fly, once a bird ceases flapping its wings, it falls. Similarly, Salanter observed that moral development, building one's life as a work of art, requires constant exertion, study, reflection, and practice.[2]

In the art of living, each individual is an apprentice. As Moses Maimonides said, "It is impossible for a person to be endowed by nature from birth with either virtue or vice, just as it is impossible that one should be skilled by nature in a particular art."[3] Life is an apprenticeship during which one has the opportunity to create the ultimate art form—one's own life.

According to Maimonides, the quest for human meaning, moral virtue, and artful existence cannot be acquired by proxy. Maimonides interpreted the well-known talmudic adage "If I am not for myself, who will be for me?" to mean that no one but one's own self can create the work of art that is one's own self.[4] Self-potential may only be realized by means of what the hasidic master Mendel of Kotsk called *arbiten auf sich*—working on oneself.[5]

The soul is a seed implanted within each of us. Each person is like a tree that may choose whether to bring forth its own fruit. At life's end, one may return a diminished form of what one received, or more than one received, at life's beginning. One has the choice to corrode or to create, to pollute or to improve, what one initially had been granted.[6]

While little Jewish genius was invested throughout the ages to create works of fine art, much Jewish genius and effort were expended on the endeavor to create lives that were works of art. Rather than concentrating on *things* of beauty, Jewish teachings focused on the creation of *people* of beauty. The primary goal was not physical prowess, or comely appearance, or even commercial success. Rather, the goal was to become a *shainer yid* – a beautiful Jew – to create one's life as a work of art.[7]

The Jewish people produced no edifices to rival Notre Dame, no paintings like those of Michelangelo or Raphael. The particular art form cultivated by the Jews was not architecture, painting, or sculpture, but human existence. The artistic masterpieces of the Jewish people do not hang in any museum. They appear in no tourist's guidebook. The great works of art that emerge from Jewish history are the lives and teachings of the greatest people it has engendered.

An artist viewing a great painting in a museum may stand in awe, gazing at its beauty, inspired by the artist's ability and creativity. Similarly, as Solomon Schechter observed, "the great saintly souls are lovely to look at just as a great piece of art is."[8]

In Greco-Roman thought, physical beauty was a good toward which one aspired. In Jewish thought, goodness is a form of beauty that one aimed to achieve. For much of secular Western aesthetics, art was a way of life. For Jewish thought, life is a way of art. Greco-Roman art elevated physical beauty over the moral act, how one appears over what one does, ontology over ethics. An example of this distinction between the Greco-Roman and the Jewish views of aesthetics was stated by Josephus in his commentary on 1 Samuel.

According to the biblical text, God sends Samuel to the place of Jesse of Bethlehem to seek out a king for Israel. Samuel sees Jesse's eldest son, Eliab, and believes him to be God's intended king. But God says to Samuel (1 Samuel 16:7), "Pay no attention to his appearance or to his stature, for I have rejected him. For not as man sees [does God see]; man sees only what is visible, but God sees into the heart." On this verse, Josephus commented and paraphrased: "God said to Samuel, 'You look at this young man's beauty, thinking none other than him is worthy to be king; but I make not of the kingdom a price for comeliness of body but for virtue of soul, and I seek one who in full measure is distinguished by this, one adorned with piety, justice, fortitude and obedience, qualities whereof beauty of the soul consists.' "[9] In this view, beauty is not determined by how one appears but by the deeds one performs. Not bodily appearance, but the values one embodies, is the criterion for determining beauty, goodness, and truth.

Great art is not simply the product of momentary inspiration. The apprentice artist who wishes to create a masterpiece of his or her own cannot rest content with a dazzled gaze at the masterpieces of the past. An apprentice must proceed to study the techniques that the master utilized in the composition of the work being admired. The apprentice must then analyze the masterpiece even more closely, studying the use of color, the subtlety of shade, the employment of lines and shapes. Still not content, the apprentice must compare the masterpiece to other works of the same master artist, or to other works of the same place and time as well as to those of different places and times. All of this is undertaken by the aspirant, with the hope and with the intention of being able to gain some insight and some knowledge to incorporate into his or her own artistic endeavors. But, study and analysis alone cannot suffice. Such study must be supplemented with constant practice. For the apprentice artist, neither talent nor skill, nor study, nor practice are sufficient in and of themselves. Only in concert can they converge to provide the potential for the emergence of a new great work of art.

Similarly, standing awestruck by the spiritual, intellectual, and moral achievements of the great personalities of the past will not suffice for one who desires to shape one's own life as a work of art. Like the novice artist, such an individual must proceed to study the masterpieces produced in the past in order to distill from them insight and information, wisdom, and inspiration that can be incorporated into the creation of one's own work of art, which, in this case, is one's own self. And, as in the case of the aspiring artist, the individual committed to cultivating the art of living cannot be satisfied with a terminal course of study. For such a person, each completion is the prelude to a new beginning; each graduation is a commencement. Continuous study, perpetual practice, and relentless self-development are the necessary ingredients toward the goal of artful living.

According to Scripture, the human being is created in the image of God (Genesis 1:26). Postbiblical Jewish religious literature takes this to mean that one should imitate the ways of God, that one should act in a godly manner, for example, "as God is merciful and compassionate, so should human beings be merciful and compassionate."[10] As God is creative, so too should human beings be creative. As God is an artist, so too should human beings be artists.

God's most superlative artwork is the human being. It is the human task to complete God's unfinished artistic masterpiece—the human person. Ethics is a way in which one creates life as a work of art. Each of us is an unfinished masterpiece of God. Like a master artist, God leaves completion of His works to His apprentices—to each of us. In a poem written on the occasion of a wedding, the ninth-century Italian Jewish poet, Ammitai ben Shephatiah, writes of God, the ultimate, awesome artist:

> A person sketches a form on the wall
> decorating it with colors, yellow and red.
> Where it is put, there must it remain.
> It stays: permanent, transfixed,
> whether its foot is gnarled or broken.

It neither speaks, nor sees, nor hears.
But God is an awesome artist:
He can create form within form
perfect and complete in every way,
capable of perception and movement.
In a pregnant woman's womb
So does He shape the embryo.[11]

The works that constitute Jewish ethical literature are masterpieces that can be perused for inspiration, studied for information, and consulted for wisdom that can be incorporated in the development of artful living. The masters who composed these works were maestros in the art of life. Blending personal quests with past wisdom, combining individual experience with inherited knowledge, they addressed the ultimate human moral issue, the most intimate personal question: How can I best live the life God has entrusted into my care?

Despite the various literary forms it adapts and the diverse views it represents, Jewish ethical literature coheres around the idea that the crucial challenge to human existence is how to manage the trust of life deposited into each of our hands. Like composers who create different melodies from various configurations of the same notes, these authors articulate a variety of visions of what and of how the individual artwork of life may be configured. However, what they share is the sense of urgency and immediacy of the challenge of initiating the enterprise of spiritual and moral self-development. For these authors, since life is like a blind date with an uncertain future, each moment is considered a summons to begin or to continue the process of self-development.

Hillel said, "If not now, when?" Commenting on this statement, a medieval Jewish writer observed that Hillel did not say, "If not today, when?" but "If not now, when?" because "even today is in doubt whether one will survive or not, for at any instant one can die."[12] Consequently, "one cannot wait even a day or two to exert oneself in the pursuit of human fulfillment."[13] This attitude is similar to that articulated by Benjamin Franklin, who advised, "Since you are not sure of a moment, throw not away an hour."

For Jewish tradition, the encounter with the tenuous nature of human life, with the reality of our own mortality, is not meant to be an invitation to morbidity, but a collision with realities that can serve as catalysts for human self-development. Being conscious of human finitude when set against the infinite plenitude of creation causes one to pause to consider how to infuse meaning into the blink of eternity that is each human life. At birth, each human person is issued a passport to transcendence, an invitation to develop one's own life as a work of art. The disposition of each human life depends on whether one chooses to accept this invitation, to make use of this passport.

Jewish ethical literature offers a variety of tour guidebooks for the journey through life.[14]

WHAT CONSTITUTES JEWISH ETHICAL LITERATURE?

One may characterize Jewish ethical literature as those works and excerpts of works from classical Jewish religious literature that address the problem of how to create an artful existence.

Unlike other characterizations of Jewish ethical literature that more narrowly circumscribe its perimeters, this approach assigns a wide port of entry to bibliographical candidates seeking inclusion. This approach considers the often sharp division among Jewish ethics, law, philosophy, and mysticism to be largely artificial.[15] While this approach would certainly include ethical treatises *per se* under its umbrella, it would not exclude extensive selections from Jewish legal codes and responsa that deal with moral issues under its purview. For example, discrete, moral treatises such as Solomon ibn Gabirol's *Improvement of Moral Virtues* would merit inclusion, but so would sections of Maimonides' legal code, the *Mishneh Torah*, that address undeniably ethical issues, such as "*Hilkhot De'ot*" ("Laws of Ethical Behavior"). Similarly, responsa treating ethical issues, for example, those treating problems in medical ethics, would also qualify for inclusion.

It is difficult, if not impossible, to surgically separate Jewish law and ethics. They are two sides of the same coin. The often-evoked distinction between law as *what* to do and ethics as *how* or *why* to do, simply does not stand up to a careful analysis of the literature.[16] Legal codes and responsa often discuss motivation and attitude, while ethical treatises often prescribe precise behavior. Such a distinction between Jewish law and ethics is often contrived.[17] Furthermore, the often-made claim that many Jewish ethical treatises were composed to challenge and to undermine halakhic authority cannot be supported by the sources. Such treatises simply intend to complement and to strengthen Jewish legal commitment. Rather than existing in opposition, Jewish law and ethics coexist as part of the organic and historical continuity of the Jewish tradition.

Though one may admit the existence of a discrete Jewish philosophical-ethical literature, this should not exclude excerpts of other philosophical or mystical works from the bibliography of Jewish ethical literature.[18] For example, Bahya ibn Pakudah's *Duties of the Heart* is justifiably considered a classic of Jewish philosophical-ethical literature despite the fact that large sections of this work deal with metaphysical and not with specifically ethical issues. On the other hand, excerpts on ethics from Jewish philosophical works that deal primarily with metaphysical issues should be included as part of Jewish ethical literature, for example, the short last chapter of Abraham ibn Daud's *Exalted Faith (Ha-Emunah ha-Ramah)* entitled "Healing the Soul."

As one cannot easily bifurcate Jewish law and Jewish ethics, one cannot clinically separate Jewish theological and Jewish ethical concerns. As a form of theological or religious ethics, Jewish ethics inevitably rests on certain theological premises.[19] It is precisely for this reason that before he can specifically address ethical issues in his *Duties of the Heart*, Bahya ibn Pakudah must first treat fundamental principles of Jewish theological concern such as the existence and nature of God.

The theological claims that God exists, that His will has been revealed through the Torah, and that human beings have been created in the divine image are premises assumed by discussions of Jewish ethical values, attitudes, and deeds. To address Jewish ethical concerns without reference to their theological underpinnings is to posit conclusions without premises, to state a fallacy. In the edifice of Jewish religious thought, theological premises establish a foundation. Jewish ethics builds upon that foundation.

The insistence that human beings act in a godlike manner, that human moral action "imitate the ways of God" (imitatio Dei), presumes a prior formulation of the nature of the divine and His preferred actions.[20] Jewish theology and Jewish ethics, Jewish theological and Jewish ethical literature, are often too inextricably intertwined to accommodate the neatly imposed, clinically discrete categories of much of contemporary, critical scholarship. An example of how Jewish law, ethics, mysticism, and theology may all be interwoven in a single text may be demonstrated by consideration of the meaning of a phrase found in various kabbalistic texts. This phrase simply identifies the *mitzvot* and the *middot*. In Nahmanides' words, "the *mitzvot* are the *middot*."[21]

Mitzvot are the commandments, the laws. By performing the *mitzvot*, a human being imitates the ways of God. He or she becomes godlike. In medieval Hebrew, *middot* (singular: *middah*) has two prominent meanings. One refers to ethical values or to moral qualities of the human soul. The other refers to divine attributes.[22] In kabbalistic literature, the term refers specifically to the *sefirot*, the manifested attributes of God expressed through the emanations or divine potencies.[23]

In this view, the laws of the Torah, the ethical values of the Torah, and the divine attributes are conceptually inseparable; they are organically linked. Through observance of God's commandments, by performance of the moral virtues, one imitates and sustains the divine attributes from which these laws and values originally derive.[24]

Beginning in the sixteenth century, the quest for the artful life is conceived as having three facets: the relationship of the individual to his or her own self, the relationship of the individual to others, and the relationship of the individual to the divine. In this view, the division between the theological and the ethical is clearly inappropriate. From this perspective, the human-divine relationship is a critical aspect of the artful life, of moral existence. Ethical living requires the cultivation of the moral virtues and of interpersonal relationships, but is incomplete without a relationship with the divine. This approach is encountered in biblical and talmudic commentaries.[25] Hence, excerpts from relevant biblical and talmudic commentaries must also be embraced by a bibliography and by a conceptual framework of Jewish ethical literature. The talmudic text that spawned these commentaries is as follows:

> Rabbi Judah said: He who wishes to be pious must fulfill the laws of *Seder Nezikin* [one of the six sections of the Mishnah; it deals with tort law]. But Raba said: [He who wishes to be pious must fulfill] the matters [dealt with in tractate] *Avot*. Still others said: [He who wishes to be pious must fulfill] matters [dealt with in tractate] *Berakhot* [that deals with laws of blessings].[26]

Commenting on this text, Samuel Edels ("Maharsha"), a leading Polish talmudist of the late sixteenth and early seventeenth century, wrote:

> A person can perform three kinds of pious deeds. These are: good [deeds] to Heaven, and good [deeds] to others, and good [deeds] to oneself. As Rabbi Judah said, one who wishes to be pious must fulfill the laws of *Nezikin*, for then one will be able to perfect one's deeds so that one will be good to others. And Raba said to fulfill the matters in *Avot*, for then one will be able to perfect one's deeds so that one will be good to oneself in [performing] the moral virtues. Still others said: Fulfill the matters in *Berakhot*, for then one will be able to perfect oneself so that one will be good to Heaven. Each one of these views reflects a single one of these three varieties of good deeds that one can perform.[27]

Edels's commentary to this talmudic passage was anticipated by the sixteenth-century Jewish mystic, Judah Loew of Prague. In his commentary to the Talmud, Loew observed:

> The explanation of this [text is] that human perfection has three independent aspects. A person must be complete within himself, complete within his relationship with other people, and he must be complete within his relationship to his Creator, i.e., in matters that relate to his Creator. These three aspects of completion [i.e., perfection] include everything. This matter is explained further in "Moses received."[28]

Loew's reference to his further elucidation of this matter in "Moses received" refers to his commentary on the text "Moses received" found in the *Ethics of the Fathers*. There, Loew wrote:

> Man must achieve the good which is his purpose, thereby justifying his existence, and when his existence has been justified, the whole universe has been justified, since all hinges on man. . . . Therefore, a person should endeavor to cultivate good qualities. And what makes a person "good" so that one might say of him: What a fine creature he is! One requirement is that he must be good in relation to himself. . . . The second category of good is that he be good toward the Lord who created man to serve Him and to do His will. The third category is that he be good to others. For a person does not exist by himself. He exists in fellowship with other people. . . . A person is not complete until he is completely pious vis-à-vis these three varieties of [human] perfection: with his Creator, with other people, and with himself as well. Then he is completely perfect.[29]

Thus, both Edels and Loew divide the moral virtues into three kinds: personal virtues, religious virtues, and social virtues. They portray three aspects of moral behavior: the individual's relation to God, the individual's relationship to himself or herself, and the individual's relationship to others.

The structure of this volume follows that suggested by Loew and Edels. Each of the three parts addresses the three areas of Jewish ethical concern, as stated above. Each part consists of five chapters, and each chapter deals with a particular Jewish ethical value addressed by that general area of ethical concern. Each chapter consists of an excerpt from Jewish ethical literature, preceded by a presentation of the ethical issue under discussion in the excerpt, the nature of the work from which the excerpt derives, the genre of Jewish ethical literature it represents (where relevant), and the life and contributions of its author.

In choosing excerpted texts, an effort has been made to offer diversity in terms of literary genre, as well as to include material from works that would be prominently featured in any bibliography of Jewish ethical literature. Each chapter title contains the term "how to" so as to express the view that the works that comprise Jewish ethical literature are "how-to" manuals in creating an artful life. By focusing each chapter on an excerpt from an important work and genre of Jewish ethical literature, the texts are provided an opportunity to "speak for themselves" without an overlay of critical embellishment.

I

God

1

How to Believe in God

J ewish ethics is a form of theological or religious ethics. As such, it rests
upon certain theological premises. The most fundamental theological
premise is the existence of God. For example, in Bahya ibn Pakudah's
Duties of the Heart—one of the mainstays of Jewish ethical literature—the
author reports that he searched for a concept that serves as the pillar of Jewish
ethics and theology. He found this in the idea of the existence of one God
who created the universe. In Bahya's words, "When I searched for the most
important pillar of our religion and the main root, I found this basic principle
in the pure assertion of the unity of our Creator. This is the first article of the
Torah. This assertion is the chief truth of our religion."[1] Similarly, Moses
Maimonides in his legal code, the *Mishneh Torah*, describes the belief in God's
existence as the basis of all theology and philosophy; indeed, of all knowledge. Maimonides wrote, "The basic principle of all basic principles and the
pillar of all knowledge is to recognize that there is a First Being [i.e., God] who
brought everything into being."[2]

Bahya and Maimonides affirm Judaism as a theistic faith, grounded in the
claim that God is; that the world is because God is; that there is evidence of
design, purpose, and meaning in the world and in human existence; that this
design and purpose are the compositions of a Designer; and that moral norms
that provide human life with meaning and purpose inhere in the Designer
(i.e., God).[3]

Judaism affirms a partisan view of reality, while tenaciously rejecting
alternative views that deny the existence of God, that disclaim a purposeful
creation, and that rebuff the affirmation that human existence has intrinsic

3

meaning. Like the British essayist G. K. Chesterton, Judaism holds that one who can believe in nothing, can believe in anything. In Jewish religious thought, the alternative to the theistic view is to affirm the existence of the universe as a sheer, unexplained brute fact, to posit either that the universe and human life have no intrinsic purpose or that such purpose is either merely apparent or a human contrivance, that moral norms inhere only in the morally precarious realm of human invention, and that the religious experience of humankind throughout the ages is but one grand delusion. In the final analysis, the theist and the nontheist disagree about more than the issue of whether or not God exists. They are divided by fundamentally different philosophies of existence.

For the theist, a reasonable means of explaining how and why we are here and what we ought to do here is available. For the nontheist, the burdens of explaining *how* and *why* we are here, and *what* the purpose of our being here is, remain open questions. The theist affirms meaning, purpose, and the presence of road maps for creating the artful life, while the nontheist must discover and build a life upon his or her own fabrications.

Neither the theist nor the nontheist can "prove" the truth of his or her position. But, the theist offers a way of explaining the universe and the human place in it. The nontheist may discard the theist's position, may reject the theist's premises and conclusions. Nevertheless, the nontheist must do more than simply debunk the theist's view. The nontheist must establish a basis for explaining how the universe came to be, from where human purpose may be derived, and how moral norms might be discerned. For the theist, the ultimate question is how to live a life consistent with the Creator's purpose, how to create an artful existence from the life entrusted into his or her care. The nontheist, on the other hand, might be led to affirming with the French existentialist Albert Camus that, "there is but one major philosophical problem and that is whether or not to commit suicide."[4] The nontheist might be led to Macbeth's view that "Life's but a walking shadow, a poor player that struts and frets his hour upon the stage and is heard no more. It is a tale told by an idiot, full of sound and fury, signifying nothing."[5]

For the theist, there is intrinsic meaning in human existence precisely because there is a God who created the world with purpose and meaning. For the nontheist, human meaning, like human life, indeed, like the universe itself, may be a product of chance, an accident waiting to happen. In this regard, Bahya observes that if we read a beautifully written poem, we cannot assume that it came to be as the result of ink spilled by accident onto a sheet of paper, conveniently situated nearby. Instead, we conclude from reading the manuscript that it has an author. Similarly, we conclude that the universe has an Author, that its composition expresses the Author, and that the Author had a purpose in composing it.[6] In a similar vein, the twentieth-century philosopher Ludwig Wittgenstein wrote, "To believe in God means to understand the question about the meaning of life. To believe in God means to see that the facts of the world are not the end of the matter. To believe in God means to see that life has a meaning."[7]

For the nontheist, an autonomous basis for morality must be affirmed for moral behavior to be justified. For the theist, the existence of God serves as the ultimate source of and justification for moral behavior. For example, a rabbinic text interprets the well-known verse from Leviticus (19:18)—"You should love your neighbor as yourself; I am the Lord"—to mean: "You should love your neighbor as yourself *because* I am the Lord, because I [God] have created him."[8]

Different expressions of Jewish religious thought offer a variety of understandings of the basis for belief in God. For example, the medieval Jewish philosophical tradition adapted a largely cognitive approach to belief in God. Many of its advocates attempted to demonstrate belief in God on the basis of logic and reason. According to Bahya, for example, faith without reason, belief devoid of cognitive understanding, is incomplete and is unworthy of the truly enlightened believer. For Bahya, faith grounded in tradition alone, or in an irrational "leap of faith," is akin to the blind leading the blind. Rather, one must look before one leaps. According to Bahya, faith through reason grants sight to the blind.[9] Faith without reason is not true belief.

The medieval Jewish philosophers were not trying to demonstrate the existence of God from scratch. Instead, they were attempting to provide a rational and logical demonstration for that which they already believed. For these philosophers, faith unaccompanied by reasonable belief is not real faith at all. It is merely a matter of personal preference. However, for the majority of Jewish religious thinkers, to demonstrate that which is already believed is deemed superfluous.[10] For many Jewish thinkers who affirmed God as the ultimate reality, demonstrating the existence of God is as unnecessary as a lover having to prove the existence of his beloved. Or, as the Danish philosopher Kierkegaard observed: What can be more impertinent than to interrupt an audience with an enthroned King to debate the King's existence?

Beginning with the Hebrew Bible, the dominant form of Jewish belief in God has been belief rooted in a personal commitment, rather than in the affirmation of intellectual propositions. Neither biblical nor rabbinic theology attempt to adduce any demonstrations for the existence of God. Most ancient and medieval Jewish thinkers posited faith in God based on revelation as transmitted by tradition. In the following excerpts, Judah Ha-Levi articulates this approach. Like other advocates of this view, Ha-Levi finds revelation, tradition, and personal commitment to be more reliable foundations for faith in God than reason alone. Reason, in this view, is a tool that can examine the validity of an argument but is incapable of establishing the validity of the premises of an argument. God, who transcends the world, certainly transcends the categories of reason and logic into which a philosopher may attempt to encapsulate Him. In the final analysis, cognitive belief in God is tenuous. Just as such belief can be established on the basis of philosophical demonstrations, so it can be eroded or even dispelled by philosophical demonstrations. Grounding faith in cognitive belief alone can lead to a rejection of the very faith and life-style cognitive belief is invoked to justify and to defend.[11]

The cognitive approach leads to a rational confirmation of the proposition that "God exists." But, what is of greater import to the Jewish religious thinker is the relationship between belief and action. In this view, intellectual affirmation of theological propositions constitutes an incomplete expression of faith, since it does not necessarily engender moral action. What is more important is belief as a result of a personal decision, as an expression of the moral will. In Nahmanides' words, "Faith in the existence of God, which He demonstrated to us with signs, with miracles, and through revelation, is the essence and the origin from which the commandments derive."[12] From this perspective, *how* one lives, rather than the cogency of the propositions one affirms, offers a validation or a refutation of one's stated personal commitments.

The dominant approach to religious belief in Judaism is not exclusively cognitive but experiential. From this perspective, there are two major varieties of experience: inherited experience (i.e., tradition), and personal experience. What binds these two together is memory. In Judaism, faith is grounded in memory. Hebrew Scripture does not command belief in God, but enjoins us to remember experiences of the divine.

Belief in God is not simply a personal endeavor. It is an effort accumulated over the centuries; it is the achievement of a continuity of the ages. Jewish belief is a recollection of events in the life of the Jewish people. Not abstract ideas, but memory of concrete events is the touchstone of Jewish belief:

> Take heed to yourself, and keep yourself diligently, lest you forget the things your eye saw, and lest they depart from your heart all the days of your life, make them known to your children and your children's children (Deuteronomy 4:9).

In the Passover liturgy for the *Seder*, called the *Haggadah*, one encounters the notion that Jewish belief is predicated upon memories rather than upon inferred propositions. In this liturgy, as in other Jewish liturgies, religious belief is predicated upon the memory of a historical event, in this case, the liberation of the Jewish people from Egyptian bondage. Faith in the present is expressed through recollection of the past. The events of the past become internalized in the present. As the Passover *Haggadah* puts it,

> In every generation each Jew is obliged to regard himself as though he personally went forth from Egypt. As it is written: And you shall tell your son on that day saying—It is because of what the Lord did for me when I went forth out of Egypt (Exodus 13:8). It was not only our forefathers whom the Holy One, blessed be He, redeemed from slavery, but us too did He redeem together with them.[13]

By recalling the past, the experiences of our ancestors become our experiences; our forebears become our contemporaries. By our appropriation of their experience, the faith derived from that experience becomes our own. Ancient moments become contemporary events. Transmitted memories become personal experiences. Memory of past events makes faith in the present possible.

Without the collective memories that constitute tradition, individual faith is impoverished. Tradition offers one a treasure house of accumulated memories. However, tradition devoid of personal memory and experience can easily allow belief to degenerate into habit.[14]

The *Shema* prayer asks us to love God with all of our heart. Solomon Schechter once observed that this indicates that faith must be a personal, as well as an inherited, experience. One must love God with one's own heart, not with one's ancestor's heart. Similarly, some Jewish prayers begin by evoking, "the God of Abraham, the God of Isaac, and the God of Jacob." One commentator suggests that each of the patriarchs is evoked because each arrived at belief in God in his own individual way. Isaac and Jacob inherited belief from Abraham, but each also formulated his relationship with the divine in his own particular way.[15] Belief includes that which is inherited from others and that which is initiated by oneself: "This is my God and I will extol Him; the God of my father and I will exalt Him" (Exodus 15:2). In the final analysis, neither inherited belief alone, nor cognitive belief alone, but rather personal experience serves as the ultimate foundation for religious faith. As the nineteenth-century Lithuanian Rabbi Simhah Zussel of Kelm wrote, "Even the wisest of people is not so much impressed with a truth grasped merely with the head as with a truth experienced in a personal way (as the Israelites did in the time of Mordecai and Esther)."[16]

❧

Belief in God through a combination of inherited tradition and personal experience is the view taken by Judah Ha-Levi in the *Kuzari*, from which an excerpt is cited below. The *Kuzari*, written in Arabic in the twelfth century, is in the form of a dialogue between a rabbi and the king of the Khazars, a people who lived in a large kingdom near the Caspian Sea, and whose leaders

converted to Judaism in the ninth century. The book opens with the king of
the Khazars having a disturbing dream. In this dream, an angel appears and
informs him, "Your intention is pleasing to the Creator, but your actions are
not pleasing." After the dream recurs, the king decides that the religion he
has been practicing must be exchanged for another. Consequently, he
decides to examine other beliefs and religions. After a dialogue with a
philosopher, a Muslim, and a Christian, he finds himself still in search of a
faith that will satisfy his quest. Reluctantly, he turns to a rabbi. Perhaps the
faith he is seeking is Judaism. Most of the book consists of a dialogue between
the king and the rabbi on the nature of Jewish faith. Eventually, the king
becomes convinced that Judaism offers not only the proper "intentions" (i.e.,
ideas), but also the actions that are "pleasing" to the Creator.

Unlike the Christian and the Muslim who refer to the God of Creation,
and unlike the philosopher who refers to the possibility that God is the First
Cause, the rabbi begins his discourse with an appeal to history, to experience.
When the king expresses his surprise at the rabbi's comparatively unconven-
tional approach to faith, the rabbi amplifies his view.

The rabbi explains that the surest foundation for faith is not abstract,
philosophical speculation, but concrete, human experience. Faith, in this
view, cannot be based upon reflections about how the world came into being
or upon other issues removed from actual experience. For Ha-Levi, faith
rooted in experience and tradition may be understood as the collective
experience of many people over an extended period of time. It is for this
reason, Ha-Levi explains, that God did not begin the Ten Commandments
by stating, "I am the Lord your God who created the world." No one
witnessed or experienced the creation of the world; no human person was
there. God's creation of the world may be demonstrated by means of rational
inference, but it is not ascertainable through direct human experience. The
Ten Commandments begin with the statement, "I am the Lord your God
who took you out of the land of Egypt" (Exodus 20:2) because the liberation
from Egypt, and the subsequent revelation at Sinai, were events experienced
by the Jewish people en masse.[17] Tradition has conveyed the memory of this
experience to later generations of Jews. Belief in revelation and redemption
are not abstract propositions of faith, but beliefs rooted in the actual
experiences of those who witnessed them and those who transmitted the
memory of these experiences to their descendants. For Ha-Levi, Jewish faith
is grounded in historical events rather than in philosophical propositions.
Individual faith is not predicated upon assent to abstract propositions, but it
is based upon experiences in the life of the individual, in memories of events
in the lives of the individual's forebears, and in the internalization of the
memory of historical events within the life of the individual. As is cited
below, the "rabbi" of the Kuzari says to the king, "I answered you as was fitting

and is fitting for the whole of [the people of] Israel, who know these things from personal experience, and afterwards through uninterrupted tradition, which is equal to the former."

The second excerpt below from Ha-Levi's works is a poem entitled, "Lord, Where Shall I Find You?" Here, Ha-Levi does not discuss the basis for belief in God, but rather he describes the relationship between the individual believer and God. For religious faith, what is of ultimate importance is not the existence of God, but the individual's relationship with the divine. Not affirming intellectual propositions but living a life consistent with one's beliefs, not only in faith but with *faithfulness* to one's relationship with God, are the primary concerns of religious thinking. To the religious person, what is of primary concern is not rational cognition of God's existence, but living a life in partnership with God and co-creating with God an improved world and an improved self.

In the poem, "Lord, Where Shall I Find You?" Ha-Levi depicts two aspects of the human relationship with God. On the one hand, God is transcendent, beyond comprehension, beyond the realm of our senses. On the other hand, God is immanent, available, closer to us than we are to ourselves. We may perceive God as being far away, but as soon as we strike out to commune with Him, we find Him rushing toward us: "When I went toward You, I found You coming towards me," Ha-Levi writes. Solomon ibn Gabirol, the great medieval Jewish poet and philosopher, goes even further. According to Ibn Gabirol, even when we flee from God, we are actually running unawares toward Him. In his classic poem *The Kingly Crown (Keter Malkhut)*, Ibn Gabirol writes, "I flee from You, to You."[18]

Judah Ha-Levi was born probably in the 1070s in Muslim Spain, probably in Toledo, possibly in Tudela. He earned his living as a physician and tradesman, and appears to have enjoyed a modicum of financial security. The *Kuzari*, twenty years in the writing, was Ha-Levi's prose *magnum opus*. Originally entitled, "The Book of Argument and Proof in Defense of the Despised Faith," and written in Arabic, this book was translated into Hebrew in the middle of the twelfth century by Judah ibn Tibbon.[19] Generally known as *Sefer ha-Kuzari*, the *Book of the Khazars*, this work achieved immense popularity, influencing future Jewish philosophy and mysticism. Shlomo Dov Goiten, an eminent twentieth-century Jewish scholar, described the *Kuzari* as "the most authentic exposition of Judaism in existence."[20]

Ha-Levi is considered by many to be the greatest Hebrew poet of the Middle Ages. We cannot be sure how many poems he composed during his literary career. However, about 800 poems of his are currently known and more may yet be discovered. Ha-Levi's surviving poetry includes both secular and religious poetry. About 350 of his *piyyutim*, or religious poems, have survived, including the poem, "Lord, Where Shall I Find You?" found below.

Some of Ha-Levi's religious poetry has been included in the traditional Jewish liturgy. A central theme both in Ha-Levi's poetry and in the *Kuzari* is the centrality of the Land of Israel to Judaism and the longing of the Jewish people (and of Ha-Levi himself) for the Holy Land. Ha-Levi's concern with the Land of Israel led him to leave Spain for Palestine in 1139. It does not seem, however, that Ha-Levi ever reached his destination. He seems to have died *en route* in 1140 or 1141. Legend describes him reaching Jerusalem only to be murdered by an Arab horseman while he was reciting the elegy he composed to Zion, traditionally recited as part of the *Tisha B'Av* liturgy.

Judah Ha-Levi
Kuzari

I was asked to state what arguments I could bring to bear against the attacks of philosophers and followers of other religions which differ from ours and against the sectaries who differ from the majority of Israel. And I remembered the arguments I had heard of a Rabbi who sojourned with the King of the Khazars, who, as we know from historical records, became a convert to Judaism about four hundred years ago: to him there appeared repeatedly a dream, in which it seemed as if an angel addressed him saying: "Thy [intention] is indeed pleasing to the Creator, but thy way of acting is not pleasing." Yet he was so zealous in the performance of the Khazar religion, that he devoted himself with a perfect heart to the service of the temple and the sacrifices. Notwithstanding this devotion, the angel came again at night and repeated: "Thy intention is indeed pleasing, but thy way of acting is not pleasing." This induced him to ponder over the different beliefs and religions, and finally he became a convert to Judaism together with many other Khazars. As I found among the arguments of the Rabbi many which appealed to me and were in harmony with my opinions, I resolved to write them down as they had been spoken. The intelligent will understand me. . . .

[The King then inquires of a philosopher, a Christian and a Muslim. Finding no acceptable response to his problem, the King reluctantly inquires of a Jew.]

[The King of the Khazars] Al Khazari: Indeed, I see myself compelled to ask the Jews, because they are the descendants of the Israelites. For I see that they constitute in themselves the evidence for the divine law on earth.

He [i.e., the king] then invited a rabbi, and asked him about his belief.

The Rabbi replied. I believe in the God of Abraham, Isaac and Israel, who led the children of Israel out of Egypt with signs and miracles; who fed them in the desert and gave them the land [i.e., Israel], after having made them traverse the sea and the Jordan in a miraculous way; who sent Moses with His law, and subsequently thousands of prophets, who confirmed His law by promises to the observant, and threats to the disobedient. Our belief is comprised in the Torah—a very large domain.

Al Khazari: I had not intended to ask any Jew, because I am aware of their reduced condition and narrow-minded views, as their misery has deprived them of all commendable qualities. Now, Jew, should you rather have said that you believe in the Creator of the world, its Governor and Guide, and in Him who created and keeps you, and such attributes which serve as evidence for every believer, and for the sake of which he pursues justice in order to resemble the Creator in His wisdom and justice?

The Rabbi: That which you express is speculative and political religion, to which inquiry leads, but it is open to many doubts. Now ask the philosophers, and you will find that they do not agree on a single action or principle, since some doctrines can be established by arguments, which are only plausible, and some even capable of being proved.

Al Khazari: That which you say now, O Jew, seems to be more to the point than the beginning. I should like to hear more.

The Rabbi: Surely the beginning of my speech was just the proof, the evidence that makes further argument superfluous.

Al Khazari: How so?

The Rabbi: Allow me to make a few preliminary remarks, for I see you are disregarding and depreciating my words.

Al Khazari: Let me hear your remarks.

The Rabbi: If you were told that the King of India was an excellent man, commanding admiration, and deserving his noble reputation, one whose actions were reflected in the justice which rules his country and the virtuous ways of his subjects, would this compel you to revere him?

Al Khazari: How could this bind me, while I am not sure if the justice of the Indian people is natural, and not dependent on their king, or due to the king or both?

The Rabbi: But if his messenger came to you bringing

presents which are known to be only procurable in India, and in the royal palace, accompanied by a letter in which it is distinctly stated from whom it comes, and to which are added drugs to cure your diseases, to preserve your health, poisons for your enemies, and other means to fight and kill them without battle, would this make you beholden to him?

Al Khazari: Certainly. For this would remove my former doubt that the Indians have a king. I should also acknowledge that a proof of his power and dominion has reached me.

The Rabbi: How would you, then, if asked, describe him?

Al Khazari: In terms about which I am quite clear, and to these I could add others which were at first rather doubtful, but are no longer so.

The Rabbi: In this way I answered your first question. In the same strain spoke Moses to Pharaoh, when he told him: "The God of the Hebrews sent me to you," that is, the God of Abraham, Isaac and Jacob. For Abraham was well known to the nations, who also knew that the divine spirit was in contact with the patriarchs, cared for them, and performed miracles for them. He did not say: "The God of heaven and earth," not "my Creator and yours sent me." In the same way God commenced His speech to the assembled people of Israel: "I am the God whom you worship, who has led you out of the land of Egypt," but He did not say: "I am the Creator of the world and your Creator." Now in the same style I spoke to you, a Prince of the Khazars, when you asked me about my creed. I answered you as was fitting, and is fitting for the whole of [the people of] Israel who knows these things from personal experience, and afterwards through uninterrupted tradition, which is equal to the former.

Judah Ha-Levi
"Lord, Where Shall I Find You?"

Lord, where shall I find You? Your place is lofty and secret. And where shall I not find You? The whole earth is full of Your glory!

You are found in man's innermost heart, yet You fixed earth's boundaries. You are a strong tower for those who are near, and the trust of those who are far. You are enthroned on the cherubim, yet You dwell in the heights of heaven. You are praised by Your hosts, but even their praise is not worthy of

You. The sphere of heaven cannot contain You; how much less the chambers of the Temple!

Even when You rise above Your hosts on a throne, high and exalted, You are nearer to them than their own bodies and souls. Their mouths attest that they have no Maker except You. Who shall not fear You? All bear the yoke of Your kingdom. And who shall not call to You? It is You who give them their food.

I have sought to come near You, I have called to You with all my heart; and when I went out towards You, I found You coming towards me. I look upon Your wondrous power with awe. Who can say that he has not seen You? The heavens and their legions proclaim Your dread—without a sound.

But can God really dwell among men? Their foundations are dust—what can they conceive of Him? Yet You, O Holy One, make Your home where they sing Your praises and Your glory. The living creatures, standing on the summit of the world, praise Your wonders. Your throne is above their heads, yet it is You who carry them all!

2

How to Thank God

The attitude of gratitude is an endemic feature of the religious personality. Thanksgiving is a recognition of divine grace, a testimony to God's providential care, an act of reciprocity for blessings already bestowed. It would be ungracious not to be grateful. A question perpetually confronts the person of faith: "How can I repay unto the Lord all God's bountiful dealings with me?" (Psalms 116:12).

Gratitude to God is an acknowledgment that no one is self-made. "A self-made man is as likely as a self-laid egg," observed Mark Twain. Thanksgiving begins with the awareness that our very existence is a gift of God, a gesture of divine largess.

Life is a gift in the form of an enigma. The surprise of being alive evokes wonder. Bearing witness to the marvels of creation elicits awe. Discovering that what is readily taken for granted is actually the miraculous in disguise, draws forth humility. In acknowledging a blessing, one reciprocates with a prayer. Appreciation becomes a vehicle for celebration, for song. With notes given by God, each individual can compose a tune, a life. Creation of one's life as a work of art is an act of reciprocity, an articulation of gratitude to God. It is gratefulness that makes the human soul great.[1]

Faith without gratitude is a premise without a conclusion, a fallacy. The creation of the artful life begins with an awareness that we are creatures as well as creators, that we can create because we have been created in the image of the Creator. As Ben Zion Bokser, a twentieth-century American rabbi, wrote:

> I did not make the air I breathe,
> Nor the sun that warms me.
> I did not place in the seed
> The secret
> That bears my bounty.
> I did not endow the muscles
> Of hand and brain
> With the strength
> To plough and plant and harvest.
> My harvest
> Is also His harvest.
> I know
> I am not
> A self-made man.[2]

In contemplating the loss of who and what is taken for granted, one may be drawn better to appreciate the plentitude of divine graciousness. In this regard, there is a story, undoubtedly an apocryphal one, of an incident that is supposed to have happened to the German writer Goethe when he was in Rome on his celebrated Italian journey. He saw a number of blind beggars crouching at their posts, displaying their crudely written appeals for coins near the entrance to St. Peter's. Goethe grew increasingly intrigued as he noticed the worshipers and the visitors pass by most of these beggars, but, almost invariably, they paused to drop a coin in a cup held out by one of them — always the same one. Often, a stroller who had thoughtlessly passed by would turn around, come back to this specially favored blind beggar, donate something, and resume his promenade. Filled with curiosity, Goethe thrust himself into the procession of visitors and he read as he moved along, again and again in one style or another, "Help the blind." Finally, he reached the station of the beggar whose sign seemed to work such wonders. It simply said, "It is springtime and I am blind."[3] This tale echoes the sentiment of a popular Yiddish proverb: "If you cannot be grateful for what you have received, then be thankful for what you have been spared."

Losing one's breath, even for a moment, may lead one to appreciate the gift of breath which is the gift of life. For this reason the talmudic rabbis insisted that "for every breath one takes, one should offer praise to the Holy One, blessed be He."[4] Gazing at one's children, one is drawn to acknowledge that "children are a gift of God, fruit of the womb His reward" (Psalms 127:3). According to the Talmud, "when one dresses, one should say, 'Blessed is God who clothes the naked.' "[5] Before partaking of bread, one offers thanks to the ultimate Source of our sustenance: "Blessed are You, God, who brings forth bread from the earth."[6] And, after a meal, one thanks God "who sustains all life with sustenance." Without the blessing of rain, the crops that sustain us would not grow, and so the Talmud enjoins one to say, "We give thanks to You for every drop You have caused to fall for us. . . . Blessed are You, God, to whom abundant thanksgiving is due."[7] Upon seeing someone who has recovered from a serious illness, one is supposed to say, "Blessed be the All-Merciful who has given you back to us and has not given you to the dust."[8] Even such a mundane act as going to the bathroom is an occasion for offering a thankful blessing to God. In this regard, the Talmud introduced a blessing into the Jewish liturgy:

> Praised are You, Lord our God, King of the universe who with wisdom fashioned the human body, creating openings, arteries, glands and organs, marvelous in structure, intricate in design. Should but one of them, by being blocked or opened, fail to function, it would be impossible to exist. Praised are You, Lord, healer of all flesh who sustains our bodies in wondrous ways.[9]

And upon arising in the morning, with the gift of life restored, one recites the words, "I am grateful to You, living, eternal King, for restoring my soul in compassion." In beginning to recite the morning liturgy one acknowledges that God "has given unto me a soul in purity. You created it and gave it form. You placed it within me. . . . While my soul dwells within my body, I shall offer thanks to You, God, and God of my ancestors, Lord of all creation, Master of all souls. Blessed are You, God who restores souls [each morning] to lifeless bodies."

As was discussed in the previous chapter, Jewish faith is rooted in memory. Expressions of gratitude for current acts of divine grace commingle in the Jewish liturgy with gratitude for recalled events in the life of the people of Israel. Memory engenders thanksgiving as well as faith. The Talmud states that "one should offer prayers of thanksgiving for God's past graciousness, and, one should offer prayers of supplication for God's future grace."[10] On Passover, for example, one expresses gratitude for past as well as present acts of divine beneficence. In the Passover *Haggadah*, we read, "We should thank and praise, laud and glorify, exalt and honor, extol and adore God who performed all the miracles for our forebears and for us. He brought us from slavery to freedom, from sorrow to joy, from mourning to festivity, from darkness to great light, and from bondage to redemption." And, on festivals such as Purim and Hanukah, the liturgy reads, "We thank You for the heroism, for the triumphs, and for the miraculous deliverance of our ancestors in other days, and in our time."

Gratitude is an act of reciprocity for an expression of grace. In this regard, Bahya wrote:

We are duty bound to thank anyone who has been good to us because of his intention to help us. . . . One is obliged to serve, praise and thank the Creator of both the goodness itself and the one who bestows it, for His goodness has no limit but is permanent and constant without any self-seeking or self-protecting motives, but only an expression of his generosity and lovingkindness to all humankind![11]

Similarly, the twentieth-century Jewish theologian, Abraham Joshua Heschel, wrote:

Indebtedness is given with our very being. . . . It experiences life as receiving, not only as taking. Its content is gratitude for a gift received. . . . Man cannot think of himself as human without being conscious of his indebtedness. Thus it is not a mere feeling, but rather a constitutive feature of being human. To eradicate it would be to destroy what is human in man. . . . There is a question that follows me wherever I turn. What is expected of me? What is demanded of me? . . . . The soul is endowed with a sense of indebtedness, and wonder, awe, and fear unlock that sense of indebtedness. Wonder is the state of our being asked. . . . I am commanded—therefore, I am. There is a built-in sense of indebtedness in the consciousness of man, an awareness of owing gratitude, of being called upon at certain moments to reciprocate, to answer, to live in a way which is compatible with the grandeur and mystery of living. . . . To the sense of indebtedness, the meaning of existence lies in reciprocity. In receiving a pleasure, we must return a prayer; in attaining a success, we radiate compassion. We have the right to consume because we have the power to celebrate. . . . The world was not made by man. The earth is the Lord's not a derelict. What we own, we owe.[12]

Awareness of blessings bestowed offers an opportunity for thanksgiving and for offering blessings. Reflecting on the sentence in the "Grace after Meals": "For all of this we thank You Lord," the hasidic master, Barukh of Medziboz, suggested that one translate this sentence as: "For all this, we thank You for being our Lord."[13]

In acknowledging our awareness of indebtedness to God, we accept our task as the stewards, the trustees of God's creation. Not to use the treasure as the Owner intended it would be negligence. Not to enjoy the products of the divine largess would be to fail to appreciate God's gifts. "In the future," says the Talmud, "one will have to render account for everything one saw but did not enjoy."[14] The traditional blessing recited upon seeing trees bloom in springtime articulates this attitude of thankful acceptance: "Blessed are You God, ruler of the universe, who have withheld nothing from Your world and have created beautiful creatures and beautiful trees for mortals to enjoy."[15]

"In this world," said Oscar Wilde, "there are only two tragedies. One is not getting what one wants, and the other is getting it. The last is the real tragedy."[16] A similar sentiment is found in the homiletical writings of the thirteenth-century preacher-philosopher, Jacob Anatoli: "If one cannot have what one wants, one ought to want what one has."[17] Gratitude is an antidote to greed, an entree to contentment.[18]

According to rabbinic tradition, of all the sacrifices that were offered at the Temple, the thanksgiving sacrifice was dearest to God. Commenting on the verse in Psalms (50:23): "He who offers a thanksgiving offering honors Me," a midrash says, "A thanksgiving offering is dearer to God than all other offerings, for the other offerings are brought only because of transgressions . . . but the thanksgiving offering is brought freely."[19] To this sentiment, the Talmud adds: "[With regard to the Thanksgiving sacrifice at the Temple] it is the same whether one gives much or little, as long as one directs one's heart to the Heavenly Father."[20] And, a midrash adds, "In time-to-come all sacrifices will cease, except the thanksgiving sacrifice which will never cease."[21]

That gratitude toward God is the ultimate act of human reciprocity for divine graciousness, that creating the artful life is the most appropriate human gift to God, is expressed in this hasidic story:

A hasidic master was once asked, "What gift can a human being give to God? Creation is His. The earth is the Lord's (Psalms 24:1). All knowledge is His; He is omniscient. All power is His; He is omnipotent. What, then, can we give to God?" The master thought for a moment, and said, "We can give a gift to God He can receive only from each of us. It is the gift that only a child can bestow upon his or her parent, a gift that each of us can bestow upon our divine Parent: *Naches fun kinder*, joy and delight from one's children."

❧

On October 3, 1789, George Washington issued a presidential proclamation establishing the Day of Thanksgiving as an everlasting holiday on the American calendar. In this proclamation, Washington stated,

> Whereas it is the duty of all nations to acknowledge the providence of almighty God, to obey his will, to be grateful for his benefits, and humbly to implore his protection and favor: And whereas both Houses of Congress have, by their joint committee, requested me to recommend to the people of the United States, a day of public thanksgiving and prayer, to be observed by acknowledging with grateful hearts the many and signal favors of almighty God. . . . Now therefore, I do recommend . . . that we may then all unite in rendering unto him our sincere and humble thanks for his kind care and protection of the people of this country."[22]

On Thursday, November 26, 1789, a Thanksgiving Day Sermon was delivered by Gershom Mendes Seixas of the Spanish and Portuguese Congregation Shearith Israel of New York. Selections from this sermon are excerpted below.[23]

The sermon or *derashah* is one of the most important genres of Jewish ethical literature. From the talmudic period, through the Middle Ages and down to modern times, sermons were delivered with the expressed intent of conveying a moral message, and with the implicit intent of linking the moral teachings of the past traditions with the ethical exigencies and challenges of the present. Success of a sermon, past or present, may be judged not by how well it informed, but by how well it managed to move its hearers or readers toward improving the moral and religious quality of their daily lives.[24]

Except for the gigantic corpus of Jewish legal writings, homiletical literature is the richest and most extensive, continuous, and widespread literary form of medieval Jewish ethical literature. In periods before the emergence of mass media newspapers, theatre, radio, television, film, and literary novels, the sermon often fulfilled aesthetic, informational, and educational functions as well as a moral one. As far as may be determined, the medieval listener reacted to the sermon first as an aesthetic form of expression and only secondarily as a behavioral guide for any situation with which he or she might be confronted. Because of the absence of mechanical recording devices until the modern period, our primary knowledge of Jewish homiletical-ethical literature derives from printed or manuscript versions of sermons, most often prepared subsequent to their oral delivery for a readership rather than for a listening audience. The majority of medieval sermons, many of which were undoubtedly delivered in the vernacular, perhaps with a sprinkling of Hebrew citations, have reached us in the form of a discursive Hebrew text. Most such texts are but fragments of what must have been more extensive compositions. It is therefore difficult to reconstruct how these sermons were actually heard and received by those present at their oral delivery.[25]

As a traditionalist art form, sermons—especially during the medieval period—used ancient sacred texts as their point of departure for a discussion of contemporary problems. Homiletics, moreover, helped smooth the way for the introduction of new ideas into traditional Judaism. In the Middle Ages, the basic text used was usually drawn from early rabbinic or biblical literature. One often can discern the level of the Jewish literacy not only of the preacher, but of his listeners, from the nature and extent of earlier classical Jewish sources quoted. One of the starting points for any preacher in the composition of a sermon is what knowledge he could take for granted as far as his listeners were concerned.

Ironically, texts of sermons actually delivered orally form a relatively small part of medieval Jewish homiletical literature. A more accessible body of material derives from texts written in sermonic form but not intended for delivery, and texts in which material originally part of a sermon was incorporated within another non-homiletical genre. Examples of texts cast in sermonic form but actually composed to be read and meditated upon include Abraham bar Ḥiyya's philosophical-ethical treatise *Hegyon ha-Nefesh—Meditation of the Sad Soul*. Written in the twelfth century, this work also has the distinction of being the first major Jewish philosophical work written in the Hebrew language, earlier works of Jewish philosophy having been composed in Arabic.[26] A second example is the collection of ethical discourses organized by subject matter in alphabetical order called *Kad ha-Kemah—The Jar of Meal*, written by the thirteenth-century biblical exegete and kabbalist, Bahya ben Asher.[27]

Beginning in the late sixteenth century, one begins to encounter sermons not only delivered, but published in European languages. By the nineteenth century in Western Europe and North America, the delivery of sermons in these languages became overwhelmingly common. Nevertheless, until the second half of the twentieth century, one still often encounters preaching in Yiddish in eastern Europe and among east European Jewish settlers in western Europe and in the Americas. Among the east European hasidic communities of the eighteenth, nineteenth, and twentieth centuries, Yiddish maintained its status as the popular language of homiletical expression. Nonetheless, most hasidic works based upon homilies were published in Hebrew subsequent to delivery either by hasidic masters themselves or by their disciples. It should be noted that Hasidism is the only religious movement in Judaism that made homiletics its dominant and, for a long time, its almost exclusive means of literary expression. Kabbalistic in ideology and moralistic in expression, hasidic literature forged a continuity with earlier homiletical literature produced in central and eastern Europe.

It was rare for a medieval Jewish preacher to deliver a sermon each Sabbath. This seems to have become standard practice only in the modern period under the influence of Protestant Christianity. Rather, extensive homilies often were delivered in central and eastern Europe only during the spring and fall holiday seasons. Of course, shorter homilies were delivered on other occasions.

Life-cycle occasions, such as weddings, bar mitzvahs, and funerals, elicited extensive homiletical addresses. While the funeral eulogy had its roots in ancient periods, other life-cycle orations were of medieval origin. Beginning in the modern period, one begins to encounter sermons, such as the one excerpted below, delivered on days of public or national celebration or sorrow, initiated not by the Jewish community, but by the national government, and observed by Jews as part of the larger body politic. For example, in 1756 we find the first sermon published in English, though delivered in Spanish, at the Sephardic synagogue of London in response to the Lisbon earthquake earlier that year. We find sermons delivered in various western

European countries and in the United States on the occasion of the death or coronation of a monarch or political leader, a great military victory, or a day of national sorrow. The sermon by Seixas excerpted below is an example of this particularly modern form of homiletical expression.

The significance of Seixas's sermon is not in its being either typical or paradigmatic of exemplary Jewish homiletics. Seixas was not a great preacher, nor was he a creative and artistic composer of sermons. As will be noted below, Seixas's knowledge of classical Jewish sources was far from extensive. One searches in vain for erudition in classical rabbinic or medieval sources in the texts of his printed sermons. Indeed, in its construction and style, Seixas's sermon is more evidently influenced by early American Protestant homiletical models than it is influenced by the long and rich history and tradition of Jewish homiletical literature. Rather, the significance of Seixas's sermon, especially for the American reader, lies in its historical context. Here we have a sermon by one of the earliest American Jewish patriots in the American English of the earliest period in American history. Utilizing the resources at his command, Seixas offers a counterpoint of biblical verses to a contemporary historical experience in order to elicit moral teachings to be conveyed to his listeners and readers. On the occasion of the first American Thanksgiving, Seixas attempts to relate ancient Jewish wisdom to the contemporary experience of Jews in the new American republic. In so doing, Seixas tries to place his discourse within the context of the long history of Jewish homiletical-ethical literature. Utilizing a biblical verse as a segue to discuss acknowledging the divine as a necessary prelude for gratitude and reciprocity as responses to divine beneficence, Seixas goes on to reflect upon the uniqueness of the American Jewish experience and the special moral obligations attendant upon Jews in his particular time and place.

Gershom Mendes Seixas was the first native-born Jewish minister in the United States.[28] Born in New York in 1746, he was appointed *hazan* of Congregation Shearith Israel in New York while in his early twenties. There being little opportunity for formal Jewish education in colonial America, Seixas's knowledge of Judaica was sparse and mostly attained autodidactically.

Seixas was the child of a Sephardic father and an Ashkenazic mother. Though he knew neither Spanish nor Portuguese (though serving as minister of The *Spanish* and *Portuguese* Congregation Shearith Israel), his correspondence indicates some knowledge of a very Germanic Yiddish. Seixas, however, chose only to preach in the synagogue in English, and as such, was one of the first to do so.

Unlike his European rabbinic contemporaries, who were grounded in classical Jewish religious literature, there is no evidence that Seixas had studied Talmud or other classical Jewish sources. He seems to have been able, however, to decipher sections from Joseph Karo's sixteenth-century code, *Shulhan Arukh*. He knew the Bible well, but mostly through its English translation. Unlike his European counterparts, however, he seems well-read and well-informed of contemporary secular thought and science.

It was not until the 1840s, three decades after Seixas's death in 1816, that the first ordained rabbi was to serve in the United States. Until then, Jewish spiritual leaders served as "ministers" or "*hazanim*," preaching, teaching, conducting Jewish rites of passage, collecting charitable funds, and providing for other religious needs of their co-religionists. This description of the American Jewish clergyman, drawn from American Protestant models, became the basis for rabbinic activities in the United States drawn to our own times. Seixas also was a pioneer in Jewish-Christian dialogue in America. He aggressively participated in communal events, which secured him a high regard among his non-Jewish clerical colleagues.

Though not a Judaic scholar or a great preacher, Seixas was an excellent pastor. When many of his wealthy congregants fled the city in times of plague, he stayed to minister to the poor, sick, and needy. He often would travel long distances, usually at his own expense, to perform a circumcision. His home, despite his many children, was always open to those who sought out his help or advice. He constantly raised funds to be sure the needy were cared for. Seixas strongly believed that the Jewish community, and not the larger community or the state, should care for the needs of its own. It was Seixas who established the precedent for honor to be afforded to, and for integrity to be characteristic of, the American Jewish clergy. He was at home personally and culturally in the general society, rubbing shoulders with individuals such as Hamilton, Burr, and John Jay. Though not a scholar, he was well read in a society where illiteracy was common. He was a leader at a critical period in American Jewish history, and his demeanor, activities, commitments, and accomplishments set an enviable precedent for those who would succeed him.

An American patriot, Seixas left New York during the Revolutionary War rather than submit to British rule, unlike most Christian ministers of New York, who chose to stay. Taking his family and the Torah scrolls of his congregation with him for safekeeping, Seixas went first to Connecticut and then to Philadelphia in a voluntary self-exile during the War of Independence, after which he returned to his former position at Shearith Israel, a position he held for fifty years, until his death. One of the earliest trustees of the New York Humane Society and of Columbia College, Seixas was elected in 1784 to the first New York Board of Regents. One of his brothers fought in the Continental Army. Another was a founder of the New York Stock Exchange. Seixas fathered 16 children; Justice Benjamin Cardozo was a descendant of one of them. In sum, Seixas was America's first native

American Jewish clergyman. His philosophy of life may have been summarized in his writing that "the only sublunary happiness man can possess" is to be "exempted from all calamities of this transient life."[29]

Gershom Mendes Seixas
"A Religious Discourse on a Day of
Public Thanksgiving and Prayer"

The subject I have chosen to expatiate on this day, is taken from the three first verses of the 100th psalm, where we find king David, in a particular manner, addresses ALL the inhabitants of the earth in these words—"Make a joyful noise unto the Lord, all ye lands," and earnestly exhorts them "to serve the Lord with gladness, to enter into his presence with singing." . . . You may here ask, how is it possible for us finite beings to attain a knowledge of God? Are we endued with faculties to comprehend that which is infinite? It is generally (though wrongly) asserted as a thing impracticable. But when we reflect on the wondrous works of his creation, that "the heavens declare the glory of God, and the firmament sheweth the works of his hands," are we not most forcibly led to exclaim, with the royal psalmist, "How wonderful are thy works, O God!" It is only through the medium of these things that we can arrive at a proportionate knowledge of God, and from a study of ourselves, we become capable of forming suitable ideas of his divine attributes; from the providential care of his creatures, we judge of his benevolence; from the manifestations of his tender mercies towards us, we judge of his beneficence; and from the various productions of nature, we judge of his omnipotence. A Being, possessed of such powers (and attributes) is forever to be adored; and we only comply with our duty, when we assemble, to render praise and thanksgiving for all his benefits towards us. The wonderful display of his divine providence, "in the course and conclusion of the late war;" the happy consequences derived therefrom, by an establishment of public liberty; the recent mercies conferred on these states, by the general approbation and adoption of the new constitution, are (ALL) blessings that demand our most grateful acknowledgements to the Supreme Ruler of the universe; more especially, as we are made equal partakers of every benefit that results from this good government; for which, we cannot sufficiently adore the God of our fathers, who hath manifested his care over us in this particular instance; neither can we demonstrate our sense of his benign goodness, for his favourable interposition in behalf of the inhabitants of this land, and for every other kind dispensation bestowed both on them and us. What return can we make to so glorious a Being? How are we to shew our gratitude? King David himself, although inspired, seemed to be at a loss to express his sense of the obligations he acknowledged to have received, as you may find in ps. cxvi. v. 12 "What shall I render unto the Lord for all his benefits towards me?" and the only mode he could devise, was by declaring he would publish the name of the Lord; as he says in the next verse—"I will take the cup of salvations, and call upon the name of the Lord;" that is, I will acknowledge the salvations, the benefits I have received, and publish the name of the Lord, to make known that he is the fountain of all good, the dispenser of all benefits. The acknowledgement of favors received by a dependent creature, is all the return he can make to his creator; the proclaiming that goodness to all men, the only thanksgiving in his power. . . .

This is a strong corroborating proof that King David, in his addressing ALL lands, anticipated what was then, and is now, to happen in the latter days, by his saying—"Know ye that the Lord he is God;" for without this ever to be desired knowledge of God, it is in vain for man to offer up praise or prayer; and he was well convinced of the necessity of knowing God, previous to any other knowledge whatever. He then proceeds to assign his reasons why we should serve the Lord with gladness, "for he hath made us, we are his (peculiar treasure) people, and the sheep of his pasture;" that he hath made us, needs no demonstration; consequently we are continually to have in mind our subjunction to him; the duties we owe him; the ready obedience we should pay to his commands; the obligations we are under to him; the necessity of strictly observing the moral and ceremonial precepts of his holy law. For, from a disinterested principle of benevolence, he hath called us into being; by his ever watchful care over us, he hath preserved us to this day; and by his own free will he can put a period to our existence. In this is comprehended the omnipotence of an eternal God. . . .

From these instructions, we are led to reflect on the great and glorious author of our existence. How does the human mind become elated with the idea of being worthy his providential care! It is then we discover the dignity of ourselves; then it is that we may truly say with Job, who, after he had suffered almost every temporal evil, exclaimed, "And from my flesh I see God;" meaning thereby, that the formation and construction of our natural bodies were manifest evidence of a God: for what power, except the omnipotent self-existing Being, could ever have formed so compleat, so complex a creature as man; endued with all the benevolent and social virtues, yet subject to the most flagrant vices, vices that are productive of destruction, both of body and soul. Man is to be viewed in two different states with respect to God, the comparative and the relative. When in the comparative, what are we? what are our lives? what are our actions? how mean! how insignificant! But when we consider the relative state we stand in towards God, that he hath formed us after his own image, how important, how dignified do we appear! Capable of reasoning on things both present and absent; searching into the mysterious operations of nature; exploring the works of an almighty Providence, in enabling the human mind to contemplate futurity; improving and increasing in knowledge; possessing faculties to comprehend the movements of the heavenly spheres, thereby admitting the necessity of a great first cause, determining rules of right, judging of things proper or improper according to their various degrees. How grateful therefore ought we to be to our Maker! Who hath of his own good-will, and not from any merit in us, bestowed on us such previous gifts; gifts that we cannot but be sensible of every moment of our lives. As we confess in our daily prayers, (in these words)—"For thy miraculous providence which is daily with us, and for thy wonders and thy goodness which are at all times, evening, morning and noon, exercised over us," for all which, we are loudly called on, to render praise and thanksgiving, as it is expressed in psal. xiii. v. 6, "I will sing unto the Lord, because he hath dealt bountifully with me." . . .

The many visitations of an almighty providence which we have experienced within these few years past, are sufficient indications, to a sensible mind, that we are suffering under his displeasure. Awaken from your lethargy, and think, before it is too late, of your dependence on him, humble yourselves before him, and implore his mercy. I mean not to impeach the innocent victims that have been made, far from it, they suffer not; for as the royal psalmist says—"Precious in the sight of the Lord is the death of his saints;" and the prophet Isaiah says, "The righteous perish and no man layeth it to heart; and merciful men are taken away because of the evil. He shall enter into peace; they shall rest in their beds, each one walking in his uprightness." But it is we that suffer; it is we that have cause to lament. Where now, ye youths, is the fostering hand of age and experience, to lead you through the slippery paths of life? In what manner can we comply with that excellent lesson given to us by our faithful legislator, "Ask thy father and he will tell thee?" Who is to plead the cause of the widow and the fatherless? Who is there left among us to support the poor and the needy? Their cries are now in vain! We have lost our benefactors; we have lost those who, in cases of necessity, were ever ready to assist us with their advice and their interest. – These, these are calamities that ought to humble you. Lay aside your pride and your vanities; strive to imitate the virtues of those worthy characters who are now no more. Be not lifted up above yourselves; but know, for a certainty, that he who exalts can depress. Let us not apply to ourselves that short but expressive sentence, "And Jeshurun waxed fat and kicked," with its fatal consequence, "and forsook the God that made him." Let us not have cause to reproach ourselves with neglect of duty: but do justice, execute judgment, and walk humbly before the Lord; for this is all that he requires. Then shall we be able to sing and rejoice both in body and spirit, and truly say, "This is the day which the Lord hath made, we will be glad and rejoice therein." . . .

From the foregoing, you will naturally observe the duties we owe our Creator: it now remains to point out the duties which we owe to ourselves, the community to which we belong.

In the first place, it is necessary that we, each of us in our respective stations, behave in such a manner as to give strength and stability to the laws entered into by our representatives; to consider the burden imposed on those who are appointed to act in the executive department; to contribute, as much as lays in our power, to support that government which is founded upon the strictest principles of equal liberty and justice. If to seek the peace and prosperity of the city wherein we dwell be a duty, even under bad governments, what must it be when we are situated under the best of constitutions? It behooves us to use our utmost endeavours to suppress every species of licentiousness, to unite, with cheerfulness and uprightness, upon all occasions that may occur in the political as well as in the moral world, to promote that which has a tendency to the public good: for, without a proper subordination to the rules (either superior or inferior) no government can (long) exist.

And, secondly, from this mode of general government may be deduced the necessity of conforming to the established rules of particular societies: for, whatever is necessary to be observed in respect to the former, may be with the greatest propriety applied to the latter.

And lastly, to conclude, my dear brethren and companions, it is incumbent on us, as Jews, in a more especial manner (seeing we are the chosen and peculiar treasure of God) to be more circumspect in our conduct [Isaiah, ch. xliv. v. 8] — that as we are at this day living evidences of his divine power and unity: so may we become striking examples to the nations of the earth hereafter, as it is mentioned in several passages of the sacred scriptures, and particularly in Exodus, ch. xix. v. 6. "And ye shall be unto me a kingdom of priests, and an holy nation;" meaning thereby that we should, in the latter days, teach the law to those who shall then enter into the covenant made with Abraham our father, for in him "shall all nations of the earth be blessed." For this purpose, let me recommend to you a serious consideration of the several duties already set forth this day; to enter into a self-examination; to relinquish your prejudices against each other; to subdue your passions; to live, as Jews ought to do, in brotherhood and amity; "to seek peace and pursue it:" so shall it be well with you both here and hereafter; which God, of his infinite mercies, grant. — Amen.

3

How to Love God

If love depends upon a |transient| thing, when that thing ceases, love ceases. When love does not depend on a [transient] thing, it never ceases."[1] This talmudic statement teaches that true love is unconditional. It requires no motivation, demands no reward, and is devoid of pragmatic value. "True love," wrote Joseph Albo, "is that which one has for the sake of the beloved alone, having no other purpose than doing the will of the beloved, because he does not love the beloved for any cause other than the beloved. Love that is due to an extraneous cause is sure to change and cease."[2]

While gratitude toward God, discussed in the previous chapter, is a desirable feature of the artful life, gratitude—unlike love—may become conditional upon the receipt of benefits. Gratitude toward God may prove too tenuous a foundation for the religious and moral life. Love of God, however, can provide a firm basis for moral action and for the creation of life as a work of art.

True love of God must not only be love, but it must also be true. It cannot be self-love masquerading as love of God, self-interest pretending to be altruism. Nor can it be a passing fancy disguising itself as a life-long commitment. Without love, an essential ingredient in creating one's life as a work of art would be absent. By reviewing how Jewish thinkers of the past understood the human love of God, one may better appreciate their comprehension of love itself.

"*You shall love the Lord your God with all your heart, and with all your soul, and with all your might*" (Deuteronomy 6:5). This verse, which is part of the *Shema*, is one of the first biblical and liturgical passages learned by each Jewish child. While belief in God is not explicitly commanded by Scripture, love is. Love is a primal emotion binding us to God and God to us.[3] In the order of the Jewish liturgy, God's love for us is affirmed before our love for God. The paragraph before the *Shema* in the morning liturgy declares, "With an everlasting love You have loved us, Lord our God."

The fundamental premise of Jewish theology is the affirmation of a permanent covenantal relationship between God and the people of Israel. An essential feature of that relationship is love. In the evening liturgy, the recitation of the *Shema*, in which the Jew reaffirms his or her love for God, is preceded by the affirmation of God's love for the people of Israel: "With an everlasting love You have loved the house of Israel. . . . Praised are You, Lord, who loves Your people Israel."

The popular description of Judaism as a religion of law devoid of love, and of Christianity as the religion of love that one often encounters in Christian polemical literature, is simply an unsubstantial claim. Love is an essential ingredient of Jewish faith and life.[4] Throughout the ages, Jewish thinkers have pondered the meaning of love. For them, love is a critical component not only of the divine-human relationship, but of all significant relationships. As the *Zohar* says, "Everything is called Love and everything is established for the sake of love."[5] For the Jewish mystics, love is a cosmic principle that unites all of existence from its supreme upper source to its most humble manifestation.[6] According to Judah Loew of Prague, love is a striving for perfection, stemming from a universal desire for individual fulfillment and completion.[7]

In their discussions of love of God, the great Jewish thinkers of the past began their inquiries by posing one or more of the following three questions:

Who *are* we?
Who *are* we *not?*
What *should* we *do?*

By asking the question of who we are in relation to discerning the nature of human love of God, Jewish thinkers were attempting to identify the essential human characteristic of the human being, the crucial component of human nature without which one would not truly be human. Their inquiries often related to the biblical description of the human being as having been created in "the image and likeness of God" (Genesis 1:26). In their view, that which we have in common with God is that which makes us human. By determining in what sense we have been created in the divine image, we can discern the characteristic that both makes us most like God and that reveals the essence of our humanity.

From this perspective, love is understood as the attraction of "like to like," i.e., two loving partners are drawn toward each other because of a shared essential quality.[8] Hence, love of God stems from the desire of the divinely implanted part of us—from the quintessentially human feature of our existence that we bear and share with God—to attain communion with the divine. In this regard, Bahya ibn Pakudah wrote, "What does the love of God mean? It is the yearning of the soul, the desire of its very substance to be attached to God's supreme light. The soul is a simple substance which inclines by its nature to the spiritual beings that are like itself."[9] As we shall see, for some Jewish thinkers, as for Ibn Pakudah, this component is the soul, while for others, like Maimonides, it is the intellect.

By asking who we are *not* in relation to determining the nature of human love of God, Jewish thinkers were attempting to identify those characteristics that essentially differentiate the human from the divine, those features God has that we lack.[10] From this perspective, love is understood to be the attraction of opposites for each other. This is the view that in love "opposites attract;" that since love is the quest for wholeness, a lack in one loving partner is fulfilled by some quality in the other loving partner. Hence, love of God is a vehicle by means of which the human person moves toward self-realization—overcoming intrinsic human shortcomings—by attachment to a perfect divinity. This type of love of God is recommended in the excerpt below, from *Sefer ha-Yashar—The Book of the Righteous*.

By asking what we should do in relation to determining the nature of human love of God, some Jewish thinkers bypassed the problem of defining the essential nature of the human being raised by the first approach, as well as the problem of the essential nature of God raised by the second approach. The question of what we should do begins with the assumption of mutual love between God and human beings, and focuses on how humans should articulate that love through concrete action. From the other two perspectives, deeds can both *lead to* one's love of God and can *flow from* one's love of God. For this third approach, performing certain deeds *is* love of God. Historically, the third approach dominates talmudic thought.[11] The other two approaches primarily reflect medieval Jewish thought.[12]

Defining the nature of God or of human beings was not a preoccupation of the talmudic rabbis. Their major concern was how to fulfill the will of God. For them, the divine will was conveyed by God through revelation. The commandments of the Torah articulate the will of God.[13] One of those commandments is "You shall love the Lord your God." "How does one love God?," asks the *Sifre*, an early rabbinic midrash. The answer: "Perform [God's commandments] out of love." The text continues:

"And these words which I [God] command you this day shall be upon your heart" (Deuteronomy 6:6). Rabbi [Judah the Prince] asked: Why did Moses say this?

Because Scripture says, "You shall love the Lord your God" (Deuteronomy 6:5). [From this verse alone] I do not know just how to love God. Therefore, Scripture goes on to say, "And these words which I command you this day shall be upon your heart," meaning, take these words to heart, for thereby you will recognize Him who spoke and the world came into being, and you will cleave to His ways."[14]

For the rabbis, love of God was not to be a rare emotion, restricted to a spiritual elite in fleeting moments of rapture, but a perpetual opportunity, an everyday activity. By loving God through one's normal behavior, one causes God to be loved by others; one sets an example for others. In the words of a midrash, " 'You shall love the Lord your God' can be taken to mean that you should cause God to be loved by others—that is, you are to cause God to be loved by humankind. Hence you are to be loving in the give-and-take of everyday life—in your goings about in the marketplace and in dealing with others."[15] In other words, a lover is delighted with the opportunity to carry out the wishes of his or her beloved. The commandments of the Torah express the will of God and consequently the command to love means that we behave toward God as a lover behaves toward his or her beloved. Performing the commandments is not a means *toward* love of God; it *is* love of God. In this view, loving is doing. Love is not a prelude to action, but action itself. Love is not an ethereal emotion, but concrete deeds. Love is expressed *as* deed. How we love and whom we love can only be expressed and verified by how we act in relation to the one we love. Love is not simply an attitude, but an act; not a disposition, but a deed; not a prelude, but a commitment.

While the talmudic rabbis emphasized love of God as being chiefly a matter of human conduct, they were not oblivious to the emotional nature of love of God. However, it was in medieval Jewish literature that the emotional and intellectual dimensions of love of God became central concerns. The talmudic rabbis were more concerned with the performance of the sacred deed than with the motivations behind it.[16] However, in medieval Jewish thought the problem of how and why to perform the commandments became a paramount concern.[17] The medievals identified love of God as a prelude to, and as a motivation for, performing the commandments. For them, love of God was a premise; religious observance a conclusion. If not predicated on love of God, religious observance became a fallacy, a fake, a gesture devoid of meaning. But, while love of God served as a stimulus for action, it was also the goal of action. For the talmudic rabbis, observance of the commandments, study of the Torah, and the cultivation of moral virtue were ends in themselves. For the medievals, however, these were not ends in themselves, but means to an end—love culminating in communion with God. Consequently, while the talmudic rabbis largely understood the commandments as having their own intrinsic value, the medievals considered the commandments as vehicles to attaining consummate love of God in communion with the divine. Some encouraged the attainment of divine communion through utilizing the commandments and by cultivating moral virtue as means to developing the part of us that is most like God, i.e., the soul or the intellect.

Maimonides' depiction of the love of God demonstrates that he was not the sober rationalist many consider him to have been. Both in his legal and his philosophical writings, Maimonides describes love of God as both the starting point and the culmination of the religious life. For Maimonides, one who loves God will perform the commandments spontaneously and automatically. Observance of the commandments and the cultivation of moral virtue will then prepare one's soul, particularly its intellectual dimension, for the higher love of God that culminates in divine communion. From this perspective, love engenders action, which leads to a higher love that becomes realized in attachment to God. In Maimonides' words:

> One who serves God out of love studies the Torah and practices the commandments and walks in the way of wisdom for no ulterior motive at all, neither out of fear of the evil that otherwise might befall him nor even in order to acquire the good. Rather he does what is true because it is good and true and good will follow in its wake. This stage is a most elevated one, and not even every sage has the wherewithal to attain it. . . . It is regarding this stage that God commanded us through Moses, "You shall love the Lord your God" (Deuteronomy 6:5). When one loves God with a love that is fitting he automatically carries out all the precepts of love. What is the love that is fitting? It is that one should love God with an extraordinary powerful love, to the extent that his soul becomes tied to the love of God so that he pines for it constantly. It should be as if he were lovesick, unable to get the woman he loves out of his mind, pining for her constantly when he sits or stands, when he eats or drinks, even more than this should the love of God be in the hearts of those who love Him and yearn constantly for Him, as He commanded us, "You shall love the Lord your God with all your heart and with all your soul." Solomon expresses this in the form of a parable, "For I am love-sick" (Song of Songs 2:5). The whole Song of Songs is a parable to illustrate this topic.[18]

For Maimonides, the highest form of love of God is complete obsession with God. In Maimonides' words, "It is known and certain that the love of God does not become closely knit in one's heart until one is continuously and thoroughly possessed by it and gives up everything else in the world for it; as God commanded us, 'with all your heart and with all your soul.' "[19] As many other medieval thinkers, Maimonides taught that attainment of this level of love of God is vouchsafed for the very few. Whereas for the talmudic rabbis, love of God is available to everyone through performance of the sacred deed, for many of the medievals, complete love of God is restricted to the spiritual elite.

In his major philosophical work, *The Guide of the Perplexed*, Maimonides describes the lower level of love of God as being available to some, but passionate love of God as being available to a highly restricted few. Those who attain passionate love of God must have first undertaken a process of deliberate ascent toward God.[20]

For Maimonides, *complete* love of God and attachment to the divine assumes that the individual already has attained the level of moral perfection which he depicts as perfection of the soul. This is accomplished through performance of the commandments and cultivation of moral virtue. But, in this view, such action is not an end in itself but a means to a higher end—intellectual perfection.[21] For Maimonides (following Aristotle), the intellect is the quality that makes one truly human. The intellect is the human feature that we share with the divine. As Maimonides wrote, "It is on account of this intellectual apprehension that it is said of man: 'In the image of God created He him' (Genesis 1:27)."[22]

Complete love of God, attained by means of intellectual self-development, represents the acme of human existence according to Maimonides. Love is the attraction of "like to like," i.e., of the human intellect, which is the essence of human beings, to the divine, which is total intellect. For Maimonides, love of God in its most exalted form is essentially an intellectual activity, not an emotional one. Maimonides' view influenced the philosopher Spinoza in coining the phrase "*amor dei intellectualis*"—the intellectual love of God.

For Maimonides, intellectual apprehension of God is the epitome of love of God. The greater the apprehension, the more intense the love. For Maimonides the philosopher, the highest love of God is the purest and most intensive sort of thinking about God. In this view, God can only be loved in proportion to the knowledge one has of Him. Where there is little knowledge, there is little love; where there is much knowledge, there is much love. As Maimonides wrote, "One only loves God with the knowledge with which one knows Him. According to the knowledge will be the love. If the knowledge will be little or much, the love will be little or much."[23]

Where there is much love, the individual achieves a state where outwardly he is with people, while inwardly he is completely preoccupied with the divine and oblivious to those around him.[24] In the state of complete love of God, the intellectual faculty of the human soul becomes attached to the divine. The love of God is realized by the cohesion of the human intellect with God.

Maimonides' portrayal of the acme of human development realized through intellectual apprehension of and cohesion with the divine was attacked by subsequent Jewish thinkers while it was accepted by others. Those who disagreed with Maimonides found three major problems with his approach. First, it was considered too elitist, restricting human spiritual fulfillment to an intellectual elite, thereby barring and discouraging the average person from trying to attain complete spiritual fulfillment. Second, it portrays the human being as essentially intellectual, not only excluding, but also denigrating, the emotional and physical aspects of human nature from the essence of the human being and from the attainment of human fulfillment. Third, it considers the commandments and moral virtues as having little or no intrinsic value, but as being merely prerequisites for the attainment of intellectual goals.[25] While all of these objections might be affirmed by the modern reader of Maimonides, the modern person would likely find Maimonides' view that the development of the intellect requires the suppression of the physical and emotional aspects of human nature to be the most problematic.

Like many of the medievals, Maimonides believed that the physical and the spiritual, the emotional and the intellectual aspects of human nature are in inevitable and intrinsic conflict. Consequently, it becomes necessary to remove the impediments posed by the body and the emotions in order for one to make manifest the spiritual and intellectual qualities of human beings that constitute the human essence. For example, in the *Guide*, Maimonides wrote:

> The philosophers have already explained that the bodily faculties impede in youth the attainment of most of the moral virtues, and all the more that of pure thought, which is achieved through the perfection of the intelligibles that lead to passionate love of God. For it is impossible that it should be achieved while the bodily humors are in effervescence. Yet in the measure in which the faculties of the body are weakened and the fire of the desires is quenched, the intellect is strengthened. . . .[26]

Because Maimonides considered the body and the emotions as impediments to the intellectual apprehension of God, it follows for him that only with death, when the intellectual faculty of the soul is free of the body, can it achieve the most superlative love of, and cohesion with, the divine. In Maimonides' words, "After having reached this condition of enduring permanence [after death], the intellect remains in one and the same state, the impediment [i.e., the body] that sometimes screened him off having been removed. And he will remain permanently in that state of intense pleasure, which does not belong to the genus of bodily pleasures."[27] In other words, for Maimonides, the goal of human development that culminates in intellectual cohesion with God is but a prelude to eternal existence in cohesion with the divine in the life after death. For Maimonides, the death of such individuals is not a tragedy, but represents ultimate human fulfillment and the attainment of life's goals. The death of such individuals, in this view, is not death, but the state in which the intellect enters into its own to adhere forever to

God. In this typically medieval view, life is but a preparation for the afterlife; true human fulfillment can only be realized in the World to Come. As Moses Hayyim Luzzatto wrote in *The Path of the Upright*, "The purpose for which man was created is not realized in this world, but in the World to Come. Human existence in this world is a preparation for existence in the next world, which is one's goal."[28]

As was noted above, an alternate view to that of love as the attraction of "like to like" is the perspective that perceives love as the attraction of opposites. A version of this second view is found in the writings of Judah Loew of Prague.[29] According to Loew, there are two kinds of opposites: complementary opposites and contradictory opposites.[30] An example of a complementary set of opposites is male and female. An example of a contradictory set of opposites is the human being and God. In both cases, love is based upon an attraction for some quality that completes the deficiency of the other. In this view, love is a striving for perfection, a desire for fulfillment and completion. Further, according to Loew, only that which is complete endures. Hence, love brings not only completion and fulfillment but endurance as well. From this perspective, human love for God stems from the human desire for completion and from the human quest for endurance, which only God represents and which only God can guarantee. In Loew's words, "God sustains the human life, but He is unlike the human being. Therefore, it is appropriate to love Him because everything that one loves should be that which brings one fulfillment and completion, and God can do this for human beings."[31]

But, what about God? If love is a mutual relationship that is realized by gaining qualities one lacks in relationship with another, to say God loves human beings is to acknowledge a need and a deficiency within God. As we shall see, while this possibility was inconceivable to the Jewish philosophers, it was an operating premise of the Jewish mystics.[32] For the Jewish mystics, both love of God and God's love presume a divine need.[33]

According to Loew, love between human beings may result in a partial fulfillment, but complete mutual fulfillment cannot be realized through human love. For example, no matter how deeply in love a man and a woman may be, they nonetheless always remain discretely separate individuals. For Loew, God, however, is complete wholeness. God endures eternally. Therefore, God is the ultimate source of complete fulfillment. Love of God is the only variety of love that can result in absolute human fulfillment.

According to Loew, human love for God differs from all other types of love. In love of God, one's love originally derives from God, the source of all. In other types of love, love derives originally from the lover. Only in love of God does one love with the love with which God has given us to love. In this regard, Loew wrote:

The love one has for God is not one's own but derives from God. It comes from God and one returns it to God. . . . Love of God is more fitting than love of anything or of anyone else. For in every kind of love that exists between two lovers, though they may cleave one to the other, nevertheless, each retains their own individuality. However, in the love of human beings for God, one completely returns one's soul to God to the extent that one loses one's individuality and completely cleaves to God, as it is written, "to love the Lord your God and to cleave to Him" (Deuteronomy 11:22). This is complete love.[34]

Judah Loew describes two levels of love of God. The lower level is *devekut*, cleaving to God, cohesion with God. This may be attained by observance of the commandments and is available to everyone who desires to achieve it. However, "complete love" – "total *devekut*" – is not simply attachment to the divine, and not even union with God, but reunion with the Source of all. This is available only to the righteous, to the very few.[35] While other varieties of love are a pilgrimage to a promised land, complete love of God is the restoration of a previous unity disjointed by creation, severed by sin and caused by alienation from God. In complete love, the human finds himself by losing himself in God. The human being attains self-realization by re-merging with the Source of Being. Through complete love of God, one discovers that God and human beings are not truly opposites, not truly separated. Once the veil of illusion has been removed, the human being becomes aware of that which is shared with God. According to Loew, the human soul is a spark of the fire that is God.[36] That which makes one human is the human soul, which is a "part of God above."[37] Complete love of God entails the purification of the human soul through sacred deeds, as the prelude to its eventual return and reunification with its source. No longer the contradictory opposite of God, the human being, through love of God, becomes absorbed in the divine flame.

This understanding of love as union and reunion is discussed in Leon Ebreo's *Philosophy of Love*, one of the few classics of Jewish religious literature written in Italian. Ebreo's views were greatly influential during the Renaissance, and beyond, and are echoed in the writings of Cervantes, John Milton, and others. According to Ebreo, love is "the actual conversion of each lover into the other, or rather the fusion of both into one, every distinction and diversity between them being eliminated as far as possible. Thus love endures in greater unity and perfection; and the lover remains continually desirous of enjoying the beloved in union; which is the true definition of love."[38] In other words, love is a self-transforming experience through encounter and union with an other. Love not only helps create life as a work of art, but love engenders a new creation – the fused union of two lovers. For Ebreo, as for Loew, human love is but an echo of divine love.

For Judah Loew, as for his fellow Jewish mystics, God's love for His creatures is a love predicated on a lack. God desires reunion with His creatures in order to become truly One again. God desires to reunite with that which is part of Himself but separate from Himself. Until then, God remains incomplete. In this bold theological view, God needs human love to recapture His surrendered oneness. It is the human being who can make God truly One.

Unlike many other Jewish mystics, Loew does not utilize erotic symbolism when discussing love of God.[39] Perhaps, for Loew, the erotic analogy is inapplicable to "complete love." In complete love, as distinguished from erotic love, a union is achieved. In erotic love, all boundaries between two individuals can be overcome, yet each retains his or her individuality. For many other Jewish mystics, however, complete union is an unachievable goal, at least in this life. They therefore focused on describing love of God as complete intimacy, as a form of cleaving to God (*devekut*), of cohesion (rather than union or reunion), in which both parties retain their distinct individuality. In presenting this variety of love of God, the erotic analogy was deemed pertinent and appropriate. For example, according to the Jewish mystics there is a feminine aspect of God called *Shekhinah*. For hasidic thought, echoing earlier kabbalistic motives, prayer, which expresses love of God, may be described as an erotic experience:

> Prayer is copulation with the *Shekhinah*. Just as there is swaying when copulation begins so, too, a man must sway at first and then he can remain immobile and attached to the *Shekhinah* with great attachment. As a result of his swaying man is able to attain a powerful stage of arousal. For he will ask himself: Why do I sway my body? Presumably it is because the *Shekhinah* stands over against me. And as a result he will attain to a stage of great enthusiasm.[40]

The idea that human deeds may help bring about an internal unity within God is often expressed in erotic terms. For example, in his mystical-ethical treatise, *Tomer Devorah*, Moses Cordovero wrote, "It is known that the *Shekhinah* is love-sick for the Union, as it is written, 'For I am lovesick' (Song of Songs 2:5). Her cure is in human hands which can bring her the good medicine she desires."[41]

For the Jewish mystics, especially for Hasidism, human passion can serve as a vehicle to love of God. For example, Elijah de Vidas wrote that a man who never passionately desired a woman is inferior to a donkey. Only through a man's passionate obsession with a woman can he achieve love of God.[42] Similarly, the Baal Shem Tov taught that only through the appreciation of a woman's beauty can a man be drawn to appreciate God, the source of all beauty. This is in keeping with the hasidic teaching that from physical desire, one can be drawn to divine worship: "When a person can arouse love through material delights, it then becomes easy to love God."[43] The physical is a vehicle to, rather than an enemy of, the spiritual.

Just as the physical can serve as an entrée to the spiritual, so can the spiritual be an invitation to the physical. Human love can serve as a path to love of God, but to be complete, love of God must be a portal to love of one's fellow.[44] In this view, communion with God is the foundation for ethical behavior. Figuratively, the verse, "You shall love your neighbor as yourself, I am the Lord" (Leviticus 19:18) was taken to refer to love of God, i.e., one's "neighbor" is God.[45] Literally, the verse was taken to refer to one's fellow human being. In other words, love of God is the premise upon which ethics rests. Through love of the Creator, one comes to a love of His creatures. As a rabbinic text states, commenting on this verse, "You shall love your neighbor as yourself *because* I am the Lord, because I have created him."[46]

꙰

The excerpt below from *Sefer ha-Yashar—The Book of the Righteous*, states both theories of love discussed above: the attraction of "like to like," and "opposites attract" to attain mutual fulfillment. However, in this text, love as the fulfillment of a missing aspect of the lover is considered the superior variety of love. Because God is deemed as having attributes that we lack, through love of God human beings can attain their self-realization.

The title "*Sefer ha-Yashar*" is of biblical origin, appearing twice in the Hebrew Scriptures: on the occasion of the sun standing still for Joshua (Joshua 10:13) and in connection with David's lament over the deaths of Saul and Jonathan (2 Samuel 1:18). In each case, reference is made to a record of the event in the *Sefer ha-Yashar*.

What *Sefer ha-Yashar* actually was is unknown.[47] It is one of the lost books mentioned in the biblical narrative, such as the *Book of the Wars of God*. Gersonides states in his biblical commentary that the *Sefer ha-Yashar* was lost during the exile of the Jewish people from the land of Israel.[48] On the other hand, Rashi indicates that *Sefer ha-Yashar* refers not to a separate book, but to the biblical book of Genesis, where the future history of the descendants of the patriarchs, i.e., the upright, is implicitly found in the text.[49] In this, Rashi reiterates a talmudic view that claims that the miracle of the sun standing still for Joshua is already hinted at in Genesis. The talmudic text reads, "What is *Sefer ha-Yashar*? . . . It is the book of Abraham, Isaac and Jacob who are designated as righteous (*yashar*). . . . And where is this episode (of the sun standing still) hinted at [in Genesis]? [In the verse]: 'And his seed [i.e., Ephraim, from whom Joshua was descended] will fill the nations' (Genesis 48:19). When shall [Ephraim's fame] reach the nations? When the sun shall stand still for Joshua."[50]

In medieval Jewish literature, two additional books bear the title *Sefer ha-Yashar*. One is a chronicle of the biblical story from creation to the time of the judges.[51] The other is a work of Jewish law in which some of the legal opinions of Rashi's grandson, Rabbenu Jacob Tam, are collected.[52] Apparently because of the identical title of the two works, our book was attributed by tradition to Rabbenu Tam. However, there is no evidence that Rabbenu Tam composed our work. A study of its literary style and the ideas it presents makes such attribution a virtual impossibility. Though modern scholars agree that Rabbenu Tam was not the book's author, they disagree as to who the author might have been. One theory identifies the writer as an anonymous follower of the Jewish pietists of medieval Germany (Hasidei Ashkenaz).[53] Another view credibly identifies the writer as the thirteenth-century Spanish writer, Jonah of Gerona, the author of the classical Jewish ethical treatise Sha'arey Teshuvah – Gates of Repentance. Nonetheless, the identity of our author remains unknown.[54] Indeed, it seems that he wanted it that way. The ultimate expression of an author's humility is to leave his name off his work. From this perspective, what is important is not the perpetuation of an author's name or fame, but the transmission of the ethical teachings he wished to convey. As is characteristic of the authors of medieval Jewish ethical literature, the intention of the author of Sefer ha-Yashar was not to inform but to transform his readers, to be both a goad and a guide. As our author wrote in the opening chapter of his work, "I have called this book Sefer ha-Yashar, the Book of Righteousness, because it will change and bring one to the right way, to the service of the divine, making it a tree of life to all who take hold of it, and happiness will be the lot of those who hold fast to it."[55]

While the identity of the author of Sefer ha-Yashar remains obscure, his teachings have had a significant and a lasting impact. Since this book's earliest publication in Constantinople in 1520, Sefer ha-Yashar has been reprinted numerous times in more than fifty editions. Sefer ha-Yashar was popular among the generations after the expulsion from Spain in 1492, and is often cited by the kabbalist Elijah de Vidas in his classical mystical-ethical work Reshit Hokhmah. It was also studied widely in Germany and Poland in the sixteenth and seventeenth centuries, and later enjoyed enormous popularity among followers of the Musar movement that flourished in Lithuania in the nineteenth century.[56]

Sefer ha-Yashar – The Book of the Righteous

We will begin with love. The matter of love is a uniting quality between the lover and the beloved. Know that love can be divided into three parts. One type of love seeks a benefit, the second type of love is the love one has for society and friends, and the third is love of the good qualities which are to be found in the beloved; this third type of love is the first and the true one. Moreover, it has the power within it of never altering or changing, because this love is sustained and bound by the qualities of the beloved and it is impossible for it to change unless the qualities of the beloved change. But it is not our intention to call to mind the qualities which change, but rather the qualities which endure, and these are the qualities of the Creator, blessed be He. For when a man loves another man because of his intellect, his wisdom, his ethics, his humility and the other good qualities, such love is firm and will never change, because the cause which brings about this love does not change. Therefore, I say that this is the true and perfect love, when a man loves his God because of His power, because He is the Creator of all things, and because He is compassionate, merciful, and patient, and possesses all the other good qualities. Such a love will never depart or be removed, for the qualities of the Creator, may He be extolled, will never depart or be altered. Of the three types of love which we have called to mind, none will endure save this one, which is the true pillar of love. The other two will not endure, for they have not within themselves the essential quality of every lover and beloved.

Know that love is joined of two parts, the qualities of the lover, and the qualities of the beloved. According to the qualities of the lover will be the strength of his love for the good qualities which exist in the one he loves. Now, I will explain the qualities of the lover and say that these are the good intellect and a pure and refined soul, and when these qualities exist in the lover even to a small degree, he will be drawn to love everyone who possesses these qualities because every kind gravitates to his kind and keeps aloof from his opposite. Therefore, a man possessing a good intellect and a pure soul is drawn to the love of God, for within the Creator are these just and good qualities, all embracing and true. Therefore, when a man is drawn to His worship, it is a sign that he, himself, has qualities of the Creator, blessed be He. Therefore, he is drawn after Him just as the intellectual man is drawn to the companionship of intellectuals. The wise man is drawn to the companionship of the wise. The fool is drawn to the companionship of fools, and the youth to the companionship of the young, the old man to the companionship of the old, and every man is drawn to the companionship of his friend, while the fowl of the heaven are drawn to the

companionship of their own kind. Therefore, when you see a
man separating himself from serving God, may He be extolled,
know that there are not within him any of the qualities of God,
but their opposites, and therefore he separates himself from the
good qualities. For if there were in him intelligence, or holiness,
or whole-heartedness, or righteousness, we would know that
these qualities are the attributes of the Creator, blessed be
He. . . . Therefore, I have said that when a man has two
qualities — and these are a good intellect and a pure soul — there
will be aroused in the man a complete love for the Creator,
blessed be He. When there will be this complete love for God,
may He be extolled, then there will grow forth reverence from
that love, for we see that whenever a man loves another man
because of good qualities that are within him, this love becomes
a yoke upon his neck and compels him to seek and fulfill the will
of the beloved. He will find no rest unless he exerts himself in
matters pertaining to the beloved and in such case, the exertion
will be sweeter to his palate more than rest. When the lover does
for the beloved a thing which finds favor in the latter's eyes,
then the soul of the lover becomes more precious in his own
eyes, because he is able to find favor in the eyes of his beloved
by doing a thing which is good in the eyes of his beloved. If the
lover should chance to do a deliberate or an unpremeditated
sinful act, or anything which does not please his beloved, then
the lover will be confounded and ashamed and he will steal
away as an entire people will steal away when they are
ashamed. This pertains to the power of love which is like an iron
yoke upon him to cause the lover to yield to the beloved, as
Scripture says (Song of Songs 8:6), "For love is as strong as
death." Since love causes the lover to yield to his beloved and do
the will of the beloved with double willingness, we must explain
why there is in love this power. We say that the love of the lover
for his beloved comes about because of the good qualities which
are in the beloved. The soul of the lover must also contain a
portion of these good qualities. Therefore, the little that is
contained of these good qualities in the lover draws him
exceedingly, just as every kind is drawn to its kind. This is a sign
of a generous soul, that he is drawn after every honorable thing,
and this is love. . . . If it should be said that one cannot compare
the love of the created to the love of the Creator, blessed be He,
he would answer that although we are created beings, still the
love which is customarily shown by man for the Creator — even

though there is a difference between the beloved who is created and the beloved who is the Creator—is the same, for there is no difference between the power of the beloved of God and the power of the mortal lover who is created, for they are one. Therefore, the Creator, blessed be He, seeks nothing of a man but that he love Him with all his power, and this will be as important in His eyes as though he loved Him according to the love that is due to Him. Now, it is interesting to note that the righteousness which we ascribe to the Creator, blessed be He, consists in this, that we are not able to do anything for His glory save that which is within our power to help our fellow men, and the Creator receives it as though we had given Him love that is worthy of Him.

Now that we have explained that love is the cause of fear and that both of them are pillars of faith, we will explain the matter of wisdom, and we say that wisdom must exist in the lover. For if the lover is without wisdom, he will not recognize the qualities which we have mentioned, nor will he recognize in his beloved his intellect, his wisdom, and the other precious qualities. If he does not know his qualities, he will not know how to love him, for the power of folly which obscures the knowledge of the precious qualities of the beloved will nullify the love of the lover, just as we have said. For the love of a fool is not love, and if this is so, we can understand that love cannot be complete if it lacks wisdom and knowledge. According to what he lacks in complete knowledge will be the lack of his love for his beloved, whose qualities are precious and perfect. As to the love of the lover for one who has few of these precious qualities, there may suffice him a little love and a little wisdom, but this cannot be called a complete or perfect love, not a perfect beloved. Our concern is not for qualities which are lacking, but rather for the complete and the perfect.

4

How to Study the Torah

How may a culture's highest value be discerned? How can one determine a culture's conception of the ideal human activity? According to an anthropological theory, a key to ascertaining which activity a social, cultural, or religious group considers most worthwhile is to identify its vision of life after death. The activity aspired for in the afterlife is often the most highly valued pursuit during life. For example, Native Americans conceive of the afterlife as a "Happy Hunting Ground." Arabs tend to portray paradise as an oasis. Vikings aspired for Valhalla, the hall of Odin, a place reserved for heroes slain in battle. In Jewish religious literature, the afterlife is often portrayed as a *yeshivah shel ma'alah*, an Academy on High.[1] Life in the World to Come is described as an eternal preoccupation with the study of the Torah, with God—the Author of the Torah, as teacher, and with those who merit eternal life as His students. It is not surprising, therefore, to find the talmudic view that the first question one will be asked by the heavenly tribunal in the afterlife will be, "Did you set aside time for study of the Torah?"[2]

For Judaism, study of the Torah is the most highly valued activity. Study is the supreme *mitzvah*, the highest value.[3] For example, the sixteenth-century legal code, the *Shulhan Arukh*, summarizes earlier teachings when it states that "the study of the Torah is equivalent to all the other commandments. If one must choose between study of the Torah and the performance of another commandment, if possible one should have the other commandment performed by others so that one's studies are not interrupted. If this is not possible, let him perform the commandment and return to his studies."[4]

That study of the Torah is the most highly valued human activity is a fundamental teaching and an innovation of the talmudic rabbis. According to the Talmud, study of the Torah is the very purpose of human existence.[5] By elevating study to this exalted status, the talmudic rabbis were establishing a firm precedent for future Jewish teachings, while simultaneously revolutionizing past Jewish teachings.

During the biblical and early rabbinic periods, when the Temple functioned in Jerusalem, not study but sacrifice was the highest religious act a Jew could perform. As the conduit to the divine, the Temple was the holiest place, the most sacred entity on earth. The primary religious act was the sacrifice. The most important religious leader was the priest, who qualified for his sacred function by virtue of patrilineal descent from a family of priests. However, the end of Jewish political independence and the destruction of the Temple by the Romans in 70 C.E. caused a crisis of immense proportions for Judaism. Could Judaism continue, now that the Temple and its sacrificial cult no longer were available?

To this question and in response to this crisis, the early talmudic rabbis advocated a revolutionary solution. Now, they proposed, the center of Jewish religious life would no longer be a place, i.e., the Temple, but a book – the Torah. The central religious figure would no longer be the priest who offers sacrifices at the Temple, but the scholar who interprets the Torah, the rabbi who studies the sacred words and elucidates their meaning.[6] The act of supremely sacred significance would no longer be the sacrifice, but continuous study of the Torah, which would perpetuate God's word, and which would convey His will for human behavior. Unlike the Temple that could function only in Jerusalem, both the Book and the scholar were portable. Hence, Judaism became portable, and thereby able to survive expulsions and diasporan existence. This ideological revolution of the rabbis helped guarantee the very survival of Judaism in the aftermath of the catastrophe of 70 C.E., as well as the subsequent tragedies that punctuated Jewish history. As long as the Torah could be perpetuated through study, Judaism could continue intact. The rabbinic insistence upon the centrality of study thereby ensured both the survival and the revival of Judaism.[7]

The talmudic rabbis deferred the rebuilding of the Temple and the restoration of the sacrificial cult to the messianic era that would come at the twilight of history. Until then, the Torah would serve as Judaism's sanctuary. Until the messianic advent, study and prayer would replace sacrifice.[8] Study and prayer would now fulfill the primary function of sacrifice – bringing one closer to God. Nonetheless, in the Talmud one already encounters the view that study of the Torah not only equals but surpasses the offering of sacrifices.[9]

Reflecting on the etymological relationship between the Hebrew word for "sacrifice" ("*korban*") and the Hebrew word for "near" ("*karov*"), the sixteenth-century Jewish mystic, Judah Loew of Prague, commented that while the sacrifices served to bring those far from God near to God, those who study the Torah *already* are close to God by virtue of their preoccupation with His Torah.[10] From this perspective, study of the Torah can serve as a conduit to knowledge of one's heritage, knowledge of one's own self, and to cohesion with the divine.[11] The text of the Torah is a door to intimacy with its Author. Study of the Torah is an entrée to love of God and to communion with God.[12]

While, in a sense, the sanctity of the synagogue—the place for prayer—replaced the Temple as the primary location for divine worship, Jewish law nonetheless elevated the sanctity of the house of study above the house of prayer, thereby indicating the priority of study of the Torah over prayer. For example, in his legal code, the *Mishneh Torah*, Maimonides affirms that "the sanctity of the school is greater than that of the synagogue."[13] Maimonides' view is based upon a talmudic observation that a place in which the Torah is magnified, i.e., a school, takes precedence over a place where prayer is sanctified, i.e., a synagogue.[14] Jewish law permits a synagogue to be converted into a school, but prohibits a school from being converted into a synagogue.[15]

One reason why study was elevated over prayer is because study was considered, at least by the kabbalists, to be a conduit to revelation. A medieval Jewish proverb says that "in prayer, we speak to God, but in study, God speaks to us." For the *Zohar* and for the Lurianic kabbalists, the experience of Moses at Sinai is a model to be emulated, a goal toward which one should aspire.[16] Study is a means to unveiling the previously concealed. It is an endless voyage, replete with discovery. In the words of the *Zohar*, "God is attentive to the voice of those who occupy themselves with the Torah, and through each new discovery made by them in the Torah, a new heaven is created."[17]

Because of the centrality given study of the Torah, the obligation to study could not be restricted to a scholarly elite, but was viewed as a lifelong endeavor, incumbent upon each person. In Maimonides' words, "Every Jew is under an obligation to study Torah, whether rich or poor, healthy or ailing, young or old, vigorous or feeble. . . . Until when in life ought one study Torah? Until the day of one's death, as it is written, 'Lest they [the words of Torah] depart from your heart all the days of your life' (Deuteronomy 4:9)."[18]

Learning is not meant to be a passing fad, a demand only put upon the young, but a lifelong quest for knowledge, wisdom, and self-understanding. With regard to this quest, the Talmud advises:

If someone tells you, "I have labored but not found,"
    do not believe him.
If he says, "I have not labored, but I have found,"
    do not believe him.
But, if he says, "I have labored and I have found,"
    then believe him.[19]

Study is the means by which Jewish ethical and religious teachings are preserved and transmitted. Without continuous study, tradition would come to an abrupt halt. Judaism would become a fossil, a relic for investigation rather than a living and lived faith. But, while study of the Torah serves to perpetuate Judaism, and while it has its own intrinsic value, study of Torah has been understood to have other goals and functions, including the creation of the artful life.[20]

The goal of study is not merely to amass information, but to bring about the spiritual transformation of the individual. In this regard, medieval Jewish scholars compared the erudite scholar who had amassed much book learning, but who neither grasped its contents nor considered its implementation, to "a donkey carrying books."[21] Erudition is a prerequisite, not a destination. Erudition alone is an empty parade of learning, marching on energetically but aimlessly. As will be discussed below (Chapter 7), wisdom—knowing what to do with what one knows—surpasses the accumulation of knowledge alone.[22]

A prominent rabbinic view maintains that "doing depends upon learning rather than *vice versa*," that proper learning leads to proper action, while action does not always lead to learning.[23] Learning informs moral behavior; "the unlearned cannot be pious."[24] Learning that does not lead to virtuous action, that does not engender self-transformation, is stillborn. As a midrash observes, "If one studies without the intention to observe, it is better that he had not been born . . . it would have been better that he had been strangled by the placenta at birth, and had never ventured into the world."[25] Similarly, in his *Ethical Letter* to his son, Nahmanides wrote, "Take care to always study Torah diligently so that you will be able to fulfill its commands. When you rise from study, ponder carefully what you have learned and see what there is in it which you can put into practice." With specific reference to the study of ethical literature, Rabbi Elijah, the Gaon of Vilna, wrote, "Reading moral words should rouse one to perform moral works."[26]

Proper study means learning why, how, and what to do in the creation of the artful life. No passive voyeur, no casual tourist surveying the landscape of learning, the student of the Torah is one committed to *live* what he or she learns. For example, Bahya ibn Pakudah condemned those who elucidate obscurities of the talmudic text while ignoring "the duties of the heart and paying no attention to what would be detrimental to their religious and moral activities . . . they cite the conflicting views of talmudic authorities on legal novellae while neglecting topics which they have no right to do—topics that affect their spiritual interests, which it is their duty to investigate." Bahya then lauds those students of the Torah "who have exerted themselves to know the duties of the heart as well as the active duties and also what is detrimental to right conduct."[27] But, worse than those who study without relating their studies to correlative moral and spiritual development, are those that sabotage the fruits of learning with immoral deeds.[28] Such an individual is described by a midrash as "soiling his learning" by his deeds.[29] Similarly, *Orhot Zaddikim* states: "What is the meaning of the verse (Hosea 2:7), 'For their mother played the harlot'? . . . When do words of Torah become like harlots? When those who study them shame them by their conduct."[30] The sentiment expressed by these texts reminds one of the jingle by Elizabeth Wordsworth:

> If all the good people were clever,
> And all the clever people were good,
> The world would be nicer than ever
> We thought that it possibly could.

Properly employed, learning serves as a critical component in the creation of the artful life. Learning can be life's greatest adventure. The Talmud recalls a proverb: "He who has knowledge has everything; he who lacks knowledge, what has he? He who has acquired knowledge, what does he lack? He who lacks knowledge, what has he acquired?"[31] But, knowledge that does not enhance self-knowledge is a *non sequitur*, a premise without a conclusion. In this regard, the hasidic master, Mendel of Kotzk, is reputed to have said the following to a scholar who was erudite but nothing more: "What good is understanding a text, if one does not thereby attain a better understanding of oneself?"[32] It is also told that an eminent scholar once approached Rabbi Mendel of Kotzk and boasted that he had gone through the entire Talmud. Unimpressed, Rabbi Mendel retorted, "So, you have gone through the Talmud, but how much of the Talmud has gone through you?"[33]

The Talmud requires one to recite a blessing thanking God for commanding one to be "occupied with words of Torah" (*la-asok be-divrei Torah*).[34] Commenting on this text, Judah Loew observes that this blessing does not state that one should merely "study" the Torah but that one should be "occupied" with the Torah. According to Loew, study is not limited to being an academic exercise, but should be an experience in which all aspects of the person are engaged. Study is meant to reflect a personal commitment. Not distinct from experience, study *is* experience.[35] It is learning how to become what one knows, how to build life as a work of art from the raw materials granted through study, how to translate classical texts into a contemporary life-style. In the words of a midrash, "Let the Torah never be for you an antiquated decree . . . but one issued this very day," and, "when one occupies oneself with the study of the Torah, one should say: It is as if I received the Torah from Sinai today."[36]

The purpose of study should not be self-aggrandizement, but love of God, knowledge of self, and spiritual self-development. Learning is to the soul what food is to the body, a source of sustenance and enrichment. As the nineteenth-century hasidic master, Shneur Zalman of Liady, wrote:

> Seeing that through the knowledge of the Torah one's soul and mind encompass the Torah and are in turn encompassed by it, the Torah is called food and the sustenance of the soul. For just as material food sustains the body and enters it and is transformed in the body into flesh and blood, by virtue of which one lives and endures, so it is with regard to knowledge of the Torah and its comprehension by one who studies with concentration until the Torah is grasped by the mind and becomes united with it.[37]

In this view, one must consume and become consumed by the Torah. Study of the Torah is a means; becoming the Torah is the goal. Commenting on the phrase "ve-zot torat ha-Adam" [literally: "and this is the Torah of man" (2 Samuel 7:19)], Mordecai of Chernobyl explained it to mean that "one becomes the Torah oneself."[38] The goal is not only to study Torah, but to *become* Torah.[39]

The talmudic rabbis read the verse describing the Torah as an inheritance (*morashah*) of Israel (Deuteronomy 33:4) as denoting the betrothal (*me-orashah*) of the people of Israel (and of each individual Jew) to the Torah.[40] As kabbalist Samuel of Uceda observed, commenting on this talmudic text, betrothal infers commitment, and commitment grants a license for intimacy.[41] The hasidic master Ephraim of Sudlykow further observed, "When one studies the Torah for its own sake, to keep it and perform it, then he brings all his limbs closer to their source whence they originated and were generated, namely the Torah . . . and he becomes identical to the Torah like the unification of man and woman."[42] This observation personifies the Torah as a beloved and the one who studies the Torah as a lover, and analogizes textual study to sexual experience. The roots of this analogy are found in talmudic literature, but for a vivid expression of this analogy, one must inevitably turn to the *Zohar*, specifically to the text excerpted below.[43]

In talmudic and midrashic literature, the revelation at Sinai is compared to a wedding between God and Israel, as well as to a wedding between the people of Israel and the Torah.[44] Other texts compare Moses to a bridegroom and the Torah to a bride at the Sinaitic revelation.[45] Moses represents the paradigmatic lover of the Torah. For the *Zohar*, the goal of the student of the Torah, of the lover of the Torah, is to emulate Moses. Just as Moses was transformed through his intimate contact with the Torah, so should the student of the Torah, the lover of the Torah, aspire for revelation, self-transformation, and self-discovery. This is one of the teachings of the texts from the *Zohar* excerpted below.

Up to this point, discussion has focused on the question of *why* to study the Torah. This issue is addressed by the following excerpts from the *Zohar*. However, these texts also relate to the question of *how* to study the Torah. In this regard, both excerpts admonish one to recognize that textual study cannot be superficial. A text is a mine requiring exploration in depth. More is always there than appears on the surface. The text is pregnant with a plethora of meanings. One is obliged to disrobe and to penetrate the text in order to elicit its meaning.

According to the *Zohar*, there are four major levels of meaning in the text. These are often denoted by the acronym *PaRDeS*, representing *Peshat, Remez, Derash,* and *Sod*. *Peshat* is usually taken to refer to the literal or contextual meaning of a text, the text's "simple" meaning. However, this is not so for the kabbalists. They relate the etymology of the word *peshat* not to the word *simple* (*pashut*) or obvious meaning of the text, but to the verb *lifshot*, meaning "to divest, to undress."[46]

Remez, meaning "hint," refers to the process of making explicit those implicit meanings buried in the text. (In the text below, the term *haggadah* is used instead of *remez*.)

Derash refers to *midrash*, characteristic of the midrashic literature of the talmudic rabbis. But, the *Zohar* itself is written in the form of a midrash. Midrash etymologically means "to search," and as such it represents a quest that includes philology, etymology, hermeneutics, homiletics, and literary imagination. A function of midrash is to re-create, to re-tell, and to re-fashion the text of the Torah to elicit new meanings from old texts, newly forged relationships between ancient texts and contemporary situations.

Sod means "mystery." This is the particularly kabbalistic understanding of Scripture, analogized by the *Zohar* to sexual relations, to becoming a "husband" of the Torah, to standing "face-to-face" with the Torah in an intimate embrace. To be sure, this level of understanding is vouchsafed only to the few, to those who have devoted themselves exclusively to translating their love of the Torah into action through long-standing diligence and complete commitment.

※

The first text below is in the form of a short allegorical fable, even a fairy tale.[47] The Torah is compared to a beautiful maiden ensconced in the tower

of a castle. The scholar is the prince, the lover, who rescues her from
isolation. This motif is common to many fables and fairy tales. Like in the
study of Rapunzel, the maiden in this tale—the Torah—has to render a bit of
assistance to her lover and redeemer. This text is an example of how Jewish
literature employs tales and allegories to make an ethical or religious point. In
reading this text, one can picture the castles of thirteenth-century Spain,
where the Zohar appeared. The maiden dwells in a small room in a minaret of
a huge castle. The narrow window of the room is her only opening to the
outside world.

The scholar—the lover of the Torah—is constantly stationed outside the
castle. He knows she is there, but he does not know how he can actually meet
her, i.e., the scholar constantly peruses the text, searching for its meaning, for
its essence, for its true message. The scholar is like a frantic lover who knows
that he is in love, with whom he is in love, but who is ignorant of how to
consummate his love. For this reason, the maiden—the Torah—has to render
him help. She appears at the window and offers him a glance of herself. Now
he knows where she is and how she looks, i.e., while he studies the text, the
scholar is vouchsafed a hint of its deeper meaning.

The maiden appears at the window and then she retracts, flirting with her
lover and hoping to lure him on. Because he is her lover, he catches the
glance that others might not notice, or that others might disregard. Seeing
her, even for an instant, his love becomes more intense, but still he remains
fumbling and frustrated by his inability to come closer to her. Consequently,
she takes matters into her own hands and brings him to her.

As they meet, she progressively reveals more of herself. These various
levels of "converse" correspond to the various levels by which the Torah may
be progressively better understood. When they are together, she begins to
speak from behind a veil. One can picture here the Spanish Arabian women
whose faces are mostly concealed with veils; only their eyes being visible to
others. This level of converse is compared to the homiletical level of understanding the text called derashah. Having initiated him into this level of
intimacy, she speaks from behind a transparent veil, i.e., the level of
haggadah. He can now perceive the meaning of hints in the text to deeper
meanings that previously escaped his attention. Finally, she reveals all, and
he understands the meaning and nature of the Torah in its greatest depth and
in its deepest sense. This description contains blatant erotic imagery and
symbolism. The term "to converse" is a talmudic euphemism for sexual
intercourse, as is the term "face-to-face" in the symbolism of the Zohar. The
maiden who begins by flirting with her lover from the seclusion of the room
in her tower eventually seduces her lover completely. In the process of his
seduction, she surrenders her seclusion and her mystery. Now, he "knows"
her. (It is not coincidental that the Bible uses the same word, yada, both for

knowledge and for sexual experience.) For the *Zohar*, the question of *how* to study the Torah is answered by comparing the one who studies to an obsessed lover whose perpetual persistence will ultimately yield the fulfillment of all his desires. For the *Zohar*, study of the Torah is an endeavor for the intellectually passionate.

According to the second text, the Torah may be compared to an iceberg in that only a small part of it is apparent to the casual viewer. The apparent meaning of the Torah, stated by its text, is important in and of itself, but it is also an entrée to the deeper levels of meaning hidden beneath the words, laws, and stories that comprise its text. This *Zohar* addresses the question of how to study the Torah, by insisting that the apparent is not necessarily the real, that what the Torah may appear to be is not what it actually is. In this view, the Torah is to be studied not as literature, not as other literary works, because it is not the same as other literary works. The Torah is considered a work replete with revealed truths. Only persistent and careful investigation of its text can lead to an apprehension and to a comprehension of its levels and depths of meaning. The narrative portions of the Torah are compared to the clothes a person wears, but clothes are not identical to the person who wears them. According to this text, only a fool would judge a person by the clothes he or she wears. The principles of the Torah that may be elicited from its narratives and laws are compared to the body of a person. Yet, the soul, and not the body, constitutes a person's essence and true nature. Just as the soul is not apparent when one looks at a person, so is the "true Torah," the Torah in essence as distinct from the Torah in manifestation, hidden from view. A deeper level of perception is required to apprehend it. What the text is saying when it restricts knowledge of this level to those "who stood on Mount Sinai," is that to Jews alone is this level of understanding vouchsafed. The text then compares the body to the "Community of Israel," the soul to the "Glory of Israel," and the "soul of the soul" of the Torah to the "Ancient Holy One." These terms refer to the symbolic understanding of God's nature developed by the Jewish mystical tradition in general, and by the *Zohar* in particular. God's "personality," as it were, is portrayed by the *Zohar* in terms of ten qualities or *sefirot* that emanate out of God's inscrutable essential nature, called *En Sof*. Each of these terms—"Community of Israel," "Glory of Israel," and "Ancient Holy One," refers to one of these *sefirot*. The text's assertion that the "soul of the soul of the Torah" will be vouchsafed only in the "future," means that the truly essential and spiritual nature of the Torah eludes even the most adept scholar during life. Only in the World to Come, the purely spiritual realm, can one apprehend the essence of the Torah in its purely essential and spiritual form. The *Zohar*, which elsewhere describes our dimension of existence as a world of veils and illusions, seems to maintain that knowledge of truths is available to us here, but that knowledge of absolute truth must escape our grasp, that knowledge of absolute truth is not a feature of earthly existence.

The *Zohar*, the Book of Splendor, Radiance, Enlightenment, is the central text of the Jewish mystical tradition.[48] It is structured as a commentary on the Pentateuch. Esoteric both by nature and design, the *Zohar* is written in its own brand of Aramaic. After the Bible, Talmud, and prayerbook, the *Zohar* is probably the most important work of Jewish religious literature. During the Holocaust, some Jews carried the *Zohar* with them into the camps, even into the gas chambers. The hasidic master, Pinhas of Koretz, once said, "Without the *Zohar*, it would be difficult to be a Jew." The *Zohar* has been called "the soul of the Torah."

Traditionally, the *Zohar* is attributed to the second-century rabbi, Simeon bar Yohai. The predominant view in modern scholarship, however, is that the *Zohar* was written by the thirteenth-century Spanish Jewish mystic, Moses de Leon. A third theory, which seems more reasonable, is that Moses de Leon was the editor rather than the author of the *Zohar*. Drawing upon earlier traditions, written and oral, he made available and "public" in a carefully crafted, edited form, a wealth of earlier traditions that were transmitted in small circles of kabbalists over many generations. After the expulsion of the Jews from Spain in 1492, the *Zohar* became the Bible of Kabbalah. The mystical-ethical literature produced during the sixteenth and seventeenth centuries helped spread the *Zohar's* teachings, as did the advent of printing with moveable type. The first two editions of the *Zohar* were printed in 1558 and 1560 in Italy.

The *Zohar* must be read simultaneously on many levels. Each text is packed with multivalent meanings, encoded by a sophisticated set of symbols and allusions. The student of the *Zohar* is constantly challenged with the task of decoding and unpacking its meanings.

Basic to the *Zohar* and to Jewish mysticism is the idea that God is manifest through ten potencies or emanations called *sefirot*, representing the divine attributes, but that the essence of God called *En Sof* (Limitless) is beyond the ken of human apprehension, comprehension, or relationship. The *Zohar* articulates the typically kabbalistic theosophical-theurgic view, i.e., that human activities can affect the Godhead. Virtuous activities affect the divine positively, while sins affect the divine negatively. In this view, the human being is a central protagonist in the drama of creation, since each action one performs affects not only himself or herself, not only one's society, but also the divine. Human actions affect either positively or negatively the balance between, and the flow down, of the divine influx from the *sefirot* described in male, female, and neuter symbolic terms.[49] Thus, the *Zohar* makes extensive use of erotic symbolism, seeing reality as the interplay, even as the intercourse between male and female forces that inhere not only in the human and natural realms, but in the realm of the divine as well. As was noted above, this use of erotic symbolism is especially pronounced in the first of the two texts from the *Zohar* excerpted below.

The Zohar

Companions, it was not just to say what I have said up to now that I entered upon this discourse with you, for certainly an old man such as I would hardly stop at one utterance, making a sound like a single coin in a jar. What a multitude of humans there are who dwell in confusion, failing to perceive the way of truth that abides in the Torah, and the Torah, in love, summons them day after day to her, but woe, they do not so much as turn their heads. It is just as I have stated, the Torah releases one word, and comes forth from her sheath ever so little, and then retreats to concealment again. But this she does only for them who understand her and follow her precepts.

She may be compared to a beautiful and stately maiden, who is secluded in an isolated chamber of a palace, and has a lover of whose existence she alone knows. For love of her he passes by her gate unceasingly, and turns his eyes in all directions to discover her. She is aware that he is forever hovering about the palace, and what does she do? She thrusts open a small door in her secret chamber, for a moment reveals her face to her lover, then quickly withdraws it. He alone, none else, notices it; but he is aware it is from love of him that she has revealed herself to him for that moment, and his heart and his soul and everything within him are drawn to her.

So it is with the Torah, who discloses her innermost secrets only to them who love her. She knows that whosoever is wise in heart hovers near the gates of her dwelling place day after day. What does she do? From her palace, she shows her face to him, and gives him a signal of love, and forthwith retreats back to her hiding place. Only he alone catches her message, and he is drawn to her with his whole heart and soul, and with all of his being. In this manner, the Torah, for a moment, discloses herself in love to her lovers, so as to rouse them to renewed love. This then is the way of the Torah. In the beginning, when she first reveals herself to a man, she gives him some sign. If he understands, it is well, but if he fails, then she summons him and calls him "simpleton," and says to her messengers: Go tell that simpleton to come to me, and converse—as it is written: "Whoso is a simpleton, let him turn in hither" (Proverbs 9:4). And when he arrives, she commences to speak with him, at first from behind the veil which she has hung before her words, so that they may suit his manner of understanding, in order that he may progress gradually. This is known as *derashah*. Then she speaks to him behind a filmy veil of finer mesh, she speaks to him in riddles and allegories—and these are called *haggadah*.

When, finally, he is on near terms with her, she stands disclosed face-to-face with him, and holds converse with him concerning all of her secret mysteries, and all the secret ways which have been hidden in her heart from immemorial time. Then is such a man a true adept in the Torah, a "master of the house," for to him she has uncovered all her mysteries, neither keeping back nor hiding any single one. She says to him: Do you see the sign, the cue, which I gave you in the beginning, how many mysteries it holds? He then comes to the realization that not one thing may be added to the words of the Torah, nor taken from them, not a sign and not a letter.

Hence should men pursue the Torah with all their might, so as to come to be her lovers, as we have shown.

Rabbi Simeon said: If a man looks upon the Torah as merely a book presenting narratives and everyday matters, alas for him! Such a Torah, one treating with everyday concerns, and indeed a more excellent one, we too, even we, could compile. More than that, in the possession of the rulers of the world there are books of even greater merit, and these we could emulate if we wished to compile some such Torah. But the Torah, in all of its words, holds supernal truths and sublime secrets.

See how precisely balanced are the upper and the lower worlds. Israel here below is balanced by the angels on high, concerning whom it stands written: "who makest your angels into winds" (Psalms 104:4). For when the angels descend to earth they don earthly garments, else they could neither abide in the world, nor could it bear to have them. But if this is so with the angels, then how much more so it must be with the Torah: the Torah it was that created the angels and created all the worlds and through Torah are all sustained. The world could not endure the Torah if she had not garbed herself in garments of this world.

Thus the tales related in the Torah are simply her outergarments, and woe to the man who regards that outer garb as the Torah itself, for such a man will be deprived of portion in the next world. Thus David said: "Open Thou mine eyes, that I may behold wondrous things out of Your Torah" (Psalms 119:18), that is to say, the things that are underneath. See now. The most visible part of a man are the clothes that he has on, and they who lack understanding, when they look at the man, are apt not to see more in him than these clothes. In reality, however, it is the body of the man that constitutes the pride of his clothes, and his soul constitutes the pride of his body.

So it is with the Torah. Its narrations which relate to things of the world constitute the garments which clothe the body of the Torah; and that body is composed of the Torah's precepts, *gufey-torah* [bodies, major principles]. People without understanding see only the narrations, the garment; those somewhat more penetrating see also the body. But the truly wise, those who serve the most high King and stood on Mount Sinai, pierce all the way through to the soul, to the true Torah which is the root principle of all. These same will in the future be vouchsafed to penetrate to the very soul of the soul of the Torah.

See now how it is like this in the highest world, with garment, body, soul, and super-soul. The outer garments are the heavens and all therein, the body is the Community of Israel and it is the recipient of the soul, that is "the Glory of Israel", and the soul of the soul is the Ancient Holy One. All of these are conjoined one within the other.

Woe to the sinners who look upon the Torah as simply tales pertaining to things of the world, seeing thus only the outer garment. But the righteous whose gaze penetrates to the very Torah, happy are they. Just as wine must be in a jar to keep, so the Torah must be contained in an outer garment. That garment is made up of the tales and stories; but we, we are bound to penetrate beyond.

5

How to Repent

One of the most popularly and regularly observed rituals in America is the annual medical check-up. Each year, millions of people are examined, tested, and evaluated in order to determine the state of their physical health and well-being. Often, one fasts in preparation for a variety of tests and procedures. One waits anxiously for test results. If an illness is detected or if a potential illness is indicated, a modification of one's behavior is required. When sickness is diagnosed, a regimen is prescribed to help restore health. What may be ascertained during the examination period can lead to a change of life-style for the rest of the year; indeed, for the remainder of one's life.

During the High Holiday season, Jews undergo a kind of spiritual "check-up." Prayer, fasting, and introspection are meant to be catalysts to aid one in evaluating the state of one's spiritual health. This process is called *teshuvah* – repentance. The task is to ascertain the health or illness of one's soul, of one's self. When a moral malady is detected, a modification of one's ethical behavior is indicated. When a spiritual disturbance is diagnosed, a regimen of moral rehabilitation is indicated.

"*Teshuvah*" means return, a return from a state of spiritual and moral dis-ease to a state of spiritual and moral health.[1] *Teshuvah* is an indispensable variety of spiritual and moral therapy. In his "Sermon for Rosh Hashanah," Bahya ben Asher wrote:

Repentance is a cure, as it is written, "Return and be healed" (Isaiah 6:10). It is a cure because sin is the sickness of the soul. Just as the physical body is subject to

59

health and sickness, so is the soul. The health of the body is indicated by its good deeds, and its sickness by its sins. Just as a physical sickness is cured by its antithesis, so is the sick, sinful soul restored to health by its antithesis.[2]

While some bodily illnesses are incurable, the restoration of spiritual health is perpetually possible and readily available through repentance. In this regard, the fifteenth-century Jewish philosopher Joseph Albo wrote:

> It is like the case of a person who is suffering from a serious illness which is regarded as incurable. Then a physician comes and says to the patient: I will tell you of a drug which will cure you of your illness. The patient thinks that since it can cure what is regarded as an incurable disease, the drug must be very costly, and extremely difficult to obtain. But the physician says: Do not think there is any difficulty in obtaining this drug.[3]

Repentance becomes necessary when sin becomes possible. Sin is a misuse of the gift of free will. But, free will is like a precious double-edged sword. With moral freedom, sin becomes likely, but without freedom, moral development is impossible. The ability to choose is meaningless unless it includes the possibility of choosing incorrectly. With choice comes error.

When Alexander Pope wrote that "to err is human," he echoed a sentiment of biblical origin: "There is no person who does not sin" (1 Kings 8:46; 2 Chronicles 6:36). This observation is both realistic and optimistic. Because human beings are imperfect by nature, they err. Nonetheless, human error can be surmounted and overcome. As the Bible has God say to Cain, "Sin couches at the door . . . yet you can be its master" (Genesis 4:7).

Though sin is real, rehabilitation and improvement are possible. According to Maimonides, were an individual to believe that there were no remedy for sin, "he would persist in his error and sometimes perhaps disobey even more because of the fact that no stratagem remains at his disposal. If, however, he believes in repentance, he can correct himself and return to a better and more perfect state than the one he was in before he sinned."

A reflection of this ongoing concern with sin and repentance is a prayer recited three times daily by observant Jews (in the *Amidah*):

> Our Father, forgive us
> for we have sinned.
> Our King, pardon us,
> for we have transgressed.
> For You forgive and pardon.

The corollary of "to err is human" is "to forgive divine."[4] The biblical assurance is that while sin is always possible, repentance and reconciliation are always available. Were sin not a persistent reality, repentance would not be an urgent necessity. Just as physical maladies require treatment for the body to function properly, so do spiritual illnesses require attention so that the individual may get on with the task of creating his or her life as a work of art.

Because life is so fragile, so precarious, initiating the process of repentance cannot be deferred. "Rabbi Eliezer said: Repent one day before your death. His disciples asked him: Master, does a person know the day of his death? To this question, he responded: Even more so then; let a person repent today, for tomorrow he might die, and all his days will have been spent in repentance."[5] In a similar vein, a midrash comments on the phrase in Psalms (144:4), "one's days are like a passing shadow." "What kind of shadow? If life is like a shadow cast by a wall it endures. . . . Rabbi Huna in the name of Rabbi Aba explained: Life is like a bird which flies past, and its shadow flies past with it. Samuel said: Life is like the shadow of a bee which has no substance at all."[6] Commenting on Hillel's often quoted phrase, "If not now, when?," Jonah Gerondi wrote:

"If not now, when?," i.e., I cannot afford to delay for one or two days my exertions on behalf of the perfection of my soul. . . . When perfection of the soul is delayed, the evil inclination grows stronger . . . and self improvement becomes difficult thereafter. . . . It may be that one's days will not be prolonged and that one will die before one has rendered his portion of repentance. . . .[7]

Repentance is a process that commences with self-awareness and results in self-renewal. Repentance is a vehicle for the re-creation of the self, for the creation of one's life as a work of art.[8] However, according to Joseph Albo, a substantial impediment to the restoration of spiritual health through repentance is the individual's failure to recognize the existence of his or her malady. Awareness of illness is the first step toward a cure. Without such an awareness, the malady can only worsen. Albo wrote:

If a person does not recognize or know that he has sinned, he will never regret doing the thing he does, nor repent, as a sick person cannot be cured as long as he does not know or feel that he is sick, for he will never seek a cure. So if one does not know he has sinned, he never will repent.[9]

Once an individual is aware of his or her malady, it can only be expected that a cure will be sought. As Bahya ibn Pakudah states in the text excerpted below, one "must have firm knowledge that repentance is the only cure for his malady, the path to recovery from his bad deed and evil act, through which he may correct his error and rectify his misdeed."[10]

In Bahya ibn Pakudah's work, as in much of the literature regarding sin and repentance, considerable discussion is devoted to factors that inhibit repentance, and which thereby prevent spiritual well-being.[11] One, already noted, is a lack of awareness of spiritual illness. A second is habit. In Bahya's words, "Another thing which makes repentance difficult is that habit makes wrong-doing almost necessary to a person, like the natural actions from which it is almost impossible for one to abstain."[12] Habit undercuts the process of repentance because it deprives the individual of moral volition, which is the underlying premise that makes rehabilitation possible. Regarding habit, Moses Hayyim Luzzatto wrote, "He who has thus become a slave to habit is no longer his own master, and cannot act differently, even should he want to. His will is held in bondage by certain habits which have become second nature with him."[13]

According to Joseph Albo, a further impediment to initiating the process of repentance is the tendency for one to blame others for his or her own mistakes. Albo terms this tendency "self-excuse." As an example, Albo refers to Adam, who tried to excuse himself for his sin by blaming Eve for his own transgression, as Eve, in turn, tried to blame the snake for hers. For Albo, the sin of Adam and Eve was not primarily that they disobeyed God by eating the forbidden fruit, but that they refused to take responsibility for their own actions. According to Albo, "self-excuse" provides no alibi, "for human beings were given reason so that they may always watch their conduct and not sin."[14]

Once the awareness of a need for repentance, for spiritual and moral renewal has been recognized, and obstacles to its initiation have been confronted and overcome, the actual process of teshuvah can commence. In much of medieval Jewish literature, intellectual resolve is the first step of a three-step process of repentance. According to Albo, "the elements of repentance by which a person may be cleansed of his iniquities and purified of his sin before God are correction of thought, speech and action."[15] In his sixteenth-century encyclopediac mystical-ethical treatise Shnei Luhot ha-Brit, Isaiah Horowitz observes that since sins are committed by thought, by speech, and by action, repentance must also include these three elements.[16] Albo defined intellectual resolve or "correction of thought" as feeling regret on account of one's sins. "Correction of speech" signifies that one should confess one's sins. "Correction of action" means that one must not repeat one's sinful actions, and should embark on a regimen of "good deeds."

Regret, remorse, and intellectual recognition of one's sins constitute the first necessary step on the road to moral recovery and to spiritual rehabilitation. According to the sixteenth-century sage, Moses ben Joseph di Trani, the intellectual factor in repentance is the most important of the three elements. In his *Beth Elohim*, di Trani states:

> The essence of repentance is regret over the past and departure from sin in the future. Without both of these elements, repentance cannot be complete. . . . Therefore, the essence of repentance is intellectual in two ways: that one have thoughts of remorse and that one intellectually resolve to depart from the sin one has committed.[17]

For di Trani, the essentials of repentance are remorse and resolve: remorse over what happened and resolve not to repeat it. Remorse without resolve indicates that the remorse is insincere because a motivation other than contrition might underlie it. It may simply be that the opportunity to repeat a specific act may just not become available; or, it may be that the sinner no longer finds the specific sin attractive any longer. Without the intellectual awareness that one has acted incorrectly, the process of repentance is thwarted at the outset. One cannot resolve to avoid repeating a mistake unless one first has recognized that an error has been committed. As Bahya ibn Pakudah states in the excerpt below, "a man's undertaking never to repeat his sins is a sign of his knowledge that what he has done is wrong. . . ."[18]

The second step in the process of repentance is confession of one's misdeeds. From an intellectual awareness of one's faults, and out of a resolve not to perpetuate them, one moves toward a specification of one's faults by making a verbal declaration. Confession translates intellectual assent into verbal commitment. As Maimonides says, "It is necessary that one make oral confession and utter the resolutions that one has made in one's mind."[19]

Confession is a concrete act by means of which one renounces one's misdeeds. It serves as a transition between the intellectually abstract and the concrete alterations of behavior that must follow to make repentance complete and that validate the sincerity of the penitent's resolve. Maimonides identifies confession as a religious obligation. Summarizing the vast biblical and rabbinic literature regarding confession that preceded him, and adding some embellishments of his own, Maimonides writes:

> With regard to all the precepts of the Torah, affirmative or negative, if a person transgressed any one of them, either willfully or in error, and repents and turns away from his sin, he is duty bound to confess before God, blessed be He, as it is written, "When a man or a woman shall commit any sin people commit, to do a trespass against the Lord, and that person be guilty, then they shall confess their sin which they have done" (Numbers 5:6–7); this means confess in words, and this confession is an affirmative commandment. How does one confess? The penitent says: "I beseech you, O Lord, I have sinned, I have acted perversely, I have

transgressed before you, and I have done such and such, and I repent and am ashamed of my deeds, and I never shall do this again." This constitutes the essence of the confession. The fuller and more detailed the confession one makes, the more praiseworthy he is.[20]

Confession of sin became both a public and a private activity. The prayerbook contains public confessionals, recited during communal prayer, such as those recited on the Day of Atonement, as well as private confessionals such as the deathbed confessional.[21] Regarding private confession, Isaiah Horowitz records that his father made private confession of his sins three times daily: "And every night before he would retire he would list the deeds he performed that day. Then, he would sit alone and contemplate them. He would scrutinize the actions he performed not only that day but all the days of his life up until that point."[22]

A similar custom was practiced by the hasidic master, Levi Yitzhak of Berditchev. Each night before he went to bed, Levi Yitzhak would recount all the improper deeds he did during the day then coming to a close. He would list them on a sheet of paper, and then he would read them aloud, saying "Today Levi Yitzhak did such and such. Tomorrow, Levi Yitzhak will not do such and such." As he would recite the list, again and again, Levi Yitzhak would become overwhelmed with remorse and contrition, so much so that he would begin to cry. Only when his tears had wiped the paper clean of ink, would Levi Yitzhak retire for the night. In his discussion of private confessional prayers, Horowitz notes the custom of a particular sage to pray that he not be allowed to become angry since "the sin in which all other sins are subsumed is the sin of anger," for anger "is the cause of all sins."

One of the texts upon which Maimonides and others base standard formulae for confession is the following talmudic citation: "Our rabbis taught: How does one make confession? (One says:) I have done wrong (*aviti*), I have transgressed (*pashati*), I have sinned (*hatati*)."[23]

The talmudic discussion that follows this citation refers to the distinction among three varieties of sin: *hait, avon, pesha*. Confession must be made for each of these types of sin. This is why the three varieties of sin are mentioned in the confessional: *Aviti* refers to *avon, pashati* refers to *pesha*, and *hatati* refers to *hait*. The Talmud distinguishes among these three by defining *hait* as an unwitting offense, *avon* as a deliberate misdeed, and *pesha* as an act of rebellion.

The type of sin called *pesha* denotes an act of human rebellion against divine sovereignty. In this view, sin is an act of treason against the Kingdom of Heaven, and against the authority of God as Sovereign of the Universe. From this perspective, repentance entails a reacceptance of God's kingship, a reaffirmation of the laws of His kingdom, a reinstatement of the individual as a citizen of the Kingdom of God, and a "return" to and reconciliation of the individual with God.[24]

Sin as rebellion means that the individual sets himself or herself up as a moral sovereign, recognizing neither God nor moral law as providing viable standards for human behavior. *Pesha* infers an individual's refusal to be accountable to any standards of morality other than those that he or she arbitrarily establishes. Actions become self-serving, rather than being aimed at serving God or at helping others. Repentance means a restoration of one's relationship with a Source beyond the self, a reaffirmation of the binding quality of God's law upon human affairs.

While fear of punishment or fear of God are accepted and often effective motives to spur one to self-examination, to rehearsing one's misdeeds, and to behavior modification, many Jewish sources consider love to be the preferable motivation for repentance, for rehabilitation, for self-renewal, and for renewal of shattered relationships. According to Isaiah Horowitz, repentance out of fear is always tainted by self-interest. He writes, "One should not repent out of fear, i.e., out of fear of punishment, for then one repents for one's own sake. Rather, one should repent out of love for the Creator and for the sake of his Name." For one who truly loves God, the alienation from God caused by sin, like the separation of any lover from his or her beloved, becomes unbearable. Reconciliation becomes not merely desirable, but crucial.[25]

Repentance out of love flows from a desire for return, for healing a rupture of relationship rather than from a hope of reward or from a fear of punishment. The more intense the love, the more significant the relationship, the greater is the yearning for reconciliation. In this regard, Elijah de Vidas wrote in his mystical-ethical treatise, *Reshit Hokhmah*:

> Sin causes to alienate the love between an individual and God, as it is written, "Your sins have separated you from your God" (Isaiah 59:2). Therefore, since a lover does not wish his beloved to become estranged from him, the one who is obliged to the other should confess his faults to his beloved, saying to her: Truly, I have sinned against you, but do not leave me because of my offense.[26]

To effect complete reconciliation, the return must be mutual. Therefore, repentance requires both a human initiative and a divine response. The corollary of human contrition is divine grace (*hesed*).[27] A midrash observes:

> Consider the parable of a prince who was far away from his father—a hundred days journey away. His friends said to him: Return to your father. He replied, I cannot; I have not the strength. Thereupon his father sent word to him saying: Come back as far as you are able, and I will go the rest of the way to meet you. So the Holy One says to Israel: "Return to Me, and I shall return to you" (Malachi 3:7).[28]

The medieval Jewish mystics maintained that God has not only a desire for, but an interest in, human repentance. According to the kabbalists, sin not only harms the soul of the sinner, but it also injures God. In the words of the Zohar: "Whosoever transgresses the laws of the Torah causes damage above, as it were, causes damage below, damages himself, and damages all worlds."[29]

In this view, repentance not only repairs the damage one's sin causes to one's own self, but it also restores God from the harm done against Him. For the Jewish mystics repentance is *for God's sake* as well as for our own. It fulfills a divine as well as a human need.[30] "Repentance," says the *Zohar*, "repairs all. It repairs what is above, and below. It repairs damage to oneself and to all worlds."[31] Repentance unifies God's Name, fragmented by human sin. Repentance must be done "for the sake of My Name" (Isaiah 48:9), "for My Name's sake" (Ezekiel 20:44).[32]

The third and final step in the process of repentance is what Albo terms "correction of action." Unless one's intellectual remorse and resolve are translated into concrete action, one's repentance is both incomplete and ineffectual. Unless one's verbal confessions engender enacted commitment, one's confession becomes a lie, rather than an expression of sincere remorse. "Correction of action" entails both the avoidance of past sins and the performance of deeds of virtue. Maimonides sums up the talmudic teachings in this way:

> What is complete repentance? When an opportunity presents itself for repeating an offense once committed, and the offender, while able to commit the offense nevertheless refrains from doing so, not out of fear or failure of vigor, but because he is truly repentant.[33]

Jonah Gerondi, who compares sin to an illness from which one ought to be cured, commented: "His soul is sick because of those (sinful) deeds, and one who begins to recover from an illness must guard against a relapse."[34] Other sources observe that, like the process of healing physical illness, the process of recovering from a moral malady is not immediate, but requires both time and effort.

The two steps that constitute "correction of action" are: "Depart from evil, and do good" (Psalms 34:15). The medieval ethical treatise *Orhot Zaddikim* lists abandonment of sin and reversing one's deeds as being among the essentials of repentance. When discussing "reversing one's deeds," this text cites a midrash: "If you have committed bundles of transgressions, counteract them by performing corresponding bundles of sacred deeds."[35]

A sin is an action that alienates an individual from himself or herself and from God. *Teshuvah* denotes return to one's own self and to God. But, because a sin against God may also be an offense against one's fellow, repentance was not deemed truly complete unless reconciliation also was made with the injured party.[36] Furthermore, in seeking God's forgiveness, one is obliged to forgive those who have trespassed against himself or herself.[37] In so doing, the individual imitates the ways of God. Like God, one grants forgiveness and practices mercy. Like God, one desires and effects reconciliation. Thereby, theology and ethics become intertwined. What characterizes God's dealings with us become features of our relationship with one another.

According to a midrash, after David sinned, he entreated God, "Master of the World, you are a great God and my sins are also great. It is only becoming for a great God that He should forgive great sins."[38] By forgiving those who have sinned against himself or herself, the human person can share in that divine greatness. By seeking the forgiveness of God and of others, the divine image each person bears, though disfigured by sin, may be restored.

Without sin, repentance would not be possible, but without repentance, true virtue would not become attainable; creation of life as a work of art would not otherwise be realizable. It is precisely for this reason that the repentant sinner is exalted even above the purest saint.[39]

❧

Bahya ibn Pakudah's *Duties of the Heart*, from which the following text on repentance has been excerpted, has been one of the most popular works of Jewish ethical literature since its translation into Hebrew from Arabic in the twelfth century. Indeed, with the possible exception of Moses Hayyim Luzzatto's *Mesilat Yesharim—Path of the Upright*, *Duties of the Heart* has emerged as the Jewish ethical text with the most significant and longlasting impact.[40] As the eminent scholar Georges Vajda wrote, this work "established itself as the single most important Jewish ethical treatise of the whole medieval and early modern period."[41] Julius Guttmann, the great historian of Jewish philosophy, notes that Bahya's treatise historically has been "widely appreciated as the truest and purest expression of Jewish piety."[42] In the introduction to his 1925 translation of Bahya's work into English, Moses Hyamson observes that Bahya's "bright intellect, wide knowledge, liberal outlook, large toleration, mild and gentle disposition, intense piety and profound humility have made *Duties of the Heart* the first and noblest example of medieval ethical and devotional literature. The place which it won in the hearts and affections of the Jewish people hundreds of years ago, it has retained to this day."[43]

Written originally in Arabic in about 1080, Bahya's treatise was translated into Hebrew by Judah ibn Tibbon in about 1161, thereby making it available to future generations of Jews. *Duties of the Heart* has been published throughout the centuries in numerous editions, including abridged editions for more popular consumption. It also has been translated into Spanish, French, Portuguese, Italian, Yiddish, German, and English. Hyamson's English translation is based on Ibn Tibbon's Hebrew rendering of the text. Menahem Mansoor's 1973 translation, from which the following excerpt is taken, is based upon Bahya's original Arabic text.[44]

Though Bahya was the inaugurator of Jewish philosophy on European soil, and the first Jewish pietistic philosopher, very little is known of Bahya's life. Though it can be established that Bahya lived in eleventh-century Spain, the dates of his birth and death are unknown. Where in Spain he lived is uncertain; some claim Cordova, while others place him in Saragossa. From Ibn Tibbon, we learn that Bahya functioned as a *dayyan*, or judge of a rabbinic court. He also was a poet and author of hymns, a number of which have been incorporated into various Jewish liturgies.

Though *Duties of the Heart* was undoubtedly influenced by non-Jewish sources, it is a profoundly Jewish work. Unlike Ibn Gabirol's earlier work, *Improvement of the Moral Qualities*, Bahya's treatise is grounded in earlier Jewish sources and attitudes, thus justifying its claim to be the first major work of Jewish ethical literature. Because Bahya affirmed that "whoever utters a wise word, even if he belongs to the Gentiles, is called a sage," he borrowed unabashedly from non-Jewish writings, especially from the works of Islamic mystics (*sufis*), pietists, and philosophers, and from the New Testament. Nevertheless, he was firmly grounded in biblical and rabbinic sources, and declared that the purpose of his book was to fill a gap in extant Jewish religious literature.

According to Bahya, religion in general and Judaism in particular "is divided into two parts. One is knowledge of the external duties of the body and its members; the other is the internal knowledge of the secret duties of the heart." Upon reviewing Jewish religious literature up until his day, Bahya discovered that while substantial attention had been given to the external duties, to "the duties of the limbs," works regarding the inner life, "the duties of the heart," were unavailable. "When I found that this knowledge, the duties of the heart, was neglected, not contained in any book comprising all its origins, forsaken, with none of its chapters collected in any one work, I was astonished," Bahya wrote. From his astonishment, Bahya moved to a question: Are the duties of the heart really necessary for human existence, for religious existence, and particularly for Jewish religious life? Basing his response on "logic" and on the "tradition of our ancient sages," Bahya answers, without qualification, in the affirmative. Bahya reasoned that since the duties of the limbs "are of no avail to us unless our hearts choose to do them and our souls desire their performance," the "duties of the heart" are not only necessary, but are essential. Without the duties of the heart, the duties of the limbs become perfunctory, devoid of motivation, stripped of meaning. It is the inner life that gives meaning, direction, purpose, and motivation for one's actions. Without the duties of the heart, religion becomes like a body without a soul, a lifeless torso. Only when the duties of the limbs are predicated upon and complemented by the duties of the heart, can religious life properly function.

On logical grounds, Bahya maintains that the duties of the limbs are fallacies without the accompaniment of the duties of the heart. Without intention and sincerity, action becomes a conclusion without a premise. Satisfied that he had established the logical need for duties of the heart, Bahya argues that tradition, as well as logic, demands that the duties of the heart are central to religious life. For example, Bahya quotes the talmudic view that "God desires the heart," that without inwardness religion becomes a fraud.[45] Following earlier rabbinic traditions, Bahya believed that when proper intention does not accompany sacred deeds, such deeds become defective and unacceptable to God.

Though Bahya treats philosophical issues in his work, he did not intend his treatise for the intellectual elite or for the philosophically adept. His goal was to compose a work for the people, a devotional treatise aimed at instructing individuals regarding the worship of God. Each of the ten chapters of Duties of the Heart deals with a step on the ladder of devotion. Each chapter treats one essential duty of the heart along with its ancillary subcategories. Each root of the inner life is examined, along with its leaves and branches.

According to Bahya, theoretical knowledge is a necessary prerequisite for the religious life. The devotional life presupposes an intellectual grasp of the foundations of religion. For Bahya, uninformed faith is deformed faith. Therefore, Bahya felt obliged to devote the beginning of his treatise to philosophical-theological issues. The first chapter of his work, entitled "On the Unity of God," deals with issues such as the existence of God, the unity of God, and the divine attributes. The second chapter is devoted to the study of creatures as witnesses to divine wisdom. Among the issues dealt with in this section are the place of man in the universe and the special grace God bestows upon human creatures. Because of the human being's place in the cosmos, and because of the grace God showers upon human beings, each person should feel obliged to respond with gratitude and with obedience to God's will. The third chapter is devoted to "our obligation of obedience to God." To fulfill these duties to God, one must practice certain virtues, such as trust in God, discussed in chapter four.

In the subsequent chapters he examines other specific virtues that are necessary for sincere and devoted worship of God. Among them are purity of action in relation to God, which entails sincerity, i.e., the correlation between intention and deed. This is discussed in chapter five. In chapter six, Bahya examines humility. In chapter seven, from which the following excerpt comes, Bahya delineates the features of repentance. Because submission to God and humiliation are features of Bahya's view of repentance, the section on repentance follows the chapter on humility. Because self-reckoning is a condition of repentance, his chapter on "self-reckoning for God's sake" follows the chapter on repentance. In chapter nine, Bahya depicts abstinence or asceticism as an essential step on the path to communion with God. However, Bahya does not advocate total asceticism, but defines the ascetic as one who directs all his actions and intentions to the service of God, while at the same time fulfilling his functions within society. The observance of the virtues, central and ancillary, that comprise the "duties of the heart" leads to the highest stage of the spiritual life, which is the love of God.

For Bahya, love of God is the synthesis and the quintessence of the other virtues that comprise the inner life. In the final chapter, chapter ten, Bahya defines love of God as "the yearning of the soul . . . to be attached to God's supreme light." Toward the end of this chapter, Bahya summarizes his work by saying:

Make reason your emir and prudence your vizier; make knowledge your leader and asceticism your companion. Go slowly in acquiring virtue, in keeping with your ability and according to the circumstances. Do it gradually lest you perish, for excess of oil extinguishes the light of the candle. Proceed gradually, with diligence and patience, and follow each stage of the virtues with the one just above it. . . . Thus you may attain the summit of the virtues and the peak of the good qualities which are pleasing to God. May you be directed by them and may you direct others to them![46]

Bahya ibn Pakudah
The Book of Direction to the
Duties of the Heart

As to the explanation of the nature of repentance, I say that repentance is when a man is reconciled to obeying God after he has failed to do so and sinned, and when he retrieves what he has lost by sinning, either through ignorance of God and the ways of obedience to Him, or because his mind was overcome by his desires, or because he had a bad companion who seduced him into disobeying his Lord, or other reasons similar to these. . . .

Deviation from obedience to God occurs in two ways: either through overlooking and leaving undone something God has commanded us to do, or through doing something God has forbidden us to do, with the purpose of rebelling against Him. If one's deviation was only neglect to do something one was obliged to do, the way to correct the failure is to exert one's efforts to perform one's obligation in the future, in addition to undertaking the necessary steps essential to repentance, which I shall explain further in this chapter. If the deviation was the doing of what had been forbidden by God, the way to correct the failure is to guard oneself against repeating the entire action, and to exert one's efforts to do its opposite, in addition to undertaking the necessary steps and conditions essential to repentance, which I shall explain further in this chapter, with God's help. . . .

The kinds of repentance are three in number, being as follows:

1. The man who repents because he can find no way to commit his act of disobedience. Whenever such a man is able to commit it, his mind is overcome by his desire and he cannot restrain himself. Only when his act is completed does he realize its evil and repent of having committed it. This man is contrite with his words only, not in his heart; he repents only with his tongue, not in his acts, and therefore he deserves God's punishment. . . .

2. The man who repents in his heart and members. His mind fights his desires, he trains his soul to overcome its appetites until he conquers it and prevents it from doing what is hateful in God's eyes. But his soul is forever trying to push him into disobeying God, because it desires the things which constitute a rebellion against Him. This man is indeed trying to defend himself, but he and his soul take turns in conquering one another. Thus he is on the way to repentance, but he does not deserve a complete pardon until he is free of all disobedience whatsoever. . . .

3. The man who fulfills all the conditions of repentance, whose mind has overcome his desire, who constantly makes a reckoning with himself, fears his Creator and is ashamed before Him. He perceives the greatness of his sins and errors and

understands the distinction of Him whose orders he has disobeyed and whose commandments he has failed to perform. He
fixes his eyes always on his sins, he faces them continuously, he
repents of them and asks God's pardon for them as long as he
lives and to the end of his days. This man deserves to be rescued
by God from sin.

How is repentance to be expressed by man? It is achieved
through knowledge of seven points:

1. He must have a firm knowledge of the evil of his acts, for
if he does not have this firm knowledge, and he is doubtful, or
ignorant of the nature of his sin, his repentance cannot be
successful, nor his begging for pardon, as it is said (Psalms
51:5): "For I know my transgressions; and my sin is ever before
me."

2. He must know in which way his act is evil and abomina-
ble, for if he is not sure of the evil of his act and the guilt of his
deed, he cannot repent of it nor undertake the conditions of
contrition for it. In this case, he is considered ignorant, is judged
as such, and he has an easy excuse, as it is said (Psalms 19:13):
"Who can discern errors? Clear Thou me from hidden faults."

3. He must know the necessity of requital for his act, for if he
does not know this, nothing prompts him to repent of his act.
But when he knows for certain that he is to be punished for it,
he follows it with repentance and begging for pardon. . . .

4. He must have the knowledge that his sin is recorded
against him and kept in the register of his bad deeds, with no
possibility of being neglected, forgotten, and overlooked. . . .
For if he were to think that it is forgotten and was never
recorded against him, he would not repent and ask for pardon,
but rather he would persist in it because punishment may be
delayed. . . .

5. He must have firm knowledge that repentance is the only
cure for his malady, the path to recovery from his bad deed and
evil act, through which he may correct his error and rectify his
misdeed. For if he does not know this, he must despair of God's
pardon, give up His mercy and never beg for His forgiveness for
his former bad deeds. . . .

6. He must make a reckoning of God's graces that he has
received and of his own acts of disobedience which have taken
the place of gratitude. He must weigh the punishment for a sin
against its pleasure, and the pleasure of the reward for a good
deed against its immediate and subsequent pains, as said our

ancient sages: "Reckon the loss incurred by the fulfillment of precept against the reward secured by its observance, and the gain gotten by a transgression against the loss it involves."[47]

7. He must take it upon himself to be firmly patient in refraining from doing the evil things he is accustomed to do, and he must determine to avoid them in his heart and conscience, as it is said (Joel 2:13): "And rend your heart, and not your garments, and turn unto the Lord your God; for He is gracious and compassionate, long-suffering, and abundant in mercy, and repenteth Him of the evil."

These seven points having been affirmed in the knowledge of the sinner, he is truly ready to repent of his sins for God's sake.

The elements essential to repentance are four in number: contrition for one's former sins, determined avoidance of them, admitting them and asking pardon for them, and undertaking in heart and conscience never to repeat them.

Contrition is a sign that a man's sins are indeed evil in his eyes. . . . We can witness the same thing among people, namely, when a sinner shows his friend that he repents of an evil deed he has committed against him, it is a major cause of the latter's forgiveness.

Avoidance is a sign of one's firm understanding of the matter of reward and punishment. . . . We can witness the same thing among people, namely, when a man who has sinned against his friend follows his repentance with an avoidance of further sins against him, he is worthy of the other's pardon and forgiveness for his sin.

Asking for pardon is a sign of humility and submission to God, and admitting one's sins leads to pardon. . . . We can witness the same thing among people, namely, when a man who has sinned against his friend turns to him, admits his misdeed and asks forgiveness, the other realizes his friend's sincere repentance, and it is not long before he forgives him, pardons his sins, and forgets his hate for him.

A man's undertaking never to repeat his sins is a sign of his knowledge that what he has done is wrong and very blameworthy. . . . We can witness the same thing among people, namely, when a man who has sinned against his friend admits his sin, undertakes never to repeat his misdeed, showing his repentance and his determined intention to avoid this misdeed in the future, then he has fulfilled the conditions for his pardon, full forgiveness, and acquittal. . . .

The conditions of asking for pardon are five, being as follows:

1. Admitting one's sins and considering them many and heavy, in heart and intention. . . .

2. Remembering them constantly, having them continually in one's mind and keeping them in living memory. . . .

3. Performing supererogatory works of obedience, like fasting by day and praying by night, when one's mind is free of other preoccupations and one's worldly affairs are finished. . . .

4. Perpetual praying and begging God to pardon one's sins, to forgive one and accept one's repentance. . . .

5. Endeavoring to warn others away from the same sin, frightening them with its punishment and urging them to repent of it. . . .

The conditions of one's undertaking never to repeat one's sins are five:

1. Comparing the immediate pleasure, which is perishable and perturbable, with the eternal pleasure, which is ceaseless and everlasting, pure, undisturbed, and immaculate. And the comparison between the immediate pain, which is perishable and finite, with the eternal pain, which is endless. . . . The sinner having understood this matter, must necessarily undertake never to repeat his deeds.

2. Imagining your death while your Lord is angry with you for your former failure to fulfill your obligations toward Him. . . . When a man thinks of this matter repeatedly, he must necessarily fear his punishment and decide never to repeat the things which make his Lord angry with him.

3. The consideration of the period during which you disobeyed your Lord and rebelled against Him, in spite of the perpetual graces that He bestows upon you. . . .

4. The avoidance of all injustice, refraining from things forbidden and abstaining from causing harm to any creature. . . .

5. The understanding of the omnipotence of God, whose orders one has disobeyed and whose Law and Worship one has discarded, together with self-reproof and self-blame for it. . . .

What is the way of arousing man to repentance? . . .

Man's strong understanding of his Lord and his meditation upon the perpetual graces that He has given him and upon his obligation to obey Him and follow His commands and prohibitions. For a man is like a slave who flees his master. When he stops to think of his master's good treatment of him, he returns obediently, asking pardon for his rebellion, against his orders and his escape from his service. . . .

Happiest is the man who returns to God in the first way. Less happy is he who returns only after he has been blamed by God. Still less happy and acceptable is he who returns only after he has noticed the misfortune of others. Least acceptable, and last to be accepted by God, is the man who rises only after he has been punished and chastised. Among the other penitents, his repentance will be the last to be accepted by God, and he will be the last to be given pardon for his sins, until he returns truly to Him, shows his repentance, avoids further sins, asks for pardon in his heart, with his tongue, and in all his movements. Only this will make him worthy of pardon, only this will make his repentance acceptable, his misdeeds forgivable. . . .

Among the things which spoil repentance is also the repetition of an act of disobedience after one has fulfilled all the conditions of repentance for it. . . .

Another is a man's hope of repenting in his old age. He thinks he will rid himself of his disobedience to God after he has achieved his purpose and satisfied his desires. This man is like one who deceives the Lord, and he was meant by our ancient sages in their saying: "A man who says 'I will sin and repent,' will be denied the opportunity for repentance,"[48] as well as by the "Admonition" which I shall add to the end of this book of mine:

My soul, make great provision, without stint,
While you still have life and power,
For the journey will be burdensome for you.
Do not say, "Tomorrow I shall provide!"
For the day turns,
And you do not know what the day will bring.
Remember that yesterday will no more return,
And all that you did then
Is weighed, is counted and assessed.
Do not say, "Tomorrow I shall act!"
For death's day is concealed from all that lives.
Make haste, prepare a portion for each day,
For death at any time can cast its arrow, or its lance.
Do not prevaricate. Prepare a measure for every day;
For as the bird flutters from her nest,
So man flutters from his place.

Another thing that spoils repentance is for the contrite sinner to repent some of his acts of disobedience to God while he

persists in others. For instance, he may abstain from all the acts
of disobedience which stand between him and the people, like
acts of injustice, treachery, stealing, and the like. . . . It is
possible for the sinner to repent of every sin, or is it not? As an
answer to this question, I say that sins are of two kinds. The first
kind of sins are those committed by man against God alone,
such as the denial of God, bad faith, evil conscience, and doing
what is forbidden concerning duties of the heart, as well as sins
concerning the duties of the members by which one does
injustice to oneself alone and so is charged only with the
disobedience of God's commands. The second kind of sins are
those committed by man against his fellow men, those which
involve some sort of injustice and evil toward them, either to
their bodies, their property, or their honor. In this kind of sin,
the sinner adds to his disobedience of the Lord, and the injustice
he does himself, also injustice to other people. . . .

As to the sins which are between man and both God and the
people, it is rather difficult to repent of them, for several
reasons. One reason is that the wronged man may not be found,
either because he has died or because he is far away. Another
reason is that the money in the hands of the oppressor may have
been lost, so that he cannot correct his injustice because he does
not have the money for it. The wronged man may refuse to
pardon the sinner for the sin committed against him, whether it
was to his body or to his honor. The sinner himself may be
ignorant of the identity of the man he wronged, or of how much
money he robbed him of, as is true of a man who robs a village
or a town, unmindful of the identity of its people or of the
amount of money he has taken from them unlawfully and with
violence. It may also be that the forbidden money has been
absorbed in many times its amount of lawful money, and it is
impossible to recover it without wasting large quantities of the
lawful money, as said our ancient sages: "If one robbed a beam
and built it in as part of a palace, the School of Shammai holds
that the robber must tear down the entire structure, so as to
restore the beam to its owner. The School of Hillel holds that the
owner is only entitled to the monetary value of the beam."[49]

Another thing which makes repentance difficult is that habit
makes wrongdoing almost necessary to a man, like the natural
actions from which it is almost impossible for one to abstain. . . .

Repentance is impossible for the sinner only because of his

bad intentions and evil conscience, but whoever desires in his heart to draw closer to God, the gate of repentance will not be shut in his face, nor will anyone hinder him from reaching it. On the contrary, the gate of righteousness will be opened to him, and God, by His grace and generosity, will lead him to the way of justice. . . .

Reckon with yourself, O my brother! Be ashamed to treat your Lord in a way that would not please you in your relations with human beings like yourself. You know that when you arouse the anger of the lowest office-holder among the ruling class, you hasten to degrade yourself before him, to beg his pardon and seek safety from his punishment, though he may have no power to inflict it. How much truer is this when the vizier is angry with you, not to speak of the emir himself! You hurry to ask his pardon, you hasten to repent, you apologize to him, because you fear his coming punishment. All this time you are aware that he is unable to execute punishment without God's will, as it is said (Proverbs 21:1): "The king's heart is in the hand of the Lord as the watercourses; He turneth it whithersoever He will." You are also aware that his rule will speedily come to an end, that his government will fall apart, that he has many interests and is preoccupied with so many different things that he neglects much and is oblivious to much, so that many obvious affairs are hidden from him, not to speak of secret ones. But you, in spite of your knowledge of all these things, you hasten without delay to ask his pardon for your sin. You rush to please him and make yourself acceptable to him.

How are you not ashamed, O my brother, before our Creator, who observes both our open and our hidden acts and thoughts, who cannot be thought of as negligent or careless, who is never preoccupied with one thing to the exclusion of the other, whose judgment we cannot escape and whose kingdom is infinite? How can we turn away from Him, how can we delay in our repentance and coming back to Him, when we are ignorant of the day of our death and the end of our life?

If a man were to warn the inhabitants of a village or a town, saying "O you people, prepare for the journey to the other world, for one among you is going to die this month, but I know not who he is," would it not be right that each one of them should be ready to die, fearing that he was the one meant by the preacher? How could he not prepare, when every month in every corner we see death killing so many creatures? Are we not obliged to fear for ourselves each month and consider the matter of our provisions for the next world before there is need of it, even one day before? As said our ancient sages: "Repent one day before thy death,"[50] and as it is said (Ecclesiastes 9:8): "Let thy garments be always white; and let thy head lack no oil."

II

The Self

6

How to Deal with the Ego

Selt-knowledge is a *sine qua non* in the creation of the artful life. To be whom one can become, the individual must be forthrightly aware of his or her abilities and limitations, accomplishments and defeats. Self-deception proves to be a formidable obstacle in the cultivation of life as a work of art. An overweening sense of self-importance or a preoccupation with self-depreciation stifles the spiritual and moral development of the self. In Jewish ethical literature, the quest for self-understanding, the challenge of managing one's ego, are inextricably related to dispelling pride and inculcating humility.

In the excerpt below from Moses Hayyim Luzzatto's *Mesilat Yesharim— The Path of the Upright*, pride is described as "an overweening sense of our own importance." Luzzatto considered the haughty person as one "who thinks that because he possesses some superiority which entitles him to respect, he ought to inspire universal awe, and everyone ought to tremble before him. . . . He overwhelms people with his arrogant replies, and he scowls all the time."[1]

The arrogant person is characterized as one who is self-indulged and self-deluded. While constantly finding faults with others, he or she remains oblivious to his or her own flaws. "Pride is literally a form of blindness," Luzzatto observed, "which prevents even one who is otherwise wise from seeing his own shortcomings. . . . A man cannot see his own faults, but his comrades can see and understand them. . . ."[2] Pride traps the individual within a prison of self-deception. Pride, counsels *The Choice of Pearls*, is "stupidity of which its possessor is unable to divest himself."[3] The arrogant person is one who closes himself or herself off not only from honest self-awareness, but from authentic relationships with others. The ego gets in the way of forming and sustaining real relationships with others.

The biblical verse, "I stood between God and you" (Deuteronomy 5:5) was interpreted by a hasidic master to mean that the "I," the ego, often stands between God and us, obstructing the divine-human relationship.[4] Indeed, many authors of Jewish ethical works considered the ego to be a potential obstacle, not only to one's relationship with God, but to any and all relationships. It is no wonder, therefore, that arrogance is considered a dangerous moral vice, obstructive in the formation of relationships, and replete with destructive potentialities. For example, in his talmudic commentary, Samuel Edels ("Maharsha") wrote that just as humility is the most exalted moral virtue, pride is the most dangerous moral vice.[5] The medieval Spanish scholar, Jonah Gerondi, describes human arrogance as the primary cause of most sins.[6] Midrashic literature characterizes the flood generation, the Tower of Babel generation, and the inhabitants of the wicked city of Sodom as arrogant, linking their arrogance to their destruction.[7] According to a midrashic source, unbridled pride is a threat to the very existence of the world.[8] "Pride precedes destruction and a haughty spirit goes before a fall," says Proverbs (16:18).

Because of the gravity with which our sources depict the sin of pride, it is not surprising that they compare pride to the most serious sins of all—idolatry and heresy. According to the Talmud, "one who is haughty of spirit is *as though* he worships idols . . . [and] as though he had denied God."[9] In hasidic thought, the analogy of pride to idolatry develops into an equation of pride with idolatry. The Baal Shem Tov, the founder of Hasidism, is quoted as stating that "pride is *actually* idolatry."[10] In this view, arrogance, impudence, and pride are equated with idolatry because they seek to replace God with the self as the object of one's ultimate concern. They represent an attitude where a human person acts as if he or she were divine.[11]

One way in which idolatry may be defined is: treating that which is relative as if it were absolute. For the religious mind, only God is absolute, ultimate, and of supreme significance; therefore, one who is exceedingly proud is like one who practices idolatry, in that he or she considers the self rather than the divine as being of absolute and supreme importance. To consider the self as the be-all and end-all of existence, as the focal point of the universe, is an exercise in self-delusion, a gesture of self-aggrandizement with no foundation in reality.

Jewish ethical literature recommends a number of antidotes to pride and arrogance. Foremost among them is for an individual to become brutally aware of life's transient nature, of the fragility of human existence. In this regard, *The Choice of Pearls* states, "I wonder at the human being whose entrance into the world is through so unclean a channel—whence has he pride."[12] This quotation is reminiscent of an ancient Christian theologian who observed that we are born between urine and feces. Or, as *The Ethics of the Fathers* puts it, we come from a putrid drop; we go to a place of worms and maggots.[13]

The existential shock of confrontation with the reality of one's own mortality can serve as a means of tempering one's tendency to aggrandize the self. "Today we are here and tomorrow in the grave," the Talmud reminds us.[14] Elsewhere, the Talmud notes, "Let a person be exceedingly humble, for the end of mortals is worms."[15] In a similar vein, Bahya ibn Pakudah wrote:

> The root of man's existence and his beginnings is in semen and blood. After corruption has entered into them, they emit an evil stench. He is nourished by unclean blood as long as he is in his mother's womb, and then he emerges weak and infirm in body and members. Later he grows by stages until he reaches maturity, growing older and older until he reaches the end of his days. . . . When a man reflects on the end of his days, and the speed with which his death comes, when all his hopes and wishes will cease and all his possessions will be abandoned, when he reflects on the hopelessness of retaining any of them for himself, or benefitting by them, when he imagines his condition in the grave, his face darkened, his body blackened and full of worms, its stench and putrefaction, the traces of his bodily beauty all effaced, while the smell grows stronger as if he had never washed or cleaned or exuded perfumed scents; when one meditates upon this and matter like this, he becomes humble and contrite. He is no longer proud or arrogant and no trace of loftiness is left in him.[16]

Other texts remind us that affliction of pain and the onset of illness can serve as antidotes to pride and as catalysts toward humility. Like the fragility of health, the tenuousness of wealth, the flightiness of fame, and the greater physical might of an adversary can quickly and easily defuse arrogance and a bloated sense of self-importance. Apprehension over losing what we possess, fear of becoming victims of the always changing vicissitudes of life, may be adequate to convince one of the ultimate unimportance of self-importance. As Luzzatto wrote:

> Let one consider the vicissitudes of life. The rich man often becomes poor, the ruler subservient, and the man of eminence sinks into obscurity. Since a man is thus liable to find himself occupying a station in life that he now looks upon with contempt, how shall he be proud because of the good fortune which he can never be sure will last? How many are the discards to which one is liable, rendering a man so helpless that he begs to be relieved? . . . Daily do we witness these occurrences. They should be sufficient to banish pride from our hearts and to imbue us with humility.[17]

Two characteristics of the haughty individual are greed and anger. Bahya characterizes the arrogant person as one who is never satisfied with what he or she has. "The whole world and everything in it," he wrote, "is not enough for the person afflicted with pride and haughtiness, because of his pretensions and scorn for what he has acquired."[18] In other words, the arrogant person whose ego is an infinitely expanding universe can never find contentment in possessions that are mere extensions of that ego. According to a medieval Jewish preacher, the arrogant person is completely preoccupied with having what he or she wants, while the humble person is content with wanting what he or she has.[19]

Of all human emotions, our sources identify anger as the emotion most closely linked to arrogance and to pride. The sixteenth-century kabbalist, Hayyim Vital, wrote that "pride and anger are a single quality."[20] Having equated pride and anger, Vital also equates anger with idolatry and heresy.[21] Similarly, the Orhot Zaddikim – The Ways of the Righteous, states, "Anger is very close to arrogance and no angry man can escape arrogance."[22] Anger places the ego at the center, displacing God and others, and causing the alienation of relationships. "He who loses his temper, even the Divine Presence is unimportant in his eyes," says the Talmud.[23]

The paradox of anger is that while focusing on the ego, it causes one to lose control of the self. Anger stifles the development of the self while revealing a person's true nature. Anger inhibits free expression by a loss of self-control, while it serves as a catalyst for exposure of one's deepest thoughts. As Orhot Zaddikim puts it:

> You often see people who when they are angry and persist in their wrath, are not conscious of what they are doing and do many things in their anger which they would not do if they were free from anger, for anger draws out the intelligence of a person from within him until his angry deeds multiply and he is plunged into strife and quarrel. Therefore, it is impossible that the wrathful person should be saved from great sins. . . . As the sages said: By three things a person is known, and one of them is his anger,[24] for when one is angry one's true nature can be recognized.[25]

Anger channeled inward at the self manifests itself as depression. Long before psychologists such as Heinz Kohut identified pride and depression as complementary aspects of narcissism, hasidic teachings described depression as the flip-side of pride.[26] In the hasidic parlance, depression, like pride, is a form of idolatry in that egocentrism replaces God as the object of ultimate concern. It places one's momentary unfulfilled needs and desires at the center of one's concerns. In this regard the Baal Shem Tov taught, "The main rule in serving God is that you should keep yourself far from sadness and depression to the very best of your ability."[27]

Anger and depression expose one to self-damnation. "He who loses his temper is exposed to all of the torments of hell," says the Talmud.[28] Anger and arrogance, being self-destructive, are described as self-afflicted diseases of the soul.[29] Yet, anger threatens to harm not only the angry person, but all those whom he or she influences. The angry person, Luzzatto wrote, "would destroy the entire world if he had the power." Luzzatto compares the person overcome by anger to a wild beast. Such a person "being at the mercy of his anger and following it blindly, is liable to commit any conceivable transgression."

Anger is dangerous, Luzzatto suggests, not simply because of what it can cause one to do, but also because of what it can cause that cannot be undone. In a fit of anger, one "is liable to commit some rash deed which can never be undone."[30] No wonder, therefore, that we read of a pious man who would pray each night that God grant him one wish—that he not become angry, for anger is the cause of most sins.[31] What anger destroys is not easily restored.

Anger and pride are depicted as corrosive diseases of the soul, whereas humility is considered a remedy for the spiritually afflicted.[32] Whereas pride is described as the most serious moral vice, humility is identified as the most exalted moral virtue.[33] Nevertheless, in certain circumstances, even humility can be a moral vice.

Like pride, expressions of humility may also be rooted in self-deception. Luzzatto discusses the temptations of both exaggerated self-esteem as well as false self-depreciation. For Luzzatto, false humility is as detestable as brazen arrogance. The individual who flaunts his humility, who is outwardly humble while inwardly proud, is one who "takes pride in his humility."[34] This is real pride but false humility. The truly humble person is the last to recognize his own humility. For the authentically humble, humility is a goal ever to be obtained, but never considered to have been attained. The truly humble person can never say, "I am humble." To do so would be a contradiction in terms.

Humility is meant to be a strength, not a weakness. When a person claims humility as an excuse for inaction, it becomes a weakness rather than a strength. According to a hasidic view, when a person claims, out of a presumed expression of humility, that his or her actions cannot make a difference, that they can have no effect on improving the quality of moral and spiritual existence, then such a person is abusing the virtue of humility rather than practicing it. Humility entails the obligation to create the artful life, to serve the needs of the divine, and to help improve the quality of one's own life and the lives of others. Authentic humility may be a conduit to great accomplishments, but it can never become an excuse for evading the challenges that face us.[35]

A feature of humility is overcoming self-delusion. Self-delusion relates as much to an unfounded emphasis on self-depreciation as it does to an overweening sense of self-importance. Self-depreciation may prove to be an obstacle rather than a conduit to instilling humility. For example, in *Kad ha-Kemah*, Bahya ben Asher states that "to be meek does not mean that one should disgrace himself in any matter or allow himself to be tread upon by others, for the human being has been created in the divine image and is therefore precious and must guard his honor."[36] In this view, humility does not entail becoming oblivious to one's own achievements and capabilities. It simply means that however superior to others one might be in certain ways, there is no justification for pride on that account. There is no reason for overemphasizing one's importance or for lording over others because of one's achievements.[37] Furthermore, a candid appraisal of one's superior abilities, when compared to others, should also entail an exercise in rigorous self-scrutiny regarding one's insufficiencies when compared to the achievements of others. In other words, humility is not the enemy of self-esteem, but of pride.[38]

Rather than condemning a person to a life of obscurity, humility can serve as a catalyst for the highest human accomplishments. In Jewish tradition, greatness and humility are not incompatible; rather, they complement each other. Moses, considered by Jewish tradition to be the greatest Jew of all, is described by Scripture as the most humble of persons (Numbers 12:3). According to the Talmud, God is great precisely because He is humble.[39]

Humility is a necessary ingredient in the creation of the artful life. In his authoritative study of creativity, psychotherapist Silvano Arieti writes, "An attitude of humility, of willingness to make even the smallest contributions and to accept a life of commitment and dedication, must be part of the potentially creative person's way of life."[40]

The truly creative person knows that setting aside the ego is necessary for the creative process to proceed unhampered. The ego can serve as an obstacle to free artistic expression. The great actor must first empty himself out of himself in order to play a dramatic role successfully. A great artist or author must divest himself or herself of the ego in order to produce a great work of art. Preoccupation with ego needs, concern with critical reviews of one's work, only deflect attention from the work at hand. A key to creative achievement is the abnegation of the ego, the temporary surrendering of self-consciousness. That self-abnegation is a necessary catalyst for artful accomplishment, for development of the artful life, and for the expression of the most profound kind of love, is an insight stressed in Jewish ethical literature, especially in hasidic texts. Humility consists not in thinking little of oneself, but of not thinking of oneself at all. This approach would have one focus on one's being absorbed on worthy aims and on service to others for their own sakes, rather than for self-satisfaction and ego reinforcement. This view offers a path to self-transcendence as an alternative to narcissistic self-preoccupation. From this perspective, love is an antidote to pride, a catalyst toward imbuing humility. In the words of Solomon Schechter:

> Infatuated with his own importance, man before long will be in opposition to man and God, who keep his due from him. The best remedy against this ugly quality is love. . . . This is a love which leaves no room for self. Man will not succeed in attaining to this love until he has acquired the virtues of humility and meekness.[41]

The truly great are humble; the truly humble are great. In the Middle Ages, human beings were described as a microcosm, a "small world," a miniature universe. Commenting on this phrase, "small world," a text observes, "If a person is a world in his own eyes, he is small. But, if a person is small in his own eyes, then he's a world."[42]

Since only God alone knows the true worth of a person, the accolades of others will not be taken to heart by the person who is truly great and truly humble. The humble person may accept praise for his or her attainments, but will not take it too seriously.[43] The truly great person would be humble enough so that pride had lost its attraction.[44] The desire for the approval and the honor of others is a vice that the humble person will successfully evade. In this regard Luzzatto wrote, "Even worse than greed is the lust for honor. A man may control his craving for wealth and pleasure, but the craving for honor is irresistible because it is almost impossible to endure being inferior to one's fellows. This is why so many people stumble and perish."[45]

According to the Baal Shem Tov, "human beings are sent into the world for the purpose of studying how to avoid the sin of pride."[46] One way of overcoming pride and of instilling humility is for an individual to contemplate one's own insignificance when compared to the overwhelming majesty of God and the vastness of His creation. In his legal code, the *Mishneh Torah*, Maimonides writes, "When a person contemplates God's great and wondrous works and creatures and from them obtains a glimpse of His wisdom which is incomparable and infinite . . . and when he ponders these matters, he will recoil affrighted and realize that he is a small creature, lowly and obscure, endowed with slight and slender intelligence. . . ."[47] Similarly, the hasidic master, Nahman of Bratzlav, stated:

> Eating and drinking are catalysts to
> pride
> A talisman for imbuing humility is to
> gaze at the heavens.[48]

The Talmud states that "he who is humble, God exalts, but he who exalts himself, God humbles." Immediately after this statement, the talmudic text reports a debate on the question of whether it would have been better for human beings to have been created or not. The final decision was that it would have been better had human beings not have been created, but since they have been created, one should continuously examine one's own deeds.[49] In this view, since human existence is a metaphysical superfluity, one should be aware of one's own insignificance when set against the panorama of the cosmos, when compared to the infinity of God. Modern existentialist philosophers who reflected on the superfluity of human existence reached a posture of nihilism and despair.[50] But, in the Jewish view, awareness of the insignificance of the individual when set against the cosmos should engender neither nihilism nor despair, but humility. It should stimulate one to create an artful existence, a life characterized by purpose, meaning, and service to others. Jewish thought encourages a balance between pride and self-depreciation. The mean between arrogance and self-abasement is humility.[51] Discussing the biblical citation "I am dust and ashes" (Genesis 18:27) and the talmudic statement, "Every person should consider himself or herself as if the world had been created for his or her own sake,"[52] the hasidic master, Bunam of Przysucha, taught:

> Each person should have two pockets. In each pocket he or she should carry a slip of paper on which is written one of these two citations. As the occasion arises, one should extract and read the slip appropriate to the specific situation. If one becomes too haughty and proud, one should be aware that "I am dust and ashes," and if one becomes too self-abusing and depressed, then one should extract the slip that reads, "For my sake the world was created."[53]

❧

The following excerpt is from *Mesilat Yesharim — The Path of the Upright*, by Moses Hayyim Luzzatto. Born in Padua, Italy, of a prominent family in 1707, Luzzatto was a child prodigy. He was equally at home in Jewish tradition and in Western culture. Besides Hebrew, he also knew Greek, Latin, and Italian. Luzzatto was an adept kabbalist, and his preoccupation with Jewish mysticism caused conflicts between him and the rabbis of his native Italy. These conflicts eventually forced him to Amsterdam in 1735, where he refrained from kabbalistic writings and teachings. It was in Amsterdam that he wrote *The Path of the Upright*. Like Bahya ben Asher's *Kad ha-Kemah — Jar of Meal*, *The Path of the Upright*, while written by a devoted kabbalist, is virtually devoid of kabbalistic terminology. In 1743, Luzzatto journeyed to the Land of Israel, and died in a plague shortly after his arrival.

Most of Luzzatto's kabbalistic works have not survived. Some of his controversial writings were burned in Frankfurt during his lifetime. Views of himself as a reincarnation of Moses who would redeem the Jewish people, the messianic overtones of the circle of mystics he led in Italy, his claim of revelation from a "spiritual intelligence" (*maggid*), and claims that he was a Sabbatean were some of the reasons why he was the focal point of controversy, especially during the years he resided in his native Italy.

Of Luzzatto's kabbalistic writings that did survive, many were claimed by him to have been written under the influence of his *maggid*. Among his kabbalistic words, *Hoker u-Mekubal* merits mention. A justification of the anthenticity of the teachings of the Jewish mystical tradition, this work is composed in the form of a debate between a rationalist (*hoker*) and a mystic (*mekubal*). Besides *The Path of the Upright*, Luzzatto wrote two additional works on theology and ethics, *Derekh ha-Shem — The Way of God* and *Da'at Tevunah The Awareness of Knowledge*. In addition, Luzzatto was a prolific author of poetry, drama, and letters. These works contain many kabbalistic and messianic motifs. His two best known plays are *The Deeds of Samson* and *The Tower of Strength*. Many prominent historians of Hebrew literature consider him to be the first modern Hebrew writer and the author of the first play written in the Hebrew language. Despite the controversy that hounded him during his lifetime, most of his surviving religious and ethical works achieved immense popularity in the generations after his death. *The Path of the Upright* was utilized both by the *hasidim* and by their Lithuanian opponents, the *mitnagdim*. Luzzatto's *The Path of the Upright* is studied today in *yeshivot* throughout the world. With the possible exception of Bahya ibn Pakudah's *Duties of the Heart*, *The Path of the Upright* is the most popularly read and studied of all the works that comprise Jewish ethical literature.

Innovation was not Luzzatto's intention in writing *The Path of the Upright*. The very first sentence of the book states, "I have not written this book to teach the reader anything new." His intention was to offer his reader a guide toward piety (*hasidut*) based upon traditional Jewish teachings. For Luzzatto, every person is a "latent saint." Every individual has a natural disposition toward piety. His work is intended as a manual to aid the individual in the cultivation of the life of piety, for like any innate quality, only through careful conscious cultivation can piety become transformed from potentiality to actuality. In Luzzatto's words, "Although uprightness is latently and fundamentally a characteristic of every person, if one is not preoccupied with cultivating these qualities, they will remain dormant, not be realized, and will have no effect." Without active, conscious, and continual effort, the moral qualities will remain dormant.[54]

The Path of the Upright is structured around the moral virtues mentioned in an often-quoted statement attributed to the talmudic rabbi, Pinhas ben Yair: "The knowledge of Torah leads to watchfulness, watchfulness to zeal,

zeal to cleanness, cleanness to abstinence, abstinence to purity, purity to piety (*hasidut*), piety to humility, humility to fear of sin, and fear of sin to holiness."[55] Except for the preface and first chapter, which treat general ethical and religious issues, each chapter of the work deals with aspects of the rungs in the ladder toward holiness described by Pinhas ben Yair: watchfulness (four chapters), zeal (four chapters), cleanness (three chapters), abstinence (three chapters), purity (two chapters), piety (four chapters), humility (two chapters), fear of sin and awe of God (two chapters), holiness (one chapter). Within this rubric, Luzzatto interjects discussion of other specific ethical issues. For example, in the course of his discussion of cleanness, he includes a discussion of anger. Sprinkled throughout his work, particularly in his discussion of piety, he discusses love of God.

The excerpt that follows contains selections from the chapters in *The Path of the Upright* dealing with cleanness and humility. In sum, Luzzatto maintains that while pride is harmful to the self and to others, "it is certain that humility removes numerous obstacles from a person's path, and brings him into close touch with much that is good."[56]

Moses Hayyim Luzzatto
Mesilat Yesharim – The Path of the Upright

As a rule, pride is an overweening sense of our own importance, and an inward belief that we deserve praise. Such conceit may be due to reasoning of the most varied character. One man may consider himself clever, another handsome, one respected, another eminent, and still another learned. Whenever a man believes he is gifted in any way, he is in danger of falling a victim to pride. When a man has become obsessed with the idea that he is important and deserving of praise, he will not stop there. Many an evil consequence comes from such self-delusion. The same cause may at first produce two opposite effects, though both, in the end, lead to the same result.

There is the vain man who, because he regards himself as deserving of praise and considers himself unique and distinguished, deems it proper to assume a dignified bearing when he walks, when he sits, when he stands up, and whenever he says or does anything. He walks leisurely, with measured step; he sits upright; he rises slowly; he speaks only with those of foremost rank, and even among them he utters only short sentences in oracular fashion. In all his behavior, in his gestures, in his eating, in his drinking, and in his dressing, he carries himself with great pompousness, as though his flesh were made of lead, and his bones of stone.

There is the proud man who thinks that because he possesses some superiority which entitles him to respect, he ought to inspire universal awe, and everyone ought to tremble before him. How dare an ordinary man speak to him, or ask anything of him! He overawes with his voice those who dare approach him. He overwhelms people with his arrogant replies, and he scowls all the time.

Another imagines that he is so great and so deserving of honor that no one can deprive him of the usual signs of respect. And to prove this, he behaves as though he were humble and goes to extremes in displaying boundless modesty and infinite humility. But in his heart he is proud, saying to himself, "I am so exalted, and so deserving of honor, that I need not have any one do me honor. I can well afford to forego marks of respect."

Another is the coxcomb, who wants to be noted for his superior qualities and to be singled out for his behavior. He is not satisfied with having every one praise him for the superior traits which he thinks he possesses, but he wants them also to include in their praises that he is the most humble of men. He thus takes pride in his humility, and wishes to be honored because he pretends to flee from honor. Such a prig usually goes so far as to put himself below those who are much inferior to him, even below the meanest, thinking that in this way he displays the utmost humility. He refuses all titles of greatness and declines promotion in rank, but in his heart he thinks, "There is no one in all the world as wise and as humble as I." Conceited people of this type, though they pretend mightily to be humble, cannot escape some mishap which causes their pride to burst forth, like a flame out of a heap of litter. Such a man has been compared to a house filled with straw. The house being full of holes, the straw keeps on creeping through them, so that after a while every one knows what is within the house. The humility of his behavior is soon known to be insincere, and his meekness nothing but pretense.

Finally, there are the proud who manage so to conceal their pride that it does not express itself in their conduct. Men of this type consider themselves great sages, and think they know the truth about everything. They consider very few their equals in wisdom, and disregard what others have to say. They imagine

that whatever they find difficult to understand cannot possibly
be intelligible to any one else. They rely upon their understanding to make everything so clear and simple to them that
they ignore all who disagree with them, whether ancient or
recent authorities. They never doubt the validity of their own
reasoning.

Such are the manifestations of pride "which foil the wise men
and make their knowledge foolish" (Cf. Isaiah 44:25). Pride
deprives of reason those who are masters of wisdom; all the
more so the disciples who have not yet served their apprenticeship; those who have hardly opened their eyes, and already
consider themselves the peers of the wisest among the wise.
Concerning all these aspects of pride, it is said, "Everyone that
is proud in his heart is an abomination to the Lord" (Proverbs
16:5). Whoever would attain the trait of cleanness must be free
from the taint of pride. He must realize that pride is literally a
form of blindness which prevents even a man of understanding
from seeing his own shortcomings. For, were he able to see and
know the truth, he would keep far away from these perverse
ways. We shall speak more of this when we come to treat of
humility, which is mentioned among the last in the scale of
virtues, because of the great effort that is required to attain
it. . . .

The principle of humility is that a man shall not think highly
of himself for any reason whatsoever. This is the very opposite
of what we understand by pride, and equally contrasted to each
other are the consequences which follow from each of these
traits respectively.

Upon examination, we find that humility depends upon both
thought and action. A man must be humble at heart before he
can adopt the ways of the meek. Whoever wishes to conduct
himself humbly, without being humble at heart, is only an evil
pretender, and of the company of those hypocrites who are the
bane of mankind.

We shall now explain the two aspects of humility. Humility in
thought means that a man should be wholly persuaded of his
unworthiness to be the recipient of praise and glory. A man of
this sort will surely find it impossible to consider himself
superior to any others. This attitude toward himself he will have
not only because he is aware of his failings, but also because he
realizes the insignificance of his attainments.

That in the awareness of his shortcomings a man should be humble is self-evident. It is impossible for any man to be altogether without faults, which may be due to nature, to heredity, to accidents, or to his own doings. "For there is not a righteous man upon earth that doeth good, and sinneth not" (Ecclesiastes 7:20). Such defects leave no room for self-esteem, despite the many excellent traits that one may otherwise possess. The defects are sufficient to eclipse the virtues. The possession of learning, for example, makes dangerously for pride and self-esteem, since it is an advantage that accrues wholly to the intellect, which is the highest faculty of the human being. Yet there is no one so learned who does not make mistakes, or who is not in need of learning from his equals, and at times even from his disciples. How, then, shall a man dare to boast of his learning?

The man of understanding will, upon reflection, realize that there is no justification for pride or vainglory, even if he was privileged to become very learned. A man of understanding, who has acquired more knowledge than the average person, has accomplished nothing more than what his nature impelled him to do, as it is the nature of the bird to fly, or of the ox to pull with all its strength. Hence, if a man is learned, he is indebted to natural gifts which he happens to possess. Any one gifted by nature with a mind like his would be just as learned. The man who possesses great knowledge, instead of yielding to pride and self-esteem, should impart that knowledge to those who are in need of it. As Rabbi Johanan ben Zakkai said, "If you have learned much Torah, take not any merit, for thereunto were you created."[57] If a man is rich, let him rejoice in his portion and help those who are poor; if he is strong, let him help those who are weak, and redeem those who are oppressed. For indeed we are like the servants of a household. Every one of us is appointed to some task and is expected to remain at his post and do the work of the household as well as possible. In the scheme of life there is no room for pride. . . .

It is certain that humility removes numerous obstacles from a man's path, and brings him into close touch with much that is good. . . .

Moreover, the company of the humble is very sweet, and people find delight in him. He is not given to anger or to strife; he does everything calmly and peacefully. Happy is he who is privileged to possess this virtue. "The fear of God, which is Wisdom's crown, is the heel of Humility's sandal," for all the wisdom in the world cannot compare with humility. . . .[58]

The habit of humility is acquired through training and reflection. The training consists in gradually habituating oneself to act humbly by always keeping in the background, and by dressing modestly; for a man's dress may be respectable without ostentation. . . .

But in the matter of reflection, there are various considerations. Consider first the dictum of Akabya ben Mahalalel. "Know whence thou camest: — from a putrid drop; whither thou art going: — to a place of dust, worms, and maggots; and before whom thou wilt have to give account and reckoning in the future: — before the Supreme King of kings, the Holy One, blessed be He."[59] Indeed these thoughts counteract pride and make for humility. . . .

If a man would recall that after all his greatness he will return to dust and be food for worms, surely then would his pride be humbled, and his arrogance forgotten. . . .

Secondly, let him consider the vicissitudes of life. The rich man often becomes poor, the ruler subservient, and the man of eminence sinks into obscurity. Since a man is thus liable to find himself occupying a station in life that he now looks upon with contempt, how shall he be proud because of the good fortune which he can never be sure will last? How many are the diseases to which one is liable, rendering a man so helpless that he begs to be relieved! How many afflictions may come upon a man so that he may have to beg favors from those whom he does not deign to greet! Daily do we witness these occurrences. They should be sufficient to banish pride from our hearts, and to imbue us with humility and lowliness. . . .

But the chief hindrance to humility is ignorance or little knowledge. You will observe that the more ignorant a man is, the more conceited he is. Our Sages said, "An arrogant disposition betrays ignorance of the Torah."[60] "When a man boasts, it is a sign that he knows nothing."[61] "When there is only one penny in the pitcher, it makes much noise."[62] "The trees that bear no fruit were once asked,'Why can one hear your rustling?' 'So that we might be heard and noticed,' was their reply."[63] We have already mentioned that Moses, who was the chosen of men, was also the meekest of men.

Associating with flatterers, or making use of their services, is another hindrance to humility. There are people who, when they want a favor, have recourse to flattery. They extol their quarry to the skies. If he happens to possess some good quality, they make it the object of exorbitant praise. They even go further and ascribe to him merits which he does not at all possess. In fact, he may even have traits that are the very opposite of those for which they laud him. Human character, after all, is fickle, weak, and easily tempted, especially in respect to those things toward which it is naturally drawn. When a man, therefore, listens to a glowing account of himself from one in whom he has confidence, it works like poison, and before long he is caught in the net of pride and is destroyed.

7

How to Be Wise

The advent of the "computer age" literally has placed infinite quantities of information at our fingertips. Knowledge has become a readily accessible commodity. Nevertheless, wisdom—the capacity to know what to do with what we know—remains rare and elusive. The biblical question continues to confront us: "Wisdom, where shall it be found?" (Job 28:12).

Information may be purchased; knowledge may be bought, but wisdom cannot be acquired in exchange for wealth: "It [i.e., wisdom] cannot be gotten for gold. Neither shall silver be weighed for the price thereof" (Job 28:15).

Of inestimable value, wisdom is difficult to attain, yet easy to relinquish. There is no wisdom at first sight. In the words of a medieval kabbalist, Judah Barzeloni, "Wisdom does not come to a person at once. It only comes after struggles, quests, anguish, and effort."[1]

Jewish tradition sets a high premium on the quest for wisdom, despite its proclivity to evade our grasp, in spite of its elusive preciousness. "One who has acquired wisdom," the Talmud observes, "has acquired everything; one who lacks wisdom, lacks everything."[2] For many medieval Jewish writers, without wisdom, human existence is devoid of purpose. "Human beings were created only to learn wisdom," wrote the medieval scholar, Abraham Ibn Ezra.[3] Without wisdom, the human soul withers and dies. "Wisdom is to the soul what food is to the body," Ibn Ezra observed.[4]

Wisdom sustains us. A person without wisdom is like a person devoid of a heart. Without a functioning heart, all of one's limbs are destined to degeneration. "Why was wisdom placed in the heart?" a midrash asks.

"Because all the limbs of the body depend upon the heart."[5] Wisdom is an indicator of a healthy soul, of a spiritually healthy individual. As the medieval Jewish philosopher, Abraham bar Hiyya, put it, "It has been said that the human soul has health and sickness. . . . Its sickness is ignorance, its health – wisdom."[6]

Though wisdom is an essential human need, it alone is not sufficient. There is a fundamental necessity to translate what we know into what we do, what we know into who we are. Wisdom must be a prolegomenon to ethics. The intellectual must become a prelude to the moral. Ethics is applied wisdom. Morality is practical wisdom. Wisdom is a critical ingredient in the creation of the artful life.

The link between wisdom and ethics is forged in the sections of the Hebrew Bible known as "Wisdom Literature." In apocryphal writings such as the Books of Sira and Barukh, in rabbinic literature, and later in medieval Jewish writings, this relationship between wisdom and ethics is amplified and expanded.

The biblical Book of Proverbs is part of the "Wisdom Literature." A verse in Proverbs (1:2) reads: "To know wisdom and moral instruction (*musar*), to comprehend the words of understanding." Commenting upon this text, a midrash says: "If [the verse requires] moral instruction, why [does it also require] wisdom? And if [it requires] wisdom, why [does it also require] moral instruction? Because if a person is wise he will therefore learn morality. But, if a person is not wise, he will be incapable of learning morality."[7]

In ancient Greek philosophy one also finds this link between moral virtue and wisdom. For Plato, "Wisdom is the essence of virtue."[8] There can be no virtue without wisdom.[9] Similarly, for Plato's disciple Aristotle, "It is impossible to be good in the full sense of the word without practical wisdom or to be a man of practical wisdom without moral excellence or virtue."[10]

According to the Talmud, wisdom that does not translate itself into action is aborted knowledge:

> The goal of wisdom is repentance and the performance of good deeds. [For example,] a person should not study Torah and Mishnah and then despise his parents and teachers or his superiors in wisdom or in rank, as it is written: "Fear of the Lord is the beginning of wisdom, a good understanding have they that do thereafter" (Psalms 111:10).[11]

Without wisdom, good deeds are blind. Without good deeds, wisdom remains mute. The performance of good deeds is wisdom's warranty. Virtuous deeds are likened to fruit that hangs on the tree of wisdom. According to a medieval proverb, "Wisdom without action is like a barren tree devoid of fruit."[12] According to *Sefer Ma'alot ha-Middot – Improvement of the Moral Virtues*, "One who has not acquired wisdom is [necessarily] devoid of morality. For as the head is the essence of the body, so is morality the essence of wisdom . . . an intellect devoid of morality is like a tree devoid of fruit."[13]

A flourishing tree is full of fruit. The branches are few—though strong and the fruits are many. Similarly, when one's wisdom engenders one's deeds, one's deeds will exceed one's wisdom. Such wisdom is destined to endure, according to the Talmud. A tree whose branches exceed its fruit cannot be described as fruitful. Similarly, the rabbis claim, when one's wisdom exceeds one's deeds, such wisdom cannot endure. The *Ethics of the Fathers* observes:

> He whose deeds exceed his wisdom, his wisdom shall endure, but he whose wisdom exceeds his deeds, his wisdom will not endure. . . . He whose wisdom exceeds his deeds is comparable to a tree whose branches are many but whose roots are few and the wind comes and plucks it up and overturns it on its face. . . . And he whose deeds exceed his wisdom is comparable to a tree whose branches are few but whose roots are many so that if all the winds in the world came and blow upon it, it cannot be stirred from its place.[14]

If ethics are the fruits of wisdom, then awe of God constitutes the roots of wisdom. As Proverbs (9:10) says, "The awe of God is the beginning of wisdom." According to *Mesilat Yesharim — The Path of the Upright*, awe of God is both the beginning and the substance of wisdom: "We read that: 'Awe of the Lord, that is wisdom' (Job 28:28). Awe of God is thus identified and declared to be the only true wisdom."[15] Similarly, the *Ethics of the Fathers* succinctly observes, "Where there is no wisdom, there is no awe [of God], where there is no awe [of God], there is no wisdom."[16]

Awe of God tempers the tendency of the wise to revel in their own wisdom. As the prophet Jeremiah reminds us (9:22–23):

> Thus says the Lord—"Let not the wise man glory in his might, nor the rich man in his riches. But let him that glories glory in this—that he understands and knows Me that I am the Lord who exercises mercy, justice, and righteousness for in these things I delight."

Awe of God reminds the wise that the source of wisdom is God, that wisdom is a divine gift as well as a human accomplishment. In the words of Proverbs (2:6): "For the Lord gives wisdom. Out of His mouth comes knowledge and discernment."

Awe of God leads to fear of sin. Fear of sin prevents the commission of immoral deeds. For wisdom to endure, for wisdom to inculcate virtue, it must be linked to the fear of sin and to the embracing of the commandments. In this regard, the *Ethics of the Fathers* notes, "He in whom the fear of sin comes before wisdom, his wisdom shall endure, but he in whom wisdom comes before fear of sin, his wisdom will not endure."[17] Also in this vein, Ben Sira advised (1:26), "If you desire wisdom, keep the commandments," and the Book of Barukh (3:9) counsels, "Hear the commandments of life, O Israel. Listen and learn wisdom."

Finally, wisdom is portrayed not only as a vehicle to awe of God, but also as an attribute of God. God's creativity is linked to His wisdom. Commenting on the verse in Proverbs (9:1), "wisdom has built her house," the Talmud states "[wisdom] is the attribute of the Holy One, blessed be He, who created the world by wisdom."[18] By cultivating wisdom, the human person shares in an attribute of God, and can, like God, become a truly creative being.

❦

The following excerpt is from the early medieval ethical work, *Mivhar ha-Peninim — Choice of Pearls*. This short treatise expresses its views as a series of aphorisms on a variety of ethical issues. The work begins with a discussion of wisdom.

Choice of Pearls is not an original work, but a compilation of epigrams from earlier Jewish and non-Jewish sources. The author was particularly influenced by an earlier collection entitled *Musrei ha-Philosofim — Maxims of the Philosophers*, compiled in Arabic by Honein ibn Ishak, a Nestorian Christian. *Maxims* includes aphorisms, statements, and stories drawn from popular Arabic, Indian, and Persian sources.[19] Upon the translation of *Maxims* into Hebrew by Judah Al-Harizi, and upon the translation of *Choice of Pearls* into Hebrew from Arabic by Judah ibn Tibbon, these non-Jewish ethical insights were provided a conduit for their eventual absorption into Jewish ethical literature. Among the most popular works in the history of Jewish ethical literature, *Choice of Pearls* was utilized both by the *Hasidei Ashkenaz* — medieval Jewish pietists — and by medieval Jewish philosophers. Published in many editions and translated into a number of languages, *Choice of Pearls* inspired a number of commentaries upon its text.[20]

Traditionally, *Choice of Pearls* is attributed to the eleventh-century Spanish poet and philosopher, Solomon ibn Gabirol. According to some scholars, Ibn Gabirol compiled *Choice of Pearls* in preparation for his later ethical treatise *Tikkun Middot ha-Nefesh — Improvement of the Moral Qualities*, which was written in Arabic in approximately 1045 and translated into Hebrew in 1167 by Judah ibn Tibbon.

Ibn Gabirol's date and place of birth are both in question. Scholars place his birthdate around 1020 and his date of death at about 1057. His birthplace seems to have been Malaga, although he grew up in Saragossa, and was orphaned at an early age. Ibn Gabirol was of a weak constitution, afflicted by a skin disease, small in stature, and ugly, according to his own testimony. As a poet and philosopher, he was dependent upon the support of wealthy patrons to pursue his work. Some of his poetry describes these patrons.

Much of Ibn Gabirol's poetry is liturgical in nature, and some of his poems have been included in the traditional Jewish liturgy, especially the Sephardic liturgy. Especially noteworthy is his long theological poem *The Kingly Crown* (*Keter Malkhut*), customarily recited by Sephardic Jews on the eve of the Sabbath.

Ibn Gabirol is often characterized as the greatest Jewish poet of the "Golden Age" of Spanish Jewry. About him, Judah al-Harizi said, "All poets before him were as nothing and after him none rose to equal him." Ibn Gabirol's poetry influenced not only Jewish liturgy, but subsequent Jewish philosophy and mysticism as well. His philosophical works, however, were not very influential upon subsequent Jewish literature.

In his magisterial work, *A History of Medieval Jewish Philosophy*, Isaac Husik characterizes Gabirol as "not merely the first Jewish philosopher in Spain, [but] . . . the first Spanish philosopher."[21] Ibn Gabirol's major philosophical work is the *Fountain of Life*, written in Arabic. The Arabic original is lost, but a twelfth-century Latin translation—*Fons Vitae*—and a partial thirteenth-century Hebrew translation—*Mekor Hayyim*—have survived. In the Latin version, the author is identified as "Avicebron," a linguistic corruption of "Ibn Gabirol." For centuries, Avicebron (or Avicebrol) was thought to have been a Christian Arab. Because of that assumption, the *Fountain of Life* enjoyed vast popularity within, and exercised considerable influence upon, late medieval Christian philosophy. Leading medieval Christian scholastics such as Thomas Aquinas and Duns Scotus often quote the *Fons Vitae*. It was not until the nineteenth-century scholar Solomon Munk demonstrated that Avicebron is none other than Solomon ibn Gabirol, that Ibn Gabirol's authorship of the *Fountain of Life* was acknowledged.

Though the *Fountain of Life* had a profound effect upon Christian philosophy, its influence upon subsequent Jewish thought has been negligible. Though Ibn Gabirol's ethical treatise, *Improvement of the Moral Qualities*, was translated into Hebrew in the twelfth century, its influence upon subsequent Jewish thought was also negligible. The reason for this lack of future impact upon Jewish ethical or philosophical literature by *Improvement* seems to be Ibn Gabirol's attempt in that work to ground ethics in the senses, without reference to the religious sources of Jewish ethical teaching. Because Ibn Gabirol presented a view of ethics that attempted to demonstrate that ethics rests on "secular" premises, without reference either to revelation or tradition, this work was largely ignored by subsequent Jewish thinkers and writers. However, as has been noted, *Choice of Pearls* did enjoy a degree of popularity.

Though Ibn Gabirol has been traditionally considered the author of *Choice of Pearls*, scholars have disputed his authorship for many generations. The sixteenth-century Jewish chronicler, David Ganz, refers to the possibility that Gabirol compiled *Choice of Pearls*, but identified Yedaya ha-Penini as the probable author. Similarly, in 1613, the first edition of the *Bibliotheca Hebraica* identifies Yedaya ha-Penini as the author of this work. Later scholars concurred with this claim. However, from a review of the vast literature regarding the question of the authorship of *Choice of Pearls*, one may conclude, with the great nineteenth-century Jewish bibliographer, Moritz Steinschneider, whose views are echoed in the *Jewish Encyclopedia* and in the *Encyclopaedia Judaica*, that authorship may be ascribed to Ibn Gabirol, although not without a lingering modicum of doubt.

Scholars who unconditionally ascribe authorship to Ibn Gabirol do so largely on the basis of a statement by Joseph Kimchi, the twelfth-century scholar who composed a metrical work in Hebrew primarily based upon the *Choice of Pearls*, entitled *Shekel Ha-Kodesh — The Holy Shekel*. Like *Choice of Pearls*, *The Holy Shekel* begins with a section on wisdom. Both *Choice of Pearls* and *The Holy Shekel* reiterate the notion discussed above that links wisdom to virtuous deeds, that requires wisdom to articulate itself as ethics. Relevant excerpts from *Choice of Pearls* follow below. In this regard, *The Holy Shekel* observes:

> If you love wisdom, choose upright action and hate rebellion [against God]. Know that wisdom is like a tree; action is its fruit. Wisdom joined to practice will guide a person to the day of death, but wisdom from which no actions flow [dies with him and] leaves nothing.[22]

Finally, the *Ethics of the Fathers* offers the following recommendation regarding the topic of this chapter — How to Be Wise. "Ben Zoma said: Who is wise? One who learns from every person."[23]

Choice of Pearls

Through wisdom the wise pay in full measure their obligation to the Creator, and [a person] attains the service of God during life and a good name after death.

There is nothing that sharpens the intellect like instruction and wisdom; and there is no truer index to the knowledgeable human mind than good conduct.

Which man is fit to rule? A sage who has been invested with power or a king who seeks wisdom? . . .

Who toils in the quest of wisdom and instruction is hampered from acquiring iniquities and transgressions; for such a person is led to despise this transitory world and love a world that is everlasting. . . .

One whom the Creator has endowed with wisdom will not be concerned when distress and trouble occur; for the sequel of wisdom is peace and tranquility, but the sequel of gold and silver, distress and trouble.

"I search not," said the sage, "for wisdom with the hope of ever coming to the end of it or attaining it completely; rather do I search for it so as not to be a fool, and the intelligent person should have none other motive than this."

The sage exhorted his son: Be not wise in words, but in deeds; for the wisdom which manifests itself in action will benefit you in the hereafter, while that of words remains here.

He further exhorted him: Seat yourself in the presence of the wise, for if you display knowledge they will praise you, if you show yourself a fool they will instruct you, and should they correct you it will be for your advantage. . . .

The sage was asked, "How is it you possess more wisdom than your fellows?" He replied, "Because I spent on oil more than they spent on wine" (i.e., he burnt the midnight lamp in study).

A body without wisdom is like a house without foundation.

Who is famed for wisdom is regarded by his fellows with respect.

Keep silent and you will escape trouble; listen and you will learn. . . .

A person is only wise during the time that he searches for wisdom; when he imagines he has completely attained it, he is a fool.

Parents can bequeath no more precious heritage to their children than wisdom; for with wisdom a person can acquire wealth, but through folly destroy wealth and be left entirely destitute.

If you will humble yourself to seek wisdom, you will be honored when others seek it of you.

Wisdom is the finest pedigree, and love the closest tie of relationship.

Kings are the judges of the earth, and the wise are the judges of kings.

The delight of the wise is in wisdom, and the delight of the fool in folly.

How goodly is the action which wisdom beautifies! How goodly the wisdom which action beautifies! And how goodly the action which gentleness beautifies!

There is no finer combination than humility and wisdom, power and clemency. . . .

He added: It is not suitable to be bashful to ask questions about what you do not know if your goal is to gain knowledge; and when you are asked concerning what you do not know, do not be ashamed to say, "I do not know." . . .

The worth of every person is proportionate to what he knows. . . .

The sage was asked, "Who are greater, the wise or the rich?" He replied, "The wise." It was then objected, "If so, how is it that there are more wise men at the doors of the rich than rich men at the doors of the wise?" He replied, "Because the wise appreciate the advantage of wealth, but the rich do not appreciate the advantage of wisdom." . . .

The first step in the acquisition of wisdom is silence, the second listening, the third memory, the fourth practice, the fifth teaching others.

When you sit among the wise, be more eager to listen than to speak. . . .

The finest human quality is to be an inquirer.

Who clothes oneself in the garment of bashfulness in the quest of wisdom will wear the vestments of foolishness; therefore rend the garment of bashfulness when seeking wisdom.

Whoever increases in pride diminishes in wisdom. . . .

How disgraceful is folly in an old man!

Teach wisdom to one who knows not, and learn from one who knows. By doing this you will know what you do not know and you will remember what you do indeed know.

The quest of wisdom in old age is like a mark made in the sand, but the quest of wisdom in youth is like an inscription on stone. . . .

Poverty cannot disgrace the wise, nor can lust enslave him. . . .

Wisdom, about which there is no discussion, is like a hidden treasure from which nothing is extracted.

There are two kinds of wisdom: the wisdom in the heart which is the wisdom that profits a person; and the wisdom in the tongue, void of action, which brings reproof from the Creator upon His creatures.

There are four mental types among human beings: the one who knows and is aware that he knows—such a person is wise, so inquire of him; the one who knows but is unaware that he knows—remind him and help him that he forget not [his knowledge]; the one who is ignorant and knows that he is ignorant—teach him; the one who is ignorant but pretends to know—he is a fool, so keep away from him.

Say not of what you do not know "I know," lest you be suspected concerning what you do indeed know. . . .

It is the practice of a fool, when doing wrong, to blame others; it is the practice of the seeker of instruction to blame himself; but it is the practice of the wise and pious man [so to act that he has occasion] to blame neither himself nor others.

Be not ashamed to receive the truth from wherever it comes, even from an inferior person.

One who acts the part of a wise man, without possessing wisdom, is like an ass working the mill, going round and round without making progress.

Pity the respected man who has sunk low, the rich man who has become impoverished and the wise man who has fallen among simpletons.

Nobody is more deserving of sympathy than a wise man upon whom has fallen the judgment of a fool.

Cast not pearls before swine, for they can do nothing with them; so deliver not wisdom to one who cannot appreciate its worth. . . .

Beware of a fool who is devout, and of a wise man who is a sinner.

The quest of wisdom is like the search for hidden treasure; gold and pearls cannot compare with it in value. . . .

The crown of the intelligent man is humility; the crown of a fool is insolence; the sequel of humility is ever peace.

Said the sage, "When I hear evil speech, I pay no attention." Somebody asked him the reason, and he replied, "Because I am afraid of hearing still worse." . . .

Somebody insulted a wise man, and one of his disciples said

to him, "Master, permit me to punish him." The sage replied, "He is not a wise man who gives another permission to do wrong." . . .

Who cannot control his temper is defective in intellect. . . .

The sage was asked, "Why do we never perceive in you a trace of anxiety?" He replied, "Because I never possessed a thing over which I would grieve had I lost it." . . .

Who is the wisest of men and the most trusting? He who accepts things as they come and go.

8

How to Be Healthy

The Hebrew word for health, *"beriut,"* derives from the word *"bara,"* to create. In Jewish thought, health and creativity are etymologically and conceptually related. Health is a prerequisite for the creation of the artful life. Furthermore, the English word "health" derives from the Old English word *"hal"* and the Old High German word *"heil,"* meaning "whole." In medieval philosophical Hebrew, the term often used for the realization of human purpose is *"shelemut,"* which derives from the Hebrew word *"shalem,"* meaning wholeness or completion. In this view, health represents the wholeness and the re-creation of human self.[1]

Health relates to the whole person, and not simply to the health of the body. The individual is a composite of body and soul, where the health of the body and the health of the soul, the illness of the body and the illness of the soul, are inextricably interrelated. For the medieval Jewish philosophers in particular, the health and illness of the soul directly relate to moral behavior.

The quest for physical and spiritual health are fundamental components in the creation of one's life as a work of art. Like so many other components of that endeavor, the quest for health is an intrinsic component of the search for self-understanding. Just as the physician must know how the body functions in order to preserve its health and remedy its maladies, so one must know one's own soul—one's own self—in order to preserve health and to remedy maladies. In this regard, Maimonides wrote:

> The improvement of the moral qualities is brought about by the healing of the soul and its activities. Therefore, just as the physician, who endeavors to cure the

human body, must have a perfect knowledge of it in its entirety and in its individual parts, just as he must know what causes sickness so that it may be avoided, and must also be acquainted with the means by which a person may be cured, so likewise, he who tries to cure the soul, wishing to improve the moral qualities, must have a knowledge of the soul in its totality and in its parts, and know how to prevent it from becoming diseased, and how to maintain health.[2]

Many medieval Jewish thinkers analogized the health of the body to the health of the soul; physical health to moral virtue. Just as medicine aims at instilling health and curing illness, so does morality aim at instilling moral virtue and curing moral vice.[3] Nevertheless, many medieval Jewish authors went further than positing an analogy between physical and spiritual or moral health. They saw them as inseparably interrelated by nature, rather than merely related by analogy. In this view, health pertains to the whole person, and not merely to the physical or to the spiritual dimensions of one's existence. To associate health with the physical alone would be to neglect the whole, to ignore the true meaning of health. To overlook the integration of bodily and moral activity, of physical and spiritual concerns, would be to deny the nature of health itself.

Medieval Jewish philosophers, such as Maimonides, echoed Plato's observation that:

> The cure of many diseases is unknown to the physicians . . . because they are ignorant of the whole [body and soul] which ought to be studied also; for the part can never be well, unless the whole is well. For all good and evil, whether in the body or in human nature, originates . . . in the soul and overflows from thence . . . and therefore, if the head and body are to be well, you must begin by curing the soul; that is the first thing."[4]

The first complete treatise on Jewish ethics was Solomon ibn Gabirol's *The Improvement of the Moral Qualities*. In this work, Ibn Gabirol links the moral virtues with the body's five senses. According to Ibn Gabirol, the moral qualities of the soul are made manifest, and in turn are influenced by, the realm of the senses. The senses may be developed to regulate the particular moral virtues associated with each of them. For example, Ibn Gabirol identifies virtues such as pride and humility with the sense of sight. One sees the greatness and the grandeur of creation, and one is inevitably led thereby to an attitude of meekness and humility.[5] The link between the senses and moral virtue is already found in the Talmud. One is cautioned, for example, not to spend too much time gazing at food or at members of the opposite sex because "one lusts for only that which the eyes see."[6] In other words, improper use of the senses, such as sight, can lead to moral vices such as gluttony and sexual promiscuity.

The connection between moral vices such as gluttony, avarice, indolence, and greed, and physical maladies of the heart, stomach, and liver is extensively addressed in medieval Jewish ethical literature. For example, in his *Treatise on Asthma*, excerpted below, Maimonides writes, "I have seen gluttons who throw their food and poke it back into their mouths like ruminating beasts. This is one of the biggest causes of many diseases. . . . Good health depends on avoidance of overeating and sinking in idleness and indolence."[7] For Maimonides, there is no real distinction between physical and moral illness. There is health and there is illness. Moral vice—the illness of the soul—is no less of an illness than is a physical malady. "I consider untrue opinions and bad morals, with all their different varieties, as types of human illness," Maimonides wrote.[8]

The nineteenth-century hasidic master, Nahman of Bratzlav, opposed treating illness on a purely physical basis. In hasidic thought, physical illness is viewed as the outward manifestation of an inner spiritual disturbance. To treat the body alone might remove the symptoms but not their cause. Such treatment would inevitably prove ineffectual. According to Nahman, the true healer cannot be a mechanic. Nahman describes physicians who neglect the spiritual dimension either of themselves or of their patients as a modern variety of "sorcerer," trying to manipulate natural forces without recourse to the spiritual.[9] In this view, the process of healing is understood as being related to the person afflicted and not only to the disease with which he or she is afflicted. As Maimonides states, "The physician should not treat the disease but the person who is suffering from it."[10]

Like health, medical ethics is not restricted to matters of physical well-being. Its scope is immeasurably larger. The primary concern of medical ethics is health; and, ethics itself, the concern with how one ought to live, is at the root of health. Just as the part cannot be complete without the whole, as the person is incomplete without the soul, so can medical ethics not be whole unless it relates to ethics *per se*, ethics here being understood as the health of the whole person—body and soul.

In the New Testament, Jesus refers to a proverb that was apparently popular in his day, "Physician, heal thyself" (Luke 4:23). Rabbinic and medieval Jewish literature might have coined a correlative proverb, "Patient, heal thyself." This latter proverb would articulate the view that one's health—physical and spiritual—is ultimately one's own responsibility. The role of the physician is to be a teacher and catalyst for helping the individual to dispel illness and to instill health. But, in the final analysis, each person—not the physician—is responsible for his or her physical and spiritual well-being, for the stewardship of his or her own life.[11]

For Maimonides, physical health is intertwined with moral health, but physical health is also the foundation upon which one may then begin to build a life of moral and intellectual virtue. As Maimonides wrote:

> The real duty of man is, that in adopting whatever measures he may for the well-being and the preservation of his existence in good health, he should do so with the object of maintaining a perfect condition of the instruments of the soul, which are the limbs of the body, so that his soul may be unhampered, and he may busy himself in acquiring the moral and mental virtues.[12]

With specific regard to physical health, Maimonides (in his *Treatise on Asthma* excerpted below) lists six "obligatory regulations" that one should attempt to observe. Before listing them, it should be noted that Maimonides offered a regimen for physical well-being not only in his medical writings such as the *Treatise on Asthma*, but also in his legal code, the *Mishneh Torah*. For Maimonides, care of the body is not merely an issue of medical concern; it is not even only an issue requiring moral advice. Care of the body is a requirement of Jewish law. Without the preservation of bodily health one cannot aspire to the higher virtues, one cannot properly serve God: "A person should aim to maintain physical health and vigor, in order that his soul may be upright, in a condition to know God. For it is impossible for one to understand sciences and meditate upon them, when one is hungry or sick, or when any of his limbs is aching."[13]

Maimonides' six obligatory regulations for the preservation of physical health are: clean air to breathe, proper diet to eat, regulation of emotion, moderate bodily exercise, proper sleep, and proper excretion.[14]

Regarding clean air, Maimonides observes that "the concern for clean air is the foremost rule in preserving the health of the body and soul."[15] Eight hundred years ago, Maimonides was concerned with the effects of air pollution on the preservation of physical health. In the area of diet, however, his prescription is more detailed.

For Maimonides, the Jewish dietary laws include not only *kashrut*, but the practice of dietary habits aimed at inducing health, preserving health, and dispelling illness. In his view, proper diet is a religious obligation, since "improper diet is like a fatal poison. It is the basis for all illness."[16] With specific reference to diet, Maimonides advises that "if a person took as good care of himself as he does of his animals, he would be saved from many illnesses."[17] Relating earlier Greek, Arabic, and Jewish sources, Maimonides' contemporary, Joseph ben Meir Zabara, himself a poet and physician, also discusses proper diet. Zabara wrote:

> Galen was asked: What is the greatest cure? Moderation in food and drink. And a certain sage has said: Who diminishes his eating will lengthen the time of his eating and will abide in health. . . . And our sages of blessed memory have said: Diminish your eating and you will diminish your disease. . . . And when Galen was asked: Why do you stint on your food?, he replied: My purpose is to eat to live; the purpose of others is to live to eat. . . . He that fills his belly each day undermines his health.[18]

Both in his medical and legal writings, Maimonides advocates a diet low in fat and high in complex carbohydrates. "Fat and coarse food should be avoided as far as possible," he counsels in the *Treatise on Asthma*.[19] In the ethical will of Ibn Tibbon excerpted in this volume (see Chapter 13), the author advises specific avoidance of "harmful sweets": "Eat no eating that prevents you from eating," writes Ibn Tibbon.[20] In *The Book of Delight*, Zabara cautions against eating too much beef. Quoting Hippocrates, he writes, "Guard yourself from eating beef and make not your stomach a graveyard for cattle."[21]

Maimonides' third criterion for health, the regulation of emotion, indicates the clear nexus between physical and moral well-being. Zabara, for example, wrote that restraint in diet leads both to physical and moral health, because such restraint articulates the virtue of elevating reason over unbridled desire, prudence over gluttony, and temperance over overindulgence.[22]

For regulating the emotions, many of the Jewish medievals advocated the "golden mean," physical as well as emotional balance. According to Ibn Gabirol, just as a physician attempts to engender health and eliminate disease by restoring a harmonious balance among the patient's bodily humors and fluids, so does the acquisition of moral virtue require that one's emotions be in a well-balanced state.[23] With regard to the "golden mean," Maimonides wrote:

> The right way is the mean in each group of dispositions common to humanity; namely, that disposition which is equally distant from the two extremes in its class, not being nearer to the one than the other. Hence, our ancient sages exhorted us that a person should evaluate his dispositions and so adjust them that they should be at the mean between extremes, and this will serve his physical health.[24]

Maimonides further observes that two substantial obstacles often hamper the attempt to attain the mean: innate dispositions and bad habits. Maimonides was keenly aware of the diverse innate physical and moral dispositions that individuate one person from another. He wrote:

> Every human being is characterized by numerous moral dispositions which differ from each other and are exceedingly divergent. [For example,] one person is choleric, always irascible; another is sedate, never angry. . . . One is a sensualist whose lusts are never sufficiently gratified; another is so pure in soul he does not even long for the few things that our physical nature needs. . . . One is so greedy that all the money in the world will not satisfy him . . . another curbs his desires that he is satisfied with little. . . .[25]

For individuals with strong negative innate dispositions, arriving at the mean is not easy. What is often required is for such individuals to go to the other extreme in order to harness the undesirable disposition. In Maimonides' words, "If any of his dispositions is at one extreme, he should move to the opposite extreme, and keep it for a long time until he has regained the right path which is the normal mean in every class of [physical and moral] dispositions."[26] Nevertheless, for Maimonides, for certain dispositions even the mean is to be avoided. One such disposition is humility.[27]

For Maimonides and for others, both physical and moral health entails the elimination of bad habits, which frustrate the effort to eliminate and prevent illness and to introduce and preserve health, and that hamper the attempt to cast off moral vice and inculcate moral virtue.[28] Since a prerequisite for moral action is moral volition, bad habits are to be avoided since they restrain choice. The habit has the person as much as the person has the habit. In this regard, Moses Hayyim Luzzatto wrote, "He who has become a slave to habit is no longer his own master, and cannot act differently, even if he should want to do so. His will is held in bondage by certain habits which have become second nature to him."[29]

Of particular interest to many medieval authors concerned with regulation of emotion are the dangerous potentialities to physical and moral health posed by anger, worry, and depression. Since these emotions were discussed earlier (see Chapter 6), suffice it here to quote a few additional observations.[30]

Ibn Gabirol states that "just as a scab is a disease of the body, so is anger a disease of the soul."[31] Or, as the *Sefer ha-Yashar—The Book of the Righteous* states, "One should not grow angry when one loses a desirable object or if business matters go awry. If a person conducts himself always in this way, his anger will grow less, and this is a healing for the soul."[32] Maimonides' younger contemporary, Joseph ibn Aknin, quotes a proverb, "Sickness is the prison of the body, and worry is the prison of the mind."[33] Finally, *Orhot Zaddikim— The Ways of the Righteous* says, "Worry and sadness destroy the heart and are physical ailments. And the most evil of all worries is the one wherein the person pursues vice and when he does not attain the gratifications of every whim and lust of his heart, he worries and feels anguish."[34]

With regard to his fourth regulation, exercise, Maimonides insists that physical exercise should relate to the "exercise of the soul" as well as to the body, that physical exercise should lead one to the development of an emotional and psychological state of happiness, joy, and contentment.[35] Physical exercise is considered an essential element in the health regimen of any individual. In his legal code, the Mishneh Torah, Maimonides wrote, "If one leads a sedentary life and does not exercise, neglects the calls of nature, or is constipated—even if he eats wholesome food and takes care of himself with medical rules—he will throughout his life be subject to ache and pains, and his strength will fail him."[36] Or, as Ibn Falaquera notes, "The exercising of the body is a bulwark against disease, and a source of strength for the limbs. . . . An overdose of exercise, however, is harmful."[37]

With regard to sleep, Maimonides advises achieving a mean between the extremes of too much and too little sleep. He also advocates short naps preceded by a bath and a massage.[38] According to Maimonides, even sleep can be a conduit, not only to physical health, but to the higher aspiration of divine worship. In the Mishneh Torah, he writes, "Even when a person sleeps and seeks repose, to calm his mind and rest his body, so as not to fall sick and be incapacitated from serving God, his sleep is in the service of the Almighty."[39]

With regard to the final element of his health regimen—proper excretion—Maimonides insists that "one should not neglect the call of nature, but should respond immediately."[40] He further counsels that "it is a leading principle of medicine that if there is constipation or if the bowels move with difficulty, grave disorders result."[41] Already in the Talmud, the normal functioning of the urinary tract and of the bowels is considered an expression of divine grace and a condition that one should strive to maintain. The following blessing, recorded in the Talmud and now part of the liturgy, is to be recited after going to the bathroom:

> Blessed is He who created human beings with wisdom, and created in each of them many orifices and many cavities. It is fully known before the throne of Your glory that if one of them should be [improperly] opened or one of them closed, it would be impossible for one to stand before You. . . . [Blessed are You] who heals all flesh and who performs wonders.[42]

According to the commentaries to this text, the phrase "who heals all flesh" means that normal excretory function is a product of divine grace, that "evacuation is a healing for the entire body." That health-threatening elements such as feces and urine exit the body through the proper orifices, while

the soul that sustains individual human life remains in place, is interpreted as
the wonder that is then performed.[43] From this perspective, the most
elemental and alimental functions of the human body can become invita-
tions to the most exalted spiritual activities.[44] Consider this talmudic text:

> Rabbi Akiva said: Once I went in after Rabbi Joshua to a privy. [From watching
> him there] I learned three things. . . . Ben Azzai said to him [i.e., to Akiva]: Did
> you dare to take such liberties with your master? He [i.e., Akiva] replied: It is a
> matter of Torah and I am required to learn. . . . Rav Kahana once hid under Rav's
> bed. He heard him [i.e., Rav] chatting [with his wife] and joking and doing what he
> required [i.e., engaging in intercourse]. He said to him: one would think Abba's
> mouth had never sipped the dish before! He [i.e., Rav] said: Kahana, what are you
> doing here?; it is rude. He [i.e., Kahana] replied: It is a matter of Torah and I need
> to learn.[45]

To suggest that the human body or its natural functions are repulsive by
nature is considered an affront to God's wisdom. In themselves, bodily organs
and functions are beautiful and good. Only when abused or misused do they
become ugly and repulsive. According to the medieval ethical treatise on
human sexuality excerpted in this volume (see Chapter 11), *Iggeret ha-
Kodesh — The Holy Letter*:

> "God saw everything He had made and behold it was very good" (Genesis
> 1:31). . . . Nothing in the human organs are created flawed or ugly. Everything is
> created with divine wisdom and is therefore complete, exalted, good and pleasant.
> But when one sins, ugliness becomes attached to these matters.[46]

In the *Mishneh Torah*, Maimonides sums up a number of the features of his
health regimen:

> A great principle of hygiene, as physicians say, is as follows: As long as a person
> takes active exercise, works hard, does not overeat, and keeps his bowels open, he
> will be free from disease and will increase in vigor. . . . Whosoever lives in
> accordance with the directions I have set forth has my assurance that he will not
> be sick until he grows old and dies; he will not be in need of a physician . . . unless
> his constitution be congenitally defective or he has acquired bad habits . . . or if
> the world should be visited by natural calamities such as pestilence or drought.[47]

In sum, Jewish religious literature takes a teleological view of the nature of
health. In creating the artful life, "a person must care for his body like an
artisan for his tools," wrote the thirteenth-century Jewish philosopher, Shem
Tov ben Joseph ibn Falaquera.[48] The concern with health is, in the final
analysis, a concern with how one lives the life divinely entrusted into one's
care. As Joseph Zabara notes, "When the brother of a certain man died, they
asked, 'What occasioned his death?,' 'His life,' was the reply."[49]

It is not surprising that many of the works of medieval Jewish ethical literature, including those excerpted in this volume, were written by practicing physicians.[50] It is also not surprising that many, if not most, medieval and early modern medical treatises written by Jews contain moral as well as medical advice and observations. It is totally appropriate to consider these medical works as a form of Jewish ethical literature, particularly as an expression of one of the major genres of that literature called "*hanhagot*" in Hebrew.[51] It is a characteristic of *hanhagot* literature to concentrate on specific practical details of moral behavior rather than to offer excursuses on general moral principles and values. The objective of *hanhagot*, as the Hebrew term implies, is to lead and to guide one through particular prescriptions toward proper behavioral patterns. Making use both of moral principles and halakhic requirements, *hanhagot* are concrete and practical rather than abstract and speculative.[52] In kabbalistic and in hasidic writings, *hanhagot* are often directed to the already spiritually developed elite.[53] However, works of medically oriented *hanhagot* are meant for a more popular readership. Indeed, many such medical works include not only moral advice, but also folk remedies and magical procedures for dispelling illness and introducing physical well-being. As has been noted above, the following excerpt comes from the medical writings of the most prominent Jewish physician and philosopher of the Middle Ages, Moses Maimonides. This excerpt from his *Treatise on Asthma* discusses most of the themes related above on how to be healthy. The *Treatise on Asthma* was written by Maimonides for the son of Saladin, the ruler of Egypt. Maimonides offers the prince instructions on how to manage this disease with which he was afflicted. However, there is little doubt that Maimonides directed his views beyond that of his patient. His advice was surely meant for a wider audience. Like Maimonides' major philosophical work, the *Guide of the Perplexed*, which was written in the form of a long epistle to one person, Joseph ibn Aknin, so a number of his medical works, including the *Treatise on Asthma*, though written ostensibly for a single person, were meant for a wider readership.

With little doubt, Moses Maimonides, or Moses ben Maimon, or "*Rambam*" (an acronym for "*Rabbeinu Moshe ben Maimon*"—our teacher Moses son of Maimon) was the most illustrious Jew of the Middle Ages. Both the extent and the impact of his writings and teachings are without parallel in Jewish intellectual history. As Abraham Joshua Heschel has written:

> The life of Maimonides seems to be more plausible as a legend than as a fact of history. The achievements that came out of the years (of his life), 1135–1204, seem so incredible that one is almost inclined to believe that Maimonides is the name of a whole academy of scholars rather than the name of an individual.

> The most distinguished physician of his time, the most creative rabbinic scholar of the millennium, an epoch-making philosopher, a notable mathematician, a nat-

ural scientist and jurist, an authority and pioneer in the field of comparative religion, a supreme master and perhaps the finest stylist in Hebrew since the days of the Bible, and adviser to his own community as well as to communities in many distant lands. . . . His unparalleled achievements in Jewish learning evoked astonishment in the eyes of experts . . . and remain incomparable and unsurpassed to this day.[54]

Born into a renowned and established Spanish-Jewish family in 1135 (or 1138), Maimonides' future seemed secure. However, with the fall of his native Cordoba to a fanatical Moslem sect, the Almohades, in 1148, there came a period of severe persecution that led Maimonides' family to leave Spain for North Africa, Palestine, and finally for Egypt, where he lived the balance of his life. In Egypt, Maimonides served as a court physician and as personal physician to Alfadhil, the vizier of Egypt, and as the leader of the Jewish community in Egypt, as well. His works may be divided into two categories: major works and minor works. His major works were his vast *Commentary to the Mishnah*, written in Arabic early in his career; his magisterial code of Jewish law, *The Mishneh Torah*, written in Hebrew toward the middle of his life; and his classic philosophical work, *The Guide of the Perplexed*, written in Arabic later in his life. His many minor works take a variety of forms and treat a plethora of different fields. For example, Maimonides' earliest works were a treatise on logic and a treatise on astronomy, dealing with the intercalculation of the Jewish calendar. His later works, written during the last ten years of his life, were a series of medical treatises that treat such diverse issues as asthma, sexuality, poisonous snakebites, air pollution, and proper diet. Between these early and later works were Maimonides' many legal responsa, his *Book of the Commandments*, his treatises on forced apostasy, on resurrection of the body, on false messiahs, and so forth. Furthermore, each of his larger works contains numerous self-contained treatises on a wide variety of subjects. Citations from and references to Maimonides' writings are scattered through this book. Any study of Jewish ethics—indeed any study of Judaism—would be incomplete without reference to Maimonides' contribution. Further information about Maimonides and his works is offered later (see Chapter 15, this volume).

Moses Maimonides
Treatise on Asthma

It is well known that the course of dietary conduct for the healthy and sick alike has been grouped by the physicians in seven categories, of which six are obligatory and unconditional and the seventh commendable. The six obligatory regulations are: (1) keeping clean the air which we breathe; (2) keeping an eating and drinking diet, (3) regulation of spiritual emotions, (4) regulation of bodily exercise, and lastly, rest, (5) sleep and waking up, (6) excretion, eventually keeping back of superfluous outflow. The seventh group is the one the body takes according to circumstance, such as bathing and massaging. . . .

Fat and coarse food should be avoided as far as possible. Furthermore avoid a too rich meal, even if it tastes well. Any food containing much residue should be avoided at all cost. It is well to take food in moderate quantities, even less than usual, and even the small amount consumed should be not too condensed or rough. The reason therefore is quite clear: in digestion the less fat and coarse foods leave behind a certain amount of unassimilated parts which escape the body in the form of gases and sweat. If more residue is left behind (from the less fatty foods) it easily escapes the body through the pores of the skin, the stool and urine or in other channels of excretion. Should, however, the residue be too solid or rough, its dissolution is beset with difficulties and its exit from the body outlets greatly hampered. It then wanders about from organ to organ and hinders evacuation. If the digestive organs are strongly resistant to the residue the latter moves to less resistant organs where they settle down and aggravate their weaknesses. . . .

In one of his sayings Galen speaks of the diligence and care to be exercised to have the openings of the digestive organs and the channels from the liver cleared and clean at all times, not only in the sick but in the healthy as well. . . .

. . . It is a most useful thing and valuable counsel for every man to beware of fat food in general. . . .

Doctors have laid down the following rule: That a man should stop eating before he experiences a sense of repletion (nausea), that is, as soon as he satisfies his appetite; even if he stays just hungry (after finishing his meal). If an animal, meaning a horse, donkey and camel to which no self-limiting (rules) were taught, can take the exact measure of its fullness and not overstep it, how can a man fail to know his proper food intake, and take more food than he can possibly cram into himself until it sticks in his throat (until it reaches his gullet)?

I have seen gluttons who throw their food and poke it back into their mouths like ruminating beasts. This is one of the biggest causes of many diseases. . . .

Says Hippocrates: Good health depends on avoidance of overeating and sinking in idleness and indolence. Galen, too, cites a most useful precept in this regard which I repeat here because I think it very important. It reads like this: inactivity is as big an evil where preservation of good health is aimed at as moderate exercise is a great boon to it. This means that a man would not become ill (so easily) were he assured of a good digestion all the time. . . .

The general rule to be followed is for healthy, vigorous people to consume all the nourishment they need at one sitting a day. On the other hand, if debilitated persons, such as old men and convalescents, take their daily meal all at once they commit an outrage against their health. They must portion it out according to the degree of their debility so that their powers do not fail them altogether and their native warmth depart.

Of the rule of diet for old people says Galen as follows: The main rule to be adhered to is that a person of limited physical strength should be given small meals within short intervals and one of full bodily vigor—a single meal at long intervals.

It is well known that clean, fresh air free of any contamination is advisable for all people, whether healthy or sick. . . .

As for the effect of psychic moods, it is generally acknowledged that the impact of mental suffering, agitation, and obstinacy is to impair mental activity and physical well-being so much so that one's appetite for food is completely lost when in mental anguish, fear, mourning, or distress. In such a condition a man cannot even use his voice properly because his agitation affects his respiratory organs and he cannot exercise them at will. The weight of the accumulated gas residue within him keeps him from walking erect, standing in an upright position and inhaling a sufficient volume of air. He experiences difficulty in exercising his other organs as well. Should this condition endure, a man cannot avoid falling ill and if it takes on a chronic character, death is not long in coming. All this is universally known and should not detain us here. On the other hand, gaiety and liveliness have the opposite effect; they gladden the heart, stimulate the movement (circulation) of the blood and the degree of mental activity stemming from such a condition is in some cases among the highest.

However, when people indulge to excess, in headlong pursuit of pleasure, which sometime happens with the ignorant and the foolish, they too invariably fall sick and may even sink altogether because in that case their soul is burdened with decay and hastens to leave the body, their hearts fail to function and death becomes inevitable.

The cure of these two kinds of psychic states and their prevention, so that a man shall not fall a prey to them, lies not in food recipes, neither in drugs alone, nor in regular medical advice. The cure of such conditions belongs rather to other spheres of professional knowledge, by which we mean the philosophical virtues taught by the philosophers who are engaged in the study of ethics, morals, etc. Undoubtedly, these psychological methods are a greater help in these emotional disorders and a better safeguard against them, for they uncover the nature of such conditions and the best way to cure them by learning from experience and failure. Furthermore, the philosophical virtues guard a man against extreme emotional states. They keep a man from falling into brutish emotionalism on mournful or joyous occasions as happens with the ignorant multitude. A man so treated reveals his mental state by resorting to friendly counsel, not by a show of explosive action, enervating anguish and the like. The same effects are possessed by moral and ethical teachings. A man should take easily the world and its phenomena and what passes for luck and ill luck. In reality these are as nothing. They are hardly to be noticed. There is no comfort in the one nor alarm in the other. In the world of our mind they are no more than ludicrous, idle specters which vanish away.

Of the good points of habit Galen speaks in his book *De usu partium*, saying this: Each man has his peculiar habits the breaking of which is fraught with the greatest danger, which holds good not only with regard to convalescents and the like but to sick men under treatment as well. . . .

The relation between the air in a town and in its streets and that found in the open country may be compared to the relation between grossly contaminated, filthy water and its clear, lucid counterpart. Town air is stagnant, turbid and "thick," the natural result of its inhabitants, their corpses and animal carcasses, food gone bad and the like. This air the winds carry stealthily inside the houses and many a man become ill even without noticing it. However, when escape seems impossible after one has grown up in the city and become used to its ways, one should at least choose for a residence a wide-open site, facing the north-east, preferably on a steep, wooded mountainside and far from ponds and marshes (for fear of mosquitoes). Should it be impossible to move to another town, a suburb residence, to the south or north, is the next best thing. Living quarters are best located on an upper floor, giving on a wide street exposed to the north wind (for Egypt) and ample sunshine, since sunshine dispels bad air and renders it fine and clear. Toilets should be located as far as possible from living rooms. The air should be kept dry at all times by sweet scents, fumigation and drying agents. The concern for clean air is the foremost rule in preserving the health of one's body and soul. . . .

Sometimes the doctor goes about his work very efficiently, no error is made either on his or the patient's part, and still no progress is made to justify all the trouble taken. This is accounted for by the fact that medicine alone is not the only factor in a cure but medicine and nature combined. . . . When the disease is stronger than the natural resistance of the organism, medicine is of no use. When one's resistance is stronger than the disease, the physician is of no use. When the two factors are balanced, the physician is called in to increase one's natural powers of resistance and assist them to oust the disease. . . .

The more a man is proficient in a given discipline, the more he thinks of it, the greater his doubts and the more weighty the problems he has to tackle. There is no end to the ideas and thoughts that surge in him and he can scarcely cope with them. On the other hand, to a man of little learning all the weighty problems seem easy to explain, all the remote things within reach, and so great is his conceit that he is prepared to come up . with a ready answer at any time and to explain things he does not grasp at all. . . . Says Hippocrates: Two things should be borne in mind, one, to help the patient, the other not to harm him. . . .

Aristotle, in his treatise on natural sciences, says as follows: The first thing required of a doctor is that he learn the nature of his patient's constitution on both healthy and sick days. Most physicians fail to establish the true facts so that, in the last resort, the doctor and his "remedy" are to blame for the patient's death. . . . It should be clear that medicine is a science essential to man, at any time, anywhere; not only in times of illness but in health as well. It may truly be said that medicine (the medical man) should be a man's constant companion. . . .

But nobody can be called a good physician who has observed

or witnessed some facts without having engaged in their theoretical study. Because medicine is not a craft like carpentry or weaving which can be acquired by practice. It is gaining perfection by changing circumstances. Training in this art implies most often a combination of practice and theory. Any sick individual presents new problems. One can never say one disease is just like the other.

There is a general rule, and I have seen great physicians acting on it (which is also in keeping with the medicine of Hippocrates and Galen) that the physician should not treat the disease but the patient who is suffering from it. . . .

Another thing I learned in Egypt is that it seldom happens, with prominent families or with the common people, that the one and the same physician should treat a patient from beginning to end. In most cases they run from doctor to doctor (to consult him), sometimes a patient, if able to afford it, is treated simultaneously by ten doctors not knowing about each other. Thus the patient leads the doctor astray by telling him he does everything ordered. The patient or the person in charge of him listens to what each doctor has to say, decides who is right and takes the medicines which he decides are the best. But the worst thing is the confusion of the patient himself who can hardly know which physician is right. . . . Says El Razi: He who lets himself be treated by many physicians is never sure if they all made no mistake.

Says the Author: This is true when all of them treat him separately. However, when they are gathered together, in consilium as is the case with kings and wealthy families, comparing their observations and deliberating on the best course to be taken, it is highly advisable and becoming. The patient has the benefit of the sum of their knowledge and ability, since no man can remember everything he learns and this art is not easy for its votaries, especially where memory is concerned, which has nothing to do with intelligence. It may well happen that a physician should not be able to muster on the spot everything he might require for his patient.

9

How to Employ Wealth

According to a hasidic legend, Levi Yitzhak of Berditchev once offered this prayer during a time of severe economic depression:

> Lord of Worlds! The prophets and sages of old compared the covenant at Sinai to a marriage between You and the people of Israel. But what kind of marriage is it? Israel brought great family lineage (*yihus*) to the marriage, for we are the children of the patriarchs, Abraham, Isaac and Jacob. What lineage did You bring? Who are Your ancestors? What did You bring to the marriage? – Wealth. As it is written, "Mine is the gold and the silver" (Haggai 2:8). This was Your contribution to the marriage. But, where is this wealth? We are in need. Therefore, keep Your part of the bargain and open Your vast treasure house to Your people, and ease our needs.[1]

In the prayer announcing the New Moon, the liturgy asks God for "a life of riches and honor."[2] Similarly in the Grace after Meals, one entreats God to "feed us, sustain us, support us, deliver us, release us from our afflictions . . . and to spare us from shame and embarrassment." These prayers recognize that fiscal security is literally the lifeblood that sustains our physical and spiritual well-being. In this regard, Hayyim ben Betzalel of Friedberg pointed out that one Hebrew term for "money" is *"damim,"* which also means "blood." "Money is called *'damim,'*" he writes, "because just as blood sustains a person's life, so is money essential for life, and one who has no money is like one who is thought of as being dead."[3] Similarly, the Talmud notes, "All the members

123

of the body depend on the heart, and the heart depends upon the purse."[4] In the words of a midrash, "Three things injure the body: heartache, stomach trouble, and an empty purse which is the worst of the three."[5] As the excerpt below from *Sefer Ma'alot ha-Middot — Improvement of the Moral Virtues* states, "when a person is rich, he vitalizes himself without grief and excessive effort, and without concern in this world about matters of livelihood and sustenance and normal human needs."[6]

According to Maimonides, a modicum of wealth is necessary for one to initiate the task of self-development. A person concerned about the source of his or her next meal, about shelter for the night, about necessary expenditures that cannot be paid, can hardly have the peace of mind required for engaging in moral and spiritual growth. Deprivation may lead one to depravity, to vice rather than to virtue. Maimonides taught that wealth is a tool. Whether it becomes good or bad depends upon how it is used. For Maimonides, proper use of wealth entails the employment of fiscal means for moral and spiritual ends. In his words, "In the pursuit of wealth, the main design in its acquisition should be to expend it for noble purposes and for the maintenance of the body and the preservation of life so that its owner may obtain a knowledge of God insofar as that is vouchsafed unto human beings."[7] With its typical elegance and brevity, the *Ethics of the Fathers* expresses a similar sentiment: "Where there is no bread, there is no Torah."[8]

In Chapter 15 we discuss how to employ wealth to help the needy, how to help provide the material means needed by others in their task of creating life as a work of art. However, the present chapter will focus on a separate issue: how to employ one's own wealth for creating one's own life as a work of art.[9] As we shall see, for much of Jewish ethical literature, wealth is both an opportunity and a danger, a promise and a peril. It all depends upon how one manages the wealth deposited into his or her care.

Two assumptions inform Jewish religious attitudes toward wealth. The first is that ultimately all wealth belongs to God, that what we own is a loan from God: "Riches and honor are Yours to dispense; You have dominion over all. . . . All is from You, and is Your gift that we have given to You" (1 Chronicles 29:12, 14). Commenting on this verse, a talmudic text affirms that what we own, we owe: "Give Him of His own, for both you and whatever is yours are His."[10]

The corollary to divine ownership is human stewardship. For example, a midrash quotes God as saying, "Honor the Lord from whatever substance God has bestowed upon you, for you are only My steward."[11] This second assumption, i.e., human stewardship of divine wealth, was known in the Middle Ages as the "doctrine of deposit."[12] In this view, God deposits His wealth with human beings as a trust. If the trustee manages God's "deposit" properly, then God's capital is well used. If not, the human trustee is liable for misappropriation of funds, even for robbery.

According to the seventeenth-century Polish talmudic commentator, Samuel Edels, there are three common motivations for the acquisition of wealth. The first is that wealth brings honors from others. The second is that one must acquire wealth to ensure that the members of one's family are provided with what they need. The third is independence. One does not want to be dependent upon the benevolence of others for one's basic sustenance.[13] In this regard, Judah Loew of Prague taught that wealth can liberate one from dependence upon others for one's sustenance, or wealth can enslave one. A person can possess riches or riches can possess the rich. For Loew, the virtue of contentment is the "golden mean" between abject dependence and passionate avarice.[14]

The virtue of contentment is summarized in the well-known talmudic statement, "Who is rich? He who is satisfied with his lot."[15] According to Solomon ibn Gabirol, the truly wealthy person is not one who has what he wants, but one who wants what he has.[16] According to Judah Loew, wealth reflects an external condition, whereas contentment indicates an inner condition. Wealth may be what one has, but not what one is.[17]

Fiscal sustenance sustains one and enables one to create life as a work of art. Economic security is not an end in itself, but a means to an end: the acquisition of wisdom, the cultivation of moral virtue, the performance of the commandments, the rendering of assistance to others. As Bahya ben Asher wrote:

> Riches enable one to perform suitable and desirable deeds through which one will find "grace and favor in the sight of God and human beings" (Proverbs 3:4). . . . Riches were created only so that one could fulfill the commandments. . . . It is known that one cannot attain perfection of wisdom without wealth. . . . Therefore, the perfection of wisdom requires riches, which are an honor and crown for the wise, for he should use them for whatever the Torah has commanded and for whatever reason dictates. . . . Riches are a crown and an honor for the wise, for such a person will use them in a way that will bring honor to himself and to others. This is the exact opposite of the wealthy fool, who, upon becoming rich, uses wealth for foolishness.

Wealth must wed wisdom. The rich must convey to their children not only riches, but the wisdom necessary for their proper employment. In the hierarchy of desirable qualities, our sources place wisdom above wealth:

> Where can wisdom be found
> Where is the source of understanding?
> No one can set a value on it . . .
> It cannot be bartered for gold,
> Silver cannot be paid out as its price.
> (Job 28:12, 15)

As one medieval text puts it, "With regard to riches—look beneath you and be grateful for your lot. But, with regard to wisdom, look above you and recognize what you lack."[18]

On this theme, a popular and often-quoted text in medieval Jewish ethical literature is the following:

> A sage was asked: Who are greater, the wise or the rich? He replied: The wise. It was objected: If so, how is it that there are more of the wise at the doors of the wealthy than rich people at the doors of the wise? He replied: Because the wise appreciate the value of riches, but the rich do not similarly value the value of wisdom.[19]

Wisdom is considered more important than wealth because wisdom may be employed in the acquisition of wealth, but wealth cannot bring about the acquisition of wisdom. The rich are often treated as if they are wise because people are attentive to them and seek their advice. In *Fiddler on the Roof*, Tevye dreams about being a rich man because then everyone would seek his counsel. But, the wealthy should not be deceived by this attention. They should recognize when they are being patronized. As the excerpt below from *Sefer Ma'alot ha-Middot* states, "All come near to the rich person, and they become related to him; among them are lovers and friends, in order to benefit from him."[20] As Bahya ben Asher wrote, "Wealth lends weight to one's words so that the opinion of the wealthy is heard." And, as the *Choice of Pearls* observes, "When a person's wealth diminishes, even his children do not accept his opinion and they contradict his words and commands."[21]

Saadya Gaon wrote that "the only reason why human beings have been endowed with the love of money is in order that they may take good care of that which God has bestowed upon them and not squander it, not for any other purpose."[22] Saadya's admonition not to squander wealth, and Bahya ben Asher's observation that wealth should not be wasted, relate to the biblical injunction of *bal tash'hit* (Deuteronomy 20:19) that enjoins one against wanton destruction or waste of God-given resources: natural, fiscal, or human. According to a midrash:

> When God created the first human beings, he took them around the Garden of Eden and said to them: "Behold My works, how beautiful and commendable they are. All that I have created in My world, I have created for your sake. Be careful not to corrupt or destroy My world; for if you do, there will be no one after you to repair it."[23]

According to the eighteenth-century preacher, Jonathan Eibshitz, of all the temptations toward immorality one faces, the greatest is posed by money.[24] As one is admonished not to waste or misuse wealth, one is warned against the temptations of avarice and arrogance that can readily afflict the wealthy.

Arrogance is considered the supreme moral vice in Jewish ethical litera ture. Pride is viewed as being rooted in self-deception and as the most significant obstacle to creating life as a work of art.[25] Contentiousness is described as the opposite of contentment. Moreover, arrogance engendered by wealth is depicted as a double self deception. Pride means that one thinks one is more than one really is. But arrogance because of wealth is an overweening sense of self-importance, not because of who one is, but because of what one has. The wise person creates life as a work of art; such a person forges his or her own pedigree. But, as a medieval proverb puts it, "Wealth is often used as a pedigree for those who lack one."[26]

"Let not a rich man say, 'My power and the might of my right hand has gotten me this wealth' (Deuteronomy 8:17)," *Sefer Ma'alot ha-Middot* states in the excerpt below. "Let the rich person understand that it is God who gives the power to acquire wealth."[27] The rich person may declare, "I am a self-made man." But, as Mark Twain said, "A self-made man is about as likely as a self-laid egg." Or, as Saadya Gaon wrote:

> If everything goes well and runs smoothly [in the accumulation of wealth], one is apt to put one's entire trust in it and to forget to make mention of his Master, and to deny his Provider, as Scripture says: "Your silver and gold is multiplied; all that you have is multiplied, then your heart is lifted up, and you forget the Lord your God" (Deuteronomy 8:13, 14).[28]

According to Bahya ben Asher, the arrogance of wealth can also lead to the desire to dominate and to oppress others in thought and in deed. In this regard, he wrote, "Wealth entails many perils, for it might cause arrogance and impertinence. . . . Because of wealth, one may want to oppress others."[29]

One of the spiritual and moral temptations associated with wealth is unbridled greed. Here wealth has the person more than the person has wealth. This passion for the limitless acquisition of wealth was recognized as a peculiar and dangerous propensity of the wealthy. As Bahya ben Asher wrote:

> It is characteristic of wealth that when one has little, one desires more, and when one attains more, one desires double of what already has been acquired, and so *ad infinitum*. Thus, a midrash teaches, "No person leaves this world with even half of his or her desires attained. If one has one hundred, one desires two hundred." . . .[30] Wealth is like a fire: the more wood one adds, the more the flame increases and the fire blazes.

Similarly, as Saadya Gaon observed:

> I have come to the conclusion that all is well with the acquisition of money so long as it comes to a person spontaneously and with ease. However, once one passionately engages in the quest for wealth, one realizes that it entails immense efforts of thought and exertion, keeping one awake at night and plagued by hardship by day, so that even when one has acquired what one desires, one is often unable to sleep properly. . . . When a person makes money the object of all his strivings and devotes himself to it with mad ambition and avidity . . . then the love of money becomes for him like a consuming fire, like a wilderness, like death or barrenness that are never sated.[31]

There are even those, the Talmud observes, who value their money more than their lives.[32]

Judah Loew pointed out that on account of human avarice, money is called *kesef* in Hebrew, from *kosef*—desire. Because money is subject to temporary ownership due to market fluctuations, coins are called *zuzim*, i.e., things that move about, or *ma'ot*, a play on the word *et*, a given time—for money is not forever. Gold, *zahav*, reflects avarice and stands for *zeh hav*—give this to me.[33]

One reason these sources admonish us not to make the acquisition of wealth the center of our existence is because of its tenuous nature. Riches are a fragile commodity—here today, gone tomorrow. In this regard, Moses Hayyim Luzzatto asks one to "consider the vicissitudes of life. The rich may become poor, the ruler subservient, the eminent obscure. Since a person is liable to find himself occupying a station in life that he now looks at with contempt, how shall he be arrogant because of the good fortune he may presently enjoy, but which he can be never sure will last?"[34] As a midrash puts it, "There is an ever rotating wheel in this world. One who is rich today, may be poor tomorrow. One who is poor today, may be rich tomorrow."[35] A final objection to avarice relates to the disruptive nature of its social and political consequences. As Maimonides wrote, "The furious desire for possessions . . . the passion of acquisition, is a primary cause of political and social tensions."[36]

Two antidotes are prescribed to treat the moral maladies of arrogance and the uncontrolled passion for limitless acquisition. These are: contemplation of loss of wealth, and contemplation of loss of life—death. A midrash articulates this prescription: "When one is born, the hands are clenched, as though to say—All the world is mine; now I shall acquire it. But when a person dies, the hands are wide open, as though to say—I have acquired nothing from this world."[37] Expressions such as "You can't take it with you" and "Shrouds have no pockets" also reflect this sentiment.

In the Talmud, there is this story about Alexander the Great:

Alexander came to the door of the Garden of Eden. He demanded: Open the gate for me. They replied: "This is the gate of the Lord, the righteous alone may enter" (Psalms 118:20). He replied: I too am a king; I am also of some account; give me something. They gave him an eyeball. He went and weighed all his gold and silver against it, and they were not equal to it. He asked the rabbis: How is this possible? They replied: It is a human eye, which is never satisfied with what it sees. He said to them: Prove it! They took some dust and covered it, and immediately the gold became heavier. This teaches that a human eye is not satisfied with all the gold, until it is covered with the earth of the grave.[38]

Wealth can be a blessing or it can be a curse. The sixteenth-century preacher, Ephraim Lunshitz, compared wealth to fire, because like fire, we cannot live without it, but if left out of control, it can destroy us.[39] As the excerpt below tells us, wealth can be "a medicine for the mind, a protection for the soul." All depends upon how we utilize it. Wealth can be a tool for self-destruction and for the destruction of others; or, wealth can be a vehicle for creating one's life as a work of art.

❦

The following excerpt comes from Sefer Ma'alot ha-Middot — Improvement of the Moral Qualities, one of the gems of Jewish ethical literature. Its author, Yehiel ben Yekutiel ha-Rofeh, was a poet, liturgist, scribe, and physician who lived in late thirteenth-century Italy.

Written with elegance and simplicity, this work offers in twenty-four chapters a road map to the principles of virtuous conduct. Directed toward the younger generation, this treatise aims at sharing inherited wisdom with those seeking direction and purpose in life. For our author, love is the sine qua non for the artful life — love of God and love of one's fellow human beings; hatred is a snare, threatening to stifle moral action, artful living, and genuine relationships. Written in a comparatively open and affluent atmosphere, this work was first published in Istanbul in 1512 under the title Beit Middot — House of Virtue, but beginning with the 1556 Cremona edition it came to be known as Sefer Ma'alot ha-Middot.

In the following excerpt, Yehiel ben Yekutiel treats a problem of his time and place, and of ours as well — the proper use of wealth. In itself, wealth in his view is neither intrinsically good or evil; it all depends upon how it is used. Wealth can help build one's own life as a work of art, and through cultivated philanthropy it can help artists and scholars create and perpetuate the cultural and spiritual resources that characterize civilized, refined living.[40]

Yehiel ben Yekutiel ha-Rofeh
Sefer Ma'alot ha-Middot —
Improvement of the Moral Virtues

My sons, come and I will teach you the quality of wealth. Know, my sons, that this quality, which comes to a person in righteousness, in faith and in justice, is one of the finest qualities. It will enable a person to inherit the life of this world as well as the life of the future world. For when a person is rich, he vitalizes himself without grief and excessive effort, and without concern in this world about matters of livelihood and sustenance and normal human needs. He is able to spare his soul from the rule of Gehinnom, for he dispenses of his money for charity and sustains the poor. . . .

Our sages say, "You shall surely tithe" (Deuteronomy 14:22), "so that you become wealthy."[41] Tithe your wealth and give of it to the poor and you merit becoming wealthy.

We find that the patriarchs tithed their resources to help the poor. Whence do we know this? From Abraham our father, of whom it is written, "And Abraham was old, well stricken in age, and the Lord had blessed Abraham in all things" (Genesis 24:1). He tithed his wealth, as it is said, "And he gave him a tenth of all" (Genesis 14:20). His house was open to every passerby. He would provide housing in his dwelling, as it is said, "And Abraham planted a tamarisk [*eshel*, also an acronym for food, drink and lodging]" (Genesis 21:33). . . .

A great quality is the quality of wealth. For when a person has wealth and does good deeds, he merits the World to Come, as it is said, "Wealth and riches are in his house; and his merit endureth for ever" (Psalms 112:3). Not only that, but he is shielded in this world from harm and evil occurrences like a person who is in a fortified city. As it is said, "The rich man's wealth is his strong city and a high wall to his own conceit" (Proverbs 18:11). A wise man said, "Wealth is a shield and a buckler."[42]

Great is the quality of wealth. Wealth comes to a person from God, as it is said, "Both riches and honor come of You" (1 Chronicles 29:12). And it is said, "Mine is the silver and Mine is the gold, says the Lord of Hosts" (Haggai 2:8). And thus he says, "For all things come of You. Of Your own have we given You" (1 Chronicles 29:14).

My sons, come and see how great is the quality of wealth. All come near to the rich person, and they become related to him; among them are lovers and friends, in order to benefit from him, as it is said, "The rich have many friends" (Proverbs 14.20). . . . My son, let not the quality of wealth be lightly regarded in your eyes, for it is the choicest of the physical qualities. Therefore, try to acquire wealth and possessions and you can transmit the wealth to your children. As it is said, "A good man leaves an inheritance to his children's children" (Proverbs 13:22). Know that wealth which comes illegally will not remain in one's hands. His wealth will be lost through a foul act, or a righteous man will inherit it, as it is said, "The wealth of the sinner is laid up for the righteous" (Proverbs 13:33). Or he will die prematurely and find no satisfaction from his money in this world, as it is said, "As the partridge that broods over young which she has not brought forth" (Jeremiah 17:11). So that he acquires riches and not by right, in the midst of his days he shall leave them. It is said too, "Wealth gotten by such vanity shall be diminished" (Proverbs 13:11).

Let not a rich man say, "My power and the might of my right hand has gotten me this wealth" (Deuteronomy 8:17). This type of talk is typical of the wicked, who flaunt their wealth which they will ultimately lose to others. Let the rich person understand that it is God who gives the power to get wealth [a paraphrase of Deuteronomy 18:8]. Therefore, let him take to heart what God has graciously given in wealth, and let him consider it as a deposit from the Creator, for this money has wings. One day a man is wealthy, possessing everything good and tomorrow he has nothing, as it is said, "Will you set your eyes upon it?" It is said, "For riches certainly make themselves wings, like an eagle that flies toward heaven" (Proverbs 23:5). As Job said, "If I had made gold my hope, and had said to the fine gold, 'You are my confidence' " (Job 31:24).

Let him continually remind himself that "The Lord makes poor, and makes rich; He brings low, He also lifts up" (1 Samuel 2:7).

All the world is like a wheel, revolving over all persons continually. Let him see and fear God's decree, as it is said, "Because that for this thing the Lord your God will bless you in all your work" (Deuteronomy 15:10).[43] Our sages said, if the [wicked] man is not impoverished, his son will be; if not his son, his grandson.[44] A wise man says, "Better than hidden measures and secreted possessions is wealth, which is like medicine for the mind, which is a protection for the soul, and he acquires a good name by his gift." . . .

You will see, my sons, what happened to Korah, who was haughty with his wealth and protested about the priesthood, what happened to him in the end. "And the earth opened her mouth and swallowed them up, and their households and all their goods" (Numbers 16:32). Also the wicked Haman prided in his wealth and said, "I will pay ten thousand talents of silver into the hands of those that have the charge of the king's business" (Esther 3:9). What happened to him in the end? "So they hanged Haman on the gallows that he had prepared for Mordecai" (Esther 7:10). And it is written, "Of them that trust in their wealth and boast themselves in the multitude of their riches" (Psalms 49:6).

Know, my sons, that some wealthy men are wise in their own eyes. When they speak to others they speak in riddles. Even if they are fools and ignoramuses, they talk by strength of their wealth and not by their mouths, as it is said, "The rich man is wise in his own eyes, but the poor that has understanding searches him through" (Proverbs 28:11). And not only that, some of them are obdurate and stubborn-minded because of their wealth upon which they depend, as it is said, "The rich answers impudently" (Proverbs 18:23).

How ugly and loathsome is the action of the rich man insulting the poor and being insolent towards the Holy One, blessed be He, because of his wealth. This is the quality of the wicked who are insolent towards the Holy One, blessed be He, because of peace and wealth, as it is said, "When they were fed, they became full, they were filled and their heart was exalted; therefore have they forgotten Me" (Hosea 13:6). It is also said, "But Jeshurun waxed fat and kicked. You did wax fat, you did grow thick, you did become gross" (Deuteronomy 32:15).

A wise man said: There are two qualities that are evil, when the donor is proud of his gift and the rich man is haughty in his riches. And he said, "The wealth of the wicked is bad for them and bad for the world. The wealth of the righteous is a pleasure to them and a pleasure for the world."

My sons, try to acquire wealth honestly so that you will be

able to live in this world and will not need the help of men, and that you will be able to use some of it for the poor. A wise man was asked, Why shall you accumulate wealth, and you are old? He answered, Better that a man die and leave his wealth to his enemies than that he should be dependent on his friends in life.[45]

My sons, if the Lord has been gracious to you with wealth and physical possessions, share them and help your kinsmen, your friends, your neighbors who are needy. For this is a command which comes from the Creator. The wise man has said, "He who does not help his beloved with his wealth, they will have to help him in the time of his need."[46]

Therefore, my sons, guard the wealth which comes to you in a just way. Do not scatter it save in time of need, and at the proper time, and to fit persons. Be grateful to God, who has been gracious to you with this wealth. Be happy in your lot for all the good that God has done for you. As our Sages have said, "Who is rich? He who is happy in his lot."[47] As it is said, "When you eat the labor of your hands, happy shall you be, and it shall be well with you" (Psalms 128:2) — happy in this world and well with you in the World to Come. Our God will open His good treasure in abundant mercy.

10

How to Die

Confronting the inevitable reality of human mortality, being conscious of individual finitude when set against the infinite plentitude of creation, causes one to pause to consider the blink of eternity that is each human life. Few statements pose the problem as poignantly as this citation from the writings of the seventeenth-century French philosopher Blaise Pascal:

> When I consider the short duration of my life, swallowed up in the eternity before and after, the little space which I fill, and even can see, engulfed in the infinite immensity of spaces of which I am ignorant and know me not, I am frightened, and I am astonished at being here rather than there; for there is no reason why here rather than there, why now rather than then? Who has put me here? By whose order and direction have this place and this time been allotted to me? The eternal silence of those infinite spaces frightens me.[1]

The transient nature of human life is also keenly recognized by classical Jewish literature. For example, in the High Holiday liturgy, we read:

> The human origin is dust and its end is dust. . . . The human creature is like a clay vessel, easily broken, like withering grass, like a fading flower, like a wandering cloud, like a fleeting breeze, like scattered dust, like an ephemeral dream.[2]

Though death is a fact of life, there is a natural human proclivity to avoid confrontation with one's own mortality. Both novelists and psychologists

have observed that it is virtually impossible for a person to contemplate his or
her own death. For example, the German author Goethe wrote, "It is entirely
impossible for a thinking being to think of its own non-existence, of the
termination of its own thinking and life." Similarly, psychiatrist Karl Menninger has written, "It may be considered axiomatic that the human mind
cannot conceive of [its] non-existence." According to Freud, there is an
intrinsic human tendency to repress death and the thought of dying.[3]

A similar perspective is found in one of the most significant modern
literary works on death and dying, Leo Tolstoy's famous story, "The Death of
Ivan Ilych." When contemplating his own death, apparently for the first time,
Ivan Ilych realizes that "what had appeared to him utterly impossible before—
that he had not lived his life as he should have done—might after all be true."
In contemplating death, Ilych also discovers the unique nature of his own
personal existence. But, in contemplating the end of that existence, Ilych
discovers that death is a subject that cannot be contemplated with detached
speculation; that death is no abstract philosophical category, but an inti-
mately personal matter. Tolstoy wrote:

> In the depth of his heart he knew he was dying, but not only was he not
> accustomed to the thought, he simply did not and could not grasp it.
>
> The syllogism he had learnt from Kiezewetter's logic: "Caius is a man, men are
> mortal, therefore Caius is mortal," had always seemed to him correct as applied to
> Caius, but certainly not as applied to himself. That Caius—man in the abstract—
> was mortal, was perfectly correct, but he was not Caius, not an abstract man, but
> a creature quite, quite separate from all others. . . . "Caius really was mortal, and
> it was right for him to die; but for me, Ivan Ilych, with all my thoughts and
> emotions, it's altogether a different matter. It cannot be that I ought to die. That
> would be terrible."[4]

Given the difficulty if not the impossibility of contemplating one's own death,
it is not surprising that an historically prominent attitude toward death has
been and continues to be escapism, an attempt to deny death's reality.

Euphemisms are used to disguise death. The deceased is referred to as
"departed," or as one who "passed on." The grave is called a "resting place" for
one who is "asleep" or "on a journey." The corpse is taken to a "parlor," a
funeral parlor where cosmetic techniques can make a person look more
"alive" after death than during life. Condolence calls become cocktail parties
characterized by levity rather than grief. Reflecting upon what has been
called "the American way of death," historian Arnold Toynbee wrote:

> The word "death" itself has become almost unmentionable in the West—particu-
> larly in the United States, which, of all the "developed" countries, is today most

extremely "developed" in the sub-human connotation of this euphemistic word. Death is "un-American"; for if the fact of death were once admitted to be a reality even in the United States, then it would also have to be admitted that the United States is not the earthly paradise that it is deemed to be. Present-day Americans, and other present-day Westerners too in their degree, tend to say, instead of "die," "pass on" or "pass away." When the mourners at a funeral pose for the cameraman, they have to put on the photographer's conventional grin, as if they were attending, not a funeral, but a wedding or the races.[5]

This escapist attitude toward death is not only a feature of contemporary society. Ancient legends, such as the *Epic of Gilgamesh*, dating from the prebiblical period, already described the perennial human desire to escape and to avoid the inevitability of death.[6] The early twentieth-century Jewish philosopher, Franz Rosenzweig, interpreted the history of Western philosophy as an attempt to "distract us from its [death's] perennial dominion," "to rob death of its poisonous sting."[7]

Despite the natural tendencies, the historical precedents, and the contemporary fashion to avoid contemplation of death, recent decades have witnessed the emergence of a new field of study—thanatology, the study of death and dying. One may ascribe the emergence of this field to five major factors.

The first factor is the pervasiveness of mass death in the twentieth century. Massive deaths during and since two world wars have demonstrated in the most blatant terms the fragility and the vulnerability of human life on an enormous scale. Discussion of the mass murder of millions of innocent people as "acceptable losses" demonstrates both the facility with which death can become the fate of enormous numbers and the use of euphemisms to mask confrontation with dimensions of death too enormous to be rationally contemplated.

The Holocaust illustrates the precariousness of human existence with the establishment of the first "death factories." The dropping of two atomic bombs—minute by today's standards—on Japan during World War II showed how technological development has reduced the time required to annihilate whole cities to a matter of minutes or even seconds. The term "genocide," coined in 1944, illustrates how our vocabulary has been enlarged to accommodate the conception of the death of whole groups of human population. Mass death, a feature of life in the twentieth century, has forced us to take death seriously, more seriously than ever before.

A second factor that may account for an increasing awareness of death and dying is the inescapable fact that we all live under the threat of nuclear holocaust. Whereas in past generations, death was an event each individual experienced by himself or herself, the present generation must confront a new and awesome possibility: the death of humankind itself. While children used to ask one another, "What will you be *when* you grow up?" it is not now uncommon for children to ask one another, "What will you be *if* you grow up?"

A third factor that has led to a progressive interest in death is a disintegration of belief in life after death. Once the belief in an existence beyond the grave is discarded, the horror and finality of death can only be amplified to unprecedented proportions. Therefore, confrontation with death and dying has become a more urgent issue than it has been before.

A fourth factor may be the omnipresence of death in the mass media. Newspapers, magazines, radio, and television place death in front of us at every turn. The media make it impossible for us to avoid the presence of death.

Finally, a fifth factor relates to the manner in which most people die today. Advances in medical technology have complicated traditional definitions of death. They have prolonged the process of dying. In the past, most people died at home in their own bed in the presence of family and friends. Today, most people die alone in hospital rooms, hooked up to tubes and machines, sedated and barely conscious that death is overtaking them. This way of death has led some to examine the issue of how one ought to die, of how one may desire to spend one's last moments of life. The accelerating collision of developments in medical technology with the inevitable end of life has raised new and challenging moral problems with regard to the process of death and dying.[8]

Jewish tradition never has avoided the inevitability or the reality of death. For example, Ecclesiastes (3:1–2) forthrightly states, "A season is set for everything, a time for every experience under heaven: a time for being born, and a time for dying." Ecclesiastes (7:2) further counsels that "it is better to go to a house of mourning than to a house of feasting: for that [i.e., death] is the end of every person, and the living one should take it to heart."

The awareness of human finitude found in Hebrew Scripture is amplified in rabbinic literature. For example, the Talmud recounts that "when Rabbi Jonathan finished the Book of Job, he used to say: the end of man is to die, and the end of a beast is to be slaughtered, and all are doomed to death. . . ."[9]

A verse in Psalms (144:4) reads, "One's days are like a passing shadow." On this verse, a midrash comments: "What kind of shadow? If life is like a shadow cast by a wall, it endures. . . . Rabbi Huna said in the name of Rabbi Aha: Life is like a bird that flies past, and its shadow flies past with it. But Samuel said: Life is like the shadow of a bee that has no substance at all."[10]

A verse in Ecclesiastes (5:14) states, "One must depart [the world] just as one entered [the world]." On this verse, a midrash comments:

As one enters [the world] so one departs. One enters with a cry and departs with a cry. One enters with tears and departs with tears. One enters in love and departs in love. One enters with a sigh and departs with a sigh. One enters devoid of knowledge and departs devoid of knowledge.

It has been taught in the name of Rabbi Meir: when a person enters the world his hands are clenched as though to say: "The whole world is mine. I shall acquire it"; but when a person departs from the world his hands are spread as though to say: "I have inherited nothing from the world."[11]

This awareness of human finitude, introduced into Judaism by the Bible and expanded upon by the talmudic rabbis, has been incorporated into the Jewish liturgy, particularly the liturgy for the High Holidays, when one is preoccupied with "who shall live and who shall die." In the *Yizkor* prayers, the memorial prayers recited on the Day of Atonement and on the pilgrimage festivals, it is customary to recite an excerpt from Psalm 90:

Man is like a breath
His days are like a fleeting shadow
In the morning he flourishes
In the evening he withers away.

The deathbed confessional prayer maintains an honest, forthright attitude toward the reality of death. In this prayer, the individual does not confront death in the abstract, but the awareness of his or her own imminent departure from life:

I acknowledge to You, Lord my God and God of my fathers, that both my cure and my death are in Your hands. May it be Your will to send me a perfect healing. Yet, if my death is determined by You, I will in love accept it at Your hand. . . . You who are the father of the fatherless and the judge of the widow protect my beloved kindred with whose soul my own is knit. Into Your hands I commend my spirit. You have redeemed me, Lord God of Truth.

This refusal to treat death as a euphemism is discussed further in medieval Jewish religious literature. For example, Bahya ibn Pakudah wrote:

When a person reflects on the end of his days and the speed with which his death comes, when all his hopes and wishes will cease and all his possessions will be abandoned, when he reflects on the hopelessness of retaining any of them for himself, or benefiting by them, when he imagines his condition in the grave, his face darkened, his body blackened and full of worms, its stench and putrefaction, the traces of his body all effaced, while the smell grows stronger, as if he had never washed or cleaned or exuded perfumed scents, when a man meditates upon this and matters like this, he humbles and degrades himself. He is no longer proud or arrogant. . . .[12]

In a similar vein, in a chapter entitled, "When one remembers, the day of death," the author of *Sefer ha-Yashar — The Book of Righteousness*, wrote:

> It is fitting for everyone who fears the word of the Lord to reflect in his heart concerning the day of death, its calamity and its terror, and let it be to him as a reminder. Let him say in his heart, "My heart, my heart, did you not know that you were not created except to return to the dust?" From the day when you first came into being why did you not remember your final end? Do you know that all the days that you live upon the earth, you are like a passing shadow and like chaff that is driven away by the whirlwind from the threshing floor, and like smoke from a window. Your days are determined and your life is cut short. Every day or night that passes over you causes a lessening in the portions of your life allotted to you. Every day you draw nearer to the grave, and you will fly away without wings. Why did you not know you are dust? Why did you not remember that you were formed of the earth? . . . Take hold of yourself and be abashed and ashamed because of your sins, and give thanks to God while still the soil is within your body before the stars of your twilight are darkened.[13]

While rejecting an escapist attitude toward death, and advocating a frank confrontation with death and dying, Jewish tradition considers the encounter with human mortality to be an invitation neither to morbidity nor to nihilism. The attitude satirized by the prophet Isaiah (22:13), "Eat, drink and be merry, for tomorrow we die," finds no place in Jewish thought. Rather, the candid awareness of human mortality is treated by Jewish religious literature as an opportunity to confront the quest for and the question of human purpose and meaning. Since life is a blind date with an uncertain future, each moment is considered a summons to begin or to continue the project of creating the ultimate work of art — one's own existence. Commenting on Hillel's famous statement, "If not now, when?" a medieval Jewish writer observed that Hillel did not say, "If not *today*, when?" but "If not *now*, when?" because "even today is in doubt regarding whether one will survive or not, for at any instant one can die."[14] Consequently, "one cannot wait even a day or two to exert oneself in the pursuit of human fulfillment."[15]

A candid confrontation with death can compel one to examine and to improve the moral quality of life. This notion is stated often in talmudic literature. For example, "Rabbi Eliezer said: Repent one day before your death. His disciples asked him: Does then one know on what day he will die? Then all the more reason to repent today, he replied, lest he die tomorrow."[16]

That contemplation of one's own death can serve as the ultimate guarantor of moral behavior is expressed in this talmudic text:

> One should always incite the good impulse [in his soul] to fight against the evil impulse. . . . If he subdues it, well and good. If not, let him study the Torah. . . . If

he subdues it, well and good. If not, let him recite the *Shema*. . . . If he subdues it, well and good. If not, let him remind himself on the day of death. . . . [17]

Reflecting on death soon after an almost fatal heart attack, the contemporary Jewish theologian, Abraham Joshua Heschel, encapsulated the Jewish attitude: "Life's ultimate meaning remains obscure unless it is reflected upon in the face of death. . . . [Judaism's] central concern is not how to escape death but rather how to sanctify life."[18]

Jewish responses to the problem of how to die are found in Jewish religious literature in preserved accounts of the deaths of sages, scholars, and saints of past generations.[19] For example, hasidic literature contains a slim volume, *Sefer Histalkut ha-Nefesh — The Book of the Departure of the Soul*, in which the deathbed scenes of a number of hasidic masters are preserved. In this collection, the following appears:

> When the hour arrived for Simha Bunam of Przysucha to depart from the world, his wife stood by his bedside. He said to her: "Be silent—why do you weep? My whole life was only that I might learn how to die."[20]

Without doubt, the most popularly known account of the death of a hasidic master is the often told story of the death of Zusia of Hanipol:

> On his deathbed, Zusia began to cry. His disciples asked: "Are you crying because you are afraid that when you stand before the Holy Tribunal, they will ask you: Why were you not like Moses?" "No," replied Zusia. "Then why do you weep?" the disciples asked. "Because I am afraid they will ask me why I was not like Zusia. Then what shall I say?"

Zusia's view is paradigmatic of Jewish responses to death. Confronting death, one is led to the awesome possibility that life has not been lived to its fullness of meaning; that one has failed to realize the potentialities unique to his or her own individual self; that one has not been adequately engaged in the creation of the artful life. Similarly, in reading Plato's account of the trial and death of Socrates, one encounters this view. At the trial that condemns him to death, Socrates proclaims that "an unexamined life is not worth living."

As was noted above, the accelerating collision of longer life expectancy and advanced developments in medical technology has made the problem of how to die even more pertinent. This situation has made the dilemma of euthanasia a compelling daily issue. The conflict between the biblical imperative to "choose life" (Deuteronomy 30:19) and the biblical observation that "there is a time to die" (Ecclesiastes 3:2) is one that demands increasing attention. It is this conflict between choosing life and recognizing that there is a time to die, between the imperative to continue preserving life and the humane desire to relieve agony, that is addressed in the excerpted text below.

⚜

The text excerpted below is a responsum. Responsa may be considered the most classical mode of Jewish moral discourse. In many responsa, the often artificial categories distinguishing law and ethics break down. Unlike any other genre of Jewish ethical literature, responsa are not primarily conceptual and abstract. They do not deal with generalizations about moral virtues. Rather, they often treat ethical issues of immediate and practical concern.

A responsum is a written legal brief dealing with some specific aspect of Jewish practice, custom, belief, or interpretation. It is a response composed to answer specific questions of current interest, usually demanding immediate resolution, i.e., cases "approaching the bench." The earliest extant responsa date from the ninth and tenth centuries and were addressed to the Geonim—the heads of the great talmudic academies of Babylonia. The deans of these academies were generally recognized as the ultimate authorities in the application and interpretation of rabbinic Judaism. By the eleventh century, a new pattern began to emerge. With the decline of the Babylonian centers and with the emergence of new Jewish communal centers in Europe and North Africa, with the rise of local rabbinates, responsa were now addressed and answered by local rabbinic authorities. This led to a decentralization of rabbinic legal authority and to the prominence of local rabbinic authorities in the promulgation of Jewish legal decisions. Responsa continue to be written today throughout the Jewish world on any and all issues of Jewish life and law.

The particular responsum that follows was written in the nineteenth century by Rabbi Hayyim Palaggi of Izmir, Turkey. The scion of a prominent rabbinic family in Turkey, his father held the office of chief rabbi, a position assumed by our author in 1857. Because of his official position in the Jewish community—a position endorsed by the Turkish sultan—and because of his personal reputation as a pious scholar, Palaggi received questions from Jewish communities all over the Near East and North Africa.

An ascetic by practice, a vehement opponent of philosophical studies, and a powerful rabbinic voice against economic corruption, Palaggi was a controversial figure in his native Turkey. As a communal leader, he was active in opposing exploitative economic monopolies, especially in the trade and sale of wine. He was instrumental in establishing a Jewish hospital and in requiring compulsory education for children. He also actively sought assistance for the victims of the Damascus "blood libel" of 1840.

An enormously prolific author, Palaggi is alleged to have written more than 70 works, but many were lost in manuscript in a fire in 1841. Though not all of his surviving or subsequently written works were published, more than twenty-five books and a number of smaller treatises of Palaggi's found their way into print. His published works include treatises on Jewish ethics, collections of homilies, supercommentaries to the Talmud and codes of Jewish law as well as to the Talmud, and a number of collections of decisions and views on Jewish law. Most prominent and influential among his published work is the two-volume collection of his responsa entitled *Hikkeke Lev* (i.e., "searchings of the heart," see Judges 5:15). The first volume was published in Salonika in 1840 and the second in 1853. The excerpt that follows is responsa no. 50 of the first volume. Palaggi died in Izmir in 1869.[21]

Hayyim Palaggi
Responsa *Hikkeke Lev*

QUESTION: A God-fearing scholar has a pious wife. Because of our many sins this woman has been afflicted with a long-term disease. For more than twenty years she has been crushed and burdened with pain. Her arms and legs have shrivelled up, forcing her to be confined to a corner of her house. This woman suffers greatly from these afflictions. Her husband, however, accepts the suffering of his wife with patience, never troubling her even for a moment. On the contrary, he shows her special affection and love so that she may have no worry on this account.

Because of her unbearable pain, the aforementioned woman has already prayed that God take her. She prefers death to life because in death she will find rest from her pain. Her husband and children, however, may God bless them, comfort her and continually bring her physicians and medicines in the hope that a remission might occur. They have even hired a maid to wait on her so that she should have no worries. Now, as if the continual pain and bitter suffering she has had up to now were not enough, her condition has worsened, bringing with it terrible agony, such as accompany dreadful diseases, leaving her totally stricken and invalid. Even the physicians have given up hope, especially since the disease has affected her internal organs, an

event which occurs twenty days before death, as written in
Tractate Semahot, "For this is the death of the righteous as
opposed to the other kinds of plagues, wounds, afflictions and
diseases."[22] Recently she began to ask others as well to pray for
her death. She especially pleads with her husband and children
to intercede on her behalf. But her husband and children,
though they are worn out with her suffering, do not listen to her
because of their love and affection, she being a righteous and
pious woman. On the contrary, they seek scholars who would
teach on her behalf so as to bring healing, and they increase
their giving of charity and paying redemption and atonement
money and buying oil for the lamps—all in order to obtain
healing for her.

Let our master in righteousness now instruct us as to whether
or not there are any grounds for prohibiting prayers that she
find rest in death. If there is no prohibition—what if her
husband and sons are so concerned with her life that they do
not want to see her die? May they pray that she not die, ignoring
her own wishes; or, since according to the physicians there is no
way she will live and there is no longer hope that she will
recover naturally, would this be against her well-being (such
that they must pray for her death)?

May the master instruct us and may his portion in heaven be
doubled.

ANSWER: First of all, it is clearly forbidden in all cases to pray
that another person die. This is so even if one is praying only
that some misfortune befall an enemy. Torah commands, for
example, that if you see the mule of one who hates you collapse
under its burden and you refuse to help, you will be abandoned
just as you abandoned the animal (Deuteronomy 22:4). Torah is
concerned here that you not cause the animal's owner any
material loss. How much more is Torah concerned that you not
cause your enemy to lose his life. Thank God no Jew is
suspected of doing this!

There is another prohibition involved, namely, that this kind
of curse, in fact any curse on one's fellow, is forbidden. This is
so even if done without explicitly naming the intended victim.
In fact, if one pronounces a curse on another by name, the
curser is flogged. . . .[23]

We turn now specifically to wishing harm to one's spouse.
Our masters, may their memories be a blessing, say, "It is
forbidden for one to marry a woman before he sees her lest

when he sees her he find something detestable in her and she be disgraced by him—for the Merciful One said, 'You should love your neighbor as yourself.' "[24] This verse, a central rule in the Torah, applies also to one's husband or wife. [Its point is that you should not get yourself in a position in which you might wish harm to your spouse.] We learn this same thing from the Talmud: "One should not marry a woman with the intention of divorcing her, for it says (in Proverbs 3:29), 'Do not plot evil against your fellow who lives trustingly with you' [i.e., your spouse]. . . ."[25] It is also stated in *Avot d'Rabbi Nathan*, "Rabbi Akiba says, 'Anyone who marries a woman who is not suitable for him transgresses five negative commands: (1) 'Do not take vengeance (Leviticus 19:18)', (2)'Do not bear a grudge (ibid.),' (3)'Do not hate your neighbor in your heart (Leviticus 19:17)', (4)'Love your neighbor as yourself (ibid.)', (5)'That your brother may live with you (Leviticus 25:36).' Further, insofar as he hates her and wishes she would die, he refrains from the command 'Be fruitful and multiply.' "[26]

[All the above speak about wishing harm to one's spouse. But the law also speaks specifically about wishing for the spouse's death.] Our masters report, for example, "He used to say, 'As for one who wishes his wife to die that he may marry her sister, or anyone who wishes his brother to die that he may marry his wife, his end will be that they [i.e. the intended victims] will bury him during their lifetimes.' As regards such a person, Scripture says (Ecclesiates 10:8), 'The one who digs the pit will fall into it; and a serpent will bite the one who breaks through the wall.' "[27] This is to say that if one hopes his wife will die so that he might marry another woman, heaven will arrange for the opposite to occur.

[Can a mere thought be the concern of the law, however?] Rabbi Hayyim Yosef David Azulai writes in *Kisei Rahamim*, "If one merely has an evil thought, the Holy One, blessed be He, does not consider it to be an evil deed, and so does not punish that person on its account." This means simply this: that a thought, being insubstantial, that is, without any overt expression, material effect or outward appearance [is not subject to legal punishment]. However, on the other hand, the Talmud says, "Whoever looks greedily upon what is not his—that which he wants will not be given to him and that which he has will be taken away."[28] [Here Talmud implies that in fact the mere thought is subject to divine punishment.]

Now, in my humble opinion, [the cases assumed by the
above rulings] are different from the case before us. All of the
aforementioned rulings are based on a particular prohibition
from the tradition. The rabbis take the command "Do not devise
evil against your fellow" (Proverbs 3:29) to apply to one thinking
about divorcing his wife; all the more so to one hoping that she
will die. There is also the positive command, "Love your
neighbor as yourself" which our rabbis, may their memories be
a blessing, apply especially to one's wife. Besides these there is
the prohibition of "not hating your brother in your heart
(Leviticus 19:17)." This applies not only to brothers, for it is clear
that one must love one's wife also and show affection for her—
as is written in the Talmud, "One who loves his wife as himself
. . . [is blessed]."[29] See also what our master and teacher Meir
ben Baruch of Rothenburg wrote in his collected responsa, "As
for one who beats his wife, I have learned that we deal with him
more harshly than with one who beats his neighbor. For he is
not obligated to honor the neighbor, but he is obligated to honor
his wife."[30] There is also the prohibition against casting the evil
eye on his wife, especially so as to cause her to die. . . .

There is an additional danger as well when he fantasizes that
his wife dies so that he can marry her sister, or that his fellow
dies so that he can marry his wife. In so doing he may have
sinful thoughts for he may think about her [i.e., the one he
wants to marry] and this thought will bear evil fruit when he has
sex, for his children will be surrogate children. . . .

It turns out that from all that has been said it is forbidden to
wish that one's wife die because of hatred. This being so, we
deduce [further] that it is absolutely forbidden to pray that
anyone die, especially as regards a wife, who is like one's own
self.

However, all this appears to apply only if the wish comes
from hatred and without the wife's knowledge and consent. But
when, to the contrary, she acquiesces to this wish because she
no longer can bear the suffering of the body, then we can say
that such a wish is permitted. I say this with the talmudic text
from tractate *Ketubot* in mind:

> On the day that Rabbi died, the sages declared a public fast and they
> prayed saying, "If anyone says, 'Let Rabbi die'—let that one be run
> through with a sword." The maidservant of Rabbi went up on the
> roof and said, "The angels seek Rabbi and the creatures seek Rabbi.

Let it be Thy will that the angels give way to the creatures." When she reflected on how often Rabbi had entered the privy and taken off his *tefilin* and put them on and how he was now suffering [she had a change of heart]. She prayed, "Let the angels have way over the creatures." But the Rabbis did not stop praying [and so Rabbi still did not die]. She finally took a jug and threw it among [the praying disciples] from the roof. They stopped praying and Rabbi [immediately] died.[31]

It is clear from this passage that the maidservant of Rabbi, when she saw how he was suffering, prayed for his death. Furthermore, we find that the ancient authorities adduced legal rulings from what Rabbi's maidservant did because she was his servant [and so would surely conduct herself as he instructed her] and also because they deemed her to be a scholar in her own right, being filled with wisdom and the fear of heaven.[32] This being so, we may adduce from this story the following: that it is permitted to pray that the sick person who is suffering greatly might die and so find rest. Were it not so, the Talmud would not have cited this story. Or, had the Talmud meant only to report the event [but with the understanding] that the maidservant acted wrongly, it should have said so explicitly.

Now you might want to argue that, on the contrary, the fact that the masters prayed for Rabbi's life without regard for his suffering ought to be the legal precedent. In response, I would argue that they at first did not pay any attention to his sufferings, while his maidservant did. Later, when they realized how much he was suffering, they in fact did stop praying. Further, it is clear that the rabbis did not disagree with what Rabbi's maidservant did, for had they disagreed they would have rebuked her straightaway, especially since they had just decreed that anyone who said, "Let Rabbi die" was to be run through with a sword. Surely this should include one who prayed that he should die. Further, had her act been wrong, you would think that the Talmud would not remain silent but would protest that what she did was improper. But since the Talmud does remain silent and since the rabbis appear in fact to agree with the maidservant's actions, the inevitable conclusion is that in the case of the afflicted woman who is ill and suffering much pain and who is begging others to pray that she die, it is certainly entirely permitted to do so. This is now clear. . . .

It seems to me that at times one may pray that a sick person die, for instance when the sick person is suffering greatly from his disease and cannot go on living much longer anyway, as we have read in *Ketubot* that when Rabbi's maidservant considered how he entered the privy regularly and always took off his phylacteries and was now suffering, said, "May it be Thy will that the angels have way over the creatures," that is, that Rabbi be allowed to die. Thus it is that the prayers of one who visits the sick are efficacious [whether they be for life or for death]. . . .

After several days I came across *Gur Aryeh Judah* by his Excellency Our Master and Teacher Aryeh Judah Leib Teomim and saw that he wrote, "As regards a sick person for whom they have given up hope and who is suffering greatly—is it permitted to pray that he die?" I looked up the place but I could find no clue as to his answer because the relevant part of the book was missing. . . . Thus I have no idea what he had written—whether I agree with his opinion that it should be permitted to pray for the patient's death, or whether I disagree because he prohibits such a prayer.[33]

It appears in my humblest of opinions that because of all this it makes sense to do as [follows]: if she is suffering very much from her many bitter afflictions, and if the physicians all say that there is no hope that she will live and they have given up in despair, then as regards even her husband and children and relatives, if they do not want to pray that she live, let them not pray explicitly that she die, either. Rather, let them sit and do nothing. For if they pray that she die, there is the chance that, heaven forbid, one out of a thousand will see this and come to the unlikely conclusion that he is praying for her death so that he might be free from her and from her demands. That is, someone might assume that he has an interest in her death. . . .

Now to pray that she live is hard because of the pain she must suffer and the bitter agonies she must endure. If you reflect on the matter you will see that it is not always preferable that she continue to live. On the other hand, as we noted, it is really not proper for them openly to pray that she die, either. However, as for others, who are strangers and not under any of the afore-mentioned suspicions—if they pray that she die so that her soul might find rest, they may do so. All is according to what is written, "God searches the heart and the innermost parts, the Lord is righteous." Our rabbis, may their memories be a blessing, have said that all that is in the heart is to God as if it were spoken. Therefore fear the Lord.

Now all this applies when the sick person is not actually in the throes of death. However, if that person is in the throes of death, there is no way that one may pray [for continued life]. It is written in *The Book of the Pious* that one ought not cry out at the time when the soul leaves the body.[34] The reason for not doing so is that the soul not be induced to return to the body and cause the patient more suffering. Why did Ecclesiastes say there is a time to die? Because when a person dies when the soul is leaving the body—they ought not cry out loud that the soul return, because the patient cannot live but a few more days anyway and during those days would suffer nothing but agonies. [This line of reasoning is not negated by the fact that Ecclesiastes] also says "a time to live" because human beings have no control over the time of death. . . .[35]

That is what, in my humble opinion, I must write, although in haste because the strength of the sufferer is weak. May Almighty God say "enough" to our troubles and save us from error and show us wonders from the Torah. May this be God's will. Amen.

III

The Self and Others

11

How to Behave Sexually

Plato described the human body as a "living tomb," as a prison.[1] Jewish tradition compares the human body to the Temple, to a house of God.[2] But, to compare the body to the Temple assumes a prior vision of the Temple.

At the center of the Temple was the Holy of Holies, the most sacred spot in the world. There one found the cherubs. What were the cherubs doing?

> Rabbi Kattina said, "Whenever Israel came up to [the Temple for] the Festival, the curtain would be removed for them and the cherubs were shown to them. Their bodies were intertwined with one another and they were thus addressed: Look! You are beloved before God as the love between man and woman."

On this text, Rashi comments, "They [i.e., the cherubs] cleaved one to the other, holding and embracing each other as the male embraces the female."[3]

These texts depict the Holy of Holies as a bedroom where the cherubs engage in the procreative act.[4] And where does God dwell? Between the cherubs.[5]

In this view, the most physical act can have the most spiritual meaning. As the *Iggeret ha-Kodesh—The Holy Letter*, states:

> If you comprehend the mystery of the *cheruhim*, you will understand what the sages of blessed memory meant in saying that which a man cleaves to his wife in holiness, the divine presence is manifested. In the mystery of man and woman, there is God. . . . Proper sexual union can be a means of spiritual elevation when it is properly practiced.[6]

Sexuality represents a stance of pro-creation and of re-creation that aligns the individual with the rest of humanity as well as with the divine image implanted within each human person. Already in Scripture, sexual experience is described as "knowing."[7] Sexual experience, coupled with love, desire, and will, can penetrate not only the mystery of sexuality, but the mysteries of knowledge of the world, of the divine, and of the self.[8]

Sexual experience can be a vehicle to self-knowledge, to self-transformation, and to the creation of life as a work of art. In the act of love, a new union is created. The two individuals who forge this union can each become irrevocably transformed thereby.[9] Each may be re-created through the procreative act. Through sexual and erotic union, one may become God's partner in the work of creation.[10]

According to Jewish religious sources from the talmudic period onward, the first human being was a hermaphrodite, male and female together. God separated them and turned them "face to face" so that procreation could occur.[11] Each subsequent human being is half a person, an unrealized self. Through encounter with one's "other half," one becomes a complete self.[12] One can thereby attain self-completion, self-realization, self-fulfillment. In Plato's *Symposium*, one finds a similar myth where the gods divide the hermaphrodite human being into its male and female components.[13] However, for Plato, the split of the human hermaphrodite is a punishment, whereas for Jewish sources it is an act of divine grace.

According to the kabbalists, who invest each human action with immense theurgic power, the procreative act not only unifies and fulfills the human being, but all of creation as well. As Meir ibn Gabbai put it, "When man and woman truly unite, all is one body and the cosmos rejoices for it becomes one complete corpus."[14] For Ibn Gabbai, the sexual act also brings about the reunification of the divine potencies, thereby causing God to become truly One.

The talmudic rabbis taught that "Whoever does not engage in procreation is deemed by Scripture as diminishing, as it were, the [divine] likeness."[15] The medieval Jewish mystics designated those who engage in the procreative act as God's partners in the prototype for all creative acts, i.e., the initial creation.[16] The sexual union is at once *imitatio Dei* and a theurgic act. The sexual act, which draws down the divine influx, fulfills not only a human but a divine need.[17]

Procreation is life affirming, demanding a future. Thus, despite the ascetic tendencies that season Jewish thought, celibacy was neither idealized nor even permitted. Procreation is a requirement of Jewish law. To deny procreation is to deny creation. Celibacy affirms the limitations of the body, the status quo. Procreation assumes that no body is complete or whole. To realize our bodily nature, a complementary other is needed.[18] With this complementary other, a partnership is formed through which a new body might be engendered. This new body, this new person, perpetuates the body of his or her parents as well as the genealogical history of his or her people. Celibacy presumes that each body is self-contained, requiring no other. But, celibacy also maintains that the body is a "dead end." According to the *Zohar*, one who does not procreate causes God's presence to depart. Willfully refraining from procreation means refusing to spread the divine image in the world.[19] The procreative act extends the image of God to successive generations. It is not surprising, therefore, that the Talmud associates God with the act of procreation: "There are three partners in the conception of a child—God, the father, and the mother."[20]

Judaism is grounded in a covenant (*brit*). The "sign" of the covenant is the mark of circumcision. The organ of generation bears the sign of the covenant to future generations. Through this organ flow the seeds for the perpetuation of the Jewish people and the human race. Just as some philosophers have separated the soul from the body, some trends of thought have severed sex from love, and sex from its procreative potential. Jewish tradition attempts to keep love and sex, procreation and sex, body and soul, inextricably inseparable.

The medieval idea of "courtly love" taught that "love can have no place between husband and wife."[21] Classical philosophy also took a decidedly antisexual stance. Influenced by the philosophers, especially Aristotle, Maimonides claimed that the sense of touch is reprehensible, that sexual relations are spiritually dangerous.[22] Maimonides wrote:

> One of the intentions of the Torah is purity and sanctification. I mean by this renouncing and avoiding sexual intercourse and causing it to be as infrequent as possible. Consequently, God states clearly in the Torah that sanctity consists in renouncing sexual intercourse.[23]

The author of *The Holy Letter*, excerpted below, found the courtly and the philosophical views of love and sex to be both unacceptable and in conflict with Jewish teachings. He even deigned to attack the great Maimonides for endorsing heretical views on this subject, views derived from Aristotle:

> The matter is not as Rabbi Moses (Maimonides) said in his *Guide of the Perplexed*. He was incorrect in praising Aristotle for stating that the sense of touch is shameful for us. Heaven forbid! The matter is not like the Greek (i.e., Aristotle) said. It smacks of imperceptible heresy.[24]

According to the author of *The Holy Letter*, to suggest, as Maimonides did, that the human body, or its natural functions—such as sexual relations—are repulsive, is an affront to God's wisdom. In themselves, bodily organs and functions are beautiful and good. Only when misused or abused can they become ugly or repulsive; but such is the result of human action, not divine intention. This text states:

> "God saw everything He had made and behold it was very good" (Genesis 1:31). . . . Nothing in the human organs are created flawed or ugly. Everything is created with divine wisdom and is therefore complete, exalted, good and pleasant. But when one sins, ugliness becomes attached to these matters.[25]

A similar view is expressed by the eighteenth-century scholar, Jacob Emden. In his commentary to the medieval legal code *Arba'ah Turim*, Emden noted that the paragraph of the code that discusses sexual relations is numbered 240, which corresponds to the Hebrew letters *resh* and *mem*. Read one way, these letters spell *"ram"*—exalted. Read backwards, they spell *"mar"*—bitterness. In other words, depending upon how it is practiced, sex can either have exalted or bitter consequences. Emden further states:

> The wise men of the other nations claim that there is disgrace in the sense of touch. But this is not the view of our Torah or of its sages. . . . To us the sexual act is worthy, good, and beneficial even for the soul. No other act compares with it; when performed with proper intention, it is certainly holy. There is nothing impure or defective about it, rather it is highly exalted.[26]

Through the performance of sacred deeds, the body, which is good by nature, becomes holy by actions. For many of the Jewish mystics, this is especially evident in sexual behavior. For example, the Baal Shem Tov is quoted as follows, commenting on the verse in Job (19:26), "From my flesh, I shall see God."

> [The *sefirah yesod* corresponds to] the sexual organ, which is the seat of one's greatest physical pleasure. This pleasure comes about when man and woman unite, and it thus results from unification. From the physical, we perceive the spiritual.[27]

Physical desire is a prerequisite for spiritual attainment, for creating life as a work of art. One who is devoid of passion disenfranchises oneself from both the physical and spiritual life. In the words of Elijah de Vidas, "He who does not desire a woman is an ass, or even less than one. From the objects of physical sensation, one may apprehend the love of God."[28] As was discussed in Chapter 3, for the Jewish mystics the procreative act is the paradigm for the ultimate religious experience: communion with God.[29]

Only through the body can the image of God become manifest. Only through the body can moral action and redemptive deeds take place. Only through the body can the mission of repairing the torn fabric of creation through restoration occur. Only through the body, with the body, and because of the body can one engage in the task of creating one's life as a work of art.[30]

⁂

The following excerpt is from *Iggeret ha-Kodesh—The Holy Letter*. This work, first published in Rome in 1546, is traditionally ascribed to Nahmanides, but is actually of unknown authorship.[31]

A variety of theories has been offered by modern scholars as to who its author might have been, but without conclusive results. What is fairly certain is that this work originated in thirteenth-century Spain. The imprint of kabbalistic ideas permeates this work.[32] The genre of Jewish ethical literature known as *iggeret* (literally: "letter") is close in meaning to the term "monograph." The purpose of an "*iggeret*" is to focus on a single topic, rather than to offer discussion of a multitude of issues. In the case of our text, one finds a presentation and examination of a single issue represented by an alternate title of this work: "a treatise on marital relations" (*hibbur ha-adam im ishto*).[33]

Iggeret ha-Kodesh is the first popular work in which kabbalistic teachings are applied to everyday human behavior. It thereby established a precedent for the emergence in the sixteenth century of the genre of Jewish mystical-ethical literature where recondite theosophical kabbalistic ideas were applied to the conduct of normal everyday behavior, including marital relations. For the kabbalistic author of *Iggeret ha-Kodesh*, it is through knowledge of *kabbalah*—the Jewish mystical tradition—that one may apprehend the true nature and the true value of marital relations.[34]

Iggeret ha-Kodesh—The Holy Letter

. . . you must understand what the sages meant when they say that a man must sanctify himself in the time of sexual intercourse. I will define the nature of this sanctification in five chapters (in order that your desire for adequate understanding of each of these matters be satisfied):

Part I, on the nature of intercourse

Part II, on the time of intercourse

Part III, on the proper diet prior to intercourse

Part IV, on the intent of intercourse

Part V, on the techniques of intercourse.

Know that the union of man with his wife is divided into two parts. Know that the sexual intercourse of man with his wife is holy and pure when done properly, in the proper time and with the proper intention. No one should think that sexual intercourse is ugly and loathsome, God forbid! Proper sexual intercourse is called "knowing" (Genesis 4:1) for good reason. As it is said, "And Elkanah knew his wife Hannah" (1 Samuel 1:19). The secret reason for this is that when the drop of semen is drawn in holiness and purity, it comes from the source of wisdom and understanding, which is the brain. Understand, therefore, that unless it involved matters of great holiness, sexual union would not be called "knowing." The matter is not as Rabbi Moses (Maimonides) of blessed memory said in his *Guide of the Perplexed*.[35] He was incorrect in praising Aristotle for stating that the sense of touch is shameful for us. Heaven forbid! The matter is not like the Greek [i.e., Aristotle] said. It smacks of imperceptible heresy, because if the accursed Greek believed the world was created purposely, he would not have said it.

We the possessors of the Holy Torah believe that God, may He be praised, created all, as His wisdom decreed, and did not create anything ugly or shameful. For if sexual intercourse were repulsive, then the reproductive organs are also repulsive. The Holy One, blessed be He, created them by His word. "Has He not made you, and established you?" (Deuteronomy 32:6): And the sages said in *Hullin* that God created in man every organ on its foundation.[36] And *Ecclesiastes Rabbah* on Ecclesiastes 2:12, "Even that which has been already done," teaches that God and his celestial court considered each individual organ, how it should be made and settled on its own foundations.[37] If the reproductive organs are repulsive, how did the Creator fashion something blemished? If that were so, we would find that his deeds were not perfect, and behold, Moses, the great master of prophecy, proclaimed, "The rock whose work is perfect" (Deuteronomy 32:4). And it is said, "God saw everything that He made, and behold it was very good" (Genesis 1:31). . . .

"And they knew that they were naked" (Genesis 3:7). And they interpreted this as follows: When the hands write a scroll of the Torah in purity, they are honored and praiseworthy. When they do something improper, they are loathsome. So it is with the sex organs of Adam and Eve. Prior to their sinning, it was one way, but after they sinned, quite different. As in every organ, there is that which is laudatory when the man performs what is good, so there is offensiveness when man does evil. So it was with the first man concerning the sex organs. Accordingly, it follows that God's ways are just, holy, and pure. All that is ugly results from man's activities.

In other words, there is nothing in all of man's organs created flawed or ugly. Thus everything created with divine wisdom is complete, exalted, good, and pleasant. But when man sins, ugliness becomes attached to these matters, as they were not repulsive or abhorrent originally. Understand this well.

Behold the mystery of knowledge that I reveal to you is the mystery of man's involvement. The mystery of man includes in his being the mystery of Wisdom, Understanding, and Knowledge. Know that the male is the mystery of wisdom and the female is the mystery of understanding. And the pure sex act is the mystery of knowledge. Such is the mystery of man and woman in the esoteric tradition.[38] If so, it follows that proper sexual union can be a means of spiritual elevation when it is properly practiced, and the mystery greater than this is the secret of the heavenly bodies when they unite in the manner of man and woman. If there were something unsanctified, the Master of the Universe would not command it, and put it in the holiest and purest place, which is on a very deep foundation. . . .

If you comprehend the mystery of the *cherubim*, you will understand what the sages of blessed memory meant in saying that when a man cleaves to his wife in holiness, the divine presence is manifested. In the mystery of man and woman, there is God. . . .

Concerning this mystery, the sages aimed at it when they said, "There are three partners in man: they are his father, his mother, and above them, God."[39] In the Talmud, in *Kiddushin*, they stated that when a man honors his father and his mother, the Holy One, blessed be He, says, "I considered it as if I had dwelled among them and they had honored me."[40]

If there is something loathsome, how could the name of God be included in such an ugly thing? . . .

When union is for the sake of heaven, there is nothing holier and purer than this union of the righteous. . . .

The union of man with his wife, when it is proper, is the mystery of the foundation of the world and civilization. Through this act they become partners with God in the work of creation. This is the mystery of what the sages said, "When a man unites with his wife in holiness, the *Shekhinah* is between them in the mystery of man and woman." This is the meaning of "Before you came forth out of the womb, I sanctified you" (Jeremiah 1:5).

At this point, I should remind you, in addition, of a great principle of the Torah: the masters of blessed memory said, "God makes the solitary to dwell in a house" (Psalms 68:7), meaning when a man and a wife are pure in intention and both intend the act for the sake of goodness, God joins with them, as it is said, "God makes the solitary to dwell in a house." . . .

Therefore, Solomon, peace be upon him, said in his very telling Proverbs, "In all thy ways acknowledge Him, and He will direct thy paths" (Proverbs 3:6). And our sages of blessed memory said, "In all your ways acknowledge Him, even in all your physical deeds both great and small."[41] And what he said, "You shall know Him," you know already what is the language. "To know" implies it is the union of the rational soul, clinging to the upper light, just as the union of a man and his wife is called knowledge. . . .

When engaging in the sex act, you must begin by speaking to your mate in a manner that will draw her heart to you, calm her spirits, and make her happy. Thus your minds will be bound upon one another as one, and your intention will unite with hers. Speak to her so that your words will provoke desire, love, will, and passion, as well as words leading to reverence for God, piety, and modesty. Tell her how pious and modest women are blessed with upright, honorable, and worthy children, students of Torah, God-fearing, and people of accomplishment and purity, worthy of the highest crown, masters of the Torah, and having the fear of God, great and holy men, as was Kimhit, who merited having seven sons who served as high priests. And when they asked her, "How is it that you merited this?" she said to them. "Never did the beams of my house see my hair." All this story emphasizes all of her virtue, modesty, and purity of deed. . . .[42]

Therefore, a husband should speak with his wife with the appropriate words, some of erotic passion, some words of fear of the Lord. He must speak with her in the middle of the night, and close to the last third of the night, as our sages have said in *Berakhot*.[43] In the third watch, a woman talks with her husband and the child sucks from the breast of his mother. A man should never force himself upon his wife and never overpower her, for the Divine Spirit never rests upon one whose conjugal relations occur in the absence of desire, love, and free will. The *Shekhinah* [God's Presence] does not rest there. One should never argue with his wife, and certainly never strike her on account of sexual matters. The Talmud in *Yoma* tells us that just as a lion tears at his prey and eats it shamelessly, so does an ignorant man shamelessly strike and sleep with his wife.[44] Rather act so that you will warm her heart by speaking to her charming and seductive words. Also speak of matters that are appropriate and worthy, so that both your intention and hers will be for the sake of heaven. A man should not have intercourse with his wife while she is asleep, for then they cannot both agree to the act. It is far better, as we have said, to arouse her with words that will placate her and inspire desire in her.

To conclude, when you are ready for sexual union, see that your wife's intentions combine with yours. Do not hurry to arouse her until she is receptive. Be calm, and as you enter the path of love and will, let her insemination come first. . . .

12

How to Treat
One's Parents

The most difficult of all the commandments of the Torah to fulfill completely, according to the second-century sage Simeon bar Yohai, is the obligation of a child to honor and to revere his or her mother and father.[1] In this regard, the following story is told of Rabbi Tarfon:

Rabbi Tarfon had a mother. When she wished to mount into bed, he would bend down to let her ascend [by stepping on him, and when she wished to descend, she would do so by stepping on him]. He went to the academy and boasted of his observance of filial piety. [Whereupon] his colleagues said to him: You have not even reached half the honor [due her].[2]

As it is stated in the Ten Commandments, the obligation of a child toward his or her parent seems clear enough: "Honor your father and your mother, that you may long endure on the land which the Lord your God is giving you" (Exodus 20:12, Deuteronomy 5:16).

This commandment differs from the other nine, because only in the case of this commandment is a reason given, i.e., "that you may long endure. . . ." In other words, the reason for observance is the promise of longevity and the threat of a curtailed life for nonobservance. Nevertheless, some medieval Jewish scholars were uncomfortable with the scriptural explanation for why one should honors one's parents. For example, Bahya ben Asher and others found this rationale inadequate and mercenary.[3] It was inconceivable to them that one should honor one's parents merely because it would help one achieve longevity. Indeed, honoring parents, they observed, should be aimed *primarily* at increasing the longevity of the *parent*, and not of the child. In their attempt to locate additional or supplementary reasons for honoring parents, our sources elicited a variety of alternative explanations.

The great sixteenth-century Jewish mystic, Judah Loew of Prague, stated that one should not honor one's parents out of expectation of reward or punishment, but simply because it is *natural* for a child to honor his or her own parents.[4] Honoring parents is a natural, universal human trait, upon which Jews have no monopoly. For this reason, the sixteenth-century halakhist, Benjamin Ze'ev ben Matityahu, said that a specific blessing is not required in this case, as it is with regard to the performance of most of the commandments, because blessings attend specifically *Jewish* commandments; of which honoring parents—being universal—is not one.[5] A second explanation as to why no blessing is recited is that a blessing is only recited over acts that can be measured, i.e., quantified, with regard to prescribed behavior, but as a mishnaic passage recited in the daily morning liturgy reminds us, honoring parents is one of those duties that "has no measure," i.e., that is limitless.[6]

The twelfth-century biblical commentator, Abraham ibn Ezra, said that one should honor one's parents because it is both natural and rational to do so. It is rational because reciprocity on the part of the child for acts of generosity and graciousness by the parent to the child should naturally and rationally evoke the gratitude of the child toward the parent.[7] This approach is also found in various other medieval sources,[8] but is rejected by a number of other medieval scholars.

The fifteenth-century commentator, philosopher, and statesman, Don Isaac Abravanel, considered it both superfluous and spiritually dangerous to locate rationales for religious observance in rationality. In his view, human rationality is too unreliable a basis upon which to predicate moral behavior. Filial devotion is a divine command, and, as such, it transcends rational analysis. One should observe simply because one is commanded by God to do so.[9]

A more sophisticated dissent is advanced by others. Some medievals believed that ethical behavior meant doing what is natural. Others believed that to do what is ethical means overcoming natural desires such as greed, lust, and so forth. Advocates of this second approach pointed out that greed, e.g., expressed through honoring parents so as to gain a good inheritance, is natural; however, ethics means overcoming greed and honoring parents *despite* the natural self-serving motives that might exist. Others, such as the seventeenth-century commentator, Moses Hafetz, pointed out that if honoring parents were indeed natural or instinctive, there would be no need for such a commandment. Indeed, Hafetz observed, precisely because it is not instinctive for a child to honor a foolish, senile, or physically incompetent parent, it is therefore necessary for honoring parents to be specifically commanded.[10]

Jeremiah (20:14–18) and Job (3:11–12), it should be remembered, cursed their parents for bestowing upon them the gift of life. This led some of the medievals to reject the reciprocity argument. For example, Bahya ibn Pakudah made a subtle psychological observation about parental motives when he wrote: "It is clear that the parent's intention is to benefit *himself* through the child, for the child is the part of the parent, who places great hopes in him."[11]

Medieval Jewish philosophers such as Maimonides and Gersonides took the question of why to honor parents, and moved it from the realm of nature and rationality to the realms of sociology and political science. Maimonides, following Plato, considered the family to be the basis of sociopolitical life.[12] When a family is weak, society is endangered. Honor of parents, in his view, helps assure a strong societal structure, a guarantee for sociopolitical continuity. Gersonides considered honoring parents to be "the beginning of proper state government where a consensus of the citizens of the state will occur, and the young will accept moral instruction from their elders."[13] Without this, they maintained, society inevitably would collapse.

Having dealt with the question of *why* to honor one's parents, we turn now to *how* to honor and to revere one's parents. Here one finds a tension in the literature between the desirable and the possible. Maimonides states, "The obligations a child owes his parents are too numerous to mention."[14] Nevertheless, specifics had to be given, and beginning with the Talmud, we find such specifics. Simply put, obligations relating to "honor" are defined as those in which the child provides personal services related to the physical needs of the parent, e.g., feeding, clothing, and bathing the parent in need; while "reverence" relates to manifesting through deeds an attitude of respect for the parent, e.g., not contradicting the parent in public, not offending the parent, showing reverence for the parent.[15] Thus, attitudes as well as deeds are required. Filial obligation is not fulfilled unless both correct action and attitude are present. As an example of a child who fulfilled his parent's physical needs, but was devoid of reverence, the Talmud tells of a man who fed his father pheasants. When his father asked how he could afford it, the son said, "What business it is of yours, old man? Just grind your teeth and eat in quiet like a dog."[16]

While Scripture demands honor and reverence from a child, it does not explicitly require love. Some commentators maintain that since love between a parent and a child is natural, it need not be commanded. Others consider love to be a form of honor, one of the attitudinal requirements of the parent–child relationship. Representatives of the Jewish mystical tradition, such as Eliezer Azikiri, describe love as a reciprocal relationship between parents and children. He describes a child's honor of his or her parent as the manifestation of a "powerful love with which they [the parents] have loved him [the child]."[17] Nevertheless, the Talmud quotes a popular contemporary proverb that embodies a keen psychological insight: "A parent's love is for his or her children. A child's love is for his or her own children."[18]

Regarding the question of *who* is covered by the commandment to honor parents, there may be some surprises. In-laws are covered, the reason for which we will examine shortly.[19] In the case of a divorce, a step-parent is covered, as long as honoring the step-parent does not detract from honoring the natural parent. Because the main activity of Jewish parenting is pedagogic, the obligation to honor parents is extended to teachers. According to the Talmud, older siblings are covered as well.[20]

Surprisingly, on the question of whether grandparents are covered, there is a difference of opinion. Despite the talmudic saying that "one's grandchildren are like one's children,"[21] this view was not universally held.[22] The reason is psychologically interesting.

The major work of the Jewish mystics, the *Zohar*, states, "a man loves his grandchildren more than his children."[23] In other words, because grandparents tend to dote on their grandchildren more than on their own children, there was an apprehension that the bond between grandparents and grandchildren might threaten the relationship between children and their parents.[24] Hence, the grandparent-grandchild relationship was deflated by some of the sources in order to try to defuse this possibility.

Many of the sources, particularly the medieval mystical sources, expand on a statement in the Talmud that finds one more individual to whom the obligation to honor parents directly extends, i.e., God. For the mystics, the essence of the person is the soul, though the person is a composite of body and soul. The human parents create the body of the child, while God creates the essence, the soul of the child. Therefore, God is the primary parent, the essential parent, the ultimate parent, the parent of all parents. In this view, discussed in the excerpt below from Nahmanides' *Commentary to the Torah*, honoring the parent is considered a commandment applicable primarily to God, and only by extension to the human parent.[25] For this reason, when there is a conflict between obeying one's human parent and obeying God's commandments, one is obliged to observe the divine commandment and to ignore the commandment of the human parent.[26] This leads to the next issue: *When* is one obliged to honor one's parent?

From the example just given, it is clear that filial devotion is not an unconditional obligation. When certain other values and issues come into conflict, it may be compromised. Let us consider a number of examples.

In an interesting responsum, the thirteenth-century Spanish Jewish scholar, Solomon Ibn Adret, dealt with the case of a conflict between filial obligations and obligations to one's spouse.[27] Here, a woman was living with her husband's parents, in a state of constant tension with her mother-in-law. This situation caused severe marital strife between husband and wife, since the mother-in-law was constantly belittling the daughter-in-law. The daughter-in-law, i.e., the wife, asked Adret whether she has a right to demand that she and her husband leave the domicile of her in-laws, despite her husband's obligation of filial devotion to his parents. In this case, Adret finds in favor of the wife. The argument made here is based upon the verse in Genesis (2:24), "Therefore a man leaves his father and mother and clings to his wife so that they become one flesh." As a midrash puts it, "Until a man marries his love centers on his parents. . . . But, when he marries, his love is bestowed on his wife—his soul cleaves to that of his wife."[28] Ironically, the notion that a husband and wife are one flesh, one person, was also used to justify the inclusion of in-laws under the category of parents.[29]

A second example has to do with the foolish or the wicked parent. Here, again, a variety of views are present in the literature. One view is that the obligations to parents are indeed unconditional. One is not obliged to emulate the foolish or the wicked parent, but neither is one free to cease honoring such a parent. A second view distinguishes between the foolish parent and the wicked parent. The foolish parent still deserves respect, though not the wicked parent. Regarding the foolish parent, the Talmud says, even if a parent throws a purse of money into the sea, or humiliates the child in public, the child is nevertheless obliged to honor such a parent.[30] However, if a parent is wicked, a number of medieval scholars, such as the twelfth-century Eliezer of Metz and the fourteenth-century Israel ben Joseph Alnakawa, released the child from the obligation to honor that parent.[31]

Essentially, two views are represented here. One view holds that filial obligations must be observed no matter how well the parent is parenting. The second view is that the child is obliged only to honor the parent who "parents" well, i.e., the parent must first fulfill his or her obligations to the child before the child can be expected to fulfill his or her obligations to the parent. In other words, honoring parents is an act of reciprocity that first assumes that the parent has fulfilled his or her religious and moral obligations to the child. The wicked parent, the incompetent parent, in this view, is unworthy of the child's honor and reverence.

In two other situations, the child is also freed from showing honor and reverence toward his or her parents. One situation is where caring for one's parent might stretch the limits of a child's physical or psychological endurance, for example, in the case of caring for a senile parent. There, even Maimonides, who considers honoring parents to be an almost unconditional obligation, concedes that in such a case, the child should seek "professional" help for the care of a parent.[32]

A second situation is where the parent is too rigid and overbearing. As the *Sefer Hasidim* states, sometimes the parent may be so overbearing as "to enrage the child so that the child has no option but to rebel." Here the unreasonable "honor" demanded by the parent can be waived. This option prevents parental inflexibility, which might lead to the moral degeneration of the child, or even in certain extreme cases, to the suicide of the child. Nevertheless, in such a case, the parent is discouraged from inviting the child's physical or psychological abuse. In other words, both too much parental rigidity and too much parental flexibility are discouraged.[33] The ultimate goal is what is of utmost importance: the moral development and character formation of the child.

Just as a child is required to perform certain deeds for his or her parent, so is the child obliged to restrain from doing certain things to his or her parent. For example, a child is enjoined from injuring a parent either through deeds or through words. Biblical law even requires the death penalty for such action, i.e., for wounding or cursing a parent (e.g., Exodus 21:15, Leviticus 20:9; see Deuteronomy 27:16). This punishment, though it appears not to have been enforced in the postbiblical era, is nevertheless reiterated by rabbinic and medieval literature, including the excerpt below from Nahmanides' *Commentary to the Torah*.[34] The underlying principle here is that a child is obliged to take pains not to distress a parent either physically or emotionally. Rather, a child is obliged to try to provide his or her parents with happiness and with joy (Proverbs 15:20):

> A wise son makes his father happy
> A fool of a man humiliates his mother.

According to one commentator, a reason one should not injure one's parents is because, in so doing, one injures oneself. Since one's parents are one's own "flesh and blood," since one's soul is "bound up" with that of one's parents, to cause injury to them is to cause injury to oneself. In this view, harming one's parents is a form of masochism.[35] A similar motif is also expressed by Abravanel. He wrote, "The benefit [of honoring parents] extends to the child who honors them. As he honors his parent so will he be honored in turn by his own children, for as one treats others so will he be treated by others."[36]

Having examined the *why*, *how*, *when*, and *whom* of honoring parents, we turn to the excerpt below, and to its author, Moses ben Nahman, or, as he is better known—Nahmanides.

꠸꠸꠸

The following text is an example of the most popular form of classical Jewish literature, i.e., commentary. While many of the works of Jewish ethical literature that adopt commentary form were written as commentaries to the biblical book of Proverbs or on the talmudic treatise *The Ethics of the Fathers*, one also finds nuggets of moral insight buried throughout the vast number of commentaries on the Torah that have been composed over the centuries.

Of the plethora of Jewish commentaries to the Torah, three stand supreme in terms of their popularity, influence, and scope. First is the commentary of "Rashi" — Rabbi Solomon ben Isaac — "the father of the commentators," who lived during the eleventh century in France. Second is the commentary of the twelfth-century Spanish exegete Abraham Ibn Ezra. Third is the commentary by the thirteenth-century Spanish scholar, Moses ben Nahman, from whose writings the following text is excerpted. This triumvirate — Rashi, Ibn Ezra, and Nahmanides — served as the foundation for all future commentaries on the Torah, the central text of Judaism.[37]

Though Nahmanides was heir to the magnificent cultural and religious traditions produced during "The Golden Age" of Spanish Jewry under Islamic rule, he was the ancestor of the extraordinary contributions made by Spanish Jewry under Christian rule. If Maimonides was the last great figure of Islamic Spain, then Nahmanides was the first great figure of Christian Spain.

Nahmanides' works are breathtaking both in the breadth of their scope and in the profundity of their depth. His versatility extends to commentary and law, poetry and polemics, responsa and mysticism, homiletics and philosophy. Moreover, Nahmanides served as a physician and was communal leader of and spokesperson for Spanish Jewry during years of internal strife and extreme oppression.

Also known by the acronym *Ramban* (Rabbi Moses ben Nahman), Nahmanides was born in the Spanish city of Gerona in about 1194. While still in his teens, Nahmanides began his literary career. His first work was a supplement to the eleventh-century legal code of Isaac Alfasi. This work established the young scholar's reputation as a legalist and talmudist of the first order. However, this was but the first of many works he composed on the Talmud and on Jewish law. His initial literary endeavor was only the prelude to two treatises aimed at defending Alfasi from his major critics. One is entitled *Sefer Zehut — The Book of Defense*, and the other is *Milhemet ha-Shem — Wars of the Lord*. Another work defended Simon Karo's *Halakhot Gedolot — Great Laws* against the criticisms leveled against it by Maimonides. This work is entitled *Mitzvot ha-Shem — The Divine Commandments*. In his extensive collection of glosses and objections to views expressed in Maimonides' *Book of the Commandments*, Nahmanides again takes issue with some of the legal and theological views of Maimonides. In these treatises, Nahmanides defends the views of earlier scholars from the intellectual onslaughts of later scholars.

Nahmanides did not merely defend the views of the past, but forged a new approach to talmudic studies for the future. In his day, two approaches dominated the study of the Talmud: that of the Franco-German tosaphists and that of the Spanish talmudists. The Spanish School had stressed the practical implications of talmudic study for legal decision. The tosaphists had emphasized a more theoretical approach to talmudic scholarship, stressing the value of textual analysis for its own sake. Nahmanides' contribution was to forge a new synthesis of these two diverse methods. In the extensive novellae (*hiddushim*) he wrote on most of the Talmud, and in his other talmudic and legal works, this new approach becomes manifest. He thereby became the first link in a chain of commentaries on the Talmud that were grounded in his method. His work became a permanent component and a required premise of subsequent advanced talmudic studies. In addition, a number of his legal responsa have been preserved, though they probably represent a fraction of the legal decisions he must have rendered during his frenetic, though illustrious, career.

Nahmanides' efforts as a synthesizer of diverse views were severely tested in a controversy that threatened to split contemporary Jewry into two perpetually feuding camps. In 1232 the "Maimonidean Controversy" exploded in France and Spain. The anti-Maimonideans condemned Maimonides' philosophical work *The Guide of the Perplexed* and the first book of his legal code, *The Mishneh Torah*, as heretical, or at least as conducive to heresy. These works were summarily put under a ban of excommunication. The pro-Maimonideans responded with a counterban. In an attempt to calm the fires of controversy, Nahmanides risked the wrath of both sides and stepped into the fray. From the anti-Maimonideans he requested the removal of their ban and an appreciation of the profound contributions Maimonides had made to Jewish scholarship and to Jewish communal life. He reminded the anti-Maimonideans that Maimonides' intentions were not to destroy the Jewish faith, but to defend it in lands where apostasy and ignorance of Judaism had been rampant. To the pro-Maimonideans, he wrote, reminding them of the dangers of philosophical study and of foreign influences upon the untutored Jewish masses, and upon Jewish intellectual, cultural, and spiritual existence. Nahmanides called for mediation, for a truce, before a schism occurred that would "divide the Torah into two Torahs and Israel into two sects." His efforts, however, went unheeded and unappreciated. As a result of his being ignored, the consequences were dire. For example, inciters of the Inquisition in France, seeing that Jews were burning Jewish books, i.e., Maimonides' writings, extended the public burning of Jewish books to the Talmud. As time progressed, the rift between the two factions deepened, and only with the end of Spanish Jewry, after the expulsion in 1492, was the matter put to an uneasy rest.

In 1263, Nahmanides became embroiled in a second dispute that could not be readily resolved. He was cast into a public disputation with Christian theologians in Barcelona. The debate took place in the presence of King James I, who guaranteed Nahmanides complete freedom of speech. The Christian scholars were led by an apostate Jew named Pablo Christiani. The disputation was clearly staged as part of an intensified program by the Church to demonstrate the superiority of Christianity, the falsity of Judaism, and to encourage the conversion of Spanish Jewry to Christianity.

Nahmanides defended Judaism with such intellectual agility that the king rewarded him with a gift. He countered every thrust of his opponents and initiated a few of his own. According to Nahmanides' own report of the debate, the king said to him, "Never have I seen a man who was wrong argue as well as you."

Nahmanides' performance at the disputation was considered a victory for him in a joust he was supposed to have lost. The pope, Clement IV, demanded that Nahmanides be punished. The Spanish clergy increased their missionary activities toward the Jews. Apparently because he felt himself in personal danger, Nahmanides was forced to flee Spain for Palestine. He arrived there in the summer of 1267. Nahmanides published his account of the debate as *Sefer ha-Vikuah, The Book of Disputation.*

One of the central issues of the debate was Messianic redemption. While still in Spain, Nahmanides composed a treatise on this subject entitled *Sefer Geulah — The Book of Redemption.* Theological as well as legal issues related to death, mourning, and the afterlife are discussed in his treatise entitled *Torat ha-Adam — The Torah of Man.* Nahmanides also wrote poetry, including poems of a liturgical nature. Of what must have been a wealth of sermonic material, Nahmanides also published four of his sermons.

Nahmanides was a mystic. Though his specifically mystical writings are sparse, one does find mystical ideas sprinkled through his works. Nahmanides' reluctance to compose any extensive or explicit mystical writings seems to derive from his conviction that mystical teachings should be conveyed orally from master to disciple, and should not be publicly disseminated through a written text. Consequently, Nahmanides alludes to mystical ideas more than he expresses them (see, e.g., the excerpt below, Leviticus 20:9). Nevertheless, despite his conscious restraint from explicating mystical ideas, Nahmanides' deep involvement with the kabbalistic teachings echoes in his writings. Only in subsequent generations would Jewish mystics make public their esoteric teachings. Nahmanides, however, preferred to keep Jewish mystical teachings hidden, referring to them only by delicately cultivated hints and carefully crafted allusions. In his commentaries to Scripture, one encounters many such echoes of Nahmanides' involvement with Jewish mysticism.

Nahmanides wrote two major works of scriptural commentary. One was his extensive commentary on Job, in which he focuses on the problem of evil

and suffering. Here Nahmanides offers the kabbalistic notion of transmigra-
tion of souls as a viable approach to explaining the problem of human
suffering. His most extensive work of biblical commentary, however, is his
Commentary to the Torah, from which the following excerpt derives. Nahmanides apparently began this massive project while still in Spain, and he
concluded it while in Palestine. In this work, he discusses a wide range of
theological, exegetical, moral, legal, and historical issues. He often criticizes
the commentaries of Rashi and Ibn Ezra, and offers his own alternative
explanations. He alludes to many kabbalistic notions, but does not explicate
them. He interprets many biblical events as being archetypes for subsequent
Jewish history. This commentary stimulated subsequent scholars to write
commentaries to the Torah that either offer a critique or a defense of
Nahmanides' views.

From the Land of Israel, Nahmanides corresponded with his family in
Spain, and about a dozen of those letters have survived. In addition, a
number of works he did not write were ascribed to him, such as *Iggeret
ha-Kodesh—The Holy Letter.*[38] One may sum up Nahmanides' accomplishments with the words of Solomon Schechter: "Nahmanides was a great
Talmudist, a great Bible student, a great philosopher, a great controversalist,
and perhaps also a great physician; in one word, great in every respect,
possessed of all the culture of his age."[39]

Nahmanides
Commentary to the Torah

"HENCE A MAN LEAVES HIS FATHER AND HIS MOTHER
AND CLEAVES TO HIS WIFE, SO THAT THEY BECOME ONE
FLESH" (Genesis 2:24).

The child is created by both of them [the father and the
mother], and in that way their flesh becomes one [in the child].
This is Rashi's comment [on this verse]. Nevertheless, this [i.e.,
Rashi's comment] offers no explanation because animals and
beasts also become one flesh in their offspring. The correct
explanation, it seems to me, is that male animals and beasts do
not *cleave* to their females. Rather, the male mates [randomly]
with any available female, and [afterwards] each goes its own
way. It is precisely for this reason the Scripture [differentiates
humans from animals and beasts. Scripture] states that the
[human] female is the bone of the bone and the flesh of the flesh
of the [human] male. [The human male] cleaves to her [i.e., to
the human female] and she stays in his bosom as his own flesh.
His desire is for her to be with him always, as it was implanted

in human nature, beginning with Adam for all subsequent generations for males to cleave to their wives, to leave their parents, and to see themselves as one flesh with their wives. In a similar sense Scripture says "For he is our brother, our flesh" (Genesis 37:27), and, "to any that is near of his flesh" (Leviticus 18:6), i.e., one's family is called "near of his flesh." Here [we see that] a man leaves the "nearness" of his parents and his relatives, and sees that his wife is closer to him than are they.

"HONOR YOUR FATHER AND YOUR MOTHER, THAT YOU MAY LONG ENDURE ON THE LAND WHICH THE LORD YOUR GOD IS GIVING YOU" (Exodus 20:12).

Having completed [presenting] all that which we are obligated to do regarding God Himself and His honor, [the text] continues to command us regarding issues relating to created beings. It [the text] begins with the father who, in relation to his offspring, is like a creator, involved in their formation. God, however, is our first Father, and our natural father who sires us is our last father. For this reason it says in Deuteronomy (5:16), "Honor your father and your mother, as the Lord your God has commanded you . . ."; i.e., just as I [God] have commanded you concerning My honor, so I command you to honor My partner(s) with Me in your creation. Scripture has not explained [why or how to honor one's parents], for it can be learned from the aforementioned honor due to God, the first Father. [As one acknowledges the Lord as God alone,] so should one acknowledge one's father as such and not deny him by claiming another as his father: [Just as one should not honor God in order to be rewarded,] so one should not honor one's father in order to receive an inheritance or for any other benefit he might expect from his father. [As one may not take God's name in vain,] so one should not take his father's name in vain or falsely swear by "the life of my father." Furthermore, there are other obligations included in honor; we are commanded regarding them and the sages have explained what they are. The sages already juxtaposed the honor due parents to the honor due to God.[40]

Because this commandment [of honoring parents] relates to terrestrial creatures, He designated its reward as longevity upon the land that He is giving you. According to the sages, the meaning of the statement, "that you may long endure . . . on the land" is that He promises that by fulfilling this commandment, all of one's days will be extended, i.e., God will extend one's days in this world, and they will also be extended in the World to Come which is without end, and that we shall dwell forever on the good land that He will give us.[41] In Deuteronomy (5:16) it states, "that you may long endure, *and* that you may fare well," thus constituting two promises [i.e., one for this world and one for the World to Come].

Exodus 20:13 . . . Of the Ten Commandments, five deal with honor due the Creator and five deal with the good of man. For "honor your father" is the honor of the Lord; it is for the honor of the Creator that he commanded that one honor one's father who participated in one's creation. Five commandments thus remain for the welfare of human beings.

"HE WHO STRIKES HIS FATHER OR HIS MOTHER SHALL BE PUT TO DEATH" (Exodus 21:15).

Our sages already have taught that his death [in punishment for this offense] is by strangulation.[42] For this reason, this verse is placed next to the verse dealing with kidnapping, for it [i.e., the type of punishment] is the same kind of death [for both offenses]. It [i.e., this verse] is separated from the verse "He who curses his father or his mother shall be put to death" (21:17) because [the punishment for that offense] is [death] by stoning, as it is written (Leviticus 20:9) "[If any man insults his father or his mother, he shall be put to death;] he has insulted his father and his mother—his blood is upon him." Whenever Scripture uses this terminology [i.e., "his blood is upon him"], it refers to stoning. This is derived from (Leviticus 20:27), "they shall be stoned with stones; their blood shall be upon them." [Since stoning was considered more severe a punishment than strangulation,] one who cursed his parents received the more severe punishment than one who struck his parents. The reason for this is because the offense of cursing is more common [than striking]. When a fool becomes angry "he rages and curses his King" (Isaiah 8:21), and his parents the entire day. Thus, the sin that is frequent [i.e., cursing] requires a more severe punishment. Furthermore, it may well be that cursing is indeed a greater offense, since in cursing one mentions God's Name [i.e., one swears falsely by God's Name and thereby takes it in vain in violation of the Ten Commandments—Exodus 20:7]. Therefore, the individual deserves to be punished both for the offense committed against his or her parents and also for transgressing against God for taking His Name in vain. Rabbi Saadya Gaon said that the matter of kidnapping is placed between them [i.e., between the verses dealing with striking and cursing a parent] because most kidnap victims are children who then are raised far from home, and consequently they do not know who their parents are.[43] [Sometime later] they might come upon the person who is their parent, and they might curse or strike them [not knowing who they are]. Therefore, it is proper for a kidnapper to be punished with death, as he [i.e., the kidnapper] is responsible for his [i.e., the child's] sin, and his [the child's] punishment falls upon him [i.e., the kidnapper].

"IF A MAN CURSES HIS FATHER OR HIS MOTHER, HE SHALL BE PUT TO DEATH; HE HAS INSULTED HIS FATHER AND HIS MOTHER—HIS BLOOD IS UPON HIMSELF" (Leviticus 20:9).

[This verse] refers back to the beginning of this section where it says, "You shall each revere his mother and father, and keep My Sabbaths; I the Lord am Your God" (Leviticus 19:3). Here it states if a man does not heed, etc. (see Deuteronomy 21:18), and curses his parents, he shall be put to death. According to the way of truth [i.e., the mystical teachings], this is stated because it has been said, "Sanctify yourselves and be you holy, for I the Lord am your God" (Leviticus 20:7), and it says, "I the Lord make you holy" (Leviticus 20:8), meaning that it is the honored Name that makes us holy, for He is "our Father and our redeemer for everlasting" (Isaiah 63:16), and He is His Name. Therefore, if one curses those who have participated in his creation, one is liable to death. . . .

"IF A MAN HAS A STUBBORN AND DEFIANT SON, WHO DOES NOT HEED HIS FATHER OR HIS MOTHER AND DOES NOT OBEY THEM, EVEN AFTER THEY DISCIPLINE HIM, HIS FATHER AND HIS MOTHER SHALL TAKE HOLD OF HIM AND BRING HIM OUT TO THE ELDERS OF HIS TOWN AT THE PUBLIC PLACE OF HIS COMMUNITY. THEY SHALL SAY TO THE ELDERS OF HIS TOWN, 'THIS SON OF OURS IS DISLOYAL AND DEFIANT; HE DOES NOT HEED US. HE IS A GLUTTON AND A DRUNKARD': THEREUPON THE MEN OF HIS TOWN SHALL STONE HIM TO DEATH. THUS YOU WILL SWEEP OUT EVIL FROM YOUR MIDST: ALL ISRAEL WILL HEAR AND BE AFRAID" (Deuteronomy 21:18–21).

In the opinion of the rabbis he [i.e., the child] cannot be a minor, since a minor is not liable to any of the punishments stated in the Torah and [he is not obliged to fulfill] any of the commandments until the onset of puberty. [Rather, the reverse relates to one who is not a minor] and is therefore liable to two punishments. One, for cursing his parents and for rebelling against them. Second, because he is "a glutton and a drunkard" thereby transgressing the commandment, "You shall be holy" (Leviticus 19:2), and the statement "worship none but Him and cleave to Him" (Deuteronomy 13:5). As I have explained, we are commanded to know God in all our ways; one who is a glutton and a drunkard does not know God's way. Though he has not yet committed a sin deserving the death penalty, he is nevertheless punished for what he will inevitably do, as our sages remind us.[44] For this reason "all Israel will hear and be afraid," for he is not executed because of the severity of his offense, but in order to chastise the public, so that he should not become a stumbling block for others. It is thus the way of Scripture to warn of the death penalty, so that his execution might serve as a deterrent and a benefit for others. . . . This [law of the stubborn and defiant child] may be considered a new commandment, or, it may be considered an explanation of "Honor your father and your mother" (Exodus 20:12) and "you shall each revere his mother and his father" (Leviticus 19:3).

13

How to Parent

Try to compose a "Help Wanted" classified advertisement for a parent. In so doing, consider all the knowledge, wisdom, and skills potential applicants would require to qualify for this job. In addition, a lifetime of total commitment would be demanded. Financial compensation would be negligible. Substantial successful experience would be a prerequisite. Specific attitudes such as unbounding devotion would be necessary. Full-time availability—meaning 24 hours a day, for at least 18 years—would be assumed.

Once such a job description has been composed, consider whether parents whom you know, or parents about whom you have heard, would qualify to be hired for this most sacred and significant lifetime career. Surprisingly, the great role models of the Bible, individuals whom we admire and revere for so many things, would be among the first group of candidates *disqualified* for this job. The great figures of Scripture were great in many ways, but not as parents. They succeeded in many things, but not in parenting.

The first parents, Adam and Eve, raised two sons in the best of all possible environments, and one murdered the other. Noah was mocked by his son. Abraham, the father of the three Western faiths, is considered by some to have been a failure as a father to his sons. Isaac and Rebecca played favorites between their sons Jacob and Esau, and tore their family apart. Jacob, who became Israel, doted obsessively on Joseph, provoking jealousy of and hostility toward Joseph. Jacob, who wrestled with the divine, responded passively to the rape of his only daughter, Dinah. Until he was on his deathbed, Jacob virtually ignored his eldest son's seduction of Jacob's concubine. Thus, the parents of the Jewish people, the patriarchs and matriarchs of the People of Israel, were poor parents.

Moses, the greatest Jew of all, is remembered for his greatness as a liberator, a prophet, a leader, and a lawgiver, but he is not recalled as an effective father. Shepherd to his people, he was an absentee father. King David, the eventual father of the Messiah, had irreconcilable differences with Absalom, his son. We cannot therefore look to the great figures of Scripture for insights in how to parent. However, we can find such insight in biblical and postbiblical Jewish religious literature.

For Jewish tradition, the primary prerogative of parenting is pedagogy. In Hebrew, it is customary for a child to refer to his or her parents as "my father, my teacher," "my mother, my teacher." The parent is the child's first and foremost teacher in creating an artful existence. The lessons the parent conveys, the values the parent tries to instill, the role model the parent strives to be are the critical aspects of parenting. The home is a school where the moral teachings of the past can be imparted to the future. Morality, including charity, begins at home.[1]

Throughout biblical, talmudic, and apocryphal literature, the duty of the parent to direct his or her child's moral development is stated. For example, the verse in Proverbs (1:8), "My son heed the instruction (musar) of your father; forsake not the teaching (torat) of your mother," was later interpreted as a clear obligation of a parent to offer, and of a child to accept, moral guidance. The apocryphal Book of Tobit explicitly records a father's moral teaching to his son. "My boy, beware of any immorality," Tobit tells his son (Tobit 4:12). A parent is expected to "guide children in a straight path," according to the Talmud.[2]

The passages in Deuteronomy (6:4–9, 11:13–21) that entered the Jewish liturgy as part of the Shema enjoin parents to teach the words of the Torah diligently and constantly to their children.[3] The Passover Seder focuses more on pedagogy than on ritual. It is an opportunity "to tell your child" (Exodus 13:8) the story of the Exodus, i.e., to convey to the child a sense of who he or she is, where he or she comes from, what is his or her spiritual heritage. What is at stake in the parent's teaching the child the constitutive moral teachings of tradition is the future moral disposition of the child. The quality of one's "parenting" becomes manifested through the activities of one's child:

> The Zhitomer rebbe was once walking along with his son when they came upon a drunken man and his drunken son, both stumbling into the gutter. "I envy that man," said the rabbi to his son. "He has accomplished his goal of having a son like himself. I do not yet know whether you will be like me. I can only hope that the drunkard is not more successful with his son than I am with you."[4]

More is at stake in parental pedagogy than the moral disposition of the child. The very existence and continuity of Jewish tradition, and the stability of society at large, are also at risk. For example, the thirteenth-century Jewish philosopher, Gersonides, considered the family to be the most fundamental political unit of society, upon which larger political units, such as cities and nations, are based. When the family functions as a conduit of moral values, the larger society gains stability. When it does not, the larger society becomes morally imperiled.[5] According to Joseph Albo, because the family serves as the essential vehicle through which tradition is perpetuated, the very existence of Judaism is vested in the pedagogic abilities of each parent to transmit moral and religious teachings to the child.[6] In this view, what is at stake in parental pedagogy is the future moral disposition of the child, the perpetuation of something of the parent in the future behavior of the child,[7] the moral and sociopolitical stability of society at large, and the continuity and perpetuation of the tradition that offers meaning and moral coherence to the lives of both the parent and the child.

From a psychological perspective, a number of sources observe that the parent who neglects the moral instruction of the child will eventually resent the child if he or she becomes a scoundrel. Similarly, the child deprived of parental guidance will inevitably come to resent the parent for the parent's neglect of his or her moral and intellectual development. Such a child may, with justification, be unable to honor or to revere a parent who has failed to convey moral instruction either pedagogically or by personal example.[8] It thus emerges that proper parental pedagogy is not only in the best interests of the child, that it is not only a fundamental parental obligation, but that it is also in the self-interest of the parent and in the best interest of a mutually beneficial parent–child relationship.

Part of the art of parental pedagogy is knowing when to be tender and when to be firm, when to be insistent and when to be flexible. It was precisely for this reason that the talmudic and the medieval sources offer parents the option of "mehilah," of foregoing their honor and their parental authority. Since the essential issue in honoring parents and in rearing children is the moral and spiritual development of the child, and not the imposition of parental authority over the child, the parent is cautioned not to provoke the child's rebellion by being overbearing or unnecessarily authoritarian. Parental inflexibility must not be permitted to become a catalyst for the moral degeneration of the child.[9] A further concern, expressed by Joseph Hahn, a seventeenth-century German rabbi, is that an oppressively overbearing parent may cause such anguish in the child, that the child will become unduly distraught, even to the point of committing suicide.[10] On the other hand, the parent is cautioned not to become so flexible so as to encourage moral anarchy on the part of the child. While the parent is occasionally encouraged to temper authority over the child, the parent is also cautioned from thereby inviting the child's physical or psychological abuse.[11] The parent is encouraged to find a middle ground—determined by the particular disposition of the child—between being apathetic and being unduly authoritarian in his or her relationship with the child.

The goal of parental instruction is the development of the child within the framework of a moral and religious tradition. The child thereby becomes a link between the past and the future. Nevertheless, the child's moral instruction is also crucial to the child's ability to function as an informed moral agent in society. As Gersonides observed, when the parent–child relationship functions properly, when the family serves as a conduit for moral values, society as a whole is enriched and improved.

The course of study that the parent is to teach the child is a course in the art of living as an individual in society. The goals of the course are to guide the child from ignorance to wisdom, from moral neutrality to virtue, from dependency to independence, from infancy to maturity. The parental obligation to prepare the child to function as an independent adult in an interdependent society is reflected in the few rabbinic statements that explicitly list the obligations of a parent toward a child. According to a talmudic text:

> The father is obligated to circumcise his son, to redeem him (if he is a firstborn, see Numbers 18:15), to teach him Torah, to have him wed, and to teach him a craft. Some say, to teach him to swim as well. Rabbi Judah said: He who does not teach his son a craft . . . is as though he taught him to steal.[12]

According to a variant reading of this text, a father is also obligated to teach his son practical citizenship (*yishuv medinah*).[13]

The parent's obligation to circumcise a son, to redeem him, and to teach him Torah, relates to the parent's duty to ensure the perpetuation of tradition and to have the child initiated into the Jewish community. In so doing, the child's history mates with his destiny. Teaching the child Torah aims not only at helping to ensure the continuation of tradition, but it attempts to assure an intellectually, morally, and spiritually developed person. The parent's obligation to have the child wed, to teach him a craft, and to teach him practical citizenship, relates to the parent's duty to permit the child to become an independent citizen of society. A crucial step toward the child's independence is his or her becoming independent from the parent. Marriage is considered a critical step in a person's independence from his or her parent. With marriage, the child's primary relationship and source of identity is as a spouse rather than as a child.[14] With marriage, a new person, a new family, a new sociopolitical unit is established. By obliging a parent to see that his or her child is married, the Talmud prods the parent not only to recognize, but to provide for, the independence of the child.

For a child to be independent, the child must be economically self-sustaining. Teaching a child a way to earn a living is deemed part of a child's moral instruction. As Rabbi Judah candidly observed, "He who does not teach his son a craft may be regarded . . . as if he is teaching him to steal."[15] On this statement Rashi comments, "Because the child has been taught no trade, he will be bereft of sustenance, and will then steal from others."[16] A means to help ensure not only a child's independent fiscal survival must be provided by the parent, but also a means to help insure a child's independent physical survival was required. It is for this reason that one talmudic opinion requires a parent to teach a child how to swim.[17] "What is the reason [why a parent should teach his child how to swim]?" the Talmud asks. "[Because] his life may depend on it," the text answers.[18] Finally, the parent is obligated to teach the child "practical citizenship" so that the child may function as an upright and productive member of society. The role of the parent as teacher encompasses not only the intellectual and the religious spheres of existence, but the social and the political dimension as well.

In Jewish tradition, to be childless is a catastrophe. To have children is a blessing: "Children are a gift from God, fruit of the womb His reward" (Psalms 127:3). Love of children is not commanded, but is assumed. The Talmud quotes a contemporary proverb: "A parent's love is for his children, a child's love is for his own children."[19] Yet, despite this expectation of parental love, medieval Jewish ethical writers keenly observed that parental love may not always be free of self-interest; it may become self-serving. The parent who supports the child fiscally and emotionally may be projecting his or her own frustrated goals and desires upon the child. Such parenting ultimately serves neither the parent nor the child. In this regard, Bahya ibn Pakudah wrote:

> It is clear that the parent's intention is to benefit himself through the child, for the child is part of the parent, who places great hopes in him. Remark how he gives preference to the child in food, drink, and clothing, how he guards him against all misfortunes and finds all the pain and trouble involved in safeguarding his peace a trifle, so strong is mercy and compassion toward his children impressed on a parent's nature.[20]

In this view, the child's fulfillment of the obligation to honor his or her parents should be based upon the quality of moral instruction conveyed by the parent to the child. As the fourteenth-century Spanish ethical work *Menorat ha-Ma'or* states, "A person should honor his or her parents more for the moral instruction they offer than for bringing one into the world. For in bringing one into the world, the parents' own pleasure may have been their motive."[21]

While duties can be specified, and while guidance may be given, selfless parental love and altruistic behavior can only be hoped for. Some maintained that since love is a natural feature of the parent–child relationship, it need not be legally required. Others claimed that if the parent–child relationship is devoid of love, to legally demand love would be impossible. Others hoped that if love were lacking, the fulfillment of the guidelines of the parent–child relationship set down by tradition might engender love.

According to one Jewish proverb, "children drive one crazy," but according to another proverb "one is crazy when it comes to one's children." The first proverb refers to the travails that inevitably characterize childrearing. The pain that may accompany childrearing may eclipse the pain that accompanies childbearing.[22] The second proverb relates to the unabashed, irrational love of a parent for a child. Plato defined love as a form of madness.[23] The loving parent may sacrifice much, including personal dignity, in manifesting devotion for a child. In this regard, a fanciful midrash records the following:

> Once it happened that a man who made out his will specified: My son shall inherit nothing of mine until he acts like a fool. Rabbi Jose bar Judah and Rabbi went to Rabbi Joshua ben Karha to get an opinion regarding the meaning of this unusual provision. When they found him (i.e., Joshua ben Karha) in the field, they saw him crawling on his hands and knees, that a reed was sticking out of his mouth, and that he was being pulled along by his child. Seeing this, they withdrew, and went to his house. When they asked him about the provision in the will, he began to laugh, and he said to them: As you live, this business you are asking about – acting like a fool – could apply to me a minute ago. Thereupon, he went on to say: When a person has children it is not unusual to act like a fool when it comes to them.[24]

While the man mentioned in the preceding story wrote a will that affected his son, he did not write an "ethical will." The tradition of writing an ethical will for one's children is one that each parent might undertake. In so doing, one offers one's children a summary of one's deepest concerns, one has the opportunity to say things that ought to be said, but never seem to get said. Writing an ethical will to one's children can be an important part of the art of parenting, both for the parent and for the child.

꧁꧂

As we have seen, biblical and rabbinic literature contain scattered statements regarding the parental obligation to instruct the child, particularly in moral matters; however, it is only with the emergence of the Jewish ethical will in about the eleventh century that one finds a specific genre of Jewish ethical literature that concentrates upon the conveyance of moral insight from parent to child. Although these Jewish ethical wills are predominantly paternal, the maternal will is not lacking. Indeed, as one traces the development of the Jewish ethical will into the modern period, one finds increasing numbers of maternal Jewish ethical wills.

Though many medieval Jewish ethical wills are pseudonymic and others are ethical treatises that use the literary form of an ethical will as a pretext for general moral exhortation, many medieval ethical wills actually do represent moral insights of a parent recorded for the benefit of his or her children. The excerpt below from the ethical will of the twelfth-century Spanish Jewish scholar, Judah ibn Tibbon, written to his son Samuel, is an example of an ethical will written by a father to his son.

The tradition of a parent writing an ethical will for his or her children never has been a requirement of Jewish law. Nevertheless, this tradition, initiated in the Middle Ages, has continued to this day. In an ethical will, a parent attempts to transmit a moral and a spiritual summation of what he or she has learned from life to his or her children.[25] A modern ethical will, written in 1965, states that the function of such a document is to represent "an inventory of precept rather than property, of concern instead of cash, of love in lieu of legacy." It is to be, in the words of Stephen Vincent Benet, "a legacy of intangibles."[26]

The following excerpt is from the ethical will of Judah ibn Tibbon.[27] Born in Granada, Spain, in about 1120, Judah fled Moslem persecution in Spain. He immigrated to Lunel (Provence), France, where he had a flourishing medical practice. Lunel was a major center of Jewish intellectual activity at that time. Because of his masterful knowledge of languages, the scholars of Lunel asked Judah to provide Hebrew translations of some of the great philosophical and ethical classics written in Arabic by Spanish and Babylonian Jews. Judah ibn Tibbon complied. Among the works he translated were Saadya's philosophical work *Beliefs and Opinions*, Jonah Ibn Janah's grammatical treatise *Book of Roots*, Ha-Levi's *Kuzari*,[28] and Bahya's *Duties of the Heart*.[29] These translations from Arabic into Hebrew made works such as these available to his contemporaries and to subsequent generations of Jews. His work earned him the title, "father of the translators." In addition, Judah translated some of Galen's medical work into Hebrew, and he also wrote an original work on science entitled *Otot ha-Shamayim—Signs of the Heavens*. Judah ibn Tibbon died in Lunel in about 1190.

Judah's ethical will is written to his son, Samuel ibn Tibbon. As was not uncommon, he apparently began this composition when his child was young, adding sections as time progressed, much like codicils are attached to modern wills. Samuel was born in Lunel in about 1150. He continued his father's project of translating Jewish philosophical works from Arabic into Hebrew. His crowning achievement was his translation of Maimonides' *Guide of the Perplexed*. In addition, Samuel translated a number of Maimonides' minor treatises as well.

Through their masterful and exacting translations, the Ibn Tibbons virtually forged the vocabulary of medieval philosophical Hebrew. In addition, Samuel ibn Tibbon also authored philosophical works such as *Yikavu ha-Mayyim* and a commentary to Ecclesiastes. He died in Marseilles in about 1230.

Before proceeding to the text, a number of observations about its contents are in order. It seems from the narrative that Judah ibn Tibbon was what we call today "a single parent." He seems to have lost his wife early in life, and was left alone to raise his children. He also seems to have vested considerably more energy in raising his son than his daughters. Consequently, throughout the text one can feel the father's complete devotion to his son, as well as his frustration regarding how his son has responded to his legion efforts to provide for his son's every need. Nevertheless, the reader also can sense that Judah ibn Tibbon's fatherly devotion is not devoid of the projection of his own needs and goals upon his son.

Judah ibn Tibbon's advice to his son covers a wide range of concerns, including how to conduct business, how to practice medicine, how to relate to one's family, how to write, and how to preserve one's health. His emphasis upon diet in the preservation of health has a contemporary ring. Despite Judah ibn Tibbon's often overbearing attitude, his ethical will seems to have struck a responsive chord in his son. It appears to have been written before Samuel ibn Tibbon made his mark on the history of Jewish literature, and may have stimulated Samuel to alter the direction of his life, thereby occasioning his scientific, literary, and philosophical achievements. For example, Judah's admonition to his son to be more diligent in his studies and less careless in his use of language seems to have been taken to heart by Samuel, as is evidenced by Samuel's literary attainments. Judah's combination of tenderness and firmness, of pushing his son away with one hand, while drawing him closer with the other hand,[30] seems to have borne fruit.

Judah ibn Tibbon
"Ethical Will"

You know, my son, that the Creator did not specify a recompense for any of the Ten Commandments except for honoring

parents. Length of days and happiness were the appointed
reward of obedience. For the Torah says: (Deuteronomy 5:16)
"Honor your father and mother . . . that your days may be long,
and that it may go well with thee;" and in the Prophecies, God
asks of Israel: "If then I be a father, where is My honor?"
(Malachi 1:6). . . .

You know, my son, how I swaddled you and brought you up,
how I led thee in the paths of wisdom and virtue. I fed and
clothed you; I spent myself in educating and protecting you, I
sacrificed my sleep to make you wise beyond your fellows, and
to raise you to the highest degree of scholarship and morality.
These twelve years I have denied myself the usual pleasures and
relaxations of men for your sake, and I still toil for your
inheritance. . . .

Seeing that God had graced you with a wise and understanding heart, I journeyed to the ends of the earth, and fetched
for you a teacher in secular sciences. I minded neither the
expense nor the danger of the ways. Untold evil might have
befallen me and thee on those travels, had not the Lord been
with us!

But you, my son! have deceived my hopes. You did not
choose to apply your abilities, hiding yourself from all your
books, not caring to know them or even their titles. Had you
seen your own books in the hand of others, you would not have
recognized them; had you need of one of them, you would not
have known whether it was with you or not, without asking me;
you did not even consult the catalogue of your library. Ben
Mishle (Samuel the Prince) says:

> He who has toiled and bought for himself books,
>   But his heart is empty of what they contain —
> Is like a lame man, who engraved on a wall
>   The figure of a foot, and tried in vain to stand!

All this you have done. Thus far you have relied upon me to
rouse you from the sleep of indolence, thinking that I would live
with you forever! You did not bear in mind that death must
divide us, and that there are daily vicissitudes in life. But who
will be as tender to you as I have been, who will take my place —
to teach you out of love and good will? Even if you could find
such a one, lo! you see how the greatest scholars, coming from
the corners of the earth, seek to profit by my society and

instruction, how eager they are to see me and my books. But you, though all this was yours without silver and price, you were unwilling; and God has not given you a heart to know, eyes to see, or ears to hearken unto this day. May God endow you with a new heart and spirit, and instill into you a desire to retrieve the past, and to follow the true path henceforward! . . .

If the Lord please to bring me back to you, I will take upon me all your wants. For whom indeed do I toil but for you and your children? May the Lord let me see their faces again in joy!

Therefore, my son! Stay not your hand when I have left you, but devote yourself to the study of the Torah and to the science of medicine. But chiefly occupy yourself with the Torah, for you have a wise and understanding heart, and all that is needful on your part is ambition and application. I know that you will repent of the past, as many have repented before you of their youthful indolence. . . .

Therefore, my son! Exert yourself while you are still young, the more so as you even now complain of weak memory. What, then, will you do in old age, the mother of forgetfulness? Awake, my son! from your sleep; devote yourself to science and religion; habituate yourself to moral living, for "habit is master over all things." As the Arabian philosopher (Al-Ghazzali) holds, there are two sciences, ethics and physics; strive to excel in both! The sage of blessed memory said: "The wise shall inherit honor," while as for wisdom, "length of days is in her right hand, in her left riches and honor" (Proverbs 3:35). And further: "Better is a poor and wise child than an old and foolish king" (Ecclesiastes 14:13). . . .

You are well aware, my son, that the companionship of the ungodly is noxious, that their example cleaves like the plague. O "enter not into the path of the wicked!" (Proverbs 4:14). Loiter not in the streets, sit not in the highway, go not with him whose society is discreditable. As the sage says: "He that walks with wise men shall be wise" (Proverbs 13:20). . . .

My son! Make books your companions, let your cases and shelves be your pleasure-grounds and gardens. Bask in their paradise, gather their fruit, pluck their roses, take their spices and their myrrh. If your soul be satiated and weary, change from garden to garden, from furrow to furrow, from prospect to prospect. Then will your desire renew itself, and your soul will be filled with delight! . . . So Ben Mishle says:

The wise of heart forsakes the ease of pleasure,
  In reading books he finds tranquility;
All men have faults, your eyes can see them,
  The wise heart's failing is—forgetfulness!
Consult a man of sense and well-beloved,
  Put not your trust in your own device;
For if you turn to your heart's desire,
  Desire will hide from you the right. . . .

Contend not with men, and meddle not "with strife not your own" (Proverbs 26:17). Enter into no dispute with the obstinate, not even on matters of Torah. On your side, too, refrain from subterfuges in argument, to maintain your case even when you are convinced that you are in the right. Submit to the majority and do not reject their decision. Risk not your life by taking the road and leaving your city, in times of disquiet and danger. Even where large sums are involved, travel only on the advice of men of mature judgment who are well disposed to you; trust not the counsel of the young in preference to that of the old. Let not the prospect of great gain blind you, to make light of your life; be not as a bird that sees the grains but not the net. Remember what the sage, of blessed memory, said: "A wise man fears and departs from evil, but the fool behaves overbearingly and is confident" (Proverbs 14:16). . . .

Show honor to yourself, your household, and your children, by providing decent clothing, as far as your means allow; for it is unbecoming for anyone, when not at work, to go shabbily dressed. Spare from your belly and put it on your back! . . .

Let your countenance shine upon the sons of men; tend their sick and may your advice cure them. Though you take fees from the rich, heal the poor gratuitously; the Lord will requite you. Thereby shall you find favor and good understanding in the sight of God and man. Thus will you win the respect of high and low among Jews and non-Jews, and your good name will go forth far and wide. You will rejoice your friends and make your foes envious. For remember what is written in the *Choice of Pearls*. "How shall one take vengeance on an enemy? By increasing one's own good qualities.". . .

My son! Examine regularly, once a week, your drugs and medicinal herbs, and do not employ an ingredient whose properties are unknown to you. I have often impressed this on you in vain when we were together.

My son! When you write, read it through a second time, for
no man can avoid slips. Let not any consideration of hurry
prevent you from revising a short epistle. Be punctilious as to
grammatical accuracy, in conjugations and genders, for the
constant use of the vernacular sometimes leads to error in this
regard. A man's mistakes in writing bring him into disrepute;
they are remembered against him all his days. As our Sages say:
"Who is it that uncovers his nakedness here and it is exposed
everywhere? It is he who writes a document and makes mistakes therein.". . .

See to it that your penmanship and handwriting is as
beautiful as your style. Keep your pen in fine working order,
use ink of good color. Make your script as perfect as possible,
unless forced to write without proper materials, or in a pressing
emergency. The beauty of a composition depends on the
writing, and the beauty of the writing on pen, paper, and ink;
and all these excellencies are an index to the author's worth. . . .

For writing, as I said above, is an art among the arts, and the
more care one takes the better is the result. Be fastidious, too, in
the alignment; the lines must be straight, and the spacing
uniform, so that one does not go up and another down. And
may your God prosper you, and make you straight in all your
ways!

And now, my son! in many of these matters, wherein you did
not obey me when I was with you, obey me at this time, when
I am far off. In all your business, your buying and selling, you
did not do me the honor to ask my advice, nor did you even
keep me informed. Whenever I asked you, you were impatient
and concealed the facts from me. If I gave you advice you
rejected it, though never did you succeed when you acted
against my counsel. Ben Mishle says:

> The father of a son who brought
>   His child to the house of the wise,
> And pointed out the way of life,
>   But he chose the path of the proud;
> Who breathed in him, to fire his mind,
>   But he refused to tend the fire;
> Leave him! and reliance place
>   On time for his discipline! . . .

Worse still, when you wrote your letters or composed your
poems to send abroad, you were unwilling to show a word to

me and you prevented me from seeing them. When I said to you, "Show me!," you would answer: "Why do you want to see?" as if thinking that my help was unnecessary. And this was from your folly, in that thou wast wise in thine own eyes. Ben Mishle says:

> Who is wise in his own sight,
> Even thinks his errors just;
> And often the cloud to him does seem
> The sun, the sun a cloud! . . .
> What good is there in life if my work
> Today remains as it was yesterday?

Therefore, my son! Strive to honor me and yourself from this day onwards. All the honor I desire is to be remembered for good because of you in life and death; that those who behold you may exclaim: "Blessed be he who begat this one, blessed be he who reared him!" For I have no son but you by whom my name may be recalled, and all my memory and glory are centered in you. Reward from God and renown from men shall accrue to you, in that you may continue my name for good! . . .

You know what I suffered in bringing you up. You have seen what the learned Rabbi Moses, son of Rabbi Judah, did. He had four sons, and he dispersed them here and there, and went and left them, to marry again. But I, from out of my compassion towards you, did not wish to bring you into the hand of another woman (i.e., a stepmother). But I bore all the anxiety, and great it was, of rearing and caring for you. You know this, and all men know it, for, but for my great devotion you would have died, or lived deformed. Remember these things, my son! and take it to your heart to hear and perform my instructions. Very important is it that you should fulfill my commands regarding your diet. Slay me not before my time! For you know my distress, my soul's sorrow, my fear for you in your sickness. Better death to me than life, that I look not on my wretchedness (see Jonah 4:3, Numbers 11:15). Yearly, as you know, you are visited with sickness (for my sins!), and the chief cause of your complaints is unwholesome food. Ben Mishle says:

> Do you desire your health to hold,
> Over your lust make long thy furrow;
> Wage war against yourself as though
> Opposed to archer or to spearman!

And now, O my son! by the God of heaven, by the obedience to me imposed by His law, by the gratitude due for my rearing and educating you, I adjure you to abstain, with all your resolution, from noxious food! Experience has taught you how much you have suffered from carelessness in this regard. Be content with little and good, and beware of hurtful sweets. "Eat no eating that prevents thee from eating." What is the use of all your wisdom if "you lay a snare for my life, to cause me to die?" (1 Samuel 28:9). Are you not ashamed before yourself and the world when all know that you are periodically sick because of your injurious diet? There is no more disgraceful object than a sick physician, who shall mend others when he cannot mend himself. Ben Mishle says:

> Turn from one who enjoins the doing
>   Of right, but himself is a man of wrong!
> How shall he heal the malady,
>   Who himself suffers from its pain?

Take care of yourself! Preserve your life, be not your own destroyer! And if you have no pity on me and on yourself, have compassion on the child of your delight, the object of your yearning! For I shall be but a little while with you. . . .

My son! I command you to honor thy wife to your utmost capacity. She is intelligent and modest, a daughter of a distinguished and educated family. She is a good housewife and mother, and no spendthrift. Her tastes are simple, whether in food or dress. Remember her assiduous tendance of you in your illness, though she had been brought up in elegance and luxury. Remember how she afterwards reared your son without man or woman to help her. Were she a hired nurse she would have earned your esteem and forbearance; how much the more, since she is the wife of your bosom, the daughter of the great, are you bound to treat her with consideration and respect. To act otherwise is the way of the contemptible. The Arab philosopher says of women: "None but the honorable honoreth them, none but the despicable despises them." . . . honor her with all your might; do not exercise too severe an authority over her; our Sages have expressly warned men against this. If you give orders, let your words be gentle. Enough is it if your displeasure is visible in your glance, let it not be vented in actual rage. Let your expenditure be well ordered. It is remarked in the *Choice of*

Pearls: "Expenditure properly managed makes half an income."
And there is an olden proverb: "Go to bed without supper and
rise without debt." Defile not the honor of your countenance by
borrowing; may God preserve you from that habit! . . .

My son! Devote your mind to your children as I did to you;
be tender to them as I was tender; instruct them as I instructed;
take care of them as I took care of you! Try to teach them Torah
as I have tried, and as I did unto you do you unto them! Be not
indifferent to any slight ailment in them, or in yourself (may
God deliver you and them from all sickness and plague), but if
you do notice any suspicion of disease in you or in one of your
limbs, do forthwith what is necessary in the case. As Hippocrates has said: Time is short, and experiment dangerous.
Therefore be prompt, but apply a sure remedy, avoiding
doubtful treatment . . . my son, honor your friends, and seek
opportunities to profit them by your wisdom, in counsel and
deed. . . .

My son! It can never be in your power to requite such
kindnesses; for no man can, all his days, repay one who has
been in advance of him in friendship. As the Scripture says (Job
41:3): "Who has given me anything beforehand that I should
repay him?" And O beware of the inimical and envious.

My son! Visit your sisters constantly in your letters, and
inquire after their welfare. Show honor to your relatives, for
they will appreciate thy courtesies.

I enjoin on you, my son, to read this, my testament, once
daily, at morn or at eve. Apply your heart to the fulfillment of its
behests, and to the performance of all therein written. Then will
you make your ways prosperous, then shall you have good
success.

14

How to Speak about Another

I n the beginning . . . God said" (Genesis 1:1, 3). In the beginning, there was the word.

Words create worlds. According to the Jewish mystics, good words create good worlds; evil words create evil worlds. Words have power: creative power and destructive power. Words can hurt or heal. They can form or deform a relationship. They can be a barrier or a window. They can endear or abuse. They can encourage tenderness or violence. Words can initiate both creativity and destructiveness, life and death. As Proverbs (18:21) says, "Life and death are in the power of the tongue." On this verse in Proverbs the Talmud comments: "One who wants life can find it through the tongue; one who desires death can find it through the tongue."[1]

In the eleventh century, Bahya ibn Pakudah wrote, "Through speech the human person expresses his or her thoughts and understands the thoughts of others. The tongue is the pen of the heart, the interpreter of the soul, the ambassador of the mind. . . . Speech is the best proof of virtue or vice. It has already been said that the human being *is* his or her heart and tongue."[2] According to Ibn Pakudah, what one says and how one speaks reveals a person's character.[3] In a similar vein, Judah Loew of Prague said, "Speech is like the fruit of a tree. One can know the nature of the tree from the fruit it produces."[4] According to Loew, how one uses language reflects one's moral virtues and one's moral deficiencies.[5] In this view, how one speaks, why one speaks, and what one says can be either an obstacle or a catalyst in the task of creating one's life as a work of art. In Judah Loew's words, "The world is actualized by human beings who were created last of all creatures, and the human being is actualized by means of speech. Speech is that which brings about the fulfillment of the human being."[6] Judah Loew further taught that the human being is a composite of the intellectual and the physical. These two characteristics coalesce in the use of the tongue. The tongue is the nexus between thought, which is intellectual, and speech, which is physical. For Loew, human nature becomes manifest in how the individual person uses the power of speech.[7] In the excerpt below from *Orhot Zaddikim – The Ways of the Righteous*, the text states that "all human affairs depend on the tongue, whether for evil or for good. With the tongue one can commit numerous great and mighty transgressions such as informing, tale-bearing, scoffing, flattery, and telling lies. And none of these bring benefit to the owner of the tongue. But with the tongue, one can also perform limitless acts of virtue."[8] In a similar vein, Judah Loew observed that the first Hebrew letter of the word *lashon*, tongue, points upward, toward God. The last letter points downward, indicating a separation of the person from God. The choice one has is whether one's speech will enhance or degrade the spiritual quality of one's life.[9]

Because of the potential harm that words can cause oneself and others, because of the immense power of the tongue – an otherwise weak and flaccid organ – Jewish ethical literature insists upon its restraint. Unlike the other facial organs, which are receptive, the tongue is active. Because of the damage it can potentially cause, the tongue is more restrained than its fellow facial organs.[10] In this regard, the talmudic rabbis observed:

> Rabbi Jose ben Zimra taught: Come and see how vicious is an evil tongue. A person has 248 body parts, some erect, some prone, some capable of being either one or the other. The tongue, however, is imprisoned with the cheeks and teeth surrounding it, and with many other restraints upon it. Yet no one can withstand it. If it were erect, think how much more vicious it could be.[11]

Not only is the tongue restrained by physiology; but, because of the dangers it poses, it must be further restrained by the application of one's will: "Many have fallen by the edge of the sword, but not so many as have fallen by the tongue" (Ecclesiastes 28:18). Another biblical verse reads, "Their tongue is a sharpened arrow that speaks deceit" (Jeremiah 9:7; see Psalms 120:4). On this verse the talmudic rabbis comment, " 'arrow' refers to the 'evil tongue,' because 'the tongue can kill like an arrow.' "[12]

Because words can destroy, because the employment of wisdom does not often accompany the use of speech, considerable value was placed upon silence over speech. As the excerpt below from *Orhot Zaddikim* says, "One who is accustomed to be silent is saved from many transgressions."[13]

Some chose the path of abstinence from speech altogether. These were

Jewish ascetics who spoke only during prayer. Others imposed upon themselves a "fast of speech." In the eastern European *yeshivot*, there were *schweig bahurim* who refrained from speech during the penitential season of the Jewish calendar year. However, for much of Jewish ethical literature, silence is a segue to prudence in speech rather than to abstinence from speaking at all. Withholding speech is an exercise in learning to appreciate both its power and its value. What Jack London said about writing is equally applicable to speaking: Pretend each word you use costs a thousand dollars. It was the abuse rather than the use of speech that often advised silence. As *Orhot Zaddikim* observes, "Humans were created with two eyes, two ears, and two nostrils, but only with one mouth because one should speak less."[14]

The virtue of silence, as Judah Loew conceived of it, is a compromise between the negative and positive aspects of speech. It is essentially restricted speech, rather than complete silence. Since the human being is a "speaking animal," speech is a necessary feature of human existence.[15] However, the use of speech or of silence requires sound judgment and prudence. As the *Choice of Pearls* says, "One who is able to make right use of speech is able to make right use of silence."[16]

"Silence is the best medicine," counsels the Talmud.[17] Specifically, it is preventative medicine. The *Choice of Pearls* recommends one to consider that "If I utter a word, it becomes my master. If I do not utter it, I remain its master." And further, "I can retract what I did not say, but I cannot retract what I already have said."[18]

"Silence," says the Talmud, "is beneficial for the wise, but how much more beneficial is it for the foolish."[19] While silence may be utilized by the wise, it is not always a sign of wisdom.[20] As Benjamin Franklin wrote, "Silence is not always a sign of wisdom, but babbling is ever a sign of folly."[21] While silence may often be preferable to speech, while silence is always preferable to abusive or foolish speech, silence may be morally wrong in certain situations. For example, silence in the face of evil is wrong because it offers evil, evil people, and morally dangerous ideas an opportunity to proliferate. The nonproliferation of evil demands that one speak out in the face of evil.[22]

In the *Ethics of the Fathers*, we read, "Simon ben Rabban Gamliel said: All my life I was raised among scholars and I found no virtue becomes a person more than silence; what is essential is not study but practice, and one who multiplies words increases sin."[23] This often-quoted citation not only endorses the prudent use of speech and silence, but it also posits the importance of translating what one knows and says into what one does. In this view, speech is a vehicle for action. What one says represents the commitments one makes. What one does either validates or denies those spoken commitments. How one's deeds relate to one's speech indicates whether one is honest or counterfeit, a person of integrity or a hypocrite. As the seventeenth-century

Italian rabbi, Leone da Modena, put it, "Words are the guide to acts; the mouth makes the first move."[24]

Already in Scripture, the requirement to correlate word and deed is stated: "That which has gone out of your lips you shall observe and you shall do" (Deuteronomy 23:24).[25] According to the Talmud, "Pleasant are the words of one who practices what one speaks."[26]

The rabbinic expression for the hypocrite is "one whose inside is not like his outside."[27] Integrity means doing what one says, being what one speaks. It means being true to others, but also to oneself. Self-deception is a common human inclination; integrity is its antidote. As was discussed above, self-deception is a major roadblock in the creation of one's life as a work of art.[28] Just as one is proscribed from deceiving others in word or deed, one is enjoined not to deceive one's own self. In this regard the hasidic master, Bunam of Przysucha, was asked: Who is a *hasid*, who is pious? He answered: One who goes above the requirements of the law. The questioner asked: What is the law? The rabbi replied: It is forbidden to deceive one's neighbor. And what is going above the letter of the law? Not deceiving one's own self.

Rabbi Bunam's disciple, Mendel of Kotsk, interpreted the commandment "You shall not steal" (Exodus 20:13) as including a prohibition against stealing from one's own self.[29] According to Isaac Aboab, the admonition against lying extends to self-deception. He wrote, "There are other matters that fall under the heading of falsehood; for example, when a person praises himself for having virtues he does not possess."[30]

In talmudic parlance, a term for deception is "stealing knowledge" (*genevut da'at*).[31] In Jewish law, a fraud in words is considered more heinous than a fraud in monetary matters, for in the latter case the money can be returned, while in the former case there can be no restitution. The latter case involves money, which is external to the person, while the former case involves a person's own existence and reputation.[32]

The biblical admonition, "You shall not wrong one another" (Leviticus 25:17) has been interpreted to apply to all kinds of deception, including deceptive business practices.[33] For example, Moses Hayyim Luzzatto interprets this verse to relate to one who advertises one's wares with extravagant praise that actually amounts to the deceit of potential customers. Luzzatto refers also to the talmudic prohibition against painting old goods to look like new goods. Luzzatto, following talmudic precedent, further distinguishes between appropriate and inappropriate advertising strategies. It is appropriate to praise good qualities that merchandise actually has, to make good merchandise more attractive for sale by the manner of its presentation to the potential customer, to proclaim the good value of a sale when such value is offered. However, any deviation from integrity or honesty is not deemed acceptable.[34] One should not, for example, camouflage defects in one's goods;

one should not indiscriminately "mark up" goods, thereby trying to convince shoppers that they are worth more than they are. In other words, honest persuasion is permitted; deception is forbidden.[35]

Luzzatto, following rabbinic precedent, includes the giving of misleading advice as a form of improper speech. He wrote, "Whether or not we have an interest in that concerning which our advice is sought, we are morally bound to state the absolute and unqualified truth plainly to anyone who asks our advice." Sometimes, Luzzatto observed, "such advice seems beneficial, but its results injure the one who sought it." According to Luzzatto, in giving advice, "the duty of the upright person is to give whatever counsel he would adopt for himself if he were similarly placed, and to be mindful only of the good of the one who consults him, and have no selfish purpose whatever." However, when asked for advice on how to do evil, one may mislead the person asking advice.[36]

According to the talmudic rabbis, truth is one of the pillars upon which the world rests.[37] Truth is the opposite of deception, of lying. The person of integrity is praised, while the liar is abhorred. According to Mendel of Kotsk, truth cannot be imitated. An imitation of truth is untrue. There is either truth or falsehood. Any deviation from truth is a lie. In Loew's words:

> The Hebrew letter *shin* stands for *sheker*—falsehood, and *tav* stands for truth. As soon as one deviates from the truth by even a single letter, one is involved in a lie. It is for this reason that these two letters are adjacent to one another in the Hebrew alphabet. Furthermore, one should not say that even if one were to lie a little, it would not really matter. . . . For example, if one removes the letter *alef* from *emet*, the word *emet* [truth] becomes *met* [dead] . . . i.e., as soon as anything deviates from truth, it no longer endures; it is dead.[38]

"Lying is a very prevalent disease," Luzzatto wrote. "There are some who actually make it their business to tell lies. They go about inventing stories without any foundation in truth, in order to have material for gossip, or to be considered clever or conversant. Of them it is said, 'Lying lips are an abomination to God' (Proverbs 12:22)."[39] A penalty for the liar, the Talmud says, is that even when such a person speaks the truth, he or she is presumed to be telling a lie.[40]

Despite the enormous value put on telling the truth, there are nonetheless situations in which one should tell a "white lie." For the talmudic rabbis, peace is exalted over truth.[41] In order not to insult another person, so as not to bring about unnecessary discord in a relationship, in order to replace conflict with peace, one is permitted to lie. The classic expression of this view is this talmudic passage:

> How does one dance before the bride? Beth Shammai says: The bride as she is [i.e., one should tell the truth. If the bride is ugly, one should say so.]. Beth Hillel says:

A beautiful and graceful bride [i.e., one should tell a "white lie" so as not to offend the bride or groom]. . . . The sages say: One's disposition with people should always be pleasant.[42]

In this view, while truth is important, it is not of ultimate importance. Truth is a value that exists for the benefit of society, and may, on occasion, be set aside if the well-being of society demands it. Interestingly, in his commentary to this talmudic text, Judah Loew of Prague observed that while it may be a "white lie" for an observer to say the bride is beautiful and graceful, it is not actually a lie since to her prospective husband, she is indeed that way.[43]

Even more important than telling the truth is *how* one tells it. For this reason, gossip is prohibited, even if true. Slander is similarly prohibited, even if true.[44] More important than truth itself is what one does with it. Already in the Talmud, harmful speech, even if true, is called "evil speech" (*lashon ha-ra*).[45]

According to Jonah Gerondi, "Slander is compared to an arrow because just as someone may shoot an arrow at random and not know who it injures, one may release a slanderous word that injures someone indiscriminately."[46] For the talmudic rabbis, slander is worse than murder. In murder, one destroys a single person. In slander, one destroys three people: the one who speaks slander, the one who hears it, and the one about whom it is spoken.[47]

"Slander is blasphemy," wrote Judah Loew.[48] "Whoever speaks slander is as though he or she denied God. . . . Of such a person, God says: He and I cannot dwell together in this world," the Talmud observes.[49]

The *Ethics of the Fathers* states, "Let your neighbor's honor be as dear to you as your own honor."[50] The *Avot d'Rabbi Natan* comments, "Just as one esteems one's own honor, one should esteem his or her neighbor's honor. Just as nobody desires his or her own reputation to be slandered, so let such a person never desire to slander his or her fellow."[51]

Suicide is proscribed by Jewish law. Yet, the Talmud states that "one should prefer to throw oneself into an oven rather than to embarrass one's neighbor in public."[52] "One who shames one's fellow in public is considered as if he shed blood. Rabbi Nahman said: That statement is correct because we see that when a person is publicly embarrassed, his face drains of blood."[53]

"Everyone is guilty of a modicum of the sin of slander," the Talmud observes.[54] Therefore, the rejection of unseemly speech involves refusal to listen to it, and to refrain from indulging in it. As the Talmud says, "Why do human fingers resemble pegs? So that if one hears something unseemly, one can plug one's fingers in one's ears. Why is the ear hard and the earlobe soft? So that if one hears something unworthy, one can plug up one's ear with the earlobe."[55]

Judah Loew observed that unlike other organs, the ears are open. Therefore, what enters cannot leave the body. If one hears evil speech, one becomes infected with it. If one hears good speech, one is ennobled by it. Both what one listens to and what one says shapes who one is.[56] The *Choice of Pearls* quotes an anonymous sage who said, "When I hear evil speech I pay no attention because I am afraid of hearing still worse."[57] Furthermore, it should be noted that the *Amidah* prayer concludes with a meditation in which one asks God to "guard my tongue from speaking evil and my lips from speaking guile, and to those who abuse me verbally may I give no heed."[58]

Because it often tends to lead to slander, gossip and idle conversation are strongly discouraged.[59] In this regard, Aboab compares one who speaks aimlessly and without purpose to an animal who cannot speak at all. Furthermore, Aboab notes that useless speech often leads to abusive speech.[60]

In the *Ethics of the Fathers*, one finds the aphorism "the more words, the more sins." In his commentary to this text, Maimonides observes that when one speaks excessively it is inevitable that one will say something improper. "A multitude of words," Maimonides stated, "is a sign of a fool."[61] Maimonides counsels that one's words should "be few but full of meaning."[62] In a similar vein, Luzzatto describes wanton speech as the prostitution of the faculty of speech.[63]

According to the Talmud, "four kinds of people are not permitted to greet the Divine Presence: mockers, flatterers, liars, and those who engage in evil talk."[64] Like gossip, flattery is discouraged because it tends toward slander or deception. In this regard, Benjamin Franklin wrote:

A flatterer never seems absurd
The flattered always takes his word.

But, as Franklin also said, "The same man cannot be both friend and flatterer." According to the Talmud, "Let no one speak in praise of one's neighbor, for through speaking his praise, one will come to disparage him."[65] "A flattering mouth works ruin," says Proverbs (26:28).

A flatterer cannot be trusted because "his lips and his heart are not one," says the Talmud.[66] Often, flattery is a manipulative, self-serving action of the flatterer. As Isaac Aboab commented, "Some lie by praising and endearing themselves to others in order eventually to exploit them."[67] In this regard, Maimonides wrote:

It is forbidden to accustom oneself to smooth speech and flattery. One must not say one thing and mean another. Inward and outward should correspond; only what we have in mind should we utter with the mouth. We must not deceive anyone. . . . Even a single word of flattery or deception is forbidden. One should always cherish truthful speech.[68]

In the following excerpt from *Orhot Zaddikim—The Ways of the Righteous*, most of the themes discussed above regarding the proper use of speech are to be found. While some authors use words for their own self-aggrandizement, such was not the case with regard to the author of *Orhot Zaddikim*. He apparently believed that conveyance of moral guidance supersedes the glory of self-identified authorship. Following a tradition endorsed by the earlier *Sefer Hasidim—The Book of the Pious* (liberally quoted in his work), our author opted for anonymity. In this view, perpetuation of the tradition, rather than the advertisement of the self, is what is important.[69]

Despite our author's apparent desire for anonymity, modern scholars have attempted to discover his identity and the approximate date and place of the composition of *Orhot Zaddikim*. While scholarly debate continues, there are a number of claims that can be established with some certainty.[70]

References and citations in the book to twelfth- and thirteenth-century Jewish literary sources indicate that *Orhot Zaddikim* is of later origin. A direct reference to the expulsion of the Jews from France in 1394 places its date of composition no earlier than the fifteenth century.[71] That citations from *Orhot Zaddikim* are liberally quoted in sixteenth-century Jewish ethical and kabbalistic texts would suggest that it was written sometime in the fifteenth century, and probably toward the end of that century. Furthermore, the best guess is that the work was not composed in southern Germany as had been assumed, but that it was written somewhere in the Mediterranean Basin, or possibly in Italy. Nonetheless, the exact identity of its author remains a mystery.[72]

The influence of *Orhot Zaddikim* upon future generations has been long-lasting and profound. First published in Prague in 1581, it had a significant impact upon the thought of Prague's most famous Jewish scholar, Judah Loew ("Maharal") of Prague.[73] Its influence was also widespread among the Jewish mystics of the Lurianic movement who flourished in sixteenth-century Safed. Also known as *Sefer ha-Middot, The Book of Ethical Values*, *Orhot Zaddikim* was widely quoted in the classic mystical-ethical work, *Reshit Hokhmah* by Elijah de Vidas, as well as by Isaiah Horowitz in his encyclopedic work of Jewish mysticism, ethics, and law, *Shnei Luhot ha-Brit*. *Orhot Zaddikim* was liberally quoted and widely read in eastern Europe from the late sixteenth century onward.[74] It was especially popular in the nineteenth-century Lithuanian *Musar* movement. Once popularly available in Yiddish translation, it was readily adopted as popular reading among east European Jews.[75] Despite the anonymity of its author, *Orhot Zaddikim* was neither anonymous nor unknown. Its more than seventy editions offered generations of Jews a self-help manual in the art form of life.

Though *Orhot Zaddikim* quotes long excerpts from earlier works, especially *Sefer Hasidim*, Bahya's *Duties of the Heart*, and from various works of Maimonides, it is nonetheless strikingly original in its structure. Unlike other classics of medieval Jewish ethical literature, it was not composed in a linear, systematic hierarchial, nor episodic form. Rather, it is replete with paradox, subtlety, dissonance, and discontinuity. In considering the structure of other classical medieval Jewish ethical works, one can illustrate how this is so.[76]

Jonah Gerondi's *Sha'arey Teshuvah—Gates of Repentance*, written in the thirteenth century, which our author often cites, deals with a single ethical issue, i.e., repentance. Gerondi takes a single moral trait and atomizes it. Not so our author, who deals with a wide variety of ethical traits.

Characteristic of the earliest specimen of Jewish ethical literature, the last chapter of Saadya Gaon's *Book of Beliefs and Opinions*, and of *Sefer Hasidim* (from which our author lifts entire sections intact), is an episodical structure. However, our author has not opted to adapt this approach.

Bahya's *Duties of the Heart* and Luzzatto's *Paths of the Upright* utilize a systematic, hierarchial structure.[77] In these works, the reader is led progressively from lower to higher ethical and spiritual stages of behavior. Each stage, each chapter, serves as the premise and prerequisite for that which follows, the final stage being the summary and quintessence of all that preceded it. Our author rejects this approach as well.

Like other medieval Jewish authors writing under philosophical influence, Bahya begins by establishing "first principles" such as belief in and knowledge of God, and then builds ethical views upon these established philosophical foundations. But, our author does not. Neither does he utilize a homiletical, aphoristic, poetic, legal, or commentary form, characteristic of much of medieval Jewish ethical literature.

At first blush, he seems to discuss singular ethical values, each in a discrete chapter, in a manner not atypical of medieval Jewish ethical literature. Like other treatises, he treats topics such as study, charity, and pride in individual chapters. However, a closer look at his table of contents reveals a novel and subtle approach. A careful perusal of his work reveals a structure that is neither hierarchial, nor singular, nor linear. Rather, his chapter titles form a series of opposites rather than a string of discrete, separated units. For example, the chapter on pride is followed by one on humility. Shame is followed by brazenness, love by hate, mercy by cruelty, happiness by anxiety, generosity by miserliness. Furthermore, within individual chapters not only the moral benefit, but also moral danger, of each virtue is presented. Not only the danger of each moral vice, but surprisingly, also its potential virtue is discussed. For example, while lauding the value of love, our author warns against loving the wicked, thereby encouraging the wicked's continued exploitation and cruelty toward others. While warning of the spiritual dangers of anger and hatred, our author demands anger and hatred toward the wicked as the prelude to taking action to effect his downfall and the threat he poses, as for example, in Mordecai's hatred of and anger toward Haman, without which Haman might have succeeded in destroying the Jews of ancient Persia. Our author recognized that it is desirable to be humble, but sometimes necessary to be brazen. It is important to remember, but sometimes better to forget. He perceived that there may not be hard and fast rules of moral attitude and behavior that are universally applicable to each and every situation. He believed that moral values must be applied to concrete individual situations, and that such situations are often characterized by complexity, paradox, and ambiguity.

For our author, the application of abstract moral values to concrete situations is complex and subtle. Therefore, moral values must be presented in all their subtlety, complexity, and ambiguity. It remains for the individual to know when and where to employ and to apply a particular moral teaching. As the hasidic master, Israel of Rhyzen, put it: Why does the Torah have five books, and the code of Jewish law, the *Shulhan Arukh*, only have four? The missing part is the individual person. For our author, like Israel of Rhyzen, moral teachings are only as good as the ethical judgment of the individual who employs them. Ultimately, the goal of *Orhot Zaddikim* is the goal of all of Jewish ethical literature – not merely to intellectually inform, but spiritually to transform its reader; not to win intellectual assent, but to alter ethical behavior; not to construct a literary structure, but to offer guidance in how to create one's life as a work of art.

Sefer Orhot Zaddikim – The Ways of the Righteous

Our Sages said "that one should not say one thing with one's mouth and another with one's heart."[78] But there are times when the Sages permitted one to lie, for example, in order to make peace between one person and another.[79] Similarly, one may praise a bride in the presence of the bridegroom and say that she is lovely and charming, even though she really is not.[80] A guest who has been well treated by the master of the house should not say in front of many people, "How good that man is in whose house I was a guest, how much honor he paid me," lest many come to that host who are not worthy to be his guests. . . .[81]

Flattery may be divided into nine categories. The first is where a man knows that his friend is a wicked man and a deceiver, that he spreads evil reports about the innocent, that he robs the money of others, and yet this man who knows all this comes and flatters him—not that he actually flatters or praises him, but rather he speaks smoothly to him saying, "You did no wrong in what you did." . . . the flatterer places a stumbling block before the sinner by saying, "You have not sinned," for then the offender will not repent of his evil deeds, and will continue to sin. This is apart from the guilt that the flatterer incurs because of the injury and pain of the people whom the sinner has injured and given pain, and whom the sinner will not reimburse for the damage nor conciliate his victims because of the flattery of the flatterer. For the flatterer justifies the wickedness, as it is said, "He that justifies the wicked and he that condemns the righteous, even they both are an abomination to the Lord" (Proverbs 17:15). All the more is this true if the wrong of the sinner is known to many, and the flatterer flatters the sinner publicly and says, "Pure and upright are you," then the flatterer has profaned the Name of God, he has shown contempt for law and judgment. . . .

There are many stumbling blocks caused by paying honor to the wicked. . . . For when one praises him, the wicked man believes him and considers himself good, and his heart will be uplifted and he will be proud and not repent. For a man who is righteous will say in his heart when people praise him, "I always knew that this was so." And thus the wicked man becomes more corrupt through the flatterer's flattery. . . . Our Sages said, "Everyone who flatters his companion in order to obtain honor, the end of the matter will be that he will depart in shame."[82]

The sixth category of flattery is he who is in a position to protest against an evil and does not protest, nor does he pay any attention to the deeds of the sinners. This thing comes close to flattery, for the sinners think, "As long as they do not protest and do not reproach us, all of our deeds must be good." But we have been commanded to root out the evil from our midst, as it is said, "So shall you put away the evil from your midst" (Deuteronomy 13:6).

And our Sages said, "Everyone for whom it is possible to protest against the sinful things of the people of his household, and he does not protest, is considered guilty of the wrongs of the men of his household. If it is possible for him to protest

against the deeds of the people of his city and he does not do so
he is held responsible for the wrongs of the people of the city. If
it is possible for him to protest against the wrongs of the whole
world and he does not do so, then he is considered guilty of the
wrongs of all the world."[83] And it is said, "And they shall
stumble one upon another" (Leviticus 26:37). And our Rabbis, of
blessed memory, explained it as meaning, "Each man for the sin
of his brother," which teaches us that all Israel are responsible,
one for another. . . .[84]

Now he who wishes to be free from the vice of flattery should
take care to remove himself from seeking honor, for one who
does not care about being honored will have no need to flatter.
And he should also be very careful not to derive benefit from
others, for most flatterers flatter a man when they think they
will obtain some benefit from him. Therefore, he who keeps
away from these two things, benefit and honor, is saved from
many transgressions. For many people do good deeds in order
to receive honor from others, and this spoils all of a person's
good work. . . .

The term "gossip" applies to anyone who tells anything that
defames his companion, even though he speaks the truth, while
one who speaks falsehood is called "one who brings forth an evil
repute." A gossip who sits and says, "Thus and thus did so and
so do? and thus and thus were his ancestors, and thus and thus
did I hear concerning him," and he says shameful things—of
him the Scriptures say, "May the Lord cut off all flattering lips,
the tongue that speaks proud things" (Psalms 12:4).

Our Rabbis, of blessed memory, said, "If one speaks gossip,
it is as though he denied God." . . .[85] And it is important to give
the full meaning in this matter, for a gossip repeats his folly; ten
times or more every day he humiliates and shames people, aside
from the damage that he does to the one he speaks against. And
even a small transgression, when done many times, becomes
great, just as although a single hair is soft and very weak, if you
gather many hairs together, you can make of them a strong
rope. . . .

Moreover, a gossip finds it difficult to repent, because he is
used to this habit and has taught his tongue to speak evil.
Furthermore, this sin appears very light in his eyes, for he says,
"I did not do anything—it was just talk." He does not consider
the great damage he does, and therefore he does not repent.
And even if he should repent, his repentance is not complete,

for he does not realize the enormity of the sin which he has committed. Moreover, he must first obtain forgiveness from those against whom he has spoken, and he cannot remember whom they all are. And it may happen that he spoke against a man, and did him evil, and caused him harm and forgot what it was that he said about that man, for gossip is always covered up; it is a blow struck in secret. The gossiper is here and smites with his tongue a person who is far away from him.[86] And this type of sinner is ashamed to let his victim know that he has done him evil. Sometimes he speaks about a defect in the family of the object of his gossip, thus injuring the generations that come after him, and there is no forgiveness for this, for our Sages said, "For one who speaks about a flaw in a family, there is no forgiveness eternally." . . .[87] We can conclude that "life and death are in the power of the tongue" (Proverbs 18:21). And it is said, "And those who love her will eat her fruit" (ibid.). This means that one who loves the tongue, that is to say a man who loves to speak constantly, it is worthy and true counsel to him that he should eat of its fruit. In other words, he should not speak idle talk, but should speak words of the Torah, or words that will teach many to do good, and he should teach them the good and keep them far from evil, and to be zealous for the truth, for there is no end to the good deeds that a man may do with his tongue. And this is the meaning of "life and death are in the power of the tongue."

Gossips may be divided into six categories. The first is he who speaks evil of people and says, "Thus did they do," when in fact they did not do so, and at times he will slander an honorable and innocent person—in which case he is both a liar and a gossip. And we have been warned by the Torah not to accept gossip because it may be false, as it is said, "You shall not utter a false report" (Exodus 23:1). And one who speaks gossip, will also be quick to accept gossip. And you should know that if one who hears gossip endorses what he has heard, then he is just as guilty as the gossiper. For all who hear that he agreed, will say, "Since he endorses it, it must be true." And even if he does not agree, but simply listens intently to the words, and appears to believe them, in the presence of people, he causes others to believe them too, and thus he helps the gossiper. For if he were to scold the gossiper, then he might restrain him from telling more, but since he pays attention and shows that he is interested, he causes him to speak even more gossip. And, behold, we have been warned by the verse, "You shall not utter a false report" that we should not believe a gossip story in our hearts, for this would leave a strong imprint in our thoughts that the words are true and cause us to despise the object of the gossip.

The second category; he who speaks gossip that is true. Even if he should remind another in private of some evil deed of his ancestors, he transgresses what is written in the Torah, "And you shall not wrong one another" (Leviticus 25:17); it is concerning wrongs done with words that the Scripture speaks.[88]

The third category of gossip is he who, in the presence of others, shames another because of something which his ancestors did. Concerning this our Sages, of blessed memory, said, "Everyone who causes the face of his companion to whiten (through shame) in public has no share in the World to Come."[89]

The fourth category of gossip is this: If one publicly makes known the abominations of someone's ancestors, although not in the presence of the victim of the gossip, in order to shame him in the eyes of people—concerning this they said, "A group which speaks gossip cannot receive the Divine Presence."[90]

The fifth category is this: If the object of the gossip is a former sinner who has repented, and someone tells about the sins that he committed before he repented, in this there is great guilt.[91] "For one who repents of his wrongdoing, his sins now become merit."[92] And this gossiper shames him with sins that, through repentance, have become his merit. Moreover, he places a stumbling block before him for the victim may think in his heart, "Just as he shamed me so shall I shame him," and enter into a quarrel with him, with the result that he perverts his repentance and returns to his former state. Moreover, others who hear of this one's shame may be restrained from repenting their evil deeds, and thus the gossiper has locked the doors of repentance. And know, that if a man sees that his companion transgressed a commandment in secret and he reveals it in public, he is guilty of a sin, for perhaps the transgressor has repented of his evil way and did not want to admit it except to an understanding Sage who would not shame him, so that he could repent of his evil deed. But one should keep away from one who has done evil until he knows that his companion has repented of his evil way. . . .

In a sense, the sin of one who gossips about something that

is true is greater than that of one who tells false gossip. For when a man tells true things about another, people believe him and the victim remains contemptible in their eyes even after he has shown remorse and repented his sin; but as for false gossip, most people will understand that it is a lie and will not believe it. But, in general, falsehood carries a greater guilt than the truth. . . .

And our Sages, of blessed memory, said, "Gossip slays three people—the one who speaks gossip, the one who listens to it and the one about whom the gossip is said."[93] And he who listens to the gossip is guiltier than he who speaks it. It is forbidden to dwell in the neighborhood of gossips, all the more so is it forbidden to sit with them and listen to their words.

There is another evil in gossip and that is that the one who speaks gossip against his companion feels proud and appears in his own eyes as a righteous person, for he thinks, "So and so did thus and thus, but I did not do anything like it." So we find that the gossip vaunts himself and claims merit for himself. . . .

Then there is he who speaks gossip by way of deceit: he tells it with seeming innocence, as though he does not know that he is indulging in gossip, and when others rebuke him he says, "I really don't know whether so and so is guilty of these things." Or he says, "This may be merely gossip." One who speaks words that cause harm to his fellow man, whether it be to his body or to his money, even though it be to distress him or to frighten him, it is gossip. If a man says something to his companion, he is forbidden to reveal it without his permission.[94] But anything which a man says in front of three people it is as though he intended it to be common knowledge and if one of the three who heard it told about it we cannot say that this is gossip. But if the teller intends to reveal more than he heard, then there is something of gossip in it. And if the speaker warns those who heard him not to reveal it, even though he speaks in the presence of many people, still if one of those who were warned does reveal it, it is a sort of gossip. . . .

And there is another sin which is called tale-bearing. Now, who is a tale bearer? One who loads himself with stories about others and goes from one to another and says, "Thus did so and so say," and "Thus and thus did I hear about that one." Even though what he tells is true, this kind of thing destroys the world. And we have been warned about this, as it is written, "You shall not go up and down as a tale-bearer among your people" (Leviticus 19:16). And what is tale-bearing? One who reveals to another things that were said about him in secret. . . .

Be very careful concerning gossip for with this you shame yourself. For he who finds others unworthy is himself unworthy, and he does not speak in praise of anyone, and his way is to find people unworthy with the fault that he himself possesses.[95] For this fault of his is constantly on his mind and when he gossips he expresses it with his mouth. . . .

A gossip always seeks out the faults of people; he is like the flies who always rest on the dirty spot. If a man has boils, the flies will let the rest of the body go and sit on the boil. And thus it is with a gossip. He overlooks all the good in a man and speaks only of the evil. There is a story about a certain man who went with a wise man in the field, and they saw a corpse. The man said, "How putrid this corpse is." And the wise man said, "How white are its teeth." Thus the wise man rebuked his companion and said in effect, "Why must you speak about its blemish; speak of its excellence, for one should always speak in commendation of the world."

If you see a man who speaks a word or does a deed which can be interpreted either favorably or unfavorably, then if he is a man who reveres God you are obliged to give him the benefit of the doubt, even if the unfavorable interpretation appears more likely. And if he is an ordinary person who guards himself from sin, but occasionally stumbles, it is still your duty to put doubt aside and decide his favor. And our Sages, of blessed memory, said: "He who judges his neighbor in the scale of merit is himself judged favorably." . . .[96]

There are a few instances where it is commendable to engage in gossip. For example, in the case of two wicked men who have taken counsel to do evil, it is permitted, by gossip, to make them hate each other and do evil to one another, in order that they do not do evil to good people. . . .

Because so many things depend upon the tongue, it is necessary to guard the tongue very much. And therefore David said, "Keep your tongue from evil" (Psalms 34:14). And our Sages, of blessed memory, recounted a story about a certain man who cried out in the streets, "Who wants to purchase the elixir of life?" Everybody came to buy. He then took out the Book of Psalms and showed them what was written in it: "Who is the man that desireth life and loveth days, that he may see good therein? Keep your tongue from evil" (Psalms 34:13–14).

And when Rabbi Yannai saw this, he took this man into his house and he fed him and he gave him drink and money. The pupils of Rabbi Yannai came to him and said to him, "Did you not know this verse before?" and he said to them, "I did know it—but I never put it in my heart to be careful concerning this. When I used to read this verse I would go over it hastily and did not realize its full meaning. And now this man came and made it mean something to me, and from now on I shall be more careful with my tongue." . . .[97]

He who is accustomed to be silent, is saved from many transgressions: from flattery, from mockery, from gossip, from lies, and blasphemies. . . . Then too, if a person is silent, others can reveal secrets to him, for inasmuch as he is not accustomed to speak much he will not reveal the secret. Moreover, it is not his habit to indulge in gossip, and concerning this it is said, "Death and life are in the power of the tongue" (Proverbs 18:21), for a man can do more harm with his tongue than he can with a sword. For a man can stand here and yet betray his companion, who is a long distance from him, and cause his death (by his word), while the sword can only slay someone who is near it. Therefore man was created with two eyes, two ears, two nostrils and one mouth to say to him that he ought to speak less. Silence is fitting for the wise, and thus all the more so for fools. "A fence around wisdom is silence."[98] "There is no better medicine than silence."[99]

The general rule here is this: When a man makes a door for the entrance to his house, there is a time to open it and a time to close it. So should he close the doors of his mouth, for there are actually two doors, the lips and the teeth. And be very careful as to when you open your mouth, and guard your tongue as you would silver and gold and pearls in your room and in your jewel case, and make a lock for the lock. Observe how the Sages of old guarded themselves from idle talk all their days. And in this way you will acquire the great virtue of praying with complete devotion for most of the interference with devotion in prayer comes from frivolous things that are stuck in one's mind. Silence is also a great fence for the reverence of God, for it is impossible to have reverence of God in one that speaks too much.

15

How to Be Philanthropic

One often hears or reads about "Judeo-Christian ethics." Underlying such references is the assumption of a continuity and a correlation, if not an identity, between Jewish ethics and Christian ethics. Spokespersons for both the Jewish and Christian communities evoke the "Judeo-Christian ethic" to describe and to justify the propriety of certain ideas, values, and social programs. But, one may ask whether "Judeo-Christian ethics" exists, and why such a notion has become part of popular parlance. To understand how and why the concept of a Judeo-Christian ethic came to be, one must look at the historical and ideological context from which it emerged.

With the Jewish Emancipation in western Europe beginning in the eighteenth century, Jews faced a choice. They could either perpetuate the ghettoized state that characterized the pre-Emancipation period, or they could seek full social and political membership in the societies in which they lived. The majority of Jews in western Europe chose the latter option. One way of attaining full social and political membership was through conversion to the dominant faith of their society, i.e., Christianity. This was the path of complete assimilation and apostasy that some Jews took, including writers such as Heinrich Heine, and composers such as Gustav Mahler. However, a second path, taken by the majority of Jews, was to try to demonstrate that Jews and Judaism deserved inclusion in society because Jews were not essentially different from other western Europeans and Judaism was similar to Christianity in terms of its essential beliefs and values. Jews tended to speak of themselves as Germans, Austrians, or Frenchmen of "the Mosaic

211

persuasion" rather than as "Jews." From this perspective there were, for example, Germans of a variety of faiths – Protestant, Catholic, and "Mosaic," all full partners in the German state, German culture, and German society. Jews spoke of themselves as "Mosaic" or as "Hebrews" to stress their identity with the "Old Testament," which Christians also held sacred, and to deemphasize their attachment to the Talmud, which Christians considered the tool by which biblical faith was perverted by the rabbis. This was part of the tactic of showing what was held in common rather than what divided Jews and Christians.

A popular definition of Judaism during this period was "Judaism is ethical monotheism." This definition stresses the essential sameness of Judaism and Christianity, i.e., both religions are monotheistic and both affirm similar, if not identical, ethical values. This emphasis on the essentially ethical nature of Judaism was influenced by the greatest philosopher of the eighteenth century, Immanuel Kant. This is ironic, since it was Kant who claimed that Judaism had no ethics at all, that Judaism was at best an amoral and at worst an immoral religion.

For Kant, a moral act had to meet two criteria. It had to be an expression of the autonomous free will, i.e., a moral act could not be synonymous with obedience to a law. Secondly, a moral act had to be universal, i.e., applicable to all human situations and not merely to those relevant to a specific group. Since, in Kant's view, Judaism requires obedience to Jewish law, and since Jewish law relates primarily if not exclusively to the behavior of Jews and not to all human beings, Jews practicing Judaism could not fulfill these Kantian criteria for moral action.[1] Kant therefore considered Judaism at best obsolete and at worst morally dangerous, and called for the "euthanasia" of Judaism. Kant considered Christianity the first great religion, a revolutionary contribution to humankind rather than an outgrowth of Judaism.

In response to Kant's influential views regarding the nature of moral action, Jews – especially in Germany and later in America – accepted Kant's assumptions regarding the nature of moral action, and attempted to refute his negative view of Judaism by demonstrating that ethics, as he defined it, is not only compatible with Judaism but is essential to Judaism.[2] In the process of responding to Kant's views, Jewish thinkers convinced few individuals other than themselves of the "Kantian" character of Jewish ethics. However, in order to make Judaism more correlative with Kantian views on ethics, they distorted the nature of Judaism and of Jewish ethics by substantially dispensing with two of its major characteristics: Jewish law and the particular relationship of Judaism to the Jewish people (in order to meet the Kantian criterion of universality). One may suggest, therefore, that Jews embraced the idea of a Judeo-Christian ethic in order to further a particular social and political agenda characteristic of the post-Emancipation period, and that they distorted the very nature of Judaism and of Jewish ethics in order to accelerate their hope for social and political acceptance in the societies in which they lived.

Christians who understood Christianity to be an organic continuation of Judaism maintained that Judaism is the premise of which Christianity is the conclusion and the fulfillment. Such Christians saw Christianity as depending upon Judaism for its roots and its authenticity. From this perspective, the affirmation of a Judeo-Christian ethic legitimizes Christianity as the continuation of Judaism, as a bough grafted onto the tree of Jewish faith.[3] Some versions of this view claim that Judaism, i.e., biblical Judaism, is but a prelude to Christianity, and that in our times, Judaism is obsolete and Jews are but potential Christians who should be shown "the light" and the "good news" of the Christian gospel. Thus, just as affirmation of a Judeo-Christian ethic served certain particularly Jewish agendas, so was it meant to serve certain particularly Christian agendas.

From what has been said, one may suggest that the idea of a Judeo-Christian ethic, beyond being an attempt to further certain self-serving Jewish or Christian agendas, is essentially a fabrication.[4] There is Jewish ethics, and there is Christian ethics. There is no Judeo-Christian ethic. The theological assumptions and categories, the textual resources, and the methodologies that characterize Jewish ethics and Christian ethics differ so substantially that to perpetuate the claim that a Judeo-Christian ethic exists would be a misunderstanding of both Judaism and Christianity. One ethical issue that can be utilized as a means of demonstrating some of the vital differences between Jewish ethics and Christian ethics is the area of social welfare and aid to the indigent.[5] It is to this issue that our attention now turns.

Whereas for Christianity, messianic redemption is a fact, for Judaism it is an expectation. Christianity assumes that the Messiah has come; Judaism assumes that the Messianic Age is yet to dawn. Consequently, Christian ethics tends to view the world in "messianic" terms while Jewish ethics tends to view the world in "messy" terms.[6] For example, many contemporary Christian ethicists call for full employment, an end to poverty, and a world at peace. Jewish ethicists perceive this view as a messianic hope rather than a realistic confrontation with the problems besetting us now in our "messy" world. For Christian ethics, the Kingdom of Heaven has been inaugurated with the advent of the Messiah in the person of Jesus Christ. For Jewish ethics, the Kingdom of Heaven is yet to be realized. At present, "the earth is given into the hands of the wicked" (Job 9.24). "In this world," says a midrash, "war, suffering, the evil inclination, Satan and the angel of death hold sway."[7] Although Judaism considers God as an ally in the struggle against evil, divine redemption is a hope rather than a fact. Human beings can and should engage in the battle to eliminate war, poverty, and evil, but only God can win this war. For Judaism, that victory is yet to begin. As Abraham J. Heschel put it, "At the end of days, evil will be conquered by the One; in historic times, evils must be conquered one by one."[8] An example of the messianic approach characteristic of a great deal of Christian ethics is the "U.S. Catholic Bishops' Pastoral Letter on the Economy." In that document, the eradication of poverty and the attainment of full employment are considered realizable goals, rather than desirable hopes. Nowhere does this document quote the biblical assumption that "there will never cease to be needy ones in your land" (Deuteronomy 15:11).[9]

With regard to social welfare, Jewish ethics assumes that there are infinite needs, but finite resources with which to address those needs. Jewish ethics considers poverty and hardship to be perennial features of life in a "messy," premessianic world. Consequently, Jewish ethics insists that the social and economic needs of the disadvantaged must be addressed and that they must be assuaged, but that it would be unrealistic to assume they could be completely eliminated. Consequently, Jewish ethical teachings regarding social and economic welfare relate more to treating the dis-ease of the individual in need rather than trying to completely cure the economic or social afflictions of society as a whole. Jewish social welfare is individual centered, "client" centered, rather than focused on the messianic task of curing society of all of its economic and social woes. Jewish ethics deals with the problems of the individual poor rather than with trying to solve the problem of poverty. Jewish ethics focuses on the individual in need and upon the specific needs of that individual, rather than being overly preoccupied with remedying the ills of society at large. Indeed, exclusive concentration upon eternal problems, rather than upon present individual needs, may lead to the benign neglect of the individual in need. Trying to solve the problem of poverty as a whole may lead to evasion of the present needs of the poor. Trying to bring about the messianic world in premessianic times inevitably leads to frustration, which in turn can lead one to despair and inaction.

Christian ethics considers helping those in need as acts of "charity" and "philanthropy." Both terms derive from etymological roots in Latin and Greek that refer to love (caritas), specifically to the love of other people (philanthropia). In this view, one should help those in need because of one's love for them. But, the poor, the indigent, the insane, and the critically ill do not usually evoke one's love, unless somebody is one of those rare saints who populate the world from time to time. Help for the needy based upon love is too unreliable to help ensure their welfare, their aid. Consequently, Jewish ethics bases help for the needy upon social obligation, rather than upon spontaneous love. While such spontaneity may be desirable, in the final analysis it is undependable. The needs of the indigent are too constant and numerous to rely upon the spontaneous altruism of the potential donor. For Jewish ethics, *zedakah* rather than "charity" is required.

"*Zedakah*" is etymologically related to "justice" and "righteousness." In this view, one regularly helps the needy because it is just; because it is right. *Zedakah* is a regular and continuous social obligation, and not the result of a passing passion.[10] For this reason, the *Orhot Zaddikim* recommends habitual giving over impulsive philanthropy:

> The quality of generosity depends on habit, for a person cannot be considered generous unless that person gives of his or her own free will at all times, at all hours, according to his or her ability. A person who gives a thousand gold pieces to a worthy person is not as generous as one who gives a thousand gold pieces on a thousand different occasions, each to a worthy cause. For the person who gave a thousand gold pieces at one time had a sudden impulse to be generous, but after that the desire left him.[11]

Biblical law could not leave the care of the needy to impulsive, though altruistic giving, to "charity" or "philanthropy." Nor could it leave too general or too vague the admonition to "open your hand to the poor and the needy" (Deuteronomy 15:14). Rather, the Bible established specific regulations for the giving of *zedakah*, which were amplified and refined during the talmudic and medieval periods, as for example in the selection from Maimonides' legal code excerpted below.[12] According to these laws, those who had, were obliged to give; those who were in need, were entitled to take. These laws not only set down the requirement to give, but they also defined the parameters of giving. *Zedakah* was more a tax, a legal obligation, than an act of capricious benevolence. Beginning with biblical law, abstract categories of justice and righteousness were translated into specific legal requirements for providing financial assistance to those in severe economic need.

The biblical laws of *zedakah* assume and address an agricultural society. According to one biblical injunction, the products of the corners of each field should not be collected by the harvesters, but should be left for the needy to take. Neither the products of a field nor of a vineyard should be totally collected; something should be left for the poor (Leviticus 19:9-10, 23:22). Each seventh year, the land is to be left fallow. Whatever the land produces during that year may be claimed by the needy (Exodus 23:10-11). In addition, that which was not reaped when a field was harvested, as well as a tithe of all one's net income, is designated for the poor (Deuteronomy 24:19, 26:12). On festivals, special contributions were made in order that the indigent could also rejoice at those times (Deuteronomy 16:9-14). Each fiftieth year, i.e., the Jubilee year, all real estate holdings are to be returned to their original owners (Leviticus 25:9-15). In this way, the impoverished could be economically restored.

Biblical law also prohibits the charging of interest (Leviticus 25:35–37, Exodus 22:24). Commenting on this law, Rashi notes that the Hebrew word for interest (*neshekh*) is related to the word for a bite (*neshikhah*). In Rashi's words:

> *Neshekh* means interest since it is like the bite (*neshikhah*) of a snake, which bites making a small wound on one's foot which he does not feel, but suddenly it blows up as far as his head. So with interest—one does not feel it and it is not at first noticeable until the interest increases and causes one to lose much money.[13]

The biblical characterization of a just society was one where the needy are cared for, where the vulnerable are protected. The unjust society, the society deserving of destruction such as Sodom and Gemmorah, is one that neglects the indigent. For example, the prophet Ezekiel observes (Ezekiel 16:49), "Only this was the sin of your sister Sodom: arrogance! She and her daughters had plenty of bread and untroubled tranquility; yet she did not support the poor and the needy."

The legal obligation of *zedakah*, established by the Bible, was developed by the talmudic rabbis, and was codified in the medieval legal codes. Through this process of development, an attempt was made to relate the laws of *zedakah* to a society that was primarily commercial rather than primarily agricultural, to an urban as well as to an agrarian society. Despite these adaptations of biblical agricultural statutes to later socioeconomic conditions, the understanding of *zedakah* as a legal duty and as a religious imperative remained constant. According to Maimonides, one who gives *zedakah* fulfills a positive commandment.[14] One who does not give *zedakah* violates a negative commandment. Furthermore, Maimonides insists, "It is our duty to be more careful in the performance of the commandment of *zedakah* than in that of any other positive commandment."[15]

Biblical law established, and rabbinic law developed, the view that everyone was obliged to donate, even the poor.[16] The medieval codes express the inevitable tension between the needs of the prospective recipients and the abilities as well as the generosity of the prospective donors. The codes therefore establish that ten percent ought to be considered as the average donation. Less brands one an evil person. One-third of a *shekel* is defined as the most minimal donation. One-fifth of one's income is established by the Talmud as the ceiling on donations to *zedakah*.[17] The ceiling of one-fifth was instituted because the rabbis apparently felt that individuals might otherwise impoverish themselves, thereby becoming clients of social welfare, through over-exuberant or compulsive giving.

Despite the emphasis upon *zedakah* as an unequivocal religious, social, and legal obligation, it would be a mistake to conclude that the idea of altruism or benevolence is absent from Judaism. Though some authors claim that the Jewish notion of *zedakah* is deficient in that it emphasizes law to the neglect of love (i.e., "philanthropy"), such a claim can hardly be substantiated by the Jewish sources themselves. Rather, Jewish religious literature seeks to strike a balance between law and love, between obligation and generosity.

Zedakah represents the minimal requirement, but more is hoped for and expected. *Zedakah* is the necessary but not sufficient expression of concern for the well-being of others. *Zedakah* is complemented by *gemilut hasadim*, acts of lovingkindness. *Zedakah* is what is required by law. *Gemilut hasadim* is an expression of love and of profound concern for others. According to Rashi, *zedakah* denotes the act of giving, while *gemilut hasadim* refers to the noble intentions infused within the act.[18] According to Judah Loew of Prague, the difference between the virtue of giving *zedakah* and the virtue of doing *gemilut hasadim* is that *zedakah* is determined by the needs of the recipient, while *gemilut hasadim* flows from the goodness of the benefactor. In *zedakah*, the recipient benefits only from the benefactor's money. In *gemilut hasadim*, the recipient enjoys the good nature of the benefactor as well. Judah Loew offers this distinction as a commentary to the following talmudic statement:

> Our rabbis taught: In three respects is *gemilut hasadim* superior to *zedakah*. *Zedakah* can be done only with one's money, but *gemilut hasadim* can be done with one's person and with one's money. *Zedakah* can be given to the poor alone, but *gemilut hasadim* can be given to the rich as well as to the poor. *Zedakah* can be given only to the living while *gemilut hasadim* can be done both to the living and to the dead.[19]

Zedakah is justice in action. *Gemilut hasadim* is mercy and love in action. "What is *gemilut hasadim*?" the author of *Sefer Ma'alot ha-Middot* asks. "That one will be merciful to all creatures, as the Creator, may He be blessed, is merciful and full of compassion."[20] By practicing *zedakah*, one fulfills social obligations. By practicing *gemilut hasadim*, one expresses *imitatio Dei*, that which we have in common with God. Through *gemilut hasadim*, one articulates one's having been created in the image of the divine.

Giving *zedakah* fulfills legal requirements; *gemilut hasadim* transcends legal demands. In his philosophical work, *The Guide of the Perplexed*, Maimonides discusses this distinction between *zedakah* and *hesed* (i.e., the root of *hasadim*). According to Maimonides, *zedakah* refers to giving one one's just due while *hesed* refers to absolute beneficence. *Zedakah* means granting something to someone who has a right of entitlement. *Hesed* is the practice of benevolence toward one who has no entitlement to what he or she receives.[21]

Among the actions identified as acts of lovingkindness, as expressions of *gemilut hasadim*, are visiting the sick, burying the dead, comforting the mourner, caring for animals, hospitality to the stranger, and giving *zedakah* without ulterior motives. While the Talmud, as was noted above, put restrictions upon how much *zedakah* one might give, acts of lovingkindness were assigned no such restrictions.[22]

Acts characterized as *gemilut hasadim*, such as burying the dead, are considered expressions of loving-kindness because such acts may be done selflessly, without thought of recompense from the recipient. For example, when Jacob is dying, he asks Joseph to treat him with "kindness (*hesed*) and with truth (*emet*)." On this verse (Genesis 47:29), Rashi comments, "The kindness that is shown to the dead is a true kindness (*hesed shel emet*), for [in such a case] one does not expect the payment of recompense [from the recipient]."

In his ethical treatise *Menorat ha-Ma'or*, Isaac Aboab wrote that "*zedakah* given selflessly for the sake of Heaven, graciously and compassionately, is called *gemilut hasadim*." Thus Aboab identifies *gemilut hasadim* as an exalted variety of *zedakah*. Aboab refuses to relegate *zedakah* to one realm and *gemilut hasadim* to another.[23] Instead, Aboab perceives a certain fluidity between dutiful and benevolent actions. For Aboab, as well as for others, actions that may benefit others embrace a wide spectrum, from self-serving and/or reluctant giving of *zedakah* to perfectly selfless acts of lovingkindness. This notion of "gradations of benevolence" underlies Maimonides' well-known eight levels of *zedakah* found in the text excerpted below.[24]

Virtually all sources agree that even the self-serving donor, even the stingy donor, even the recalcitrant donor fulfills the *mitzvah* of *zedakah* though his intentions may be far from honorable or benevolent. The primary goal is that the needy be cared for. Nevertheless, virtually all sources also agree that what is hoped for is that "the donor of *zedakah* will give for the sake of Heaven, i.e., selflessly, that his or her intention in giving will not be public acclaim or acknowledgement."[25] This tension between the always present requirements of the needy and the desired virtue of the donor pervades the literature regarding *zedakah*. According to some traditions, the act of *zedakah* is essential; the motivation of the donor is secondary. The donor whose primary intention is the expectation of reward, protection from harm, social approval, or personal aggrandizement is still adjudged as having fulfilled the *mitzvah* of *zedakah*, even though helping the needy might not have been the central motivation behind his gift. What is paramount is that the indigent be served. On the other hand, some traditions refuse to consider recalcitrant or self-serving giving as fulfilling the *mitzvah* of giving *zedakah*. For these sources, *zedakah* given with improper intentions perverts the very aim of the entire institution of *zedakah*—the establishment of a just society; such actions are examples of good deeds badly done.[26]

Besides the tension between the actions and the intentions of the donor, the literature regarding *zedakah* articulates a further tension between the obligation and the ability of the donor to give. On the one hand, *zedakah* is viewed as an obligatory tax with defined minimal and maximal amounts. On the other hand, *zedakah* is perceived as a gift, an expression of generosity, limited only by the beneficence of the donor. For example, the view that the obligations of the wealthy to the needy transcend the limits of the law is summarized by the rabbinic aphorism, "In accordance with the camel is its burden."[27]

The endeavor of Maimonides and others to identify levels of *zedakah* may be an attempt to diffuse these tensions presented by the literature on *zedakah*. Rather than presenting opposing views as contradictions, Maimonides places these diffuse and often conflicting opinions as points on a spectrum. On one side of the gamut is the altruistic donor, who preserves the individuality and the dignity of the person in need. On the other side is the self-serving recalcitrant donor, who must be cajoled into reluctant giving. A spectrum of attitudes and motivations links these two extremes. The *mitzvah* of *zedakah* covers a wide field, from selflessness to niggardliness, from minimal legal obligation to extreme selfless generosity, from self-serving intentions to the saintly service of others.

The obligation to help the needy rests upon two theological assumptions: all wealth ultimately belongs to God and human beings must properly fulfill their roles as stewards of God's possessions by aiding those in need.[28] From this perspective, one who can give but who does not give is viewed as a thief, as one who misuses and abuses the trust deposited into his or her hands by God. In this regard, the *Sefer Hasidim* quotes God as saying to the person with means who does not give:

> I have supplied you with abundance so that you may give to the needy to the extent of your means. Yet, you did not give. I [i.e., God] shall punish you as if you have stolen from those people and as if you have denied having in your possession something that I entrusted into your care. The wealth I put into your hand for distribution to the poor, you appropriated for yourself.[29]

The requirement to give *zedakah* is based upon the biblical assumption that in premessianic times there will always be those in need. Unlike certain Christian (particularly Calvinist) traditions, which consider poverty to be a divine punishment, Judaism considers poverty to be a human tragedy. Jewish sources condemn the view of the uncharitable that disparages the poor in an attempt to surrender their social responsibility toward the poor. As Abraham Cronbach wrote, "To the contention that the poor are devoid of decency, the answer is that the poor are devoid of iniquity."[30] According to the *Zohar*, the poor are not alienated from God because of their sins. Rather, they are endeared to God because of their impoverished state. The *Zohar* teaches:

The prayers of the poor are received by God ahead of all other prayers. "Happy is he who is considerate of the poor" (Psalms 41:2). . . . How great is the reward that the poor merit of the Lord . . . for they are closest to God. . . . The poor man is closer to God than anyone else . . . for God abides in these broken vessels, as it is written, "I dwell on high, amid holiness, but also with the contrite and humble in spirit" (Isaiah 57:15). . . . Therefore we have been taught that he who reviles the indigent scoffs at the Divinity. . . . Happy is he who encounters a poor man, for this poor man is a gift sent to him by God.[31]

Were poverty a divine punishment, then *zedakah* would not be the fulfillment of a religious imperative, but an intervention in God's execution of justice.[32] While *zedakah* is invariably portrayed as a virtue, poverty is rarely so portrayed. According to one talmudic source, poverty deprives a person of his senses, i.e., poverty can make one mad.[33] Another talmudic source compares poverty with death,[34] and a third source observes that "poverty in one's home is worse than fifty plagues."[35] A fourth text summarizes this view of poverty as a calamity: "There is nothing in the world more grievous than poverty—the most terrible of all sufferings. . . . Our teachers have said: If all troubles were assembled on one side and poverty on the other, poverty would outweigh them all."[36]

The calamity of poverty was understood not only as posing a physical and a psychological danger as far as the poor were concerned, but a moral danger as well. Driven by destitution, the indigent person might become prone to immoral acts such as robbery, the *Me'il Zedakah* observes. For precisely this reason, the nineteenth-century hasidic master, Aaron of Karlin, taught that "one must have a greater fear of a poor person than of a sword." Thus, poverty, like wealth, has its temptations. *Zedakah* is a way not only of physically and fiscally helping the needy, but a way of aiding the impoverished person morally as well. In this view, *zedakah* and *gemilut hasadim* are means to helping both the giver and the recipient to proceed with the task of creating his or her life as a work of art.

Despite the obligation to give, Jewish religious literature recognizes that the needs of the indigent always surpass the resources of their benefactors. The realization that the needs of the poor seem infinite may lead many potential donors to the conclusion that any philanthropic effort is ultimately futile. The *Me'il Zedakah* argues against this conclusion. Because the impossible cannot be realized is no reason for being dissuaded from achieving the possible. The enormity of the need and the inability to eliminate it completely cannot serve as a justification for not taking action to reduce it.

In considering the incongruity between resources and needs, the literature on *zedakah* discusses the prioritization of needs, while not losing sight of the individuality of the requirements of the needy. Already in the talmudic period our sources were aware that needs vary both in kind and in degree.

The various levels of *zedakah* outlined by Maimonides, as well as by others, parallel a recognition that needs could also be manifest on a variety of levels. Just as there are levels and degrees of aid, so are there levels and degrees of need. It is noteworthy, and perhaps not coincidental, that Maimonides identifies eight levels of *zedakah*, while a midrash notes that biblical Hebrew has eight words to denote the poor.[37]

The literature on *zedakah* relentlessly observes that need cannot be quantified on the basis of objective criteria. An individual's needs cannot be determined through calculating the objective minimum that any person might require to be sustained. The sources refuse to "objectify" another person's need. Rather, each person is perceived as an individual with subjective, individualistic, and even idiosyncratic needs. The demands of his or her personality, past experience, self-respect, and personal dignity are never overlooked. The goal in Jewish social welfare—not always attainable, though never forgotten—is to provide the individual that which is "sufficient for *his* need" (Deuteronomy 15:8). That the individual need of the client is of paramount concern is expressed in the following talmudic text.[38] Commenting on the verse, "Rather, you must open your hand and lend him sufficient for whatever he needs" (Deuteronomy 15:8), the Talmud says:

> "For whatever he needs" (Deuteronomy 15:8) [includes] even a horse to ride and a slave to run before him. It is related about Hillel the Elder that he bought for a certain poor man who was of a good family a horse to ride upon and a slave to run before him. On one occasion he could not find a slave to run before him, so he himself ran before him for three miles.

In his legal code, Maimonides refers to this text.[39] Maimonides interprets the text to mean that the poor man mentioned in the text was not simply of a good family, but once was rich. Since poverty is more psychologically debilitating for a person who lost his wealth than to a person who never had wealth, the needs of the formerly wealthy are greater. To ensure the dignity of such a person, more than the gift of a dole is required. Maimonides' demand that the personal experience and economic history of the individual must be considered when giving him *zedakah* is talmudic in origin:

> It has been taught that if a person [who was rich] has become poor and requires public assistance, if he had been used to vessels of gold, they give him vessels of silver; if of silver, they give him vessels of copper; if copper, they give him vessels of glass. Rabbi Mena said: They give him vessels of silver or glass only for his personal use. How about that teaching which said that if a man had been used to wearing clothes of fine wool, they give him clothes of fine wool? Again, these are only for his personal use.[40]

Zedakah is person-centered and need-centered. The gift must be appropriate both to the person and to his or her particular present need. As Maimonides wrote:

> You are commanded to give the poor man according to what he lacks. If he has no clothing, he should be clothed. If he has no house furnishings, they should be brought for him. If he has no wife, he should be helped to marry. If it is a woman, she should be given in marriage. Even if it had been his wont to ride a horse, with a manservant running in front of him, and he has now become poor and has lost his possessions, one must buy him a horse to ride and a manservant to run before him, as it is said, "Sufficient for his need in that which he needs" (Deuteronomy 15:8). You are obliged to fill his want; you are not, however, obligated to restore his wealth.[41]

To help safeguard the dignity of the poor, efforts were made to ensure the anonymity both of the donor and of the recipient of *zedakah*. Especially in cases in which the rich had lost their possessions, joining the ranks of the poor, anonymity was desired: "Just as there was a 'vestry of secret givers' in the Temple, so there was one in every city, for the sake of noble people, who had come down in life, so that they may be helped in secret."[42]

According to a talmudic tale, Mar Ukba had a poor man in his neighborhood. So as not to embarrass this poor man, Mar Ukba used to throw four coins into his house through the door socket every day. One day the poor man decided to discover the identity of his benefactor. When Mar Ukba saw that the man was watching as he approached the house, Mar Ukba ran away and hid in a furnace from which the fire had been just swept out. When Mar Ukba's extreme measures to escape being known were questioned, the Talmud explained them by quoting the well-known rabbinic adage: Better to throw oneself in a fiery furnace than publicly to shame one's neighbor.[43] Elsewhere the Talmud states, "A person who gives *zedakah* in secret is greater than Moses, our teacher."[44]

According to Maimonides' eight levels of charity, reproduced below, giving anonymously to a poor person who does not know the identity of his benefactor is the next to highest kind of *zedakah*. It protects the dignity of the recipient and expresses the altruism of the benefactor. However, according to Maimonides and many other sources, the highest form of *zedakah* is not a gift, but a loan. By giving a loan or by entering into partnership with the needy person, his or her dignity is preserved by allowing him or her to maintain a facade of self-sufficiency. In such cases, to be sure, there is no requirement or even an expectation that the loan be repaid. Nor is any interest attached to the loan. The goal of this form of *zedakah* is not only to preserve the dignity of the needy, but to help extricate him or her from being needy and to offer an opportunity for economic self-sufficiency.

Here, too—in the case of giving *zedakah* as a loan—one finds a special sensitivity toward the needs of the previously wealthy. For example, the Talmud recounts that Rabbi Jonah examined how to fulfill the *mitzvah* of *zedakah*:

What did Rabbi Jonah do? When he saw a previously wealthy poor person he would say: I have heard that you have inherited some wealth. Take this loan now and you will repay me. After he took it, he [i.e., Rabbi Jonah] would say. It is a gift for you.[45]

This view that a loan is better than a gift has firm talmudic precedent: "One who lends [money to the poor] is greater than he who gives a charitable gift; and he who forms a partnership [with the poor] is greater than all." On this text, Rashi comments that a loan is better than a gift, because a poor person who might be ashamed to accept a gift, would readily agree to a loan. Also, a donor might be willing to make a loan of a greater sum than he might be willing to make as a gift.[46] According to a number of sources, lending is superior to giving because loans are common between the rich as well as the poor, while *zedakah* is for the poor alone. A dole demeans by the very fact that the recipient is on a level subordinate to that of the donor, while in the case of a loan both parties are deemed equal.

The aim of giving a loan to the poor is to help him or her to exchange dependency for self-sufficiency. Just as rabbinic sources are concerned about the need to rescue the poor from poverty, so are they preoccupied with the need to prevent one from sliding into indigence. *Zedakah* is not only to be therapeutic, but preventative as well. Commenting on the phrase in Leviticus (25:35), "then you shall uphold him," Rashi warns:

Do not let him come down until he falls [completely] for then it will be difficult to raise him. Rather, uphold him at the time that his means [begin to] fail. To what is this comparable? To a burden that rests on a donkey. While it is still on the donkey, one [person can] hold it and set it back in place, but if it fell to the ground even five people cannot set it back in its place.

In order to ensure that communal funds were distributed to the truly needy, means to investigate the authenticity of need were developed and employed. Funds were always too sparse to expend on "deceivers." In addition, as the *Me'il Zedakah* observes, the presence of "cheats" was often used as an excuse by recalcitrant potential donors not to contribute. Regarding impostors, the Mishnah taught:

He that does not need to take yet takes shall not depart from this world before he falls in need of his fellows. . . . And if a man is not lame or dumb or blind or halting, yet he makes himself like unto one of them, he shall not die in old age until he becomes like one of them, as it is written (Proverbs 11:27), "He that searches after mischief, it shall come upon him."[47]

Furthermore, as Maimonides notes, community officials would investigate the claims of potential clients seeking communal welfare so as to remove impostors from community welfare roles.

According to Maimonides, if a person asks for food, i.e., for the fulfillment of an immediate need that may be life-threatening, such a person's need is not investigated. The need may be too severe to endure an inquiry. However, if a person asks for other types of aid such as clothing, the need is not immediate and life-threatening; therefore, an investigation into the grounds for the request is warranted.[48]

In his code, Maimonides also deals with the case of the truly needy person who is hesitant or who refuses to accept aid. In such a case, Maimonides counsels that aid should be given as a gift or as a loan. Maimonides' source seems to be this talmudic statement:

> Our rabbis taught: If a person has no means and does not wish to be maintained [out of the poor funds], he should be granted [the sum he requires] as a loan and then it can be presented to him as a gift; so [says] Rabbi Meir. The sages, however, said that it is given to him as a gift and then it is granted to him as a loan.[49]

According to Maimonides, who relies on talmudic sources, the deceiver is accursed, and the indigent, who is too proud to accept help needed to survive, is self-destructive.[50] But, the truly needy are entitled to receive. Nevertheless, every effort for self-support must be made before one begins to receive public aid: "One should always restrain himself and submit to privation rather than be dependent upon other people or cast himself upon public charity."[51]

The constant disparity between available funds and ever-present need requires some prioritization in the dispensing of aid. For Maimonides, charity begins at home. The first priority is the support of one's family. Maimonides wrote, "A poor man who is one's relative has priority over all others, the poor of one's own household have priority over the other poor of his city, and the poor of his city have priority over the poor of another city. . . ."[52] Similarly, Aboab insists that a person's first obligation is self-support, then support of one's parents, support of one's children, and only then is one obliged to render support for the needy.[53]

The belief that giving zedakah would ensure one a place in the afterlife, communal pressures to contribute to the public welfare, or sheer selfless altruism might lead one to contribute more than one could afford, thereby transferring the donor and his or her family to the ranks of the indigent. For this reason, restrictions upon the percentage of one's possessions one was able to contribute was limited to twenty percent by rabbinic decree.[54] While one is required to help the indigent, one is forbidden to impoverish oneself in the process.

Safeguards were established to protect the overzealous from joining the ranks of the impoverished, and thereby becoming public charges. About the nineteenth-century hasidic master, Levi Yitzkhak of Berditchev, it is told that after he would collect his salary he would begin to walk home to deposit it with his wife for household expenses. On the way, he would inevitably meet people in need. Giving each individual a portion of his salary, he would arrive home empty handed. Eventually, his wife was so desperate for funds that she brought suit against Levi Yitzkhak for failing to support his wife and his children. The judge found Levi Yitzkhak guilty, and ordered that the salary be paid directly to her. Being the rabbi of the town, Levi Yitzkhak was not only the defendant in the case, but the judge as well.

In meeting the needs of others, priorities were established. As was already noted, one is obliged to care for one's own family before one is required to take care of another's family. Immediate needs such as hunger supersede other, less pressing needs.[55] A woman's needs take precedent over those of a man because she is considered more vulnerable to harm or to abuse. The needs of orphans are given priority because they have no family; no one else but the community could care for them.

Communal funds aided not only the indigent, but others as well. Brides were provided with dowries, newlyweds with house furnishings. The dead were buried, the sick cared for and attended. Interest-free loans were made. Newly arrived immigrants were cared for until they could plant roots of their own.

In the rabbinic period and throughout the Middle Ages, Jews were held for ransom by kings, pirates, and other extortionists. Therefore, ransoming of captives—especially women and children—became priorities of communal zedakah funds.[56]

All the needs for which communal funds were expended would have been left unattended if observance of the mitzvah of zedakah had been neglected. Dispensing of funds assumes the giving of funds. For this reason, the Talmud considers "zedakah as important as all the other commandments combined."[57] For this reason, Maimonides' observation, made in the twelfth century, always has remained accurate: "We have never seen nor heard of a Jewish community without a zedakah fund."[58]

✿

The following excerpt is from Maimonides' code of Jewish law, the Mishneh Torah. While some information about Maimonides and his work has been provided in Chapter 8, some additional observations relating to the *Mishneh Torah* are pertinent here.[59]

The *Mishneh Torah* was completed by Maimonides in 1178 after ten years of unstinting labor. As a legal code, it is unsurpassed in post-talmudic Judaism. It is distinct in a number of ways. First, it is unique because of its literary style. In his attempt to elicit a renaissance of the Hebrew language and of the study of the Mishnah, Maimonides wrote the *Mishneh Torah* in Mishnaic Hebrew. Finding biblical Hebrew inadequate to his task, and talmudic Aramaic too obstruse, he chose to compose his legal *magnum opus* in a felicitous and fluent, though precise and elegant Hebrew style modeled after the classical Hebrew of the Mishnah.

Second, the *Mishneh Torah* is unique in its scope. Maimonides included both theoretical and practical aspects and issues of Jewish law. He addressed those laws currently in practice as well as those (such as laws of sacrifices) not then in practice. His code includes obvious as well as abstruse matters of Jewish legal concern. Third, Maimonides fused actions with ideas, law with philosophy, theological discourse with moral edification. He painstakingly established metaphysical and theological foundations upon which he then constructed his legal edifice. Theological girders and moral principles form the conceptual underpinnings for his presentation of the specific demands of Jewish law.

Fourth, the *Mishneh Torah* brought order out of chaos. The vast and unsystematic corpus of rabbinic law was rearranged in a structured, topical order. To the disorganized "sea of Talmud" with its many tides and streams, Maimonides brought a penchant for order and a proclivity toward making distinctions aimed at promoting conceptual clarity. Abandoning the sequence of the Mishnah and rejecting commentary as a style of codification, Maimonides created a new topical arrangement and structure for Jewish legal discourse. In so doing, he composed a new kind of legal composition that rearranged the themes of former composers, while not violating the integrity of their melodies. For such an endeavor, there is neither precedent nor sequel in Jewish history or literature.

The *Mishneh Torah* was designed to be an all-embracive re-formation of Judaism in a structured and systematic manner. As Maimonides noted in his introduction, "I have entitled this work *Mishneh Torah* ["the repetition of the Torah"] so that a person who first reads the written Torah and then this compilation, will know from it the whole oral Torah [i.e., rabbinic tradition], without having occasion to consult any other book between them."

Because the term "Mishneh Torah" is used by Scripture as another name for the Book of Deuteronomy, subsequent Jewish tradition found Maimonides' title too bold. Therefore, some refer to this work as the "*Yad ha-Hazakah*," the "strong hand." In Hebrew, each letter is also a number, and the

Hebrew word "*yad*" has the numerical value of fourteen, referring to the fourteen books that comprise this massive work.

Each of the fourteen books deals with a major area of Jewish religious practice, which is then divided into subsections. For instance, Book Three, *Sefer Zemanim*, discusses laws relating to Jewish religious festivals. One of the subsections of *Sefer Zemanim* deals with laws that relate to observance of the Sabbath. Maimonides continued his process of subdivision by dividing each subsection into chapters that deal with specific issues within the purview of the area and subarea under discussion. Finally, he subdivided each chapter into paragraphs, each of which deals with a very specific issue related to the topic under discussion.

One may compare the *Mishneh Torah* to a huge office building complex consisting of fourteen separate buildings. Each building—each book—is devoted to one of the fourteen areas of Jewish law and tradition depicted by Maimonides. Each floor in each building—each subsection of each book—deals with a particular issue related to the major area assigned to that individual building. Each suite of offices on each floor—each chapter—handles a particular matter related to the subarea assigned to the floor. Each individual office—each paragraph—treats a very specific matter handled by the suite of which it is a part. By so structuring this complex, Maimonides made it pedagogically, conceptually, and practically simple to locate the particular place where the most specific issue is treated. Thus, Maimonides' process of classification is a process of clarification. The product of this process is a masterpiece of codification.

In Book One, *Sefer ha-Mada—The Book of Knowledge*, Maimonides begins his exposition with a treatise called "Basic Principles of the Torah." In this first subsection of the *Mishneh Torah*, Maimonides identifies and explicates the fundamental theological and philosophical foundations of Judaism. For Maimonides, Jewish law flows from Jewish belief. The laws ultimately rest upon a theological foundation. Therefore, before delineating the legal specifics of Judaism, Maimonides felt obliged by logic to portray the ideological presuppositions presumed by the laws. From theological premises, Maimonides moves to ethical assumptions in the second subsection of *The Book of Knowledge*. Ethical principles derive from theological premises and articulate themselves in specific legal requirements. In the third subsection, he treats study of the Torah. Without study, one is bereft of knowing what is required. Knowledge leads to action. Knowing is the necessary prelude to doing. In the fourth subsection, Maimonides discusses idolatry. For Maimonides, both here and in *The Guide of the Perplexed*, idolatry is the antithesis of Judaism. Therefore, to practice Judaism one must be familiar with its antithetical alternative, with its ideological enemy. Finally, Maimonides devotes a subsection of *The Book of Knowledge* to repentance. Because humans are fallible, they will inevitably violate the law. Through repentance, the ability to repair and rectify errors in actions may be effected.

In Book Two, *Sefer Ahavah—The Book of Love*, Maimonides treats various aspects of worship. He discusses, for example, laws of prayer, blessings, circumcision, etc. In Book Three, *Sefer Zemanim—The Book of Seasons*, Maimonides discusses various Jewish festivals and their observance. In Book Four, *Sefer Nashim—The Book of Women*, Maimonides discusses laws of marriage, divorce, and other laws relating to women. Book Five, *Sefer Kedushah—The Book of Holiness*, deals with laws of "the permitted and the forbidden." Here Maimonides discusses laws relating to sexual relations and the Jewish dietary laws. Book Six, *Sefer Hafla'ah—The Book of Asseverations*, deals with legal obligations and responsibilities engendered by a person's spoken words. Here Maimonides treats laws relating to oaths, vows, and promises. According to Maimonides, the purpose for most of the laws in Book Seven, *Sefer Zera'im—The Book of Seeds*, is "instilling pity for the weak and the wretched, giving strength in various ways to the poor, and inciting us . . . not to afflict the hearts of the individuals who are in a weak position." The excerpt below is drawn from the second section of this book, which is entitled "Laws of Gifts to the Poor."

As was noted above, Maimonides' code is comprehensive in scope, including not only laws currently in effect, but also laws and traditions no longer in effect. Book Eight, *Sefer Avodah—The Book of Temple Service*, deals with the Temple and with the sacrificial cult. While these were not practical issues in his day, Maimonides looked forward to the time of messianic redemption when the Temple would be rebuilt, and when the sacrificial cult would be reinstituted. When this occurred, it would be important to have these laws clearly and carefully explained. In Book Nine, *Sefer Korbanot—The Book of Sacrifices*, Maimonides continues his discussion of the sacrificial cult by discussing specific features of sacrifices to be offered at particular occasions. For instance, the first subsection of this book treats various aspects of the paschal sacrifice to be offered on Passover.

When the Temple stood in Jerusalem, the laws of "purity" were of special relevance, since one who was impure was enjoined from participating in the sacrificial cult. In Book Ten, *Sefer Taharah—The Book of Purity*, Maimonides discusses the concept of ritual purity and the laws related to it. In this section, he also discusses those aspects of ritual purity still in effect, such as the use of *mikvaot*, ritualariums or ritual baths.

In Book Eleven, *Sefer Nezikin—The Book of Torts*, Maimonides treats various aspects of civil and criminal law, such as murder, theft, torts, and restitution. Book Twelve, *Sefer Kinyan—The Book of Acquisitions*, is concerned with ways one may acquire property, and with rights and responsibilities related to the ownership of property. Here Maimonides also has occasion to treat contract law, commercial fraud and misrepresentation, and laws of sale. In Book Thirteen, *Sefer Mishpatim—The Book of Judgments*, Maimonides continues his explication of Jewish civil law. Here he deals with relationships between employers and their employees, as well as those between creditors and debtors, bailors and bailees, and estates and their heirs.

The fourteenth and final book of the *Mishneh Torah* is *Sefer Shoftim—The Book of Judges*. It is primarily concerned with procedural aspects of law, such as laws of evidence, court procedure, punishment of convicted criminals, the qualifications of judges, and the structure of courts. Some of these laws, such as those relating to the Sanhedrin, which no longer exists, are theoretical. Some, such as those laws relating to community leadership, are practical and currently relevant. However, the final section of the final book of the *Mishneh Torah* was thoroughly theoretical at the time of its composition, as it deals with laws of Jewish kings and Jewish wars. With the emergence of the State of Israel, this section, which treats the proper exercise by Jews of military and of political power, suddenly became remarkably pertinent. Finally, in the very last chapters of this last section of this last book, Maimonides discusses the nature of the Messiah and of the Messianic Age. In the Messianic Age, the expectation was that the entire range and scope of laws discussed in the *Mishneh Torah* would be in effect. Indeed, one modern scholar has suggested that Maimonides's *Mishneh Torah* was written as the "constitution" for the Jewish republic to be established in the messianic era.[60]

Moses Maimonides
Mishneh Torah—The Book
of Agriculture

When one harvests his field, he may not harvest all of it, but should rather leave for the poor some of the standing corn at the end of the field, as it is said, "You shall not wholly reap the corner of thy field when you reap" (Leviticus 23:22). . . .

Just as one is obliged to leave corner crop in the field, so is he obligated to leave it in trees: when he gathers their fruit, he must leave some for the poor.

If he transgresses and harvests the entire field or gathers all the fruit of the tree, he must take some of what he had harvested or gathered and give it to the poor, inasmuch as the giving of it is a positive commandment, as it is said, "You shall leave them

for the poor and for the stranger" (Leviticus 23:22). Even if he
has ground it into flour, kneaded it, and baked it into bread, he
must give corner crop out of it to the poor. . . .

In all these gifts for the poor the owner has no option as to the
recipient; rather the poor may come and take them regardless of
the owner's wishes. Even if he is the poorest person in Israel,
these gifts must be extracted from him. . . . the poor of the
heathens may not be excluded from these gifts; rather they may
come together with the poor of Israel and take of them, for the
sake of promoting ways of peace. . . .

There is another . . . gift that is due to the poor out of the
yield of the land, namely the tithe given to the poor. This is the
so-called poor man's tithe. . . .

The owner of a field who has a number of the poor pass by
him while the poor man's tithe is still there, must give to each
one enough of the tithe to satisfy his hunger, as it is said, "That
they may eat within your gates, and be satisfied" (Deuteronomy
26:12). . . .

The owner has no optional right in the apportionment of the
poor man's tithe that is distributed at the threshing floor; rather
the poor may come and take their share, even against the
owner's will. Even if the owner is himself the poorest person in
Israel, the poor man's tithe may be taken out of his hand. . . .

If a poor man and a poor woman come to the house together,
one should give to the woman first, dismiss her, and then give
to the man. . . .

It is a positive commandment to give alms to the poor of
Israel, according to what is fitting for them, if the giver can
afford it, as it is said, "You shall surely open your hand unto
him" (Deuteronomy 15:8), and again, "Then you shall uphold
him; as a stranger and a settler shall he live with you . . . that
your brother may live with you" (Leviticus 25:35–36).

He who seeing a poor man begging turns his eyes away from
him and fails to give him alms, transgresses a negative commandment, as it is said, "You shall not harden your heart, nor
shut your hand from your needy brother" (Deuteronomy 15:7).

You are commanded to give the poor man according to what
he lacks. If he has no clothing, he should be clothed. If he has no
house furnishings, they should be bought for him. If he has no
wife, he should be helped to marry. If it is a woman, she should

be given in marriage. Even if it had been his wont to ride a horse, with a manservant running in front of him, and he has now become poor and has lost his possessions, one must buy him a horse to ride and a manservant to run before him, as it is said, "Sufficient for his need in that which he needs" (Deuteronomy 15:8). You are thus obligated to fill his want; you are not, however, obligated to restore his wealth. . . .

If the poor man comes forth and asks for enough to satisfy his want, and if the giver is unable to afford it, the latter may give him as much as he can afford. How much is that? In choice performance of this religious duty, up to one-fifth of his possessions; in middling performance, up to one-tenth of his possessions; less than this brands him as a person of evil eye. At all times one should not permit himself to give less than one-third of a *shekel* per year. He who gives less than this has not fulfilled this commandment at all. Even a poor man who lives entirely on alms must himself give alms to another poor man

If a poor man unknown to anyone comes forth and says, "I am hungry; give me something to eat," he should not be examined as to whether he might be an impostor—he should be fed immediately. If, however, he is naked and says, "Clothe me," he should be examined as to possible fraud. If he is known, he should be clothed immediately according to his dignity, without any further inquiry.

One must feed and clothe the heathen poor together with the Israelite poor, for the sake of the ways of peace. In the case of a poor man who goes from door to door, one is not obligated to give him a large gift, but only a small one. It is forbidden, however, to let a poor man who asks for alms to go empty-handed, just so you give him at least one dry fig, as it is said, "O let not the oppressed turn back in confusion" (Psalms 74:21). . . .

If a poor man refuses to accept alms, one should get around him by making him accept them as a present or a loan. If, on the other hand, a wealthy man starves himself because he is so niggardly with his money that he would not spend of it on food and drink, no attention need be paid to him.

He who refuses to give alms, or gives less than is proper for him, must be compelled by the court to comply, and must be flogged for disobedience until he gives as much as the court estimates he should give. The court may even seize his property in his presence and take from him what is proper for him to give. One may indeed pawn things in order to give alms, even on the eve of the Sabbath.

A munificent person who gives alms beyond what he can afford, or denies himself in order to give to the collector of alms so that he would not be put to shame, should not be asked for contributions to alms. Any alms collector who humiliates him by demanding alms from him will surely be called to account for it, as it is said, "I will punish all that oppress them" (Jeremiah 30:20). . . .

A poor man who is one's relative has priority over the other poor of his city, and the poor of his city have priority over the poor of another city, as it is said, "Unto your poor and needy brother, in your land" (Deuteronomy 15:11). . . .

The ransoming of captives has precedence over the feeding and clothing of the poor. Indeed there is no religious duty more meritorious than the ransoming of captives, for not only is the captive included in the generality of the hungry, the thirsty, and the naked, but his very life is in jeopardy. . . .

Captives may not be ransomed for more than their fair value, for the sake of good world order, lest the enemies should seek them out in order to capture them. Nor may they be assisted to escape, for the same reason, lest the enemy should make their yoke heavier and guard them more vigilantly. . . .

A woman takes precedence over a man as far as feeding, clothing, and redemption from captivity are concerned, because it is customary for a man to go begging from door to door, but not for a woman, as her sense of shame is greater. If both of them are in captivity, and both are exposed to forcible sin, the man takes precedence in being ransomed, since it is not customary for him to submit to such sin.

If two orphans, male and female, are about to be given in marriage, the female should be wed before the male, because a woman's sense of shame is greater. . . .

In every city inhabited by Israelites, it is their duty to appoint from among themselves well-known and trustworthy persons to act as alms collectors, to go around collecting from the people every Friday. They should demand from each person what is proper for him to give and what he has been assessed for, and should distribute the money every Friday, giving each poor man sustenance sufficient for seven days. This is what is called "alms fund." . . .

We have never seen nor heard of an Israelite community that does not have an alms fund. . . .

It is our duty to be more careful in the performance of the commandment of almsgiving than in that of any other positive commandment, for almsgiving is the mark of the righteous man who is of the seed of our father Abraham, as it is said, "For I have known him, to the end that he may command his children," etc., "to do righteousness" (Genesis 18:19). The throne of Israel cannot be established, nor true faith made to stand up, except through charity, as it is said, "In righteousness shall you be established" (Isaiah 54:14); nor will Israel be redeemed, except through the practice of charity, as it is said, "Zion shall be redeemed with justice, and they that return of her with righteousness" (Isaiah 1:27).

No man is ever impoverished by almsgiving, nor does evil or harm befall anyone by reason of it, as it is said, "And the work of righteousness shall be peace" (Isaiah 32:17).

He who has compassion upon others, others will have compassion upon him, as it is said, "That the Lord may . . . show thee mercy, and have compassion upon you" (Deuteronomy 13:18).

Whosoever is cruel and merciless lays himself open to suspicion as to his descent, for cruelty is found only among the heathens, as it is said, "They are cruel, and have no compassion" (Jeremiah 50:42). All Israelites and those that have attached themselves to them are to each other like brothers, as it is said, "You are the children of the Lord your God" (Deuteronomy 14:1). If brother will show no compassion to brother, who will? And unto whom shall the poor of Israel raise their eyes? Unto the heathens, who hate them and persecute them? Their eyes are therefore hanging solely upon their brethren.

He who turns his eyes away from charity is called a base fellow, just as is he who worships idols. Concerning the worship of idols Scripture says, "Certain base fellows are gone out" (Deuteronomy 13:14), and concerning him who turns his eyes away from charity it says, "Beware that there be not a base thought in your heart" (Deuteronomy 15:9). Such a man is also called wicked, as it is said, "The tender mercies of the wicked are cruel" (Proverbs 12:10). He is also called a sinner, as it is said, "And he cry unto the Lord against you, and it be sin in you" (Deuteronomy 15:10). The Holy One, blessed be He, stands nigh unto the cry of the poor, as it is said, "You hear the cry of the poor." One should therefore be careful about their cry, for a covenant has been made with them, as it is said, "And it shall come to pass, when he cries unto Me, that I will hear, for I am gracious" (Exodus 22:26).

He who gives alms to a poor man with a hostile countenance and with his face averted to the ground, loses his merit and forfeits it, even if he gives as much as a thousand gold coins. He should rather give with a friendly countenance and joyfully. He should commiserate with the recipient in his distress, as it is said, "If I have not wept for him that was in trouble, and if my soul grieved not for the needy?" (Job 30:25). He should also speak to him prayerful and comforting words, as it is said, "And I caused the widow's heart to sing for joy" (Job 29:13).

If a poor man asks you for alms and you have nothing to give him, comfort him with words. It is forbidden to rebuke a poor man or to raise one's voice in a shout at him, seeing that his heart is broken and crushed, and Scripture says, "A broken and contrite heart, O God, You will not despise" (Psalms 51:19), and again, "To revive the spirit of the humble, and to revive the heart of the contrite ones" (Isaiah 57:15). Woe unto him who shames the poor! Woe unto him! One should rather be unto the poor as a father, with both compassion and words, as it is said, "I was a father to the needy" (Job 29:16).

He who presses others to give alms and moves them to act thus, his reward is greater than the reward of him who gives alms himself, as it is said, "And the work of righteousness shall be peace" (Isaiah 32:17). Concerning alms collectors and their like Scripture says, "And they that turn the many to righteousness [shall shine] as the stars" (Daniel 12:3).

There are eight degrees of almsgiving, each one superior to the other. The highest degree, than which there is none higher, is one who upholds the hand of an Israelite reduced to poverty by handing him a gift or a loan, or entering into a partnership with him, or finding work for him, in order to strengthen his hand, so that he would have no need to beg from other people. Concerning such a one Scripture says, "You shall uphold him; as a stranger and a settler shall he live with you" (Leviticus 25:35), meaning uphold him so that he would not lapse into want.

Below this is he who gives alms to the poor in such a way that he does not know to whom he has given, nor does the poor man know from whom he has received. This constitutes the fulfilling of a religious duty for its own sake, and for such there was a Chamber of Secrets in the Temple, whereunto the righteous would contribute secretly, and wherefrom the poor of good families would draw their sustenance in equal secrecy. Close to such a person is he who contributes directly to the alms fund.

One should not, however, contribute directly to the alms fund unless he knows that the person in charge of it is trustworthy, is a Sage, and knows how to manage it properly, as was the case of Rabbi Hananiah ben Teradion.

Below this is he who knows to whom he is giving, while the poor man does not know from whom he is receiving. He is thus like the great among the Sages who were wont to set out secretly and throw the money down at the doors of the poor. This is a proper way of doing it, and a preferable one if those in charge of alms are not conducting themselves as they should.

Below this is the case where the poor man knows from whom he is receiving, but himself remains unknown to the giver. He is thus like the great among the Sages who used to place the money in the fold of a linen sheet which they would throw over their shoulder, whereupon the poor would come behind them and take the money without being exposed to humiliation.

Below this is he who hands the alms to the poor man before being asked for them.

Below this is he who hands the alms to the poor man after the latter has asked for them.

Below this is he who gives the poor man less than what is proper, but with a friendly countenance.

Below this is he who gives alms with a frowning countenance.

The great among the Sages used to hand a perutah to a poor man before praying, and then proceeded to pray, as it is said, "As for me, I shall behold Your face in righteousness" (Psalms 17:15).

He who provides maintenance for his grown sons and daughters—whom he is not obligated to maintain—in order that the sons might study Torah, and that the daughters might learn to follow the right path and not expose themselves to contempt, and likewise he who provides maintenance for his father and mother, is accounted as performing an act of charity. Indeed it is an outstanding act of charity, since one's relative has precedence over other people. Whosoever serves food and drink to poor men and orphans at his table, will, when he calls to God, receive an answer and find delight in it, as it is said, "Then shall you call, and the Lord will answer" (Isaiah 58:9). . . .

One should always restrain himself and submit to privation rather than be dependent upon other people or cast himself upon public charity, for thus have the Sages commanded us, saying, "Make the Sabbath a weekday rather than be dependent upon other people." Even if one is a Sage held in honor, once he becomes impoverished, he should engage in a trade, be it even a loathsome trade, rather than be dependent upon other people. It is better to strip the hides off animal carcasses than to say to other people, "I am a great Sage, I am a priest, provide me therefore with maintenance." So did the Sages command us. Among the great Sages there were hewers of wood, carriers of beams, drawers of water to irrigate gardens, and workers in iron and charcoal. They did not ask for public assistance, nor did they accept it when offered to them.

Whosoever is in no need of alms but deceives the public and does accept them, will not die of old age until he indeed becomes dependent upon other people. He is included among those of whom Scripture says, "Cursed is the man that trusts in man" (Jeremiah 17:5). On the other hand, whosoever is in need of alms and cannot survive unless he accepts them, such as a person who is of advanced age, or ill, or afflicted with sore trials, but is too proud and refuses to accept them, is the same as a shedder of blood and is held to account for his own soul, and by his suffering he gains nothing but sin and guilt.

Whosoever is in need of alms but denies himself, postpones the hour, and lives a life of want in order not to be a burden upon the public, will not die of old age until he shall have provided maintenance for others out of his own wealth. Of him and of those like him it is said, "Blessed is the man that trusts in the Lord" (Jeremiah 17:7).

Notes

INTRODUCTION

1. This statement is attributed to Menahem Mendel Morgenstern of Kotsk, a hasidic master of nineteenth-century Poland. See *Emet mei-Kotsk Tizmah* (Bnei Brak: Nezah, 1961), pp. 51–52. A similar statement is attributed to Israel Friedmann, the Maggid of Ruzhyn. See *Kenesset Yisrael* (Warsaw: N.p., 1906), pp. 16–17.

2. Noted by Louis Ginzberg, "Rabbi Israel Salanter," chap. in his *Students, Scholars and Saints* (Philadelphia: Jewish Publication Society, 1928), p. 174.

3. Moses Maimonides, *Shemonah Perakim*, chap. 8. See Joseph I. Gorfinkle, ed. and trans., *The Eight Chapters of Maimonides on Ethics* (New York: Columbia University Press, 1912), p. 42 (Heb. sec.), p. 84 (Eng. sec.).

4. Idem, *Commentary to the Mishnah*, *Avot* 1:14. See Arthur David, trans., *Moses Maimonides—The Commentary to Mishnah Abot* (New York: Bloch, 1968), p. 14.

5. See Abraham J. Heschel, *Kotsk*, 2 vols. [Yiddish] (Tel Aviv: Menorah, 1973), vol. 1, pp. 131–136.

6. See Byron L. Sherwin, *Mystical Theology and Social Dissent* (London: Oxford University Press, 1982), p. 119.

7. See, e.g., Heschel, *The Earth is the Lord's* (New York: Henry Schuman, 1950), p. 9. The Yiddish term *"a shainer yid"* conveys a particularly Jewish notion of aesthetics. Beauty is characterized by action and life-style rather than by appearance and by sheer being. In this regard, note Jacob Petuchowski, "The Beauty of God," chap. in Joseph Edelheit, ed., *The Life of Covenant* (Chicago: Spertus College of Judaica Press, 1986), pp. 125–131.

8. In a letter from Solomon Schechter to Solomon Solis-Cohen, dated July 11, 1904, quoted in Norman Bentwich, *Solomon Schechter: A Biography* (New York: Burning Bush Press, 1964), p. 238.

9. Josephus, *Antiquities*, J. Thackeray, trans. (Cambridge, MA: Harvard University Press, 1934), vol. 5, Book 6, paras. 159–160, p. 247. Note Samuel S. Cohon, *Judaism* (New York: Schocken, 1948), pp. 3–6.

10. *Sifre on Deuteronomy*, Louis Finkelstein, ed. (Berlin: Gesellschaft zur Forderung der Wissenschaft des Judentums, 1939), "*Ekev*," para. 49, p. 114.

11. For the Hebrew original, see Yonah David, ed., *The Poems of Amittay* [Hebrew], (Jerusalem: Achshav, 1975), pp. 20–24. Translation here by Byron L. Sherwin.

12. See the commentary of Samuel of Uceda on *Ethics of the Fathers* 1:14 in his *Midrash Shmuel* (Jerusalem: Brody-Katz, n.d.), p. 16a.

13. See Jonah Gerondi, *Sha'arey Teshuvah* (*Gates of Repentance*), 2 vols., Shraga Silverstein, ed. and trans. (New York: Feldheim, 1971), 2:26, p. 115.

14. Sections of the preceding discussion are drawn from Byron L. Sherwin, *In Partnership with God* (Syracuse, NY: Syracuse University Press, 1990), chap. 3, and from Sherwin, "Jewish Ethics as Theological Ethics," *Shofar* 9:1 (Fall 1990): 2–13.

15. The approach to Jewish ethical literature taken here sharply differs with that taken by a number of contemporary authors on the subject, most notably Joseph Dan. While one cannot fail to appreciate the extraordinary contribution made by Dan to the study of Jewish ethical literature, there are fundamental difficulties with his conceptual approach. First is his attempt to sharply distinguish between Jewish ethics and Jewish law. Second is his characterization of major works of Jewish ethical literature, such as Bahya ibn Pakudah's *Duties of the Heart*, as "radical and revolutionary," to the point of being virtually subversive of the Jewish legal system. Third is his characterization of Jewish ethical literature as something radically new that appears in the medieval period rather than as being an organic outgrowth of preceding tradition, with deep roots in what came before. Indeed, as Dan himself is aware, most authors of significant works in this area stress the lack of novelty in their work and emphasize their continuity with prior Jewish religious literature. Fourth is Dan's restriction of Jewish ethical literature to specific literary forms and to the medieval and early modern period. This is not the place to offer a full-scale analysis of Dan's approach; however, see his "Ethical Literature" in *Encyclopedia Judaica*, vol. 6, pp. 922–942, esp. pp. 922–923; idem, *Jewish Mysticism and Jewish Ethics* (Seattle: University of Washington Press, 1986); and, idem, *Sifrut ha-Musar ve-ha-Derush* (Jerusalem: Keter, 1975).

16. Compare Dan, *Jewish Mysticism and Jewish Ethics*, p. 13, where such a distinction is made. The literature on the relationship between Jewish law and ethics is vast and beyond the scope of discussion here. See, e.g., Louis Newman, "Ethics as Law, Law as Religion: Reflections on the Problem of Law and Ethics in Judaism," *Shofar* 9:1 (Fall 1990): 13–32.

17. See, e.g., *Orhot Zaddikim*'s discussion of repentance, where both attitudinal issues and precise prescriptions for behavior are to be found. Such texts demonstrate that a distinction of ethics and law in terms of why/how and what to do are not only artificial but are not always characteristic of classical works of Jewish ethical literature, even as Dan defines the parameters of this literature. Furthermore, the discussion of attitudinal and motivational issues in codes of Jewish law and responsa, and in talmudic/midrashic literature that Dan excludes from Jewish ethical literature, dem-

onstrates the inappropriateness of this distinction from another perspective. For example, with regard to issues such as children's obligations toward parents, prayer, repentance, and other issues discussed in the following chapters, the Talmud and medieval legal codes do indeed deal with attitudinal and motivational issues, i.e., with *why* to act in a specific manner and not simply with *what* to do.

18. Dan lists philosophical-ethical literature and kabbalistic-ethical literature as being two major genre of medieval Jewish ethical literature. See his "Ethical Literature," pp. 925, 930.

19. See, e.g., Sherwin, *In Partnership with God*, chap. 3.

20. See, e.g., Alexander Altmann, "*Homo Imago Dei* in Jewish and Christian Theology," *Journal of Religion* 48 (1968): 235–259; Norbert Samuelson, "Gersonides," in Sherwin, ed., *Solomon Goldman Lectures*, vol. 5 (Chicago: Spertus College of Judaica Press, 1990), pp. 114–115.

21. Moses Nahmanides, *Kitvei Rabbenu Moshe ben Nahman*, 2 vols., Charles B. Chavel, ed. (Jerusalem: Mosad ha-Rav Kook, 1964), vol. 2, p. 538.

22. See, e.g., Jacob Klatzkin, *Otzar ha-Munahim ha-Philosophi'im*, 2 vols. (New York: Feldheim, 1986), s.v. "*Middah*," vol. 2, pp. 146–147.

23. See the discussion of the relationship between *mitzvot* and *middot* in Hayyim Vital, *Sefer Sha'arei Kedushah* (Jerusalem: Aravah, 1967), 1:1,2, pp. 11–16.

24. See Daniel C. Matt, "The Mystic and the *Mizwot*," chap. in Arthur Green, ed., *Jewish Spirituality* (New York: Crossroad, 1986), p. 378.

25. In biblical commentary, see, e.g., the commentary of Rabbi Elijah, the Gaon of Vilna, on Proverbs 2:9, in *Sefer Mishlei im Biur ha-Gera* (Petah Tikvah: N.p., 1985), p. 39. On talmudic commentary, see nn. 27, 28.

26. *Baba Kamma* 30a.

27. Edels's commentary to the Talmud is found in standard editions of the Babylonian Talmud. For an anthology of texts from his commentary dealing with ethical issues, see Abraham Mase-Zahav, ed., *Tokhahat Musar* (Jerusalem: N.p., 1962). The citation quoted is there on pp. 30–31. See also Edels's commentary to *Sota* 5a quoted in the anthology, p. 92.

28. Judah Loew, *Hiddushei Aggadot*, 3 vols. (New York: Judaica Press, 1969), vol. 3, p. 4.

29. Idem, *Derekh Hayyim* (New York: Judaica Press, 1969), 1:2, p. 24; see also "Introduction," p. 9.

CHAPTER 1

1. Bahya ibn Pakudah, *The Book of Direction to the Duties of the Heart*, Menahem Mansoor, trans. (London: Routledge and Kegan Paul, 1973), p. 109. On Bahya, see this volume, chap. 5.

2. Moses Maimonides, *Mishneh Torah—Sefer ha-Mada*, "*Hilkhot Yesodei ha-Torah*" 1:1. Moses Hyamson, trans., *The Book of Knowledge* (Jerusalem: Boys Town Jerusalem Publishers, 1965), "Basic Principles of the Torah," 1:1, p. 34a.

3. See, e.g., Louis Jacobs, *Faith* (New York: Basic Books, 1968), pp. 62–64.

4. Albert Camus, *The Myth of Sisyphus*, Justin O'Brien, trans. (New York: Knopf, 1955), p. 3.

5. William Shakespeare, *Macbeth*, Act 5, Scene 5.

6. Bahya, p. 121.

7. Ludwig Wittgenstein, *Notebooks 1914–1916*, G. E. M. Anscome, trans. (New York: Harper and Brothers, 1961), p. 74.

8. *Avot d'Rabbi Natan*, Solomon Schechter, ed. (Vienna, 1887), "A" chap. 16, end. Judah Goldin, trans., *The Fathers According to Rabbi Nathan* (New Haven, CT: Yale University Press, 1955), p. 86.

9. Bahya, p. 113. On "belief" in Saadya, see Saadya Gaon, *The Book of Beliefs and Opinions*, Samuel Rosenblatt, trans. (New Haven, CT: Yale University Press, 1948), pp. 14–16. Saadya (p. 15) characterizes as "a reprehensible fool" one "who sets up his personal conviction as his guiding principle, assuming that reality is patterned after his belief."

10. See, e.g., Judah Loew of Prague as discussed in Byron L. Sherwin, *Mystical Theology and Social Dissent* (London: Oxford University Press, 1982), p. 56.

11. See, e.g., Simon Mendel of Givurtchav, ed., *Sefer ha-Besht*, 2 vols. (Jerusalem: Horeb, 1961), vol. 1, p. 176, no. 141. On how the reduction of Judaism to rational philosophical demonstrations can lead to dispensing with Jewish moral values, see e.g., Yitzhak Baer, *A History of the Jews in Christian Spain*, 2 vols., L. Schoffman, trans. (Philadelphia: Jewish Publication Society, 1966), vol. 1, p. 241.

12. Nahmanides in his commentary to Maimonides, *Sefer ha-Mitzvot – Book of the Commandments*, "Positive Commandments," no. 1. On Nahmanides, see this volume, chap. 12.

13. See M. *Pesahim* 10:5; Maimonides, *Mishneh Torah – Seder Zemanim*, "Hilkhot Hametz u-Matzah" 7:6.

14. See *Sefer ha-Besht*, vol. 1, p. 176, no. 141.

15. See Meir Eisenstadt, *Panim Me'irot* (Amsterdam, 1715), no. 39. Quoted in Abraham J. Heschel, *Man is Not Alone* (New York: Farrar, Straus and Giroux, 1951), p. 164.

16. Simhah Zussel of Kelm, *Hokhmah u-Musar* (New York, 1957), no. 57. On Simhah Zussel, see Dov Katz, *Tenuat ha-Musar*, 5 vols. (Jerusalem: Brody-Katz, 1974), vol. 2, pp. 26–219.

17. See Joseph Albo, *Sefer ha-Ikkarim – Book of Principles*, 6 vols., Isaac Husik, trans. and ed. (Philadelphia: Jewish Publication Society, 1946), vol. 1, chaps. 19-20, pp. 165–173.

18. Israel Davidson, ed., *Solomon ibn Gabirol: Selected Religious Poems* (Philadelphia: Jewish Publication Society, 1924), p. 118, line 563. On Ibn Gabirol, see this volume, chap. 7. Compare the song of the hasidic master, Levi Yitzhak of Berditchev, "Wherever I wander, You"; quoted in Martin Buber, *Tales of the Hasidim: Early Masters*, Olga Marx, trans. (New York: Schocken, 1947), p. 212.

19. On Judah ibn Tibbon, see this volume, chap. 13.

20. Shlomo Dov Goiten, "The Biography of Rabbi Judah Ha-Levi in Light of Cairo Geniza Documents," *Proceedings of the American Academy of Jewish Research* 28 (1959): 42.

CHAPTER 2

1. See Abraham J. Heschel, *Man's Quest for God* (New York: Scribners, 1954), p. 5.

2. Ben Zion Bokser, *The Gift of Life and Love* (New York: Hebrew Publishing Co., 1975), p. 118.

3. Quoted in Edmund Cahn, *The Moral Decision* (Bloomington, IN: Indiana University Press, 1955), pp. 49–50.

4. *Genesis Rabbah* 14:9.

5. *Berakhot* 60b.

6. *Berakhot* 35a.

7. *Berakhot* 59b.

8. Ibid.

9. *Berakhot* 60b.

10. *Berakhot* 54a. See also *Midrash Tadsheh* [*Midrash Pinhas ben Yair*] in Judah D. Eisenstein, ed., *Otzar ha-Midrashim*, 2nd ed. (New York: Grossman, 1956), "*Midrash Pinhas ben Yair*," para. 19, p. 483.

11. Bahya ibn Pakudah, *Duties of the Heart*, Menahem M. Mansoor, trans. (London: Routledge and Kegan Paul, 1973), Part 3, Introduction, p. 176.

12. Heschel, *Who is Man?* (Stanford, CA: Stanford University Press, 1963), pp. 108, 110, 111, 112, 118.

13. Quoted in Louis Newman, *The Hasidic Anthology* (New York: Schocken, 1963), p. 326.

14. *P. Kiddushin* 4:2.

15. *Berakhot* 43b.

16. Quoted in Heschel, *Who is Man?* p. 87.

17. Jacob Anatoli, *Malmed ha-Talmidim* (Lyck, 1866), "*Mattot*," p. 152b. Anatoli's statement was anticipated and may have been influenced by Solomon ibn Gabirol, *The Improvement of the Moral Qualities*, Stephen S. Wise, trans. (New York: Columbia University Press, 1901), p. 79: "If it be impossible for a man to have what he desires, he must desire what he has."

18. On contentment, see, e.g., Yehiel ben Yekutiel of Rome, *Sefer Ma'alot ha-Middot* (Jerusalem: Eshkol, 1968), "*Ma'alot ha-Histapkut*," pp. 266–288.

19. *Midrash on Psalms*, Solomon Buber, ed. (Vilna, 1891), 50:3, p. 140b. See also *Leviticus Rabbah* 9:2; *Midrash Tanhuma*, Solomon Buber, ed. (Vilna, 1885), "*Tzav*," para. 8, p. 9a.

20. *Shevuot* 15a.

21. *Pesikta d'Rav Kahana*, Solomon Buber, ed. (Lyck, 1868), 9:12, p. 79a; see n. 98 for variants.

22. Quoted in Gershom Mendes Seixas, *A Religious Discourse: Thanksgiving Sermon* (New York: Jewish Historical Society of New York, 1977), Introduction, p. vii. See Rose S. Klein, "Washington's Thanksgiving Proclamations," *American Jewish Archives* 20:2 (Nov. 1968): 156–162.

23. Ibid., pp. 1–16.

24. On homiletics as a significant form of Jewish ethical literature, see, e.g., Joseph

Dan et al., "Homiletic Literature," *Encyclopedia Judaica*, vol. 8, pp. 946–960. See also Dan, *Sifrut ha-Musar ve-ha-Derush* (Jerusalem: Keter, 1975).

25. See the extensive discussion on the relationship between oral delivery and written form of Jewish sermons as well as an illuminating discussion of other aspects of Jewish homiletical literature in Marc Saperstein, *Jewish Preaching* (New Haven, CT: Yale University Press, 1989), Introduction, pp. 1–109. The earlier work by Israel Bettan, *Studies in Jewish Preaching* (Cincinnati: Hebrew Union College Press, 1939) is also indispensable for a study of this largely neglected area of Jewish scholarship. The present discussion of Jewish homiletics is indebted to the scholarly researches of Bettan, Dan, Saperstein, and others.

26. See Abraham bar Hiyya, *The Meditation of the Sad Soul*, Geoffrey Wigoder, trans. (London: Routledge and Kegan Paul, 1969). For the view that this is the first homiletical work in the Middle Ages written in Hebrew, see Dan, *Sifrut*, pp. 69–70.

27. See Bahya ben Asher, *Kad ha-Kemah* (Lwow, 1892). In English translation: Charles B. Chavel, trans., *Encyclopedia of Torah Thoughts* (New York: Shilo, 1980). See also Bettan, pp. 89–130.

28. On Seixas, see, e.g., Jacob Rader Marcus, *Early American Jewry*, vol. 1 (Philadelphia: Jewish Publication Society, 1951), pp. 94–98: idem, "The Handsome Young Priest in the Black Gown: The Personal World of Gershom Seixas," *Hebrew Union College Annual* 70/71 (1969/1970): 409–467; Thomas Kessner, "Gershom Mendes Seixas," *American Jewish Historical Quarterly* 78:4 (June 1969): 445–471; David Da Sola Pool, *Portraits Etched in Stone* (New York: Columbia University Press, 1952), pp. 344–375.

29. Quoted in Marcus, "Handsome Young Priest," p. 463.

CHAPTER 3

1. *Avot* 5:16.

2. See, e.g., Joseph Albo, *Sefer ha-Ikkarim – The Book of Principles*, 6 vols., Isaac Husik, trans. (Philadelphia: Jewish Publication Society, 1946), vol. 3, p. 330.

3. A major issue related to the love of God is the relationship between love of God and "fear of God" (*Yirat Shamayim*). This issue is beyond the scope of this chapter. An entire literature has been written about it. One should note, however, that in most of biblical literature, the primary emotion used to describe God's relationship with Israel is love, while the primary emotion used to describe the individual's relationship with God is *yirah*. In this context, *yirah* can mean both "fear" and "awe." In Deuteronomy, however, love appears as the desired human emotion in relation to God. Later sources distinguish between two types of *yirah*, i.e., fear of punishment, and awe of God. Once this distinction was made, debate ensued as to whether awe or love of God is superior. The issue is never resolved in classical Jewish religious literature. For discussion of these themes, see, e.g., Bernard Bamberger, "Fear and Love of God in the Old Testament," *Hebrew Union College Annual* 6 (1929): 34–55; Adolph Buchler, *Studies in Sin and Atonement* (London: N.p., 1928), pp. 118–175; Louis Jacobs, *Jewish Values* (London: Vallentine, Mitchell, 1960), pp. 31–50; Byron L. Sherwin, "Fear of God,"

chap. in Arthur A. Cohen and Paul Mendes-Flohr, eds., *Contemporary Jewish Religious Thought* (New York: Scribner's, 1987), pp. 245–255; Isaiah Tishby, *Mishnat ha Zohar* (Jerusalem: Mosad Bialik, 1961), vol. 2, pp. 280–306.

4. See, e.g., Byron L. Sherwin, "Law and Love in Jewish Theology," *Anglican Theological Review* 60:4 (October 1982): 467–481.

5. See, e.g., Elijah de Vidas, *Reshit Hokhmah*, "Sha'ar ha-Ahavah," chap. 2, beginning, quoting *Zohar* 3: 267b. See Elijah de Vidas, *Reshit Hokhmah ha-Shalem*, 2 vols. (Jerusalem: Or ha-Musar, 1984), p. 367.

6. This idea is expressed by De Vidas and also by Leon Ebreo (Judah Abarbanel) in his *Philosophy of Love*.

7. Judah Loew, *Netivot Olom*, 2 vols. (New York: Judaica Press, 1969), "*Netiv Ahavat ha-Shem*," chap. 1, p. 38.

8. On love as the attraction of like to like, see, e.g., Albo, vol. 3, chap. 37, pp. 336–338. See also discussion and sources noted in Alexander Altmann, *Studies in Religious Philosophy and Mysticism* (Ithaca, NY: Cornell University Press, 1969), pp. 5–7.

9. Bahya ibn Pakudah, *The Book of Direction to the Duties of the Heart*, Menahem M. Mansoor, trans. (London: Routledge and Kegan Paul, 1973), chap. 10, p. 427.

10. On both theories of love, i.e., the attraction of like to like and the attraction of opposites, see Plato, *Laws*, Book Nine, para. 837; Loew, pp. 38–39.

11. On love of God in talmudic literature, see, e.g., George Foot Moore, *Judaism*, 2 vols. (Cambridge, MA: Harvard University Press, 1927), vol. 2, pp. 96–101; C. G. Montefiore and H. Loewe, *A Rabbinic Anthology* (New York: Meridian, 1963), pp. 58–86, 93–116; Ephraim E. Urbach, *The Sages*, Israel Abrahams, trans. (Cambridge, MA: Harvard University Press, 1987), pp. 400–419.

12. For an extensive discussion of these talmudic and medieval approaches to love of God, see, e.g., Louis Jacobs, *A Jewish Theology* (New York: Behrman House, 1973), pp. 152–173; Idem, *Jewish Values*, pp. 50–73. On the love of God in medieval Jewish literature, including *Sefer ha-Yashar*, see the important work, Georges Vajda, *L'Amour de Dieu dans la Theologie Juive du Moyen Age* (Paris, 1957).

13. See, e.g., Urbach, pp. 365–367.

14. *Sifre on Deuteronomy*, Louis Finkelstein, ed. (Berlin: Gesellschaft zur Forderung der Wissenschaft des Judentums, 1939), paras. 32–33, pp. 54–59.

15. *Seder Eliyahu Rabbah*, Meir Friedmann, ed. (Vilna: Ahiyasaf, 1903), chap. 26, p. 140.

16. Urbach, p. 365.

17. See, e.g., Daniel C. Matt, "The Mystic and the Mitzvot," chap. in Arthur Green, ed., *Jewish Spirituality* (New York: Crossroad, 1986), pp. 367–404.

18. Moses Maimonides, *Mishneh Torah – Sefer ha-Mada*, "Laws of Repentance," 10:3.

19. Ibid., 10:6.

20. See Moses Maimonides, *Guide of the Perplexed*, Book III, chap. 51.

21. See, e.g., Menachem Kellner, *Maimonides on Human Perfection* (Atlanta: Scholars Press, 1990).

22. Maimonides, *Guide of the Perplexed*, Shlomo Pines, trans. (Chicago: University of Chicago Press, 1963), Book I, chap. 1, p. 22.

23. Maimonides, "Laws of Repentance," 10:6. See also, Albo, chap. 35, p. 318.

24. Maimonides, *Guide*, Book 3, chap. 51, p. 623.

25. See, e.g., the writings of Hayyim ben Betzalel of Friedberg, the brother of Judah Loew of Prague. For a summary of his views in this regard, see Byron L. Sherwin, "In the Shadow of Greatness: Rabbi Hayyim Ben Betsalel of Friedberg," *Jewish Social Studies* 37:1 (January 1975): 51–55.

26. Maimonides, *Guide*, Book 3, chap. 51, p. 627.

27. Ibid., p. 628.

28. Moses Hayyim Luzzatto, *Mesilat Yesharim — The Path of the Upright*, Mordecai M. Kaplan, trans. (Philadelphia: Jewish Publication Society, 1936), p. 28.

29. On love of God in Judah Loew's writings, see Abner Weiss, "Rabbi Judah Loew of Prague: Theory of Human Nature and Morality" (Ph.D. dissertation: Yeshiva University Press, 1969), pp. 330–347.

30. On Loew's theory of opposites, see Byron L. Sherwin, *Mystical Theology and Social Dissent* (New York: Oxford University Press, 1982), pp. 70–75.

31. Loew, p. 38.

32. The idea of God's essential self-sufficiency is a basic teaching of medieval Jewish philosophy. See, e.g., Joseph ibn Zaddik, *Ha-Olam ha-Katan*, S. Horovitz, ed. (Breslau: Shatzky, 1903), pp. 54–56. This assumption has led some medieval Jewish philosophers, such as Maimonides, to claim that since God is self-sufficient, He neither desires nor has any relationships. For example, in the *Guide* (Book I, chap. 52, p. 118), Maimonides wrote, "There is, in truth, no relation in any respect between God and His creatures." From this starting point, it is difficult for Jewish philosophers to find a basis for religion predicated upon the divine–human relationship. It also sets severe parameters upon the nature of love of God, for how can there be love without relationship?

33. On human fulfillment of a divine need (*tzorekh gavoah*) in Jewish mysticism, see, e.g., Morris Faierstein, "God's Need for the Commandments in Medieval Kabbalah," *Conservative Judaism* 36:1 (Fall 1982): 45–59. On the human influence on the divine in Jewish mysticism, see, e.g., Moshe Idel, *Kabbalah: New Perspectives* (New Haven, CT: Yale University Press, 1988), pp. 173–200.

34. Loew, p. 39.

35. On *devekut* in Loew's thought, see Sherwin, *Mystical Theology*, pp. 131–141. On *devekut* in general, see, e.g., Idel, *Kabbalah*, pp. 35–73; Gershom Scholem, *The Messianic Idea in Judaism* (New York: Schocken, 1971), pp. 203–227; Sherwin, *Mystical Theology*, pp. 124–142; Mordecai Pachter, "The Concept of Devekut in the Homiletical Ethical Writings of 16th Century Safed," chap. in Isadore Twersky, ed., *Studies in Medieval Jewish History and Literature*, vol. 2 (Cambridge, MA: Harvard University Press, 1984), pp. 171–231. The equation of love of God with *devekut* was common among Jewish mystics, for example, in the extensive discussion about love of God in Elijah de Vidas's *Reshit Hokhmah*, this equation is assumed. See, e.g., the discussion in Pachter, p. 211.

36. Judah Loew, *Nezah Yisrael* (New York: Judaica Press, 1969), chap. 51, p. 195.

37. The phrase "a part of God above" was not used by Loew, but was used (and perhaps coined) by his disciple Shabbtai Sheftel ha-Levi Horowitz. This term, describing the human soul, became immensely popular in hasidic sources. See Sherwin, *Mystical Theology*, pp. 137–138.

38. Leon Ebreo, *The Philosophy of Love*, F. Friedeberg-Seeley and Jean H. Barnes, trans. (London: Soncino, 1937), p. 54.

39. See, e.g., Moshe Idel, *The Mystical Experience in Abraham Abulafia* (Albany, NY: SUNY Press, 1988), pp. 179–227.

40. Quoted in Simon Givurtchav, ed., *Sefer ha-Besht*, 2 vols. (Jerusalem: Horeb, 1961), vol. 1, p. 144, n. 65 from *Za'avat ha-Rivash*.

41. Moses Cordevero, *Tomer Devorah—The Palm Tree of Deborah*, Louis Jacobs, trans. (London: Vallentine, Mitchell, 1960), chap. 5, p. 94

42. Elijah de Vidas, *Reshit Hokhmah, "Sha'ar ha-Ahavah,"* chap. 4, p. 426.

43. Menahem Nahum of Tchernobyl, *Ma'or Einayim* (Jerusalem: Ma'or Einayim, 1966), "Ve-Ethanan," p. 188.

44. That love of God can lead to love of one's fellow human being is true for the talmudic rabbis and for some of the Jewish mystics, but not usually for the Jewish philosophers. For the philosophers, human love and ethics are but preludes to eventual attachment to the divine.

45. See Rashi to *Shabbat* 31a; also see *Exodus Rabbah* 27:1.

46. *Avot d'Rabbi Natan*, Solomon Schechter, ed. (Vienna: N.p., 1887), "A," chap. 16 end, p. 32b.

47. See, e.g., Samuel Sandmel, *The Hebrew Scriptures* (New York: Oxford University Press, 1978), pp. 45–47. Sandmel notes that the Septuagint refers to biblically mentioned *Sefer ha-Yashar* as "The Book of Song," based on the emended reading *sefer ha-shayar*.

48. Levi ben Gerson (Gersonides), *Commentary to the Torah* [Hebrew] (Venice: Bomberg, 1547), to Joshua 10:13.

49. Rashi on 2 Samuel 1:18.

50. *Avodah Zarah* 25a.

51. This book is attributed to Joseph ben Gorion ha-Kohen. Its first printing was Venice, 1625.

52. This volume was first published in Vienna, 1811. The standard edition was edited by Shraga Fish Rosenthal, Berlin, 1898.

53. See, e.g., Joseph Dan, *The Esoteric Theology of Ashkenazi Hasidism* [Hebrew] (Jerusalem: Mosad Bialik, 1968), p. 211.

54. For a summary of the discussion regarding authorship of *Sefer ha-Yashar*, see *Sefer ha-Yashar*, Seymour J. Cohen, trans., pp. xii–xvi and sources noted there. See also Shimon Shokek, "*Sefer ha-Yashar* within the Framework of Thirteenth-Century Hebrew Ethical Literature" (Ph.D. dissertation: Hebrew University, 1986), and sources noted there.

55. *Sefer ha-Yashar*, Cohen, trans., pp. 8–9.

56. See, e.g., Jacob Elbaum, *Petihot ve-Histagrut* (Jerusalem: Magnes Press, 1990), p. 229, and Dov Katz, *Tenu'at ha-Musar*, vol. 1 (Jerusalem: Brody-Katz, 1974), p. 50.

CHAPTER 4

1. See, e.g., *Pesahim* 53b, and many references in Jewish liturgical texts, especially in prayers for the dead.

2. In the talmudic reference this is not the first question in sequence of the text, but Maimonides considers it first in sequence and in importance. See *Shabbat* 31a; Moses Maimonides, *Mishneh Torah – Sefer ha-Mada*, "Laws of Study of the Torah" 3:5.

3. See, e.g., *P. Peah* 1:1, *Shabbat* 127a. This text has been incorporated into the daily liturgy. According to the Lurianic kabbalists, an angel is created when one performs a *mitzvah*, but angels created through study are of greater spiritual quality than angels created through the performance of other commandments. See, e.g., Hayyim Vital, *Sha'ar Ruah ha-Kodesh* (Jerusalem: Eshel, 1963), p. 9.

4. Joseph Karo, *Shulhan Arukh – "Yoreh Deah"* 246:18. See also Maimonides, *Mishneh Torah – Sefer ha-Mada*, "Laws of Study of the Torah" 3:3.

5. In the Talmud, see, e.g., *Ethics of the Fathers* 2:8; *Sanhedrin* 99b. In medieval Jewish ethical literature, see, e.g., Bahya ben Asher, *Kad ha-Kemah* (Lwow, 1892), "Torah," p. 93a: "Human beings were created primarily to study Torah."

6. This attitude is expressed, for example, in talmudic statements such as: "A learned bastard takes precedence over an ignorant High Priest." A king takes precedence over a High Priest, but a scholar takes precedence over a king, "for if a scholar dies, there is none to replace him." See *Horayot* 13a. In *Avodah Zarah* 3a, we read, "Even a gentile who is occupied with study of the Torah is like the High Priest."

7. For an example of the view that study of the Torah is the key to Jewish survival, see, e.g., the well-known parable of the fox and the fish attributed to Rabbi Akiva, *Berakhot* 61b.

8. On prayer as an equivalent replacement of sacrifice, see, e.g., *Berakhot* 26a-b. On the equation of Torah study with sacrifice, see, e.g., *Menahot* 110a.

9. See, e.g., *Rosh ha-Shanah* 18a. That prayer not only replaces but surpasses sacrifice, see, e.g., *Midrash Tanhuma* [*ha-Nidpas*] (Jerusalem: Levin-Epstein, 1964), "*va-yerah*," para. 1, p. 24b.

10. Judah Loew, *Netivot Olom*, 2 vols. (New York: Judaica, 1969), vol. 1, "*Netiv ha-Torah*," chap. 9, p. 40.

11. For the purpose of study of Torah as self-knowledge, see, e.g., Alexander Altmann, ed., *Or Zaru'a*, n.s. 9, *Kovetz al-Yad* (1980): 249.

12. On study of the Torah as a catalyst for love of God and communion with God, see, e.g., *Sefer ha-Hinukh*, attributed to Aaron ha-Levi of Barcelona (Jerusalem: Eshkol, n.d.), no. 418, p. 253; Loew, pp. 31, 39.

13. Maimonides, *Mishneh Torah – Sefer ha-Mada*, "Laws of Study of the Torah" 4:19. See also the view in the midrash that the school represents a higher level of sanctity in *Midrash Tehillim*, Solomon Buber, ed. (Vilna: Romm, 1891), 84:4, p. 186a.

14. *Megillah* 26b-27a.

15. See Jacob ben Asher, *Arba'ah Turim*, and Joseph Karo, *Shulhan Arukh*, "*Orah Hayyim*," para. 153.

16. For alerting me to the presence of this notion in the *Zohar*, I am grateful to Professor Moshe Idel. In Lurianic Kabbalah, see, e.g., Isaiah Horowitz, *Shnei Luhot ha-Brit*, 3 vols. (Jerusalem: Edison, 1960), "*Masekhet Shavuot*," vol. 2, pp. 88–89. See also Lawrence Fine, *Techniques for Mystical Meditation for Achieving Prophecy and the Holy Spirit in the Teachings of Isaac Luria and Hayyim Vital* (Ph.D. dissertation: Brandeis University, 1976).

17. *Zohar* 1:4b.

18. Maimonides, Mishneh Torah – Sefer ha-Mada, "Laws of Study of the Torah" 1:8, 10.

19. Megillah 6b.

20. See, e.g., Ethics of the Fathers 3:17 on learning and ethical behavior. The idea of Torah lishmah is often misunderstood as study for its own sake, for its own intrinsic value; Torah lishmah actually means study for God's sake, study as a means of divine worship. The idea that study has its own intrinsic value is characteristic of Jewish teaching, but is not the same as Torah lishmah. On study for its own sake, i.e., for the sake of the Torah, see, e.g., Taanit 7a. See Nedarim 62a where study for the sake of self-aggrandizement is repudiated. For study of Torah as a means of spiritual self-development, see, e.g., Loew, pp. 9, 22, 34.

21. On the expression, "a donkey carrying books," see, e.g., Israel Davidson, Otzar ha-Mashalim ve-ha-Pitgamim (Jerusalem: Mosad ha-Rav Kook, 1969), no. 2851, p. 171, n. 39. See, e.g., Bahya ibn Pakudah, Sefer Hovvot ha-Levavot – Duties of the Heart, 2 vols. (Hebrew-English edition), Moses Hyamson, trans. (Jerusalem: Boys Town, 1965), "Shaar Avodat ha-Elohim," sec. 4, pp. 218–219.

22. See this volume, chap. 7.

23. Sifre on Deuteronomy, Louis Finkelstein, ed. (Berlin, 1939), "Ekev," para. 41, pp. 84–85 on Deuteronomy 5:1. See the well-known talmudic discussion of whether study or deeds takes precedence in Kiddushin 30b, and see Judah Loew's commentary on it, Loew, p. 8. Here Loew insists that "Torah study precedes all the commandments." There is, of course, the opposite view that practice takes precedence; see, e.g., Ethics of the Fathers 1:17; Yevamot 109b.

24. Ethics of the Fathers 2:5.

25. Leviticus Rabbah 35:7; P. Berakhot 1:2.

26. See Nahmanides' Iggeret ha-Musar, printed in many prayer books, and in Israel Abrahams, ed., Hebrew Ethical Wills (Philadelphia: Jewish Publication Society, 1926), p. 98. See the ethical will of the Gaon of Vilna, in Abrahams, p. 322.

27. Bahya ibn Pakudah, pp. 220–221.

28. See, e.g., Yoma 86a.

29. Yalkut Shimoni, 2 vols. (New York: Pardes, 1944), "Proverbs," vol. 2, no. 947, p. 492b.

30. Orhot Zaddikim – The Ways of the Righteous, Seymour J. Cohen, trans. (New York: Feldheim, 1969), "Torah," pp. 560–563, commenting on Ruth Rabbah 1:2.

31. Nedarim 41a.

32. See Abraham J. Heschel, A Passion for Truth (New York: Farrar, Straus and Giroux, 1973), p. 107.

33. Cited in Abraham J. Heschel, The Earth is the Lord's (New York: Henry Schuman, Inc., 1950), p. 83.

34. Berakhot 11a.

35. Loew, p. 32.

36. Pesikta de-Rav Kahana, Solomon Buber, ed. (Lyck: Mekitzei Nirdamim, 1868), 12:12, p. 102a; Midrash Tanhuma, S. Buber, ed. (Vilna, 1885), "Yitro," para. 7, p. 37a.

37. Shneur Zalman of Liady, Lekutei Amarim [Tanya] (Brooklyn: Otzar ha-Hasidim, 1965), chap. 5, pp. 18–19. The analogy between study and eating is earlier; see, e.g., Seder Eliyahu Zuta, chap. 14, in Seder Eliyahu Rabba ve-Seder Eliyahu Zuta,

Meir Friedmann, ed. (Vilna: Ahiyasaf, 1904), p. 195. See also *Exodus Rabbah* 25:9.

38. Mordecai of Chernobyl, *Lekutei Torah* (New York: Noble Printing Co., 1954), "*Le-Rosh ha-Shanah,*" p. 22b.

39. See, e.g., Loew, p. 34.

40. *Sifre*, para. 345, p. 402; *Pesahim* 49b. See also, e.g., *Exodus Rabbah* 33:7.

41. Samuel of Uceda, *Midrash Shmuel* (Jerusalem: Body-Katz, n.d.), pp. 61a–b.

42. Moses Hayyim Ephraim of Sudylkow, *Degel Mahaneh Ephraim* (Jerusalem: Hadar, 1963), "*Aharei,*" p. 175.

43. For the personification of the Torah, see, e.g., Solomon Schechter, *Aspects of Rabbinic Theology* (New York: Macmillan, 1909), chap. 9 and sources noted there.

44. On the Torah and Israel, see, e.g., *Exodus Rabbah* 30:5, 33:7; *Song of Songs Rabbah* 8:11. Note Byron L. Sherwin, "Law and Love in Jewish Theology," *Anglican Theological Review* 64:4 (October 1982): 467–481, and sources noted there.

45. *Numbers Rabbah* 12:8.

46. See, e.g., Moshe Idel, *Kabbalah: New Perspectives* (New Haven, CT: Yale University Press, 1988), p. 388, n. 184.

47. For a discussion of the "palace motif" and its use in this and other medieval texts, and for an erudite examination of the use of allegory in medieval Jewish literature, see Frank Talmage, "Apples of Gold: The Inner Meanings of Sacred Texts in Medieval Judaism," chap. in Arthur Green, ed., *Jewish Spirituality* (New York: Crossroads, 1986), pp. 313–355. For an analysis of the texts from the *Zohar* excerpted below, see Idel, pp. 227–230. Compare Gershom Scholem, "The Meaning of the Torah in Jewish Mysticism," chap. in his *On the Kabbalah and Its Symbolism* (New York: Schocken, 1965), pp. 55–65.

48. On the *Zohar*, see, e.g., Daniel C. Matt, ed., *Zohar: The Book of Enlightenment* (New York: Paulist Press, 1983); Gershom Scholem, *Major Trends in Jewish Mysticism* (New York: Schocken, 1961), pp. 156–244; Isaiah Tishbi, *Mishnat ha-Zohar*, 2 vols. (Jerusalem: Mosad Bialik, 1957–1961); Eng. trans., David Goldstein, *The Wisdom of the Zohar* (London: Oxford University Press, 1988).

49. See, e.g., Abraham J. Heschel, "The Mystical Element in Judaism," chap. in Louis Finkelstein, ed., *The Jews: Their History, Culture, and Religion* (Philadelphia: Jewish Publication Society, 1960), pp. 932–953.

CHAPTER 5

1. Parts of the present discussion of repentance are drawn from my more extensive discussion of this problem in Byron L. Sherwin, *In Partnership with God* (Syracuse, NY: Syracuse University Press, 1990), pp. 119–130, 242–246.

2. Bahya ben Asher, *Kad ha-Kemah* (Lwow: N.p., 1892), p. 66a. English translation: Charles B. Chavel, *Encyclopedia of Torah Thoughts* (New York: Shilo Publishing House, 1980), pp. 587–588. See also Bahya ibn Pakudah, *The Book of Direction to the Duties of the Heart*, Menahem Mansoor, trans. (London: Routledge and Kegan Paul, 1973), pp. 330, 333; *Orhot Zaddikim*, Seymour J. Cohen, trans. (New York: Feldheim, 1969), pp. 460–461; Isaac Aboab, *Menorat ha-Ma'or* (Jerusalem: Mosad ha-Rav Kook,

1961), p. 593; Eliezer Azikiri, *Sefer Hareidim* (Jerusalem: N.p., 1957), chap. 62, p. 240.

3. Joseph Albo, *Sefer ha Ikkarim*, 6 vols., Isaac Husik, trans. (Philadelphia: Jewish Publication Society, 1946), vol. 4, sec. 25, p. 224.

4. Alexander Pope, "An Essay on Criticism," in *Alexander Pope: Selected Works*, L. Kronenberger, ed. (New York: Modern Library, 1948), p. 47.

5. *Shabbat* 153a. See *Ethics of the Fathers* 2:15.

6. *Ecclesiastes Rabbah* 1:1.

7. Jonah Gerondi (Jonah ben Abraham of Gerona), *Sha'arey Teshuvah—Gates of Repentance*, 2 vols., Shraga Silverstein, trans. and ed. (New York: Feldheim, 1971), 2:26, 30, 31, pp. 116–119.

8. This idea of repentance as a means to self-renewal is expressed by the talmudic comparison of the penitent to a new "creation"; see, e.g., *P. Rosh ha-Shanah*, chap. 2; *Leviticus Rabbah* 29:12. There is also the saying, "A penitent is as a newborn child" (*Ba'al teshuvah ke-Nolad Damei*).

9. Albo, p. 237. See also Gerondi, 2:8, pp. 80–81.

10. Bahya, p. 333.

11. In most of the medieval literature on *teshuvah*, twenty-four obstacles to repentance are listed. See, e.g., Maimonides, *Mishneh Torah—Sefer ha-Mada*, "Hilkhot Teshuvah," 4:1–6; Gerondi, pp. 69–71; Menachem Meiri, *Hibbur ha-Teshuvah*, A. Schreiber, ed. (New York: Schulzinger, 1950), pp. 72–112; *Orhot Zaddikim*, pp. 480–489; Israel ibn Al-Nakawa, *Menorat ha-Maor*, 4 vols. Hyman G. Enelow, ed. (New York: Bloch, 1931), vol. 3, pp. 48–51. The eleventh-century codifier, Yitzhak Al-Fasi is the first scholar to list these twenty-four obstacles to teshuvah in his commentary to the end of the talmudic tractate *Yoma*. He appears to be quoting an earlier source, but this source was unknown to later commentators. For example, the fourteenth-century commentator, Rabbenu Nissan, in his super-commentary to Al-Fasi observed, "I do not know where this has been (previously) taught." Similarly, in a responsum, Maimonides states that an earlier source than Al-Fasi is also unknown to him; see Maimonides, *Teshuvot ha-Rambam*, 3 vols., J. Blau, ed. (Jerusalem: Mikize Nirdamim, 1948), vol. 1, no. 121, pp. 216–217.

12. Bahya, p. 346.

13. Moses Hayyim Luzzatto, *Mesilat Yesharim—The Path of the Upright*, Mordecai M. Kaplan, trans. (Philadelphia: Jewish Publication Society, 1966), p. 122.

14. Albo, pp. 237–238.

15. Ibid., p. 235.

16. Isaiah Horowitz, *Shnei Luhot ha-Brit*, 3 vols. (Jerusalem: Edison, 1960), "Hilkhot Teshuvah," vol. 3, 173b. In *Reshit Hokhmah*, "Shaar Teshuvah," chap. 2, p. 108a, Elijah de Vidas relates action, speech, and deeds to the three levels of the human soul, i.e., *nefesh, ruah, neshamah*. See Elijah de Vidas, *Reshit Hokhmah* (Tel Aviv: Esther Press, n.d.).

17. Moses di Trani, *Beth Elohim* (Warsaw: Goldman, 1852), p. 29b. Di Trani may have been anticipated by the twelfth-century Jewish philosopher Joseph ibn Zaddik in his *Olam ha-Katan*, S. Horovitz, ed. (Breslau: Schatzky, 1903), 4:1, p. 71.

18. Bahya, p. 334.

19. Maimonides, "*Hilkhot Teshuvah*" 2:2. Note Jacob ben Asher, *Arba'ah Turim*—

"*Orah Hayyim*," para. 607. For further sources regarding confession, see Hayyim Abramowitz, *Heikhal ha-Teshuvah* (Bnei Brak: Nezah, 1961).

20. Maimonides, "*Hilkhot Teshuvah*" 1:1.

21. A form of private confession not usually identified with Judaism is confession to another person. While not pervasive in Judaism, this form of confession was practiced both by the medieval German *hasidim* and by adherents to various schools of nineteenth-century eastern European Hasidism, especially the Bratzlaver *hasidim*. In both these movements, confession was made to a spiritual mentor who would then assign the penitent tasks to perform (i.e., penances) to effect the realization of repentance. For this practice among the German *hasidim*, see Ivan Marcus, *Piety and Society* (Leiden, Holland: E. J. Brill, 1981), pp. 77–78, 131, 14–165. In later Hasidism, see Aaron Wertheim, *Halakhot ve-Halikhot ba-Hasidut* (Jerusalem: Mosad ha-Rav Kook, 1960), pp. 22–23. Note Louis Jacobs, *A Jewish Theology* (New York: Behrman House, 1973), pp. 257–258. On confession to a friend in Hasidism, see Joseph Weiss, *Studies in Eastern European Jewish Mysticism*, David Goldstein, ed. (New York: Oxford University Press, 1985), pp. 160–167. On Bratzlaver Hasidism, see, e.g., Arthur Green, *Tormented Master: A Life of Rabbi Nahman of Bratslav* (University, AL: University of Alabama Press, 1979), pp. 45–46, and Ada Rappoport Albert, "Confession in the Circle of Rabbi Nahman of Bratslav," *Bulletin of the Institute of Jewish Studies* 1 (1973): 65–75.

22. Horowitz, p. 171b.

23. *Yoma* 36b. See also *Tosefta Yoma* 2:1 and *Sifra* (Vienna: Shlossberg, 1862), "*Aharei*" 2:9.

24. See Solomon Schechter, *Aspects of Rabbinic Theology* (New York: Macmillan, 1909), pp. 219–263, 293–343.

25. See, e.g., *Yoma* 86b; Horowitz, p. 175b; Albo, 4:25, pp. 225–226. Albo does not consider repentance motivated by fear of punishment or by fear of death to be repentance at all. On attitudes of fear, love, and reverence for God, see Byron L. Sherwin, "Fear of God," chap. in Arthur A. Cohen and Paul Mendes-Flohr, eds., *Contemporary Jewish Religious Thought* (New York: Scribners, 1987), pp. 255–261.

26. De Vidas, *Reshit Hokhmah*, "*Shaar ha-Teshuvah*," chap. 3, p. 113a. See Maimonides, "*Hilkhot Teshuvah*" 7:6, 7.

27. Albo, pp. 232, 464.

28. *Pesikta Rabbati* 44:9.

29. *Zohar* 3:122a.

30. See, e.g., Horowitz, p. 180a.

31. *Zohar* 3:122a.

32. On repentance in the *Zohar*, see Isaiah Tishbi, *Mishnat ha-Zohar*, 2 vols. (Jerusalem: Mosad Bialik, 1961), vol. 2, pp. 735–744.

33. Maimonides, "*Hilkhot Teshuvah*" 2:1. In the Talmud, see, e.g., M. *Yoma* 6:2, 8:9; *Yoma* 86b; *Taanit* 16b.

34. Gerondi, 1:36, pp. 50–51.

35. *Orhot Zaddikim*, p. 473, citing *Leviticus Rabbah* 21:5.

36. See, e.g., *Rosh ha-Shanah* 17b; Maimonides, "*Hilkhot Teshuvah*" 2:9.

37. See, e.g., *Yoma* 85b, 87a; *Baba Kamma* 110a.

38. *Leviticus Rabbah* 5:8.

39. See, e.g., *Berakhot* 34b; *Zohar* 2:106b. See discussion of this talmudic text in Bahya, p. 345.

40. On Luzzatto, see this volume, chap. 6.

41. George Vajda, "Bahya ibn Pakudah," *Encyclopedia Judaica*.

42. Julius Guttmann, *Philosophies of Judaism*, David W. Silverman, trans. (New York: Holt, Rinehart and Winston, 1964), p. 118.

43. Moses Hyamson, "Foreword" to his translation of Bahya ibn Pakudah, *Duties of the Heart*, 2 vols. (Jerusalem: Boys Town, 1965), p. 10.

44. Pakudah, Mansoor, trans.

45. *Sanhedrin* 106b. The previous citations are from Bahya's introductory chapter.

46. Bahya, Mansoor trans., p. 444.

47. *Ethics of the Fathers* 2:1.

48. *Yoma* 88b.

49. *Taanit* 16a.

50. *Ethics of the Fathers* 2:10.

CHAPTER 6

1. Moses Hayyim Luzzatto, *Mesilat Yesharim – The Path of the Upright*, Mordecai M. Kaplan, trans. (Philadelphia: Jewish Publication Society, 1936), pp. 207–208.

2. Ibid., pp. 212, 422.

3. (Attributed to) Solomon ibn Gabirol, *Choice of Pearls*, A. Cohen, trans. (New York: Bloch, 1925), no. 626, p. 128. Compare Reinhold Niebuhr, *The Nature and Destiny of Man*, vol. 1 (New York: Scribner's, 1941), p. 207: "The self is afraid of being discovered in its nakedness behind these veils and of being recognized as the author of the veiling deceptions."

4. Quoted in Martin Buber, *Tales of the Hasidim, Early Masters*, Olga Marx, trans. (New York: Schocken, 1947), p. 149.

5. Samuel Edels's ("Maharsha") commentary to the Talmud, in standard editions of the Talmud with commentaries, to *Sanhedrin* 88b. Quoted in Abraham Mase-Zahav, ed., *Tokhahat Musar* (Jerusalem, 1962), p. 71. See also Bahya ben Asher, *Kad ha-Kemah* (Lwow, 1892), "Ga'avah," p. 486.

6. Jonah Gerondi's Commentary on *Ethics of the Fathers* (Jerusalem: Makhon Torah Shelemah, 1969), 4:4, p. 60. See also Jacob Joseph of Polnoye, *Toldeot Ya'akov Yosef* (Jerusalem, 1967), "Bereshit," p. 30, in the name of Jacob Yaabetz. Note Solomon Schechter, "Saints and Saintliness," in his *Studies in Judaism* (New York: Meridian, 1958), p. 138.

7. *Seder Eliyahu Rabbah*, Meir Friedmann, ed. (Vienna, Ahiyasaf, 1904), chap. 29, p. 158.

8. Ibid., chap. 16, p. 74.

9. *Sotah* 4b. See Solomon Schechter, *Some Aspects of Rabbinic Theology* (New York: Macmillan, 1909), pp. 233–224.

10. Jacob Joseph of Polnoye, *Ketonet Pasim*, "Ki Tissah." Quoted in *Leshon Hasidim* (Lwow, 1876), p. 39.

11. "The haughty person is as if he makes himself God." See *Mishnat Rabbi Eliezer,* Hyman G. Enelow, ed. (New York: Bloch, 1933), ch. 10, p. 194. For modern views, see, e.g., Will Herberg, *Judaism and Modern Man* (New York: Meridian, 1959), p. 31. Note Jean Paul Sartre's view that to be human means trying to become God. See *The Philosophy of Jean Paul Sartre,* Robert D. Cumming, ed. (New York: Random House, 1965), p. 293, "Man is the being whose project is to be God."

12. *Choice of Pearls,* no. 624, p. 128.

13. *Ethics of the Fathers* 3:1. It was Tertulian who said, "*Inter faeces et urinas nascimur.*"

14. *Berkahot* 28b.

15. *Ethics of the Fathers* 4:4.

16. Bahya ibn Pakudah, *Duties of the Heart,* M. M. Mansoor, trans. (London: Routledge and Kegan Paul, 1973), pp. 311–312. See also Yehiel ben Yekutiel of Rome, *Sefer Ma'alot ha-Middot* (Jerusalem: Eshkol, 1968), p. 173.

17. Luzzatto, p. 414.

18. Bahya, p. 324.

19. Jacob Anatoli, *Malmed ha-Talmidim* (Lyck, 1866), "*Matot,*" p. 152b. Anatoli seems to have borrowed this statement from ibn Gabirol. See Solomon ibn Gabirol, *The Improvement of the Moral Qualities,* Stephen Wise, trans. (New York: Columbia University Press, 1901), p. 79. See *Sefer Ma'alot ha-Middot* on contentment (*histapkut*), pp. 266–278.

20. Hayyim Vital, *Sefer Sha'arey Kedushah* (Jerusalem: Aravah, 1967), 1:2, p. 17.

21. Ibid., 1:2, p. 15. Vital refers here to *Zohar* 1:27b where anger and idolatry are not equated, but compared. Vital, however, equates them. See also Vital, 2:4, p. 52.

22. *Orhot Zaddikim,* Seymour J. Cohen, trans. (New York: Feldheim, 1969), p. 243.

23. *Nedarim* 22b. See *Orhot Zaddikim,* p. 231.

24. *Erubin* 65b.

25. *Orhot Zaddikim,* pp. 230–232. *Orhot Zaddikim* also discusses a positive side to anger, i.e., anger is a necessary spur to survival, and anger is a necessary stimulus in confronting evil and evil people.

26. See, e.g., Heinz Kohut, *The Analysis of the Self* (New York: International Universities Press, 1971).

27. See sources quoted in Aryeh Kaplan, *The Light Beyond: Adventures in Hasidic Thought* (New York: Maznaim, 1981), pp. 287–300.

28. *Nedarim* 22a.

29. *Orhot Zaddikim,* pp. 231.

30. Luzzatto, p. 214.

31. Isaiah Horowitz, *Shnei Luhot ha-Brit,* 3 vols. (Jerusalem: Edison, 1960), "*Hilkhot Teshuvah,*" p. 171a.

32. *Orhot Zaddikim,* pp. 231. See also Edels on *Sabbath* 67.

33. Edels on *Sanhedrin* 88b. See also Hayyim ibn Attar, *Or ha-Hayyim* on Exodus 34:30, in standard editions of the Pentateuch with commentaries. For the hasidic master, Elimelekh of Lizensk, "Humility is the source, the root and the sustainer of everything that is sacred." See his teachings in *Noam Elimelekh,* Gedaliah Nigal, ed. (Jerusalem: Mosad ha-Rav Kook, 1978), "*Ekev*" (beginning), p. 487 (p. 90d in the first

edition, Lwow, 1787).

34. Luzzatto, p. 208.

35. Jacob Joseph of Polnoye, *Toledot Ya'akov Yosef*, "*Ekev*," p. 633. Similarly, Jonah Gerondi in his commentary to the *Ethics of the Fathers* 2:17, p. 36, warns that self-deprecation should not become an excuse for failing to embark on a process of repentance because one feels inadequate to the task.

36. Bahya ben Asher, *Kad ha-Kemah*, "*Ga'avah*," p. 52a-b. To be sure, a stance in Jewish ethical literature does teach that humility entails self-deprecation. See, e.g., Moses Cordevero, *The Palm Tree of Deborah*, Louis Jacobs, trans. (London: Vallentine Mitchell, 1960), chap. 2, pp. 76–77: "Humility chiefly means that man finds no worth in himself, but values himself as nought . . . until he becomes despicable in his own eyes."

37. Menahem Nahum of Chernobyl, *Yismah Lev* in his *Me'or Einayim* (Jerusalem: Me'or Einayim, 1966), pp. 353–354. See the English translation in Louis Jacobs, *Hasidic Thought* (New York: Behrman House, 1976), pp. 92–93.

38. See Bahya ibn Pakudah's notion that there are good and bad varieties of pride and that self-esteem necessary for spiritual development is a good form of pride. Bahya, p. 324. *Orhot Zaddikim*, p. 15, encourages pride when confronting the wicked and offers the example of Mordecai's confrontation with Haman. Edels (to *Sotah* 5a) recommends that a scholar not be self-demeaning lest it lead to the demeaning of the honor due the learning of the Torah that he represents.

39. *Megillah* 31a.

40. Silvano Arieti, *Creativity* (New York: Basic Books, 1976), p. 380.

41. Schechter, "Saints and Saintliness," pp. 138–139. See also Louis Jacobs, *Jewish Values* (London: Vallentine Mitchell, 1960), pp. 113–116.

42. See *Zohar* 3:168a (bottom); Vital, 2:4, p. 51. This statement is also attributed to Rabbi Nahman of Bratzlav.

43. See Menahem ha-Meiri's Hebrew *Commentary to the Ethics of the Fathers* (Jerusalem: 1944), 6:5, p. 202. This attitude is stressed in Hasidism and is called *hishtavut*, ataraxy. The word "*hishtavut*" derives from "*shaveh*" – equal, meaning that everything that happens to an individual should be considered equal in his eyes, no one thing being more important than another. This attitude is discussed extensively in ancient Stoic philosophy. For example, see *Za'avat ha-Rivash*, "The principle of *hishtavut* is important. It means that you should not care whether people consider you to be learned or ignorant in the whole Torah. Constant communion with God, the Creator, is what makes this possible because when you are occupied with achieving communion with God, you are so busy establishing your connection with God that you have no time to think about such lowly things." For a translation of this text, see Joseph Dan, ed., *The Teachings of Hasidism* (New York: Behrman House, 1983), p. 139.

44. See Jacobs, *Jewish Values*, p. 111.

45. Luzzatto, p. 224.

46. Pinhas of Koretz, *Midrash Pinhas* (Jerusalem, 1961), no. 20, p. 13a.

47. Moses Maimonides, *Mishneh Torah* – *Sefer ha-Mada*, "Hilkhot Yesodei ha-Torah" 2:1.

48. Nahman of Bratzlav, *Sefer ha-Middot* (New York, 1965), "*ga'avah*," pp. 63–64.

49. *Eruvin* 13b.

50. See, e.g., Jean Paul Sartre's novel *Nausea* and Albert Camus's novel *The Stranger*.

51. Maimonides, *Eight Chapters*, Joseph I. Gorfinkle, ed. and trans. (New York: Columbia University Press, 1912), chap. 4, p. 55. However, compare Maimonides, *Mishneh Torah — Sefer ha-Mada*, "Hilkhot De'ot" 2:3.

52. *Sanhedrin* 37a.

53. Quoted in a slightly different form by Buber, *Tales of the Hasidim: Later Masters*, pp. 249–250. For the original Hebrew, see the definitive anthology of classical Jewish sources on pride and humility that has been consulted in the preparation of this chapter with much benefit, Israel Jacob ben Mordecai, *Torat ha-Middot — Anavah u-Ga'avah* (Jerusalem: Levin-Epstein, 1966), p. 391.

54. Luzzatto, pp. 2–8. On Luzzatto, see, e.g., Joseph Dan, "Moses Hayyim Luzzatto," *Encyclopedia Judaica*, vol. 11, pp. 599–604; idem, *Sifrut ha-Musar ve-ha-Derush* (Jerusalem: Keter, 1975), pp. 247–263; Simon Ginzburg, *The Life and Works of Moses Hayyim Luzzatto* (Philadelphia: Dropsie College, 1931); Shalom Spiegel, *Hebrew Reborn* (New York: Meridian, 1962), pp. 29–45; Israel Zinberg, *A History of Jewish Literature*, vol. 6, Bernard Martin, trans. (New York: Ktav, 1975), pp. 173–190. For a bibliography of various editions of Luzzatto's published work, see Naftali ben Menahem, *Kitvei Rabbi Moshe Hayyim Luzzatto* (Jerusalem: Mosad ha-Rav Kook, 1951) and for some of his kabbalistic work published from manuscript, see Meir Benayhu, *Kitvei ha-Kabbalah she-le-Ramhal* (Jerusalem, 1979).

55. M. *Sotah* 9:5; *Avodah Zarah* 20b. Luzzatto's works are, by and large, unusually well structured. See, e.g., *Derekh ha-Shem — The Way of God*, Aryeh Kaplan, trans. (New York: Feldheim, 1988). A second English translation of *Mesilat Yesharim* by Shraga Silverstein has been published as *The Path of the Just* (New York: Feldheim, 1989). Silverstein also translated Luzzatto's *Da'at Tevunot* as *The Knowing Heart* (New York: Feldheim, 1989).

56. Luzzatto, p. 408.

57. *Ethics of the Fathers* 2:8.

58. P. *Shabbat* 1:3.

59. *Ethics of the Fathers* 3:1.

60. *Sanhedrin* 24a.

61. *Zohar* on Numbers 22:5.

62. *Baba Metzia* 85b.

63. *Genesis Rabbah* 16:3.

CHAPTER 7

1. Judah Barzeloni, *Peirush Sefer Yetzirah*, Z. H. Halberstein, ed. (Jerusalem: Makor, 1971), p. 94.

2. *Nedarim* 41a.

3. Abraham ibn Ezra on Job 4:21, in standard editions of Hebrew Scripture with commentary.

4. Ibn Ezra on Isaiah 55:1, in standard editions of Hebrew Scripture with commentary.

5. *Yalkut Shimoni*, "Proverbs," para. 929.

6. Abraham bar Hiyya, *Sefer Hegyon ha-Nefesh—Meditation of the Sad Soul*, Geoffrey Wigoder, trans. (London: Routledge and Kegan Paul, 1969), p. 46.

7. *Yalkut Shimoni*, "Proverbs," para. 929.

8. Plato, *Epinomis* 977.

9. Idem, *Meno* 88a; *Phaedo* 69a.

10. Aristotle, *Nichomachean Ethics*, Book 6, end.

11. *Berakhot* 17a.

12. Samuel ha-Nagid, quoted in Israel Davidson, *Otzar ha-Mashalim ve-ha-Pitgamim* (Jerusalem: Mosad ha-Rav Kook, 1969), p. 102, no. 1594.

13. Yehiel ben Yekutiel of Rome, *Sefer Ma'alot ha-Middot* (Jerusalem: Eshkol, 1968), p. 240.

14. *Ethics of the Fathers* 3:22.

15. Moses Hayyim Luzzatto, *Mesilat Yesharim—The Path of the Upright*, Mordecai M. Kaplan, trans. (Philadelphia: Jewish Publication Society, 1936), p. 12.

16. *Ethics of the Fathers* 3:21. On awe of God in Jewish thought, see Byron L. Sherwin, "Fear of God," chap. in Arthur Cohen and Paul Mendes-Flohr, eds., *Contemporary Jewish Religious Thought* (New York: Scribners', 1987), pp. 245–255.

17. *Ethics of the Fathers* 3:11.

18. *Sanhedrin* 38a.

19. Honein ibn Ishak [Isaac], Judah Al-Harizi, trans., *Musrei ha-Philosophim*, Abraham Leventhal, ed. (Cracow, 1896).

20. The first edition of *Mivhar ha-Peninim* is Soncino, 1484. For a bibliographical study of this work, see A. M. Habermann in *Sinai* 25 (1943): 53–63. On Judah ibn Tibbon, see this volume, chap. 13.

21. Isaac Husik, *A History of Medieval Jewish Philosophy* (Philadelphia: Jewish Publication Society, 1940), p. 60.

22. Joseph Kimchi, *Shekel ha-Kodesh—The Holy Shekel*, Hermann Gollancz, trans. (London: Oxford University Press, 1919), p. 3.

23. *Ethics of the Fathers* 4:1.

CHAPTER 8

1. For a general discussion on the nature of health, see, e.g., *International Encyclopedia of the Social Sciences*, D. L. Sills, ed. (New York: Macmillan, 1968–74), s.v. "Health," vol. 5, pp. 330–336; *Encyclopedia of Bioethics*, T. L. Beauchamp and L. Walters, eds. (Belmont, CA: Wadsworth, 1982), chap. 2; Leon Kass, "Regarding the End of Medicine and the Pursuit of Health," chap. in Hunt and Arras, eds., *Ethical Issues in Modern Medicine* (Palo Alto: Mayfield, 1977), pp. 83–515. On medicine in Jewish thought, see, e.g., David M. Feldman, *Health and Medicine in the Jewish Tradition* (New York: Crossroad, 1986), Byron L. Sherwin, "Health, Healing and Tradition," chap. in his *In Partnership with God: Contemporary Jewish Law and Ethics* (Syracuse, NY: Syracuse University Press, 1990), chap. 4.

2. Moses Maimonides, *Eight Chapters*, Joseph I. Gorfinkel, ed. and trans. (New

York: Columbia University Press, 1912), chap. 1, p. 38. See also Maimonides, *Mishneh Torah — Sefer ha-Mada*, "Hilkhot De'ot" 2:1.

3. See, e.g., Abraham ibn Daud, *Emunah Ramah* (Frankfurt, 1852), vol. 3, p. 98; Solomon ibn Gabirol, *The Improvement of the Moral Qualities*, Stephen S. Wise, trans. (New York: Columbia University Press, 1901), p. 16, n. 3; Abraham S. Halkin, "Classical and Arabic Material in ibn Aknin's 'Hygiene of the Soul,' " *Proceedings of the American Academy for Jewish Research* 4, pp. 25–147; the ethical will of Joseph ibn Kaspi in *Hebrew Ethical Wills*, Israel Abrahams, ed. and trans. (Philadelphia: Jewish Publication Society, 1926), p. 136.

4. Plato, *Charmides* 156–157. Compare Aristotle, *Nichomachean Ethics* 1:13.

5. Ibn Gabirol, "Introduction," and 4:1, especially pp. 84–85.

6. See, e.g., *Sanhedrin* 45a; note *Berakhot* 12b.

7. Moses Maimonides, *Treatise on Asthma*, Suessman Muntner, ed. and trans. (Philadelphia: Lippincott, 1963), pp. 24–25.

8. Maimonides, *Pirke Moshe — The Medical Aphorisms of Moses Maimonides*, Fred Rosner and S. Muntner, eds. and trans. (New York: Yeshiva University Press, 1971), 25:9, p. 203.

9. See Arthur Green, *Tormented Master* (University, AL: University of Alabama Press, 1979), p. 234.

10. Maimonides, *Asthma*, p. 89.

11. See, e.g., Ephraim Lunshitz's *Klei Yakar* on Deuteronomy 4:9, in standard editions of Hebrew Scripture with commentaries.

12. Maimonides, *Eight Chapters*, chap. 5, p. 71.

13. Maimonides, "Hilkhot Deot" 3:3.

14. Maimonides, *Asthma*, p. 6.

15. Ibid., p. 36. See also Maimonides, *Hanhagat ha-Beri'ut*, S. Muntner, ed., and Moses ibn Tibbon, trans. (Jerusalem: Mosad ha-Rav Kook, 1957), pp. 67–68.

16. Maimonides, "Hilkhot Deot" 4:15.

17. Maimonides, *Asthma*, p. 24, see also pp. 73–74; *Hanhagat ha-Beri'ut*, p. 31; *Medical Aphorisms*, chap. 20. Note Abraham ibn Ezra to Exodus 23:25 that all illnesses come from improper diet.

18. Joseph ben Meir Zabara, *The Book of Delight*, Moses Hadas, trans. (New York: Columbia University Press, 1932), pp. 116–118.

19. Maimonides, *Asthma*, p. 8.

20. Abrahams, *Hebrew Ethical Wills*, p. 76.

21. Zabara, p. 120.

22. Ibid., p. 123.

23. See, e.g., Ibn Gabirol, p. 16, n. 3.

24. Maimonides, "Hilkhot Deot" 1:4.

25. Ibid., 1:1.

26. Ibid., 2:2.

27. Ibid., 2:3.

28. See, e.g., Maimonides, *Guide of the Perplexed*, Shlomo Pines, trans. (Chicago: University of Chicago Press, 1963), 1:33, 3:12, pp. 81, 445.

29. Moses Hayyim Luzzatto, *The Path of the Upright*, Mordecai M. Kaplan, trans. (Philadelphia: Jewish Publication Society, 1936), chap. 9, p. 122.

30. See this volume, chap. 6.

31. Ibn Gabirol, p. 85.

32. *Sefer ha-Yashar—The Book of Righteousness*, Seymour J. Cohen, trans. (New York: Ktav, 1973), chap. 7, pp. 156–159.

33. See Halkin, p. 111. Note S. Muntner, "A Medieval Treatise on Melancholy," *Ha-Rofe ha-Ivri* (1953), part 1, pp. 62–80.

34. *Orhot Zaddikim—The Ways of the Righteous*, Seymour J. Cohen, trans. (New York: Feldheim, 1969), pp. 214–215.

35. Maimonides, *Medical Aphorisms*, chap. 18, p. 51.

36. Maimonides, "*Hilkhot Deot*" 4:14. See also Maimonides' treatise on hemorrhoids.

37. Quoted in Israel Chodos, "A Critical Edition of Shem Tov Ben Joseph Falaquera's *Bate Hanhagat Guf ha-Bari*," *Ha-rofeh ha-Ivri* (1938), part 1, pp. 114, 191. While physical exercise is encouraged, the rabbinic disapproval of sports in the hellenistic period articulates the rabbis' objection to making the body an end in itself. In this regard, Saul Lieberman wrote, "The physical care of the body played a prominent part in everyday life of the Gentile, and undoubtedly it began to occupy an important place in Jewish life also. The Rabbis, of course, felt a deep contempt for the one who pays excessive attention to the development of the body, but there is no Biblical law forbidding physical training. The Rabbis did not miss the opportunity to condemn sport as an occupation." See Saul Lieberman, *Greek in Jewish Palestine* (New York: Feldheim, 1965), p. 92.

38. Maimonides, *Asthma*, pp. 49–50.

39. Maimonides, "*Hilkhot Deot*" 4:3.

40. Ibid., 4:1.

41. Ibid., 4:13.

42. *Berakhot* 60b.

43. According to the Talmud, "He who prolongs his stay in the privy prolongs his days and years" (*Berakhot* 55a).

44. For example, on evacuation of the bowels as a potential act of cosmic reparation (*tikkun*), see Hayyim Vital, *Pri Etz Hayyim* (Tel Aviv: Eshel, 1966), "*Shaar ha-Tefilah*," chap. 5, p. 22. See also Louis Jacobs, "Eating as an Act of Worship in Hasidic Thought," in S. Stein and R. Loewe, eds., *Studies in Jewish Religious and Intellectual History* (University, AL: University of Alabama Press, 1979), pp. 157–167.

45. *Berakhot* 62a.

46. *Iggeret ha-Kodesh—The Holy Letter*, Seymour J. Cohen, ed. and trans. (New York: Ktav, 1976), pp. 45–48. This text is excerpted below, chap. 11.

47. Maimonides, "*Hilkhot Deot*" 4:14, 20. For further discussion of Maimonides' views on "perfection of the body," see, e.g., Byron L. Sherwin, "Moses Maimonides on Perfection of the Body," *Listening* 9:1/2 (1974): 28–37, and Alexander Altmann, "Maimonides' Four Perfections," *Essays in Jewish Intellectual History* (London: University Press of New England, 1981), pp. 65–77.

48. Chodos, p. 193.

49. Zabara, p. 103.

50. For example, Judah ha-Levi, Moses Maimonides, Moses Nahmanides, Judah ibn Tibbon, Yehiel ben Yekutiel of Rome.

51. See Zeev Gries, *Sefer ha-Hanhagot* (Jerusalem: Mosad Bialik, 1989), pp. 6, 93–99.

52. See Joseph Dan, "Ethical Literature," *Encyclopedia Judaica*, vol. 6, p. 924.

53. See Louis Jacobs, *Holy Living* (London: Jason Aronson, 1990), chap. 7.

54. Abraham J. Heschel, *The Insecurity of Freedom* (New York: Farrar, Straus and Giroux, 1966), p. 285. See also Heschel, *Maimonides: A Biography*, J. Neugroshel, trans. (New York: Farrar, Straus and Giroux, 1982).

CHAPTER 9

1. See Samuel H. Dresner, *Levi Yitzhak of Berditchev* (Bridgeport, CT: Hartmore House, 1974), p. 80.

2. Based on *Berakhot* 16b.

3. Hayyim ben Betzalel, *Sefer ha-Hayyim* (Jerusalem: Weinfeld, 1968), part 3, chap. 5, p. 58.

4. *P. Terumot* 8, end.

5. *Ecclesiastes Rabbah* 7:26.2.

6. Yehiel ben Yekutiel of Rome, *Sefer Ma'alot ha-Middot* (Jerusalem: Eshkol, 1978), pp. 248–249.

7. Moses Maimonides, *The Eight Chapters of Maimonides on Ethics*, Joseph I. Gorfinkle, trans. (New York: Columbia University Press, 1912), chap. 5, p. 70.

8. *Ethics of the Fathers* 3:17.

9. See this volume, chap. 15.

10. *Ethics of the Fathers* 3:7.

11. *Pesikta Rabbati*, Meir Friedmann, ed. (Vienna: Herausgebers, 1880), chap. 25, p. 126b.

12. On the "doctrine of deposit," see Hayyim Hillel Ben-Sasson, *Hagut ve-Hanhagah* (Jerusalem: Mosad Bialik, 1959), pp. 75–89; idem, "Wealth and Poverty in the Teachings of the Preacher Ephraim Lunshitz" [Hebrew], *Zion* 19 (1954): 142–166.

13. Samuel Edels ("Maharsha") on *Shabbat* 125b, in standard editions of the Talmud with commentaries. The desirability of nonreliance on others for sustenance is expressed in the Grace after Meals, "May we never be dependent upon the gifts of others, nor upon their favors."

14. See, e.g., Abner Weiss, "Rabbi Loew of Prague: Theory of Human Nature and Morality" (Ph.D. dissertation: Yeshiva University, 1969), pp. 315–321.

15. *Ethics of the Fathers* 4:1.

16. Solomon ibn Gabirol, *The Improvement of the Moral Qualities*, Stephen S. Wise, trans. (New York: Columbia University Press, 1901), p. 79. Gabirol seems the original source for this proverb, though it is usually ascribed to the thirteenth-century Jewish philosopher Jacob Anatoli in his *Malmed ha-Talmidim* (Lyck, 1886), p. 34a.

17. Judah Loew, *Netivot Olom*, 2 vols. (New York: Judaica Press, 1969), "Netiv ha-Osher," vol. 2, pp. 223–230. On wealth as an external condition, see also Bahya ben Asher, *Kad ha-Kemah* (Lwow, 1892), "Osher," pp. 28a–30a. All citations of Bahya ben Asher in this chapter are from this source.

18. Samuel of Uceda, *Midrash Shmuel* (Jerusalem: Brody-Katz, n.d.), 4:1, p. 70b.

19. This is widely quoted in medieval Jewish ethical literature. See, e.g., Solomon ibn Gabirol, *Choice of Pearls*, A. Cohen, trans. (New York: Bloch, 1925), p. 31, Yehiel ben Yekutiel, *Sefer Ma'alot ha-Middot*, p. 251.

20. Yehiel ben Yekutiel, *Sefer Ma'alot ha-Middot*, p. 250.

21. Ibn Gabirol, *Choice of Pearls*, p. 119.

22. Saadya Gaon, *The Book of Beliefs and Opinions*, Samuel Rosenblatt, trans. (New Haven, CT: Yale University Press, 1948), book 10, chap. 8, p. 380.

23. *Ecclesiastes Rabbah* 7:12.1.

24. Jonathan Eibshitz, *Ya'arot Devash* (Lwow, 1863), part 1, sermon 7, p. 57b.

25. See this volume, chap. 6.

26. The original source is the Hebrew version of the Christian Arab, Honein ibn Ishak, *Musrei ha-Philosophim*, trans. to Hebrew by Judah al-Harizi (Cracow, 1896), 2:21, p. 40. This work is often quoted in medieval Jewish ethical literature, including *Choice of Pearls* and *Sefer Ma'alot ha-Middot*.

27. Yehiel ben Yekutiel, p. 252. Bahya ben Asher expressed a similar view.

28. Saadya, p. 380.

29. The tendency of the wealthy to oppress others is a major theme in the writings of Ephraim Lunshitz. See Ben-Sasson, *op cit.*

30. *Ecclesiastes Rabbah* 1:13.1.

31. Saadya Gaon, p. 379.

32. See, e.g., *Berakhot* 61b.

33. Loew, pp. 227–228. Compare *Numbers Rabbah* 22:8.

34. Moses Hayyim Luzzatto, *Mesilat Yesharim – The Path of the Upright*, Mordecai M. Kaplan, trans. (Philadelphia: Jewish Publication Society, 1936), p. 415.

35. *Exodus Rabbah* 31:3.

36. Moses Maimonides, *Guide of the Perplexed*, Shlomo Pines, trans. (Chicago: University of Chicago Press, 1963), book 3, chap. 39, p. 553.

37. *Ecclesiastes Rabbah* 5:14.1.

38. *Tamid* 52b.

39. See Israel Bettan, *Studies in Jewish Preaching* (Cincinnati: Hebrew Union College Press, 1939), p. 291.

40. On the book and its author, see Shlomo Zalman Havlin, "Jehiel ben Jekutiel ben Benjamin ha-Rofe," in *Encyclopedia Judaica*; Israel Zinberg, *A History of Jewish Literature*, vol. 2., Bernard Martin, trans. (Cleveland: Case Western University Press, 1792), pp. 187–191.

A discussion of Jewish views on the use of wealth would be incomplete without a reference to the sumptuary laws enforced by medieval Jewish communities upon their inhabitants. The purpose of these laws was to restrain extravagance with regard to personal attire, private celebrations, and individual levity. These laws were motivated by a desire to teach the proper uses of wealth. However, they were also motivated by the awareness of potential jealousy both on the part of Gentiles and on the part of the Jewish poor. For a discussion of these laws as well as for some textual examples, see, e.g., Jacob Marcus, ed., *The Jew in the Medieval World* (New York, Atheneum, 1969), pp. 193–197.

41. This is a play on the word *"asher,"* "tithe," which is close to the word *"ashir,"* "wealthy."

42. Honein ibn Ishak, *Musrei ha-Philosophim* 2:21:39.

43. *"Biglal,"* "because," reminds one of *"galgal,"* "wheel."

44. *Shabbat* 151b.

45. *Musrei ha-Philosophim* 2:2:46.

46. Ibid., 2:2:21.

47. *Ethics of the Fathers* 4:1.

CHAPTER 10

1. Blaise Pascal, *Pensées*, para. 68. A. J. Krailsheimer, trans. (London: Penguin, 1966), p. 48.

2. Translation is by Byron L. Sherwin. From the *Unetaneh Tokef* prayer. See Morris Silverman, ed., *High Holiday Prayerbook* (Hartford: Prayerbook Press, 1951), p. 148. See Psalm 90:3–6.

3. See Paul Edwards, s.v. "My Death," in Paul Edwards, ed., *Encyclopedia of Philosophy*, 8 vols. (New York: Macmillan, 1967).

4. Leo Tolstoy, *The Death of Ivan Ilych and Other Stories* (New York: The New American Library, 1960), pp. 131–132. A similar observation is made by Simhah Zussel of Kelm, *Hokhmah u-Musar* (New York, 1957), no. 27. See an English translation in Louis Jacobs, *Jewish Ethics, Philosophy and Mysticism* (New York: Behrman House, 1969), p. 47.

5. Arnold Toynbee et al., *Man's Concern with Death* (New York: McGraw-Hill, 1968), p. 131.

6. See A. Heidel, *The Gilgamesh Epic and Old Testament Parallels* (Chicago: University of Chicago Press, 1963).

7. Franz Rosenzweig, *The Star of Redemption*, William H. Hallo, trans. (New York: Holt, Rinehart and Winston, 1970), pp. 3–5.

8. There is a growing literature on Jewish views of euthanasia. See, e.g., Byron L. Sherwin, "A View of Euthanasia," chap. in his *In Partnership with God: Contemporary Jewish Law and Ethics* (Syracuse, NY: Syracuse University Press, 1990), chap. 5; Daniel Sinclair, *Tradition and the Biological Revolution* (Edinburgh: Edinburgh University Press, 1989); Louis E. Newman, "Woodchoppers and Respirators," *Modern Judaism* 10:1 (1989).

9. *Berakhot* 17a.

10. *Ecclesiastes Rabbah* 1:1.

11. Ibid., 5:14, 1.

12. Bahya ibn Pakudah, *Duties of the Heart*, Menahem M. Mansoor, trans. (London: Routledge and Kegan Paul, 1973), pp. 311–312.

13. *Sefer ha-Yashar—The Book of the Righteous*, Seymour J. Cohen, trans. (New York: Ktav, 1973), chap. 17, pp. 250–252.

14. See the commentary of Samuel of Uceda on *Ethics of the Fathers* 1:14 in his *Midrash Shmuel* (Jerusalem: Brody-Katz, n.d.), p. 16a.

15. Jonah Ocrondi, *Shaarey Teshuvah (Gates of Repentance)*, 2 vols., Shraga Silverstein, ed. (New York: Feldheim, 1971), 2:26, p. 115.

16. *Shabbat* 153a. See chap. 6 in this volume on contemplation of death as a way of eliminating pride and instilling humility.

17. *Berakhot* 5a.

18. Abraham Joshua Heschel, "Reflections on Death," *Conservative Judaism* 28:1 (Fall 1973): 3.

19. See, e.g., *Ketubot* 103a; "The Passing of Nathaniel Trabotti," in Israel Abrahams, ed. and trans., *Hebrew Ethical Wills* (Philadelphia: Jewish Publication Society, 1926), pp. 259–285; Louis Jacobs, *Holy Living*, pp. 111–121.

20. Benjamin Mintz, *Sefer ha-Histalkut* (Tel Aviv, 1930).

21. See "Hayyim Palaggi," *Encyclopedia Judaica*; Israel Isaac Hasidah, *Rabbi Hayyim Palaggi and His Work* [Hebrew] (Jerusalem: n.p., 1968); Peter J. Haas, "Toward a Semiotic Study of Jewish Moral Discourse: The Case of Responsa," *Semeia* 34 (1985): 59–85. This responsa by Palaggi is quoted in modern discussions of euthanasia, e.g., see Sherwin, pp. 96–97; in Leopold Greenwald, *Kol Bo Al Avelut* (New York, 1947), 1.9, p. 20, n. 14; Solomon B. Freehof, *Reform Responsa* (Cincinnati: Hebrew Union College Press, 1960), pp. 120–121.

22. *Semahot* 3:11. *Semahot* is one of the "minor" tractates of the Talmud. See Eng. trans. by Dov Zlotnick, *The Tractate Mourning* (New Haven, CT: Yale University Press, 1966).

23. Palaggi refers here to *Temurah* 4b; Maimonides, *Mishneh Torah—Book of Judges*, "Sanhedrin" 26:1; Asher ben Yehiel, *Arba'ah Turim*, and Joseph Karo, *Shulhan Arukh*, "Hoshen Mishpat," para. 27:1, as prooftexts for his view.

24. *Kiddushin* 83a.

25. *Yebamot* 37b. Palaggi refers here also to Karo, *Shulhan Arukh*, "Even ha Ezer," para. 119, top.

26. *Avot d'Rabbi Nathan*, Solomon Schechter, ed. (Vienna, 1887), chap. 26.

27. Ibid., chap. 3, beginning.

28. *Sotah* 9a. Azulai's work, *Kiseih Rahamim* (Livorno, 1803), is a commentary on *Avot d'Rabbi Natan*. He lived in the nineteenth century.

29. *Yebamot* 72b.

30. Meir ben Baruch of Rothenburg lived in the thirteenth century. Reference here is to his collected responsa 81:30.

31. *Ketubot* 104a.

32. Palaggi here refers to *Moed Katan* 17a, Karo, *Shulhan Arukh—*"Hoshen Mishpat," para. 40:34, and other sources.

33. The reference here is to Aryeh Judah Leib Teomim, a nineteenth-century Galician rabbi's work, *Gur Aryeh Judah* (Zulkav, 1827), "Hiddushei Yoreh Deah," para. 260:52.

34. The reference here is to the thirteenth-century pietistic work, *Sefer Hasidim*, para. 234.

35. Palaggi refers here to Moses Isserles's gloss to Karo, *Shulhan Arukh—*"Yoreh Deah," para. 339.

CHAPTER 11

1. Plato, *Phaedrus* 250.

2. See, e.g., Abraham Ibn Ezra on Exodus 25:40, in standard editions of Hebrew Scriptures with commentary; Bahya ben Asher, *Kad ha-Kemah* (Lwow, 1892), "*Zenut*," p. 80.

3. *Yoma* 54a and Rashi there.

4. Compare *Numbers Rabbah* 11:3 and *Midrash Tanhuma*, Solomon Buber, ed., 2nd ed. (Jerusalem, N.p., 1964), "*Ba-Midbar – Naso*," p. 17a, where the function of the Temple is stated as procreation.

5. See Numbers 7:89, and discussion in Abraham J. Heschel, *Torah min ha-Shamayim*, vol. 1 (London: Soncino, 1962), pp. 59–64.

6. *The Holy Letter*, Seymour J. Cohen, trans. (New York: Ktav, 1976), pp. 50, 48.

7. See, e.g., Genesis 4:1, 1 Samuel 1:19; *Iggeret ha-Kodesh*, p. 40.

8. On desire, love, and will, see *Iggeret ha-Kodesh*, p. 142. On love, and love of God, see this volume, chap. 3.

9. See Leone Ebreo, *The Philosophy of Love*, F. Friedeberg-Seeley and Jean H. Barnes, trans. (London: Soncino, 1937), p. 54.

10. *The Holy Letter*, p. 60.

11. See, e.g., *Berakhot* 61a; *Erubin* 18a; *Genesis Rabbah* 8:1; *Zohar* 1:49b; Ebreo, pp. 347–351. On the hermaphrodite in rabbinic thought, see, e.g., Ephraim Urbach, *The Sages*, Israel Abrahams, trans. (Cambridge, MA: Harvard University Press, 1987), pp. 228–229. On the hermaphrodite in Jewish mysticism, see, e.g., Moshe Idel, *Kabbalah: New Perspectives* (New Haven, CT: Yale University Press, 1988), pp. 128–136.

12. See, e.g., Ebreo, p. 345.

13. See Plato, *Symposium* 190. See also the discussion by Ebreo, pp. 343–345. Ebreo assumes that Plato derived this myth from Jewish sources.

14. Meir ibn Gabbai, *Avodat ha-Kodesh* (Jerusalem: Levin-Epstein, 1954), sec. 4, chap. 13, p. 122b. Here the notions of the hermaphrodite, the "half body" of the human individual, the unification of the "whole" person, and human intercourse as being paralleled by and causative of the upper union, including the union of the elements of the divine name and the male and female aspects of the divine, are portrayed in succinct fashion. For these ideas in the *Zohar*, see, e.g., Isaiah Tishbi, *Mishnat ha-Zohar*, vol. 1 (Jerusalem: Mosad Bialik, 1957), p. 139.

15. *Tosefta-Yevamot* 8:4, end; see *Genesis Rabbah* 34:14, where refraining from procreation and murder are compared. Both impair the divine image.

16. See *The Holy Letter*, pp. 59–61. See the engaging essay by Charles Mopsik, "The Body of Engenderment in the Hebrew Bible, the Rabbinic Tradition and the Kabbalah," chap. in Michel Feher, ed., *Fragments for a History of the Human Body*, part 1 (New York: Zone, 1989), pp. 48–74.

17. See, e.g., Idel, *Kabbalah*, p. 211. For a wealth of sources and insights regarding sexuality in Jewish thought, particularly in Jewish mysticism, see idem, "Sexual Metaphors and Praxis in the Kabbalah," chap. in David Kraemer, ed., *The Jewish Family* (New York: Oxford University Press, 1989), pp. 197–225.

18. See, e.g., *Yebamot* 63a, "A man who has no wife is no proper man for it is said, 'Male and female created He them and called their name Adam' (Genesis 1:27).

Adam equals the human. Only when male and female are united are they called Adam."

19. *Zohar* 1:264b.

20. *Niddah* 31a. The *Shekhinah* is said to be present during intercourse; see *Sotah* 16a; *Zohar* 1:176; *The Holy Letter*, pp. 60, 62–63.

21. This citation is from Andreas Capellanus, *The Art of Courtly Love*, J. J. Parry, trans. (New York: 1941), p. 100. On courtly love, see, e.g., Denis de Rougemont, *Love in the Western World*, Montgomery Belgion, trans. (Princeton: Princeton University Press, 1983); Irving Singer, *The Nature of Love*, vol. 2 (Chicago: University of Chicago Press, 1984). On courtly love and medieval Jewish concepts of love, see, e.g., Monford Harris, "The Concept of Love in *Sepher Hasidim*," *Jewish Quarterly Review* 50 (1959): 13–44.

22. On the sense of touch, see Aristotle, *Nicomachean Ethics*, Martin Oswald, trans. (New York: Bobbs-Merrill, 1962), III, 10, 1118b, p. 79. Moses Maimonides, *Guide of the Perplexed*, Shlomo Pines, trans. (Chicago: University of Chicago Press, 1963), book 2, chap. 36, p. 371. See also Bahya ben Asher, *Kad ha-Kemah*, "*zenut*," p. 80a. On negative views of sex in Judaism, see, e.g., the views of Abulafia, who was influenced in this regard by Maimonides. According to Abraham Abulafia, "Intercourse is a matter of disgust and one ought to be ashamed of the act." Quoted from a manuscript of *Oẓar Eden Ganuẓ* in Moshe Idel, *Mystical Experience in Abraham Abulafia* (Albany, NY: SUNY Press, 1988), p. 204. For antisexual views in Hasidism, see, e.g., Elimelekh of Lizensk in *Noam Elimelekh* (Lwow, 1787), "*Bereshit*": "The way of the true *tzaddik* is not to have any thought, desire or passion, even for his wife. Even during intercourse with his wife, he should think of the higher worlds and remain oblivious to the fact that he is with his wife." On Nahman of Bratzlav, see Arthur Green, *Tormented Master* (University, AL: University of Alabama Press, 1979). Unlike other Jewish thinkers who saw the study of the human body as a source of wonder, Nahman, like Jean-Paul Sartre, saw it as a source of disgust. On Mendel of Kotsk, see Abraham J. Heschel, *A Passion for Truth* (New York: Farrar, Straus and Giroux, 1973), pp. 216–225.

23. Maimonides, *Guide*, book 3, chap. 33, p. 533.

24. *The Holy Letter*, pp. 40–42.

25. Ibid., pp. 45, 48.

26. Jacob Emden, *Mor Uktziah* (Altoona, 1771–1778), "*Orah Hayyim*," to para. 240. This excerpt from Emden is translated by David Feldman, *Birth Control in Jewish Law* (New York: New York University Press, 1968), pp. 89–102.

27. Jacob Joseph of Polnoye, *Toledot Yaakov Yosef*, 2 vols. (Jerusalem: N.p., 1960), "*Lekh Lekhah—Mitzvat Milah*," vol. 1, p. 57.

28. Elijah de Vidas, *Reshit Hokhmah*, 2 vols. (Jerusalem: Or ha-Musar, 1984), "*Sha'ar ha-Ahavah*," vol. 1, chap. 4, end, p. 426.

29. See this volume, chap. 3.

30. Parts of this essay were published in Byron L. Sherwin, "The Body: A Window to the Divine," chap. in Abraham J. Karp et al., eds., *Three Score and Ten: Essays in Honor of Seymour J. Cohen* (New York: Ktav, 1991).

31. On Nahmanides, see this volume, chap. 12.

32. On the authorship of *Iggeret ha-Kodesh*, see *The Holy Letter*, trans. Cohen, pp.

7–19; Gershom Scholem, "Did Nahmanides Compose the *Iggeret ha-Kodesh?*" [Hebrew], *Kiryat Sefer* 21 (1944/1945): 179–186; Nahmanides, "*Iggeret ha-Kodesh,*" chap. in Charles B. Chavel, ed., *Kitvei Rabbenu Moshe ben Nahman*, 2 vols. (Jerusalem: Mosad ha-Rav Kook), vol. 2, pp. 315-337; Yosef Dan, *Sifrut ha-Musar ve-ha-Derush* (Jerusalem: Keter, 1975), pp. 150–152.

33. This is a play on words, since *hibbur* can refer both to sexual relations and to a literary composition. Other alternative titles cited in English translation are: "He Who Teaches a Man to Know," "Canopy of the Groom," "The Gates of Righteousness," "The Door of the Holy," "The Gates of Holiness," "Knowledge of the Holy."

34. See Idel, *The Mystical Experience in Abraham Abulafia*, p. 226. Compare Monford Harris, "Marriage as Metaphysics," *Hebrew Union College Annual* 33 (1962): 197–220. Note Yosef Dan, "*Iggeret ha-Kodesh,*" in *Encyclopedia Judaica*.

35. Maimonides, *Guide of the Perplexed*, book 2, chap. 36.

36. *Hullin* 56b.

37. *Ecclesiastes Rabbah* 4:14.

38. The text alludes here to the kabbalistic doctrine of the *sefirot*, the divine potencies.

39. *Niddah* 31a.

40. *Kiddushin* 30b.

41. *Berakhot* 63a.

42. *P. Megillah* 1:12.

43. *Berakhot* 3a.

44. Correctly, *Pesahim* 49b.

CHAPTER 12

1. *Midrash Tanhuma*, Solomon Buber, ed. (Vilna, 1885), "*Ekev,*" no. 3, p. 9a. For a more extensively documented discussion of obligations of children to parents in Jewish religious literature, see Byron L. Sherwin, "Parent-Child Relations in Jewish Tradition," chap. in his *In Partnership with God: Contemporary Jewish Law and Ethics* (Syracuse, NY: Syracuse University Press, 1990), chap. 8.

2. *Kiddushin* 31b. See also *P. Peah* 1:1.

3. See, e.g., Bahya ben Asher, *Kad ha-Kemah* (Lwow, 1892), "*Kibbud Av,*" p. 107a: "One must not serve one's parents for the sake of an eventual inheritance, for some honor which may be derived from such service, or for any selfish consideration."

4. Judah Loew of Prague, *Gur Aryeih*, 5 vols. (Bnei Brak: Judaica, 1972), on Deuteronomy 5:16, vol. 5, p. 36.

5. On honoring of parents by non-Jews, see, e.g., *Kiddushin* 31a. Benjamin Ze'ev ben Mattitayhu, *Responsa Benjamin Ze'ev* [Hebrew] (Venice, 1539), no. 169. This work was unavailable to me. I rely on Abramowitz's invaluable Hebrew anthology on parent–child relations, where it is quoted. See Hayyim Abramowitz, *Ha-Dibrah ha-Hamishit* (Jerusalem: Reuven Mass, 1971), p. 116.

6. *M. Peah* 1:1; *Shabbat* 127a. See also Eliezer of Metz, *Sefer Yere'im* (Livorno, 1835), no. 56, pp. 49b–50a.

7. Abraham ibn Ezra on Exodus 20:12 in his commentary to the Torah, in standard editions of Hebrew Scriptures with commentaries.

8. See, e.g., *Sefer ha-Hinukh*, ascribed to Aaron ha-Levi of Barcelona (New York: Feldheim, 1978), "Yitro," no. 33, pp. 181–183.

9. Don Isaac Abravanel's Hebrew *Commentary to the Bible*, 6 vols. (Jerusalem: Bnei Abarbanel, 1964), to Leviticus 19:13, vol. 2, pp. 109–111.

10. Moses Hafetz, *Malekhet Mahshevet* (Warsaw: Cahana, 1914), to Deuteronomy 5:16, p. 148b.

11. Bahya ibn Pakudah, *Duties of the Heart*, Menahem M. Mansoor, trans. (London: Routledge and Kegan Paul, 1973), p. 177.

12. See Plato, *Laws* 790, and Moses Maimonides, *Guide of the Perplexed*, Shlomo Pines, trans. (Chicago: University of Chicago Press, 1963), 3:41, p. 562.

13. Levi ben Gershon (Gersonides), *Commentary to the Torah* [Hebrew], 2 vols. (Venice: Bomberg, 1547), to Exodus 20:12, pp. 50b–51a.

14. Maimonides, *Commentary to the Mishnah* [Hebrew] (Jerusalem: Mosad ha-Rav Kook, 1975), to M. *Kiddushin* 1:7, p. 197. See also Maimonides, *Sefer ha-Mitzvot*, Joseph Kapah, ed. (Jerusalem: Mosad ha-Rav Kook, 1971), nos. 210, 211, p. 166.

15. *Kiddushin* 31b. See also *Tosefta*, M. Zuckermandel, ed. (Jerusalem: Wahrmann, 1970), *Kiddushin* 1:11, p. 336.

16. P. *Kiddushin* 1:7, and Rashi to *Kiddushin* 31a-b. See also Eliezer Azikiri, *Sefer Hareidim*, where this kabbalist writes that "the essence of the commandment to honor parents means to honor with the heart, for the Merciful One requires the heart in the performance of each of the commandments." See Azikiri, *Sefer Hareidim* (Jerusalem: N.p., 1987), "Commandments Related to the Heart," chap. 9, nos. 36–38, pp. 68–69.

17. Azikiri, chap. 9, nos. 37–38, p. 69; *Zohar* 3:281a–b.

18. *Sotah* 49a.

19. *Mekhilta de Rabbi Ishmael*, Hayyim Horovitz and Israel Rabin, eds. (Jerusalem: Wahrmann, 1960), "Yitro," chap. 1, p. 190; *Yalkut Shimoni*, "1 Samuel," no. 133; Joseph Karo, *Shulhan Arukh*—"Yoreh Deah," para. 240:24.

20. *Ketubot* 103a.

21. *Yebamot* 62b; *Kiddushin* 4a.

22. See, e.g., *Sotah* 49a.

23. *Zohar* 2:233a.

24. See, e.g., *Genesis Rabbah* 94:5; Rashi's and Nahmanides' commentaries to Genesis 46:1; Moses Isserles's gloss to Karo, *Shulhan Arukh*—"Yoreh Deah" 240:24.

25. See *Niddah* 31a; *Zohar* 1:49, 3:219b—*Raya Mehemna* on Leviticus 19:3. See also Nahmanides on Exodus 20:12 in the excerpt below.

26. See, e.g., *Sifra* on Leviticus 19:3.

27. Solomon ibn Adret, *Responsa*, part 4 [Hebrew] (Pietrikov: Belhatavsky, 1883), no. 168, p. 25b. See also Gerald Blidstein, *Honor Thy Father and Mother* (New York: Ktav, 1975), pp. 83–98, 100–109.

28. *Pirke de Rabbi Eliezer*, chap. 32. See Nahmanides' commentary on Genesis 2:24 in the excerpt below.

29. See, e.g., Azikiri, chap. 12, p. 76.

30. See, e.g., *Kiddushin* 32a; Maimonides, *Mishneh Torah*—*Sefer Shofetim*, "Laws of Rebels" 6:7.

31. Eliezer of Metz, no. 56, p. 49b; Israel ben Joseph Alnakawa, *Menorat ha-Maor*, Hyman G. Enelow, ed. (New York: Bloch, 1932), vol. 4, p. 18. Contrast this to Maimonides, "Laws of Rebels" 6:11.

32. Maimonides, "Laws of Rebels" 6:10. See also Karo, *Shulhan Arukh*—"*Yoreh Deah*" 240:10.

33. *Sefer Hasidim*, Reuven Margaliot, ed. (Jerusalem: Mosad ha Rav Kook, 1960), nos. 152, 565, pp. 153, 372. See also Maimonides, "Laws of Rebels" 6:8. See the discussion in Blidstein, pp. 126–127, 155–156.

34. *Sanhedrin* 84b–85b; Maimonides, "Laws of Rebels," chap. 5; Karo, *Shulhan Arukh*—"*Yoreh Deah*" para. 241; Nahmanides to Exodus 21:15, Leviticus 20:9, Deuteronomy 21:18–21.

35. Moses Hafetz, *Malekhet Mahshevet* to Leviticus 20:9.

36. Abravanel on Deuteronomy 5:16.

37. See Edward Greenstein, "Medieval Biblical Commentaries," chap. in Barry W. Holtz, ed., *Back to the Sources* (New York: Summit, 1984), pp. 213–261.

38. See this volume, chap. 12.

39. Solomon Schechter, "Nahmanides," chap. in his *Studies in Judaism* (New York: Meridian, 1958), p. 193. On Nahmanides, see, e.g., Charles B. Chavel, *Rabbenu Moshe ben Nahman* (Jerusalem: Mosad ha-Rav Kook, 1967); Israel Zinberg, *A History of Jewish Literature*, vol. 3, Bernard Martin, trans. (Philadelphia: Jewish Publication Society, 1973), pp. 21–27; Isadore Twersky, ed., *Rabbi Moses Nahmanides* (Cambridge, MA: Harvard University Press, 1983); Yitzhak Baer, *A History of the Jews in Christian Spain*, 2 vols., L. Schoffman, trans. (Philadelphia: Jewish Publication Society, 1966), vol. 1, pp. 102–106, 152–157, 245–249; C. Henoch, *Ha-Ramban ke-Hokeir u-Mekubal* (Jerusalem, 1978). Nahmanides' *Commentary to the Torah* is found in standard editions of Hebrew Scripture with commentary and has been edited by Charles B. Chavel in two vols. (Jerusalem: Mosad ha-Rav Kook, 1959). See also David Novak, "Nahmanides' *Commentary to the Torah*," chap. in Byron L. Sherwin, ed., *The Solomon Goldman Lectures*, vol. 5 (Chicago: Spertus College of Judaica Press, 1990), pp. 87–105.

40. *Kiddushin* 30b.

41. *Kiddushin* 39b.

42. *Sanhedrin* 84b.

43. Quoted in Abraham ibn Ezra's commentary to Exodus 21:16, in standard editions of the Pentateuch with commentaries.

44. *Sanhedrin* 72a.

CHAPTER 13

1. On the role of the parent in Jewish tradition, see Byron L. Sherwin, *In Partnership with God* (Syracuse, NY: Syracuse University Press, 1990), chap. 8, and sources noted there.

2. *Yebamot* 62b.

3. See *Kiddushin* 29a; Moses Maimonides, *Mishneh Torah*—*Sefer ha-Mada*, "*Hilkhot Talmud Torah*" 1:1. Eng. trans., Moses Hyamson, *The Book of Knowledge*

(Jerusalem: Boys Town Jerusalem Publishers, 1965), p. 57a; Joseph Karo, *Shulhan Arukh—"Yoreh Deah"* 245:1.

4. Quoted in *Beit Pinhas* (Bilgorayi Weinberg, 1926), pp. 9b 10a, n. 11.

5. Levi ben Gerson (Gersonides), *Commentary to the Torah*, 2 vols. (Venice, 1547) [Hebrew], on Exodus 20:12.

6. Joseph Albo, *Sefer ha-Ikkarim—The Book of Principles*, 6 vols., Isaac Husik, trans. (Philadelphia: Jewish Publication Society, 1946), vol. 3, chap. 26, pp. 251–252. See also Don Isaac Abravanel's *Commentary to the Bible*, 6 vols. (Jerusalem: Bnai Abravanel, 1964) [Hebrew], on Exodus 20:12.

7. *Shabbat* 127a (bottom); *Pesahim* 113a (bottom).

8. See, e.g. *Yalkut Shimoni*, "Proverbs," no. 950, on Proverbs 13:25 and Rashi on Proverbs 13:25. The question of whether a child is obliged to honor his or her parents unconditionally is debated in the sources, particularly in medieval Jewish ethical literature. One view is that the child's obligation is unconditional; namely, it is unrelated to the parent's moral or religious behavior and to the quality of parenting provided to the child by the parent. A second view is that since the most important feature of the parent–child relationship is parental pedagogy, then the parent who fails as a moral and religious teacher of the child and who is not a viable role model for the child releases the child from the obligation of parental reverence. An extreme example of this latter view is expressed by Eliezer of Metz, *Sefer Yereim* (Livorno: Rokeah, 1837), no. 56, ". . . if one's parent is wicked even by failing to observe a single commandment written in the Torah, one is free from honoring such a parent." See also Israel ben Joseph ibn Al-Nakawa, *Sefer Menorat ha-Ma'or*, 4 vols., Hyman G. Enelow, ed. (New York: Bloch, 1932), vol. 4, p. 14:

> A person who teaches Torah to his child is due manifold honor, more honor than for siring the child. As the parent is obliged to teach the child ethics, to set the child on the right path, to guide the child in the performance of the commandments and of virtuous deeds, so is the child obliged to heed the parent, to accept the parent's words, and to obey the parent's commands, even regarding secular matters. But, if the parent is a sinner, and his intention is to mislead his child and to prevent his child from doing the will of the Creator—for example, if the parent teaches the child to rob or to steal or to murder, or something similar, or even to transgress a single religious precept—then the child is obliged to reject the commands of his parent, to rebel against the parent's dicta and to refuse [to obey] the parent's words. . . .

9. See *Kiddushin* 32a; Maimonides, *Mishneh Torah—Sefer Shofetim*, "Hilkhot Mamrim" 6:8. Eng. trans., Abraham M. Hershman, *The Book of Judges* (New Haven, CT: Yale University Press, 1949), p. 156; *Sefer Hasidim*, Reuven Margaliot, ed. (Jerusalem: Mosad ha-Rav Kook, 1960), nos. 565, 152. See also Gerald Blidstein, *Honor Thy Father and Mother* (New York: Ktav, 1975), pp. 126–127, 155–156.

10. Joseph Yuspa Hahn, *Yosif Ometz* (Frankfurt: Herman, 1928), p. 279.

11. Ahai Gaon, *She'iltot* (Jerusalem: Mosad ha-Rav Kook, 1960), no. 60 (end).

12. *Kiddushin* 29a. See variant readings in P. *Kiddushin* 1:7, *Numbers Rabbah* 17:1, *Ecclesiastes Rabbah* 9:8, *Midrash Tanhuma*, Solomon Buber, ed. (Vilna, 1885), "Shelah," no. 26, vol. 2, p. 36a.

13. *Mekhilta de Rabbi Ishmael*, Hayyim Horovitz and Israel Rabin, eds. (Jerusalem: Wahrmann, 1960), "Bo," chap. 18, p. 73.

14. See, e.g., *Pirke de Rabbi Eliezer* (Warsaw, 1852), chap. 32, p. 73a; Nahmanides, *Commentary to the Torah* [Hebrew] on Genesis 2:24, in standard editions of the Pentateuch with commentaries.

15. *Kiddushin* 29a.

16. Rashi on *Kiddushin* 29a.

17. *Kiddushin* 29a and *Mekhilta* "Bo," chap. 18, p. 73.

18. *Kiddushin* 30b.

19. *Sotah* 49a.

20. Bahya ibn Pakudah, *The Book of Direction to the Duties of the Heart*, Menahem M. Mansoor, trans. (London: Routledge and Kegan Paul, 1973), chap. 3, p. 177.

21. Al-Nakawa, p. 17.

22. Note *Genesis Rabbah* 20:6.

23. On love, see this volume, chap. 3.

24. *Midrash on Psalms* 92:13; *Yalkut Shimoni* "Psalms," no. 846.

25. On ethical wills, see Joseph Dan, *Sifrut ha-Musar ve-ha-Derush* (Jerusalem: Keter, 1975), pp. 92–104; Israel Abrahams, ed. and trans., *Hebrew Ethical Wills* (Philadelphia: Jewish Publication Society, 1926); Jack Riemer and Nathaniel Stampfer, eds., *Ethical Wills* (New York: Schocken, 1983).

26. Riemer and Stampfer, p. 131.

27. On Judah ibn Tibbon, see Abraham Halkin, "Judah ben Saul ibn Tibbon," in *Encyclopaedia Judaica*, vol. 15, pp. 1129–1130.

28. See this volume, chap. 1.

29. See this volume, chap. 5.

30. *Sotah* 47a.

CHAPTER 14

1. *Arakhin* 15b.

2. Bahya ibn Pakudah, *The Book of Direction to the Duties of the Heart*, Menahem M. Mansoor, trans. (London: Routledge and Kegan Paul, 1973), p. 167.

3. See also Isaac Aboab, *Menorat ha-Ma'or* (Jerusalem: Mosad ha-Rav Kook, 1961), sec. 2, p. 132.

4. Judah Loew, *Netivot Olom*, 2 vols. (New York: Judaica Press, 1969), vol. 2, "Netiv ha-Tzni'ut," chap. 3, p. 108; see also "Netiv ha-Lashon," vol. 2, chap. 3, p. 70.

5. Loew, "Netiv ha-Tzni'ut," vol. 2, chap. 4, p. 110.

6. Ibid., chap. 3, p. 105; see "Netiv ha-Shetikah," chap. 1, p. 98.

7. Loew, "Netiv ha-Lashon," chap. 2, p. 70, and elsewhere. In the teachings of the Baal Shem Tov, see, e.g., Simon Mendel of Givurtchav, *Sefer ha-Besht*, 2 vols. (Jerusalem: Horeb, 1961), "Bereshit," vol. 1, p. 75, n. 93.

8. *Orhot Zaddikim — The Ways of the Righteous*, Seymour J. Cohen, trans. (New York: Feldheim, 1969), p. 445.

9. Loew, "Netiv ha-Lashon," chap. 4, p. 73.

10. Ibid., chap. 3, p. 69.

11. See *Arakhin* 15b and parallels, e.g., *Midrash on Psalms*, chap. 39; 52:5. This text

is often quoted in medieval Jewish ethical literature. See, e.g., Loew, "*Netiv ha-Lashon*," chap. 1, p. 65; *Orhot Zaddikim*, p. 443.

12. *Arakhin* 15b. See Aboab, p. 123.

13. *Orhot Zaddikim*, p. 355.

14. Ibid., p. 355.

15. See *Targum Onkeles* to Genesis 2:7, where "Man became a living being" is translated as "a speaking being." This is quoted and elaborated upon by Loew, "*Netiv ha-Lashon*," chap. 2, p. 67.

16. Solomon ibn Gabirol, *Choice of Pearls*, A. Cohen, trans. (New York: Bloch, 1925), p. 81.

17. *Megillah* 18a.

18. *Choice of Pearls*, p. 78.

19. *P. Pesahim* 9:9. See the discussion by Loew, "*Netiv ha-Shetikah*," chap. 1, p. 97.

20. See, e.g., *Ethics of the Fathers* 3:13: "Silence is the gate to wisdom."

21. All citations from Benjamin Franklin are from *Poor Richard's Almanack*.

22. See, e.g., *Shabbat* 54b, 119b; *Sanhedrin* 19a–b, 106a; *Orhot Zaddikim*, pp. 357, 405; Jonah Gerondi, *Sha'arey Teshuvah* (Jerusalem: Eshkol, 1978), part 3, end, p. 126; Israel Meir ha-Kohen (Hafetz Hayyim), *Sefer Shmirat ha-Lashon* (Jerusalem: N.p., 1964), on *Avot* 1:17, pp. 26–27.

23. *Ethics of the Fathers* 1:17.

24. The precise source of this quote could not be located.

25. See also Numbers 30:3.

26. *Tosefta Yebamot* 8:7; *Genesis Rabbah* 34:14.

27. See, e.g., *Yoma* 72b; *Berakhot* 28a. See also *Sotah* 41b–42a.

28. See this volume, chap. 6.

29. On the teachings of Mendel of Kotsk regarding truth and deception, see Abraham J. Heschel, *A Passion for Truth* (New York: Farrar, Straus and Giroux, 1973). It should be noted that the teachings of Mendel of Kotsk were greatly influenced by those of Judah Loew of Prague.

30. Aboab, sec. 2, p. 103.

31. On the equation of lying with robbery, see, e.g., *Tosefta-Baba Kamma* 7:8; *Sotah* 42a. On *genevut da'at*, see Aboab, pp. 116–118.

32. See, e.g., Moses Maimonides, *Mishneh Torah—Sefer Kinyan*, "*Hilkhot Mekhirah*," 14:18.

33. *Hullin* 94a. See also Leo Jung, *Business Ethics in Jewish Law* (New York: Hebrew Publishing Co., 1987); Basil F. Herring, *Jewish Ethics and Halakhah for Our Time*, vol. 2 (New York: Yeshiva University Press, 1989), pp. 221–231, and sources noted there; Seymour J. Cohen, *Affirming Life* (Hoboken, NJ: Ktav, 1987), pp. 244–268.

34. *Baba Metzia* 60a–b.

35. Moses Hayyim Luzzatto, *Mesillat Yesharim—The Path of the Upright*, Mordecai M. Kaplan, trans. (Philadelphia: Jewish Publication Society, 1936), chap. 11, pp. 144–156.

36. Luzzatto, pp. 178–182.

37. *Ethics of the Fathers* 1:18. On "truth" in Jewish thought, see Louis Jacobs, *Jewish Values* (London: Vallentine, Mitchell, 1960), pp. 145–155.

38. Loew, vol. 1, *"Netiv ha-Emet,"* chap. 1, p. 195.

39. Luzzatto, p. 188.

40. *Sanhedrin* 89b.

41. See *Yebamot* 65b. On truth and peace, see also Jacobs, *Jewish Values,* pp. 155–160.

42. *Ketubot* 17a.

43. Loew on *Ketubot* 17a in his *Netivot Olom,* vol. 1, *"Netiv ha-Emet,"* chap. 1, p. 200. The great philosopher, Immanuel Kant, insisted that one should always tell the truth, no matter what. But other philosophers disagreed. For example, the French philosopher, Jean-Paul Sartre, writing about World War II in Nazi-occupied France, said that in certain cases it would be immoral to tell the truth. The example he gave was that of a French resistance fighter captured by the Nazis and asked if certain named individuals were members of the resistance and therefore liable to be executed if caught by the Nazis. In such a case, counseled Sartre, one is obliged to reject Kant's "categorical imperative" always to tell the truth. In this case, Sartre insisted, one is morally obliged to tell a lie.

44. See, e.g., Aboab, sec. 2, p. 122.

45. On "evil speech" (*lashon ha-ra*) in talmudic literature, see, e.g., George Foot Moore, *Judaism in the First Centuries of the Christian Era,* 2 vols. (Cambridge, MA: Harvard University Press, 1927), vol. 2, pp. 147–154; Max Kadushin, *Worship and Ethics* (Evanston, IL: Northwestern University Press, 1963), pp. 206–209. In the writings of the early twentieth-century scholar, the Hafetz Hayyim, the idea of *"lashon ha-ra"* plays a major role; see, e.g., Israel Meir ha-Kohein (Hafetz Hayyim), *Kol Sifrei ha-Musar al Inyanei Shemirat ha-Lashon* (Jerusalem: Va'ad Shemirat ha-Lashon, 1965).

46. Gerondi, p. 131.

47. *Arakhin* 15b.

48. Loew, *"Netiv ha-Lashon,"* chap. 8, p. 79.

49. *Arakhin* 15b.

50. *Ethics of the Fathers* 21:10.

51. *Avot d'Rabbi Natan,* Solomon Schechter, ed. (Vienna, 1887), chap. 15, p. 30b.

52. *Sotah* 10b.

53. *Baba Metzia* 58b–59a.

54. *Baba Batra* 164b–165a.

55. *Ketubot* 5b. See Loew, *"Netiv ha-Tzni'ut,"* chap. 2, pp. 116–117.

56. Loew, *"Netiv ha-Zeni'ut,"* chap. 2, pp. 106–107.

57. *Choice of Pearls,* p. 39.

58. This prayer is based on *Berakhot* 17a.

59. Idle gossip inevitably leads to slander, wrote Bahya ben Asher, *Kad ha-Kemah* (Lwow, 1892), *"Lashon ha-Ra,"* pp. 127–130. On gossip, see *Orhot Zaddikim,* pp. 421–449.

60. Aboab, sec. 2, p. 137.

61. Moses Maimonides, *Commentary to the Mishnah-Avot* 1:17.

62. Maimonides, *Mishneh Torah – Sefer ha-Mada,* *"Hilkhot Deot"* 2:4.

63. Luzzatto, p. 166.

64. *Sotah* 42a.

65. *Arakhin* 16a. See also *Erubin* 16a, *Baba Batra* 164b.

66. *Pesahim* 113b.

67. Aboab, sec. 2, p. 104.

68. Moses Maimonides, *Mishneh Torah—Sefer ha-Mada*, "*Hilkhot De'ot*" 2:6. On flattery, see also *Orhot Zaddikim*, pp. 395–421; Bahya ben Asher, "*Hanufah*," pp. 82b–84b.

69. *Sefer Hasidim*, Reuven Margaliot, ed. (Jerusalem: Mosad ha-Rav Kook, 1960), para. 367, pp. 270–271.

70. See, e.g., *Orhot Zaddikim*, Cohen, trans., ix–xii; Jacob Elbaum, *Petihot ve-Histagrut* (Jerusalem: Magnes, 1990), "Appendix II," pp. 390–394; Hayyim Zalmen Dimitrovsky, "Al Derekh ha-Pilpul," chap. in *Sefer ha-Yovel le'Salo Baron* (Jerusalem: 1975), pp. 174–176; Y. Reifman, "Some Notes About *Sefer Orhot Zaddikim*," *Ha-Karmel* 2 (1862): 271–272.

71. Cohen, trans., p. 579.

72. See Dimitrovsky, pp. 174–176; Elbaum, p. 390.

73. See Elbaum, p. 229.

74. See M. Halamish, "The Problem of the Identity of the Book '*Beth Middot*' Mentioned in the Books *Sefer Hareidim* and *Reshit Hokhmah*" [Hebrew], *Kiryat Sefer* 47 (1962): 169–178; M. Pechter, "On the Citations from *Orhot Zaddikim* in the Ethical Literature of the Sages of Safed" [Hebrew], *Kiryat Sefer* 47 (1962): 487–492.

75. The first printed version of *Orhot Zaddikim* was actually published in Yiddish in Isny, 1542, almost twenty years before its first publication in Hebrew. This led some scholars to conclude that the work was originally written in Yiddish, and later translated into and published in Hebrew. However, the investigations of Zinberg and others demonstrate that *Orhot Zaddikim* was indeed originally written in Hebrew. See, e.g., Israel Zinberg, *A History of Jewish Literature*, vol. 7, Bernard Martin, trans. (Cincinnati: Hebrew Union College Press, 1975), pp. 148–153. See also Hayyim Shmeruk, "A Bibliography of Polish Books in Yiddish Until 1648–1649," [Hebrew] in his *Sifrut Yiddish he-Polin* (Jerusalem, 1971), p. 50.

76. On the structure of *Orhot Zaddikim*, see Hillel Goldberg, "Israel Salanter and *Orhot Zaddikim*: Restructuring Musar Literature," *Tradition* 23:4 (Summer 1988): 14–47.

77. On Bahya ibn Pakudah, see this volume, chap. 5; on Luzzatto, see this volume, chap. 6.

78. *Baba Metzia* 49a.

79. *Yehamot* 65b.

80. *Ketubot* 17a.

81. *Arakhin* 16a.

82. *Avot d'Rabbi Nathan* 29.

83. *Shabbat* 54b.

84. *Sanhedrin* 27b.

85. *Arakhin* 15b; see P. *Peah* 1:1.

86. *Arakhin* 15b; *Genesis Rabbah* 98:19.

87. P. *Baba Kamma* 8:10.

88. *Baba Metzia* 58b.

89. *Ethics of the Fathers* 3:11.

90. *Sotah* 42a.

91. *Baba Metzia* 58b.
92. *P. Peah* 1:1.
93. *Arakhin* 15b.
94. *Yoma* 4b.
95. *Kiddushin* 70a.
96. *Shabbat* 127b.
97. *Leviticus Rabbah* 16:2.
98. *Ethics of the Fathers* 3:13.
99. *Megillah* 18a.

CHAPTER 15

1. See, e.g., Michael A. Meyer, *Response to Modernity* (New York: Oxford University Press, 1988), pp. 64–66; Sidney Ayinn, "Kant on Judaism," *Jewish Quarterly Review* 59 (July 1968): 9–23.

2. A significant and influential example is Moritz Lazarus, *The Ethics of Judaism*, 2 vols., Henrietta Szold, trans. (Philadelphia: Jewish Publication Society, 1900), especially vol. 1, pp. 123–138.

3. This analogy derives from 2 Romans, chap. 11.

4. For other views regarding the rejection of the notion of a Judeo-Christian ethic, see, e.g., Arthur A. Cohen, *The Myth of the Judeo-Christian Tradition* (New York: Schocken, 1971); Irwin M. Blank, "Is There a Common Judeo-Christian Ethical Tradition?" chap. in Daniel Jeremy Silver, ed., *Judaism and Ethics* (New York: Ktav, 1970), pp. 95–113.

5. For an erudite and penetrating comparison of early rabbinic and early Christian views on this issue, see Ephraim E. Urbach, "*Magamot Datiot ve-Havratiot be-Torat ha-Zedakah shel Hazal*," *Zion* 16 (1951): 18–27.

6. This terminology and distinction between "messianic" and "messy" views of ethical problems was brought to my attention by Rabbi Walter Wurzburger.

7. *Midrash Va-Yosha*, in Adolf Jellenick, ed., *Beit ha-Midrash*, 6 vols. (Jerusalem: Wahrmann, 1938), vol. 1, p. 55.

8. Abraham Joshua Heschel, *God in Search of Man* (Philadelphia: Jewish Publication Society, 1955), p. 377.

9. For further discussion, see Byron L. Sherwin, "The U.S. Catholic Bishops' Pastoral Letter on the Economy and Jewish Tradition," chap. in Charles R. Strain, ed., *Prophetic Views and Economic Realities* (Grand Rapids, MI: Eerdmans Publishing Co., 1989), pp. 81–93.

10. Parts of the following are derived from a more extensive and more highly documented discussion in Byron L. Sherwin, *In Partnership with God* (Syracuse, NY: Syracuse University Press, 1990), pp. 102–119, 239–242.

11. *Orhot Zaddikim*, Seymour J. Cohen, trans. (New York: Feldheim, 1969), "On Generosity," p. 303.

12. Unless otherwise noted, all citations in this chapter from Maimonides come from the section of his legal code dealing with the ethics of giving and receiving: *Mishneh Torah—Sefer Zera'im*, "Laws Regarding Gifts to the Poor." An English

translation by Isaac Klein is available: *The Book of Agriculture* (New Haven, CT: Yale University Press, 1979). On *zedakah* in the Talmud, see, e.g., Roger Brooks, *Support for the Poor in the Mishnaic Law of Agriculture: Tractate Pe'ah* (Chico, CA: Scholars Press, 1983).

13. Rashi to Exodus 22:24.

14. Maimonides 7:1–2.

15. Maimonides 10:1.

16. *Gittin* 7a.

17. *Ketubot* 50a. In the codes, see Maimonides 7:5; Joseph Karo, *Shulhan Arukh—"Yoreh Deah,"* 249:1–2.

18. Rashi on *Sukkah* 49b. Judah Loew, *Netivot Olom*, 2 vols. (New York: Judaica Press, 1969), "*Netiv Gemilut Hasadim*," vol. 1, chap. 2, p. 154.

19. *Sukkah* 49b.

20. Yehiel ben Yekutiel, *Sefer Ma'alot ha-Middot* (Jerusalem: Eshkol, 1968), p. 84.

21. Maimonides, *Guide to the Perplexed*, Shlomo Pines, trans. (Chicago: University of Chicago Press, 1963), book 3, chap. 53, pp. 630–632.

22. See M. *Pe'ah* 1:1.

23. Isaac Aboab, *Menorat ha-Ma'or* (Jerusalem: Mosad ha-Rav Kook, 1961), p. 420. See also *Tosafot* to *Avodah Zarah* 17b.

24. Maimonides 10:7–14. Maimonides' influence is clear in later codes such as Jacob ben Asher, *Arba'ah Turim—"Yoreh Deah,"* sec. 294, and Karo, *Shulhan Arukh—"Yoreh Deah"* 249:6–12. These codes list the gradations in ascending order. Others list them in descending order; see, e.g., Moses of Coucy, *Sefer Mitzvot Gadol*, and Israel ibn Al-Nakawa, *Menorat ha-Ma'or*, 4 vols., Hyman G. Enelow, ed. (New York: Bloch, 1931), vol. 1, pp. 82–84. See also Abraham Cronbach, "The Gradations of Benevolence," *Hebrew Union College Annual* 16 (1941): 163–187.

25. Aboab, p. 417.

26. See, e.g., Rashi to *Hagigah* 5a.

27. *Ketubot* 67a.

28. See, e.g., Solomon Schechter, "Notes of Lectures in Jewish Philanthropy," chap. in his *Studies in Judaism: Third Series* (Philadelphia: Jewish Publication Society, 1924), pp. 238–277. Also see this volume, chap. 9.

29. *Sefer Hasidim*, Reuven Margaliot, ed. (Jerusalem: Mosad ha-Rav Kook, 1960), para. 415, p. 297.

30. Abraham Cronbach, "The Me'il Zedakah," *Hebrew Union College Annual* 12/13 (1938): 637.

31. See Yitzhak Baer, *A History of the Jews in Christian Spain*, 2 vols. (Philadelphia: Jewish Publication Society, 1966), vol. 1, p. 265, and sources noted there.

32. See, e.g., *Baba Batra* 10a.

33. *Erubin* 41b.

34. *Nedarim* 64b.

35. *Baba Batra* 116a.

36. *Exodus Rabbah* 31:12, 14.

37. *Leviticus Rabbah* 34:6.

38. *Ketubot* 67b.

39. Maimonides, 7:3.

40. *P. Peah* 8:8.

41. Maimonides, 7:3. See also Jacob ben Asher, *Arba'ah Turim—"Yoreh Deah,"* para. 250. These codes are based upon *Sifre on Deuteronomy*, Louis Finkelstein, ed. (Berlin: Gesellschaft zur Forderung der Wissenschaft des Judentums, 1939), *"Re'eh,"* sec. 118, p. 177, and *Ketubot* 67b.

42. *Tosefta, Shekalim* 2:16.

43. *Ketubot* 67b.

44. *Baba Batra* 9b.

45. *P. Shekalim* 5:4.

46. *Shabbat* 63a. See also *Avot d'Rabbi Natan*, Solomon Schechter, ed. (Vienna, 1887), chap. 41.

47. *M. Peah* 8:9. See also *Ketubot* 68a and *Avot d'Rabbi Natan*, chap. 3.

48. Maimonides, 7:6.

49. *Ketubot* 67b. Maimonides, 7:9.

50. Maimonides, 10:19.

51. Maimonides, 10:18.

52. Maimonides, 7:13.

53. Aboab, pp. 410–411.

54. *Ketubot* 50a.

55. Maimonides, 6:12.

56. *Baba Batra* 6b; Maimonides, 8:10–12.

57. *Baba Batra* 9a.

58. Maimonides, 9:3.

59. On Maimonides' code, see the definitive work by Isadore Twersky, *Introduction to the Code of Maimonides* (New Haven, CT: Yale University Press, 1980).

60. See Solomon Zeitlin, *Maimonides: A Biography* (New York: Bloch, 1955).

References

This bibliography is divided into two sections: classical Jewish sources and other sources. The first section primarily lists Hebrew works from the ancient and medieval periods. The second section lists other works utilized in the preparation of this book.

CLASSICAL JEWISH SOURCES

Aboab, Isaac. *Menorat ha-Ma'or.* Jerusalem: Mosad ha-Rav Kook, 1961.

Abravanel, Don Isaac. *Commentary to the Bible* [Hebrew]. 6 vols. Jerusalem: Bnei Abarbanel, 1964.

Ahai Gaon, *She'iltot.* 6 vols. Edited by S. K. Mirsky. Jerusalem: Mosad ha-Rav Kook, 1964.

Albo, Joseph. *Sefer ha-Ikkarim — The Book of Principles.* 6 vols. Translated by Isaac Husik. Philadelphia: Jewish Publication Society, 1946.

Anatoli, Jacob. *Malmed ha Talmidim.* Lyck. N.p., 1866.

Avot d'Rabbi Natan. Edited by Solomon Schechter. Vienna, 1887. Translated by Judah Goldin. *The Fathers According to Rabbi Nathan.* New Haven, CT: Yale University Press, 1955.

Azikiri, Eliezer. *Sefer Hareidim.* Jerusalem: N.p., 1957.

Azulai, Hayyim Joseph David. *Kiseih Rahamim.* Livorno, 1803.

Bar Hiyya, Abraham. *The Meditation of the Sad Soul.* Translated by Geoffrey Wigoder. London: Routledge and Kegan Paul, 1969.

Barzeloni, Judah. *Peirush Sefer Yetzirah.* Edited by Z. H. Halberstein. Jerusalem: Makor, 1971.

Beit ha-Midrash. 6 vols. Edited by Adolf Jellenick. Jerusalem: Wahrmann, 1967.

Beit Pinhas. Bilgoray: Weinberg, 1926.

Ben Asher, Bahya. *Kad ha-Kemah.* Lwow: 1892. Translated by Charles B. Chavel. *Encyclopedia of Torah Thoughts.* New York: Shilo, 1980.

Ben Asher, Jacob. *Arba'ah Turim.* 1550. Reprint. New York: Grossman, n.d. [with commentaries].

Ben Betzalel, Hayyim. *Sefer ha-Hayyim.* Jerusalem: Weinfeld, 1968.

Ben Gershon, Levi. See Gersonides.

Ben Mattitayhu, Benjamin Ze'ev. *Responsa Benjamin Ze'ev* [Hebrew]. Venice: 1539.

Ben Shephatiah, Amittai. *The Poems of Amittay* [Hebrew]. Edited by Yonah David. Jerusalem: Achshav, 1975.

Ben Yekutiel, Yehiel. *Sefer Ma'alot ha-Middot.* Translated by Seymour J. Cohen. Jerusalem: Eshkol, 1968.

Cordevero, Moses. *Pardes Rimonim.* 2 vols. Jerusalem: N.p., 1962.

———— . *Tomer Devorah.* Venice: 1588. Translated by Louis Jacobs. *The Palm Tree of Deborah.* London: Vallentine Mitchell, 1960.

De Vidas, Elijah. *Reshit Hokhmah.* Tel Aviv: Esther Press, n.d.

———— . *Reshit Hokhmah ha-Shalem.* 2 vols. Jerusalem: Or ha-Musar, 1984.

Di Trani, Moses. *Beth Elohim.* Warsaw: Goldman, 1852.

Ebreo, Leone. *The Philosophy of Love.* Translated by F. Friedeberg-Seeley and Jean H. Barnes. London: Soncino, 1937.

Edels, Samuel. *Hiddushei Halakhot ve-Aggadot.* In Talmud [with commentaries].

Eibshitz, Jonathan. *Ya'arot Devash.* Lwow: 1863.

Eisenstadt, Meir. *Panim Me'irot.* Amsterdam: 1715.

Eliezer of Metz. *Sefer Yere'im.* Livorno: Rokeah, 1837.

Elijah of Vilna. *Sefer Mishlei im Biur ha-Gra.* Petah Tikvah: N.p., 1985.

Elimelekh of Lizensk. *Noam Elimelekh.* Lwow: 1787. Edited by Gedaliah Nigal. Jerusalem: Mosad ha-Rav Kook, 1978.

Emden, Jacob. *Mor Uktziah.* Altoona: 1771–1778.

Emet mei-Kotsk Tizmah. Bnei Brak: Nezah, 1961.

Gerondi, Jonah. *Commentary to the Ethics of the Fathers* [Hebrew]. Jerusalem: Makhon Torah Shelemah, 1969.

———— . *Sha'arey Teshuvah (Gates of Repentance).* Translated and edited by Shraga Silverstein. 2 vols. New York: Feldheim, 1971.

———— . *Sha'arey Teshuvah.* Jerusalem: Eshkol, 1978.

Gersonides (Levi ben Gershon). *Commentary to the Torah.* 2 vols. [Hebrew]. Venice: Bomberg, 1547.

Ha-Kohen, Israel Meir (Hafetz Hayyim). *Kol Sifrei ha-Musar al Inyanei Shemirat ha-Lashon.* Jerusalem: Va'ad Shemirat ha-Lashon, 1965.

———— . *Sefer Shmirat ha-Lashon.* Jerusalem: N.p., 1964.

Halevi, Aaron, of Barcelona. *Sefer ha-Hinukh.* Jerusalem: Eshkol, n.d.

Halevi, Judah. *Kuzari.* Translated by Hartwig Hirschfield. New York: Schocken, 1964.

———— . *Kuzari.* Chapter in Isaac Heinemann, ed. *Three Jewish Philosophers.* Philadelphia: Jewish Publication Society, 1960.

———— . *Selected Poems of Judah Ha-Levi.* Edited by Heinrich Brody. Translated by Nina Salaman. Philadelphia: Jewish Publication Society, 1924.

Hafetz, Moses. *Malekhet Mahshevet*. Warsaw: Cahana, 1914.

Hahn, Joseph Yuspa. *Yosif Ometz*. Frankfurt: Herman, 1928.

Hanakdan, Derechiah. *Fables of a Jewish Aesop*. Translated by Moses Hadas. New York: Columbia University Press, 1967.

Hebrew Ethical Wills. Edited and translated by Israel Abrahams. Philadelphia: Jewish Publication Society, 1926.

Honein ibn Ishak. *Sefer Musrei ha-Philosophim*. Translated by Judah al-Harizi. Edited by Abraham Leventhal. Cracow, 1896.

Horowitz, Isaiah. *Shnei Luhot ha-Brit*. 3 vols. Jerusalem: Edison, 1960.

Ibn Adret, Solomon. *Responsa*. Part 4 [Hebrew]. Pietrikov: Belhatavsky, 1883.

Ibn Aknin, Joseph. "Ibn Aknin's *Hygiene of the Soul*." Translated by Abraham Halkin. In *Proceedings of the American Academy for Jewish Research* 14 (1933).

Ibn Al-Nakawa, Israel ben Joseph. *Sefer Menorat ha-Ma'or*. 4 vols. Edited by Hyman G. Enelow. New York: Bloch, 1931.

Ibn Attar, Hayyim. *Or ha-Hayyim*. In *Mikraot Gedolot*.

Ibn Daud, Abraham. *Emunah Ramah*. Frankfurt, 1852.

Ibn Ezra, Abraham. *Commentary to the Torah* [Hebrew]. 5 vols. Tel Aviv: Moreib, 1961. Also in *Mikraot Gedolot*.

Ibn Falaquera, Shem Tov ben Joseph. *The Book of the Seeker—Sefer ha-Mabaqqesh*. Translated by M. H. Levine. New York: Yeshiva University Press, 1976.

――――. "A Critical Edition of Shem Tov Ben Joseph Falaquera's *Bate Hanhagat Guf ha-Bari*. Edited by Israel Chodos. In *Ha-Rofeh ha-Ivri* (1938).

Ibn Gabbai, Meir. *Avodat ha-Kodesh*. Jerusalem: Levin-Epstein, 1954.

Ibn Gabirol, Solomon. *Mivhar ha-Peninim*. 1484. *Choice of Pearls*. Translated by A. Cohen. New York: Bloch, 1925. (Also translated by B. H. Ascher. London, 1859.)

――――. *The Foundation of Life*. A partial translation by H. E. Wedneck. New York: Philosophical Library, 1962.

――――. *The Improvement of the Moral Qualities*. Translated by Stephen S. Wise. New York: Columbia University Press, 1901.

――――. *[Keter Malhut]. The Kingly Crown*. Translated by Bernard Lewis. London: Vallentine, Mitchell, 1961.

――――. *Selected Religious Poems of Solomon Ibn Gabirol*. Translated by Israel Zangwill. Philadelphia: Jewish Publication Society, 1923.

――――. *Solomon Ibn Gabirol: Selected Religious Poems*. Edited by Israel Davidson. Philadelphia: Jewish Publication Society, 1924.

Ibn Pakudah, Bahya. *Sefer Hovot ha-Levavot*. 2 vols. (Hebrew-English edition). Translated by Moses Hyamson. Jerusalem: Boys Town, 1965. Also *The Book of Direction to the Duties of the Heart*. Translated by Menahem M. Mansoor. London: Routledge and Kegan Paul, 1973.

Ibn Zaddik, Joseph. *Ha-Olam ha-Katan*. Edited by S. Horovitz. Breslau: Schatzky, 1903.

Iggeret ha-Kodesh The Holy Letter. Translated by Seymour J. Cohen. New York: Ktav, 1976.

Israel of Ruzhyn. *Knesset Yisrael*. Warsaw: N.p., 1906.

Isserles, Moses. *Mappah*. [In Joseph Karo. *Shulhan Arukh* with commentaries].

Jacob Joseph of Polnoye. *Toldeot Ya'akov Yosef.* Jerusalem: N.p., 1967.

Karo, Joseph. *Shulhan Arukh.* Reprint. Vilna: Romm, 1911 [with commentaries].

Kimchi, Joseph. *Shekel ha-Kodesh — The Holy Shekel.* Translated by Herman Gollancz. London: Oxford University Press, 1919.

Kook, Abraham Isaac. *Orot ha-Teshuvah.* Translated by A. Metzger. *Rabbi Kook's Philosophy of Repentance.* New York: Yeshiva University Press, 1968.

Leshon Hasidim. Lwow, 1876.

Loew, Judah. *Derekh ha-Hayyim.* New York: Judaica Press, 1969.

———. *Gur Aryeih.* 5 vols. Bnei Brak: Judaica Press, 1972.

———. *Hiddushei Aggadot.* 4 vols. New York: Judaica Press, 1969.

———. *Netivot Olom.* 2 vols. New York: Judaica Press, 1969.

———. *Nezah Yisrael.* New York: Judaica Press, 1969.

Lunshitz, Ephraim. *Klei Yakar.* In *Mikraot Gedolot.*

Luzzatto, Moses Hayyim. *Da'at Tevunot — The Knowing Heart.* Translated by Shraga Silverstein. New York: Feldheim, 1989.

———. *Derekh ha-Shem — The Way of God.* Translated by Aryeh Kaplan. New York: Feldheim, 1988.

———. *Mesilat Yesharim [The Path of the Just].* Translated by Shraga Silverstein. New York: Feldheim, 1989.

———. *Mesilat Yesharim — The Path of the Upright.* Translated by Mordecai M. Kaplan. Philadelphia: Jewish Publication Society, 1936.

Maimonides, Abraham. *The Highways to Perfection.* Translated by Samuel Rosenblatt. New York: Columbia University Press, 1927.

Maimonides, Moses. *Commentary to Mishnah Aboth.* Translated by Arthur David. New York: Bloch, 1968.

———. *Commentary to the Mishnah* [Hebrew]. Jerusalem: Mosad ha-Rav Kook, 1975.

———. *Eight Chapters.* Edited and translated by Joseph I. Gorfinkle. New York: Columbia University Press, 1912.

———. *Ethical Writings of Maimonides.* Edited by Raymond L. Weiss and Charles E. Butterworth. New York: New York University Press, 1975.

———. *Guide of the Perplexed.* Translated by Shlomo Pines. Chicago: University of Chicago Press, 1963.

———. *Hanhagat ha-Beri'ut.* Edited by S. Muntner. Translated by Moses ibn Tibbon. Jerusalem: Mosad ha-Rav Kook, 1957.

———. *Maimonides' Commentary on the Aphorisms of Hippocrates.* Translated by Fred Rosner. Haifa: Maimonides Research Institute, 1987.

———. *Mishneh Torah.* 6 vols. New York: Friedman, 1963.

———. *Mishneh Torah — Sefer ha-Mada.* Translated by Moses Hyamson. *The Book of Knowledge.* Jerusalem: Boys Town Jerusalem Publishers, 1965.

———. *Mishneh Torah — Sefer Shofetim.* (*The Book of Judges.*) Translated by Abraham M. Hershman. New Haven, CT: Yale University Press, 1949.

———. *Mishneh Torah — Sefer Zera'im.* (*The Book of Agriculture.*) Translated by Isaac Klein. New Haven, CT: Yale University Press, 1979.

———. *Moses Maimonides' Glossary of Drug Names.* Edited and translated by Fred Rosner. Philadelphia: Jewish Publication Society, 1979.

_____ . *On Sexual Intercourse.* Translated by Morris Gorlin. Brooklyn: Rambash, 1961.

_____ . *On the Causes of Symptoms.* Edited by J. O. Leibowitz and S. Marcus. Berkeley: University of California Press, 1974.

_____ . *Pirke Moshe — The Medical Aphorisms of Moses Maimonides.* Edited and translated by Fred Rosner and S. Muntner. New York: Yeshiva University Press, 1970–1971.

_____ . *The Preservation of Youth.* Translated by Hirsch L. Gordon. New York: Philosophical Library, 1958.

_____ . *Sefer ha-Mitzvot.* Edited by J. Kapah. Jerusalem: Mosad ha-Rav Kook, 1971.

_____ . *Sefer ha-Mitzvot.* Jerusalem: Epstein, 1965.

_____ . *Teshuvot ha-Rambam.* 3 vols. Edited by J. Blau. Jerusalem: Mikize Nirdamim, 1948.

_____ . *Treatise on Asthma.* Edited and translated by Suessman Muntner. Philadelphia: Lippincott, 1963.

_____ . *Treatise on Hemorrhoids.* Translated by Fred Rosner and Suessman Muntner. Philadelphia: Lippincott, 1969.

_____ . *Treatise on Poisons and Their Antidotes.* Translated by Suessman Muntner. Philadelphia: Lippincott, 1966.

_____ . *Treatises on Poisons, Hemorrhoids, Cohabitation.* Translated by Fred Rosner. Haifa: Maimonides Research Institute, 1984.

Meiri, Menahem. *Commentary to the Ethics of the Fathers* [Hebrew]. Jerusalem: 1944.

_____ . *Hibbur ha-Teshuvah.* Edited by A. Schreiber. New York: Schulzinger, 1950.

Mekhilta de Rabbi Ishmael. Edited by Hayyim Horovitz and Israel Rabin. Jerusalem: Wahrmann, 1960.

Menahem Nahum of Chernobyl. *Yismah Lev* in his *Me'or Einayim.* Jerusalem: Me'or Einayim, 1966.

Midrash Rabbah. Vilna: Romm, 1921 [with commentaries].

Midrash Tadsheh. [In *Otzar ha-Midrashim*].

Midrash Tanhuma [*ha-Nidpas*]. Jerusalem: Levin-Epstein, 1964.

Midrash Tanhuma. Edited by Solomon Buber. Vilna: 1885.

Midrash Tehillim. Edited by Solomon Buber. Vilna: Romm, 1891. Translated by William G. Braude. *Midrash on Psalms.* New Haven, CT: Yale University Press, 1959.

Mikraot Gedolot. [Hebrew Scripture with commentaries]. 5 vols. New York: Tanach, 1959.

Mishnah [with commentaries]. Jerusalem: Horeb, 1952.

Mishnat Rabbi Eliezer. Edited by Hyman G. Enelow. New York: Bloch, 1933.

Mordecai of Chernobyl. *Lekutei Torah.* New York: Noble Printing Co., 1954.

Moses Hayyim Ephraim of Sudlykow. *Degel Mahaneh Ephraim.* Jerusalem: Hadar, 1962.

Moses of Coucy. *Sefer Mitzvot Gadol.*

Nahman of Bratzlav. *Sefer ha-Middot.* New York: N.p., 1965.

Nahmanides (Moses ben Nahman). *Commentary to Maimonides' Sefer ha-Mitzvot — Book of the Commandments* [Hebrew]. In Maimonides, *Sefer ha-Mitzvot.* Jerusalem: Levin-Epstein, 1965.

_____ . *Commentary to the Torah* [Hebrew]. 2 vols. Edited by Charles B. Chavel. Jerusalem: Mosad ha-Rav Kook, 1959. Also in *Mikraot Gedolot*.

_____ . *Iggeret ha-Musar*. [In *Hebrew Ethical Wills*].

_____ . *Kitvei Rabbenu Moshe ben Nahman*. 2 vols. Edited by Charles B. Chavel. Jerusalem: Mosad ha-Rav Kook, 1964.

Or Zaru'a. In n.s. 9, *Kovetz al-Yad* (1980). Edited by Alexander Altmann.

Orhot Zaddikim — The Ways of the Righteous. Translated by Seymour J. Cohen. New York: Feldheim, 1969.

Orhot Zaddikim. Jerusalem: Eshkol, 1967.

Otzar ha-Midrashim. Edited by Judah D. Eisenstein. 2nd ed. New York: Grossman, 1956.

Palaggi, Hayyim. *Hikkeke Lev*. Salonika: 1840.

Palestinian Talmud [with commentaries]. Krotoschin, 1886.

Pesikta d'Rav Kahana. Edited by Solomon Buber. Lyck: Mikitzei Nirdamim, 1868.

Pesikta Rabbati. Edited by Meir Friedmann. Vienna: Herausgebers, 1880.

Pinhas of Koretz. *Midrash Pinhas*. Jerusalem, 1961.

Pirke de Rabbi Eliezer. Warsaw, 1852. Reprint. New York: Ohm, 1946. Translated by Gerald Friedlander. London: N.p., 1916.

Rashi on the Bible. [In *Mikraot Gedolot*].

Rashi to Talmud. [In *Talmud* with commentaries].

Saadya Gaon. *The Book of Beliefs and Opinions*. Translated by Samuel Rosenblatt. New Haven, CT: Yale University Press, 1948.

Samuel of Uceda. *Midrash Shmuel*. Jerusalem: Brody-Katz, n.d.

Seder Eliyahu Rabba ve-Seder Eliyahu Zuta. Edited by Meir Friedmann. Vilna: Ahiyasaf, 1904.

Sefer ha-Besht. 2 vols. Edited by Simon Mendel of Givurtchav. Jerusalem: Horeb, 1961.

Sefer Hasidim. Edited by Reuven Margaliot. Jerusalem: Mosad ha-Rav Kook, 1960.

Sefer ha-Yashar. Jerusalem: Eshkol, 1966.

Sefer ha-Yashar — The Book of the Righteous. Translated by Seymour J. Cohen. New York: Ktav, 1973.

Semahot. Translated by Dov Zlotnick. *The Tractate Mourning*. New Haven, CT: Yale University Press, 1966.

Shneur Zalman of Liady. *Lekutai Amarim [Tanya]*. Brooklyn: Otzar ha-Hasidim, 1965.

Sifra. Vienna: Schlossberg, 1862. Reprint. New York: Ohm, 1947.

Sifre. Edited by Louis Finkelstein. Berlin: Gesellschaft zur Forderung der Wissenschaft des Judentums, 1939.

Tales of Sendebar. Translated by Morris Epstein. Philadelphia: Jewish Publication Society, 1967.

Talmud [with commentaries]. Vilna: Romm, 1895.

Teomim, Judah Leib. *Gur Aryeh Judah*. Zulkav, 1827.

Tosefta. Edited by M. Zuckermandel. Jerusalem: Wahrman, 1970.

Vital, Hayyim. *Pri Etz Hayyim*. Tel Aviv: Eshel, 1966.

_____ . *Sefer Sha'arey Kedushah*. Jerusalem: Aravah, 1967.

_____ . *Sha'ar Ruah ha-Kodesh*. Jerusalem: Eshel, 1963.

Yalkut Shimoni. 2 vols. New York: Pardes, 1944.

Zabara, Joseph ben Meir. *The Book of Delight.* Translated by Moses Hadas. New York: Columbia University Press, 1932.

Zahalon, Jacob. *A Guide for Preachers on Composing and Delivering Sermons: The Or ha-Darshanim of Jacob Zahalon.* Edited by Henry Sosland. New York: Jewish Theological Seminary, 1987.

Zohar. 3 vols. Vilna: Romm, 1882. Partial translations: *The Zohar.* 5 vols. Translated by Harry Sperling and Maurice Simon. London: Soncino, 1933. Daniel C. Matt. *Zohar: The Book of Enlightenment.* New York: Paulist Press, 1983. Gershom Scholem. *The Zohar.* New York: Schocken, 1949.

Zussel, Simhah of Kelm. *Hokhmah u-Musar.* New York: 1957.

OTHER SOURCES

Aberbach, Moses. "Smoking and Halakhah." *Tradition* 10:3 (1969).

Abraham, Abraham S. *Medical Halacha for Everyone.* New York: Feldheim, 1980.

Abramowitz, Hayyim. *Ha-Dibrah ha-Hamishit.* Jerusalem: Reuven Mass, 1971.

_____ . *Heikhal ha-Teshuvah.* Bnei Brak: Nesah, 1961.

Agus, Jacob. *The Vision and the Way: An Interpretation of Jewish Ethics.* New York: Ungar, 1966.

Albert, Ada Rappoport. "Confession in the Circle of Rabbi Nahman of Bratslav." *Bulletin of the Institute of Jewish Studies* 1 (1973).

Altmann, Alexander. "*Homo Imago Dei* in Jewish and Christian Theology." *Journal of Religion* 48 (1968).

_____ . "Maimonides' Four Perfections." Chapter in his *Essays in Jewish Intellectual History.* London: University Press of New England, 1981.

_____ . *Studies in Religious Philosophy and Mysticism.* Ithaca, NY: Cornell University Press, 1969.

Arieti, Silvano. *Creativity.* New York: Basic Books, 1976.

Aristotle. *Nichomachean Ethics.* Translated by Martin Ostwald. New York: Bobbs-Merrill, 1962.

Ayinn, Sidney. "Kant on Judaism." *Jewish Quarterly Review* 59 (July 1968).

Baer, Yitzhak. *A History of the Jews in Christian Spain.* 2 vols. Translated by L. Schoffman. Philadelphia: Jewish Publication Society, 1966.

Bamberger, Bernard. "Fear and Love of God in the Old Testament." *Hebrew Union College Annual* 6 (1929).

Baron, Salo, ed. *Essays on Maimonides.* New York: Columbia University Press, 1941.

_____ . "Yehudah Ha-Levi: An Answer to an Historic Challenge." *Jewish Social Studies* 3 (1941).

Beauchamp, T. L., and Walters, L., eds. *Encyclopedia of Bioethics.* Belmont, CA: Wadsworth, 1982.

Ben Menahem, Naftali. *Kitve Rabbi Moshe Hayyim Luzzatto.* Jerusalem: Mosad ha-Rav Kook, 1951.

Ben Mordecai, Israel Jacob. *Torat ha-Middot – Anavah u-Ga'avah.* Jerusalem: Levin-Epstein, 1966.

Ben Sasson, Hayyim H. *Hagut ve-Hanhaga*. Jerusalem: Mosad Bialik, 1959.

———. "Wealth and Poverty in the Teachings of the Preacher Ephraim Lunschitz" [Hebrew]. *Zion* 19 (1954).

Benayhu, Meir. *Kitvei ha-Kabbalah she-le-Ramhal*. Jerusalem: 1979.

Bentwich, Norman. *Solomon Schechter: A Biography*. New York: Burning Bush Press, 1964.

Bergman, Judah. *Ha-Zedakah B'Yisrael*. Jerusalem: Tarshish, 1944.

Bettan, Israel. *Studies in Jewish Preaching*. Cincinnati: Hebrew Union College Press, 1939.

Blank, Irwin M. "Is There a Common Judeo-Christian Ethical Tradition?" Chapter in Daniel Jeremy Silver, ed. *Judaism and Ethics*. New York: Ktav, 1970.

Bleich, J. David. *Contemporary Halakhic Problems*. New York: Ktav, 1977.

———. *Judaism and Healing*. New York: Ktav, 1981.

Blidstein, Gerald. *Honor Thy Father and Thy Mother: Filial Responsibility in Jewish Law and Ethics*. New York: Ktav, 1975.

Bloch, Abraham P. *A Book of Jewish Ethical Concepts*. New York: Ktav, 1984.

Blumenthal, David, ed. *Approaches to Judaism in Medieval Times*. Chico, CA: Scholars Press, 1984.

Bokser, Ben Zion. *The Gift of Life and Love*. New York: Hebrew Publishing Co., 1975.

Borowitz, Eugene. *Choosing a Sex Ethic*. New York: Schocken, 1970.

———. *Exploring Jewish Ethics*. Detroit: Wayne State University Press, 1989.

Breslauer, S. Daniel. *Contemporary Jewish Ethics*. New York: Greenwood, 1985.

———. *Modern Jewish Ethics*. New York: Greenwood, 1986.

———. *A New Jewish Ethics*. New York: Edwin Mellen Press, 1983.

Brooks, Roger. *Support for the Poor in the Mishnaic Law of Agriculture: Tractate Pe'ah*. Chico, CA: Scholars Press, 1983.

Buber, Martin. *Tales of the Hasidim: Early Masters*. Translated by Olga Marx. New York: Schocken, 1947.

———. *Tales of the Hasidim: Later Masters*. Translated by Olga Marx. New York: Schocken, 1948.

Buchler, Adolf. *Studies in Sin and Atonement*. 2nd ed. New York: Ktav, 1967.

Buijs, Joseph. *Maimonides*. Notre Dame, IN: Notre Dame University Press, 1988.

Cahn, Edmund. *The Moral Decision*. Bloomington, IN: Indiana University Press, 1955.

Camus, Albert. *The Myth of Sisyphus*. Translated by Justin O'Brien. New York: Knopf, 1955.

Capellanus, Andreas. *The Art of Courtly Love*. Translated by J. J. Parry. New York: 1941.

Carmi, T., ed. *The Penguin Book of Hebrew Verse*. Philadelphia: Penguin Books and Jewish Publication Society, 1981.

Chavel, Charles D. *Rabbenu Moshe ben Nahman*. Jerusalem: Mosad ha-Rav Kook, 1967.

Chipkin, Israel. "Judaism and Social Welfare." Chapter in *The Jews*. Edited by Louis Finkelstein. Philadelphia: Jewish Publication Society, 1949.

Choron, Jacques. *Death and Western Thought*. New York: Collier Books, 1963.

Cohen, Arthur A. *The Myth of the Judeo-Christian Tradition.* New York: Schocken, 1971.

Cohen, Arthur A., and Mendes-Flohr, Paul, eds. *Contemporary Jewish Religious Thought.* New York: Scribners, 1987.

Cohen, Seymour J. *Affirming Life.* Hoboken, NJ: Ktav, 1987.

Cohon, Samuel S. *Judaism: A Way of Life.* New York: Schocken, 1948.

Cooperman, Bernard, ed. *Jewish Thought in the Sixteenth Century.* Cambridge, MA: Harvard University Press, 1983.

Cronbach, Abraham. "The Gradations of Benevolence." *Hebrew Union College Annual* 16 (1941).

———. "The Maimonidean Code of Benevolence." *Hebrew Union College Annual* 20 (1947).

———. "The Me'il Zedakah." *Hebrew Union College Annual* 11 (1936).

———. "The Me'il Zedakah." *Hebrew Union College Annual* 12/13 (1937–1938).

———. "The Me'il Zedakah." *Hebrew Union College Annual* 14 (1939).

———. "Social Thinking in the *Sefer Hasidim.*" *Hebrew Union College Annual* 22 (1949).

Cumming, Robert D., ed. *The Philosophy of Jean Paul Sartre.* New York: Random House, 1965.

Dan, Joseph. *The Esoteric Theology of Ashkenazi Hasidism* [Hebrew]. Jerusalem: Mosad Bialik, 1968.

———. "Ethical Literature." In *Encyclopaedia Judaica.*

———. "Homiletic Literature." In *Encyclopaedia Judaica.*

———. *Jewish Mysticism and Jewish Ethics.* Seattle: University of Washington Press, 1986.

———. "Moses Hayyim Luzzatto." In *Encyclopaedia Judaica.*

———. *Sifrut ha-Musar ve-ha-Derush.* Jerusalem: Keter, 1975.

———, ed. *The Teachings of Hasidism.* New York: Behrman House, 1983.

Davidson, Israel. *Otzar ha-Mashalim ve-ha-Pitgamim.* Jerusalem: Mosad ha-Rav Kook, 1969.

DeRougemont, Denis. *Love in the Western World.* Translated by Montgomery Belgion. Princeton, NJ: Princeton University Press, 1983.

De Sola Pool, David. *Portraits Etched in Stone.* New York: Columbia University Press, 1952.

Diesendruck, Zvi. "Samuel and Moses Ibn Tibbon on Maimonides' Theory of Providence." *Hebrew Union College Annual* 11 (1936).

Dimitrovsky, Hayyim Zalmen, ed. *Sefer ha-Yovel le'Salo Baron.* Jerusalem: 1975.

Dresner, Samuel H. *Levi Yitzhak of Berditchev.* Bridgeport, CT: Hartmore House, 1974.

Dresner, Samuel H., and Sherwin, Byron. *Judaism: The Way of Sanctification.* New York: United Synagogue of America, 1978.

Edelheit, Joseph, ed. *The Life of Covenant.* Chicago: Spertus College of Judaica Press, 1986.

Edwards, Paul. "My Death." In *Encyclopedia of Philosophy.*

Efros, Israel. "Some Aspects of Judah Ha-Levi's Mysticism." *Proceedings of the American Academy for Jewish Research* 11 (1941).

Elbaum, Jacob. "Aspects of Hebrew Ethical Literature in Sixteenth-Century Poland." Chapter in Bernard Dov Cooperman, ed. *Jewish Thought in the Sixteenth Century.* Cambridge, MA: Harvard University Press, 1983.

_____ . *Petihot ve-Histagrut.* Jerusalem: Magnes Press, 1990.

Encyclopedia Judaica. Edited by Cecil Roth. Jerusalem: Keter, 1971.

Encyclopedia of Philosophy. Edited by Paul Edwards. New York: Macmillan, 1967.

Epstein, Isadore. "Judah Ha-Levi as Philosopher." *Jewish Quarterly Review* 25 (1935).

_____ , ed. *Moses Maimonides: Anglo-Jewish Papers in Connection with the Eighth Centenary of His Birth.* London: Soncino, 1935.

Epstein, Louis. *Marriage Laws in the Bible and Talmud.* Cambridge, MA: Harvard University Press, 1942.

_____ . *Sex Laws and Customs in Judaism.* New York: Bloch, 1948.

Faierstein, Morris. "God's Need for the Commandments in Medieval Kabbalah." *Conservative Judaism* 36:1 (Fall 1982).

Falk, Zeev. *Jewish Matrimonial Law in the Middle Ages.* New York: Oxford University Press, 1966.

Feher, Michael, ed. *Fragments for a History of the Human Body.* New York: Zone, 1989.

Feldman, David M. *Birth Control in Jewish Law.* New York: New York University Press, 1968.

_____ . *Health and Medicine in the Jewish Tradition.* New York: Crossroad, 1986.

Fine, Lawrence, ed. *Safed Spirituality.* New York: Paulist Press, 1984.

_____ . *Techniques for Mystical Meditation for Achieving Prophecy and the Holy Spirit in the Teachings of Isaac Luria and Hayyim Vital.* Ph.D. dissertation: Brandeis University, 1976.

Fox, Marvin. *Interpreting Maimonides.* Chicago: University Press, 1990.

_____ , ed. *Modern Jewish Ethics.* Ohio: Ohio State University Press, 1975.

Freehof, Solomon B. *Reform Responsa.* Cincinnati: Hebrew Union College Press, 1960.

Friedenwald, Harry. *The Jews and Medicine.* 2 vols. Baltimore: Johns Hopkins University Press, 1944.

Frisch, Ephraim. *An Historical Survey of Jewish Philanthropy.* New York: Cooper Square Publishers, 1969.

Gershfield, Edward, ed. *Studies in Jewish Jurisprudence.* New York: Sefer Hermon, 1971.

Ginzberg, Louis. *Students, Scholars and Saints.* Philadelphia: Jewish Publication Society, 1928.

Ginzburg, Simon. *The Life and Works of Moses Hayyim Luzzatto.* Philadelphia: Dropsie College, 1931.

Goiten, Shlomo Dov. "The Biography of Rabbi Judah Ha-Levi in Light of Cairo Geniza Documents." *Proceedings of the American Academy for Jewish Research* 28 (1959).

_____ . *A Mediterranean Society: The Jewish Communities of the Arab World as Portrayed by the Documents of the Cairo Geniza.* 4 vols. Los Angeles: University of California Press, 1967–1981.

Goldberg, Hillel. "Israel Salanter and *Orhot Zaddikim.*" *Tradition* 23:4 (Summer 1988).

Goldstein, David, ed. and trans. *The Jewish Poets of Spain.* New York: Penguin, 1965.

Goodman, Lenn E., ed. *Rambam: Readings in the Philosophy of Moses Maimonides*. New York: Viking, 1976.

Goodman, Philip, and Goodman, Hannah. *The Jewish Marriage Anthology*. Philadelphia: Jewish Publication Society, 1975.

Gordis, Robert. *Jewish Ethics for a Lawless World*. New York: Jewish Theological Seminary, 1986.

_____ . *Love and Sex*. New York: Farrar, Straus and Giroux, 1978.

_____ . *Sex and the Family in Jewish Tradition*. New York: United Synagogue of America, 1967.

Green, Arthur. *Tormented Master: The Life and Spiritual Quest of Rabbi Nahman of Bratslav*. Woodstock, VT: Jewish Lights Publishing, 1992.

_____ , ed. *Jewish Spirituality*. New York: Crossroad, 1986.

Greenstein, Edward. "Medieval Biblical Commentaries." Chapter in Barry W. Holtz, ed. *Back to the Sources*. New York: Summit, 1984.

Greenwald, Leopold. *Kol Bo Al Avelut*. New York: Moriah, 1947.

Gries, Zeev. *Sefer ha-Hanhagot*. Jerusalem: Mosad Bialik, 1989.

Guardini, Romano. *The Death of Socrates*. Translated by B. Wrighton. New York: Meridian Books, 1962.

Guberman, Karen. "The Language of Love in Spanish Kabbalah. An Examination of the *Iggeret ha-Kodesh*." Chapter in David R. Blumenthal, ed. *Approaches to Judaism in Medieval Times*. Chico, CA: Scholars Press, 1984.

Gudemann, Moritz. *Ha-Torah ve-ha-Hayyim*. Vol. 2. Warsaw: 1899.

Guttmann, Jacob. "Die ethische Schrift Sefer hajashar und ihre philosophischen Anschauungen." *Monatschrift fuer Geschichte und Wissenschaft des Judentums* 63 (1919).

Guttmann, Julius. *Philosophies of Judaism*. Translated by David W. Silverman. New York: Holt Rinehart and Winston, 1964.

Haas, Peter J. "Toward a Semiotic Study of Jewish Moral Discourse: The Case of Responsa." *Semeia* 34 (1985).

Halamish, Moshe. "The Identity of the Book 'Sefer ha-Middot' Mentioned in *Sefer Hareidim* and *Reshit Hokhmah*" [Hebrew]. *Kiryat Sefer* 47 (1972).

Halkin, Abraham. "Judah ibn Tibbon." In *Encyclopaedia Judaica*.

Harris, Monford. "The Concept of Love in *Sefer Hasidim*." *Jewish Quarterly Review* 50 (1959).

_____ . "The Dirty Word: A Theological Analysis." *Central Conference of American Rabbis Journal* 17 (April 1970).

_____ . "Marriage as Metaphysics: A Study of the *Iggeret ha-Kodesh*." *Hebrew Union College Annual* 33 (1962).

Hartman, David. *Maimonides: Torah and Philosophic Quest*. Philadelphia: Jewish Publication Society, 1976.

Harvey, Warren. "Love: The Beginning and the End of Torah." *Tradition* 15:4 (Spring 1976).

Hasidah, Israel Isaac. *Rabbi Hayyim Palaggi and His Work* [Hebrew]. Jerusalem: 1968.

Heidel, A. *The Gilgamesh Epic and Old Testament Parallels*. Chicago: University of Chicago Press, 1963.

Heinemann, Benno. *The Maggid of Dubno and His Parables.* New York: Feldheim, 1978.

Henoch, C. *Ha-Ramban ke-Hokeir u-Mekubal.* Jerusalem, 1978.

Herberg, Will. *Judaism and Modern Man.* Woodstock, VT: Jewish Lights Publishing, 1997.

Herring, Basil F. *Jewish Ethics and Halakhah for Our Time.* New York: Ktav, 1984.

_____. *Jewish Ethics and Halakhah for Our Time.* Vol. 2. New York: Yeshiva University Press, 1989.

Heschel, Abraham J. *The Earth Is the Lord's.* Woodstock, VT: Jewish Lights Publishing, 1995.

_____. *God in Search of Man.* Philadelphia: Jewish Publication Society, 1955.

_____. *The Insecurity of Freedom.* New York: Farrar, Straus and Giroux, 1966.

_____. *Kotsk* [Yiddish]. Tel Aviv: Menorah, 1973.

_____. *Maimonides: A Biography.* Translated by Joachim Neugroshel. New York: Farrar, Straus and Giroux, 1982.

_____. *Man is Not Alone.* New York: Farrar, Straus and Giroux, 1951.

_____. *Man's Quest for God.* New York: Scribners, 1954.

_____. "The Mystical Element in Judaism." Chapter in Louis Finkelstein, ed. *The Jews: Their History, Culture, and Religion.* Philadelphia: Jewish Publication Society, 1960.

_____. *A Passion for Truth.* Woodstock, VT: Jewish Lights Publishing, 1995.

_____. "Reflections on Death." *Conservative Judaism* 28:1 (Fall 1973).

_____. *Torah min ha-Shamayim.* 3 vols. London: Soncino, 1962, 1965, 1990.

_____. *Who is Man?* Stanford, CA: Stanford University Press, 1963.

Holtz, Barry W. *Back to the Sources.* New York: Summit, 1984.

Husik, Isaac. *A History of Medieval Jewish Philosophy.* Philadelphia: Jewish Publication Society, 1940.

Idel, Moshe. *Kabbalah: New Perspectives.* New Haven, CT: Yale University Press, 1988.

_____. *The Mystical Experience in Abraham Abulafia.* Albany, NY: SUNY Press, 1988.

_____. "Sexual Metaphors and Praxis in the Kabbalah." Chapter in David Kraemer, ed. *The Jewish Family.* New York: Oxford University Press, 1989.

Jacobs, Louis. "Eating as an Act of Worship in Hasidic Thought." Chapter in S. Stein and R. Loewe, eds. *Studies in Jewish Religious and Intellectual History.* University, AL: University of Alabama Press, 1979.

_____. *Faith.* New York: Basic Books, 1968.

_____. *A Guide to Yom Kippur.* London: Jewish Chronicle, 1957.

_____. *Hasidic Thought.* New York: Behrman House, 1976.

_____. *Holy Living.* London: Jason Aronson, 1990.

_____. *Jewish Ethics, Philosophy and Mysticism.* New York: Behrman House, 1969.

_____. *A Jewish Theology.* New York: Behrman House, 1973.

_____. *Jewish Values.* London: Vallentine Mitchell, 1960.

_____. *Principles of the Jewish Faith.* New York: Basic Books, 1964.

_____. *We Have Reason to Believe.* London: Vallentine Mitchell, 1957.

Jakobovits, Immanuel. *Jewish Medical Ethics.* New York: Bloch, 1959.

Jegen, Carol Francis, and Sherwin, Byron L. *Thank God.* Chicago: Liturgy Training Publications, 1989.

Josephus. *Antiquities*. Translated by J. Thackery. Cambridge, MA: Harvard University Press, 1934.

Jung, Leo. *Business Ethics in Jewish Law*. New York: Hebrew Publishing Co., 1987.

Kadushin, Max. *Worship and Ethics*. Evanston, IL: Northwestern University Press, 1964.

Kaham, I. M. *Israel Meir ha-Kohen Looks at Life*. Jerusalem: Likutei Chafetz Chaim, 1987.

Kaminetsky, Joseph, and Friedman, Murray, eds. *Building Jewish Ethical Character*. New York: Fryer Foundation, 1975.

Kaplan, Aryeh. *The Light Beyond: Adventures in Hasidic Thought*. New York: Maznaim, 1981.

Karp, Abraham, et al., eds. *Three Score and Ten: Essays in Honor of Seymour J. Cohen*. New York: Ktav, 1991.

Kass, Leon. "Regarding the End of Medicine and the Pursuit of Health." Chapter in Hunt and Arras, eds. *Ethical Issues in Modern Medicine*. Palo Alto, CA: Mayfield, 1977.

Katz, Dov. *Tenuat ha-Musar*. 5 vols. Jerusalem: Brody-Katz, 1974.

Kayser, Rudolf. *The Life and Times of Jehudah Halevi*. New York: Hubner, 1949.

Kellner, Menahem Marc, ed. *Contemporary Jewish Ethics*. New York: Sanhedrin, 1978.

——— . *Maimonides and the Jewish People*. Albany, NY: SUNY Press, 1991.

——— . *Maimonides on Human Perfection*. Atlanta: Scholars Press, 1990.

Kessner, Thomas. "Gershom Mendes Seixas." *American Jewish Historical Quarterly* 78:4 (June 1969).

Klatzkin, Jacob. *Otzar ha-Munahim ha-Philosophi'im*. 2 vols. New York: Feldheim, 1968.

Klein, Isaac. *A Time to be Born, A Time to Die*. New York: United Synagogue of America, 1976.

Klein, Rose S. "Washington's Thanksgiving Proclamations." *American Jewish Archives* 20:2 (1968).

Kohler, Kaufman. *Jewish Theology*. 2nd ed. New York: Ktav, 1968.

Kohut, Heinz. *The Analysis of the Self*. New York: International Universities Press, 1971.

Kraemer, David, ed. *The Jewish Family*. New York: Oxford University Press, 1989.

Kumove, S. *Words Like Arrows: A Collection of Yiddish Folk Sayings*. New York: Schocken, 1985.

Lamm, Maurice. *The Jewish Way in Death and Mourning*. New York: Jonathan David, 1969.

Lamm, Norman. *The Good Society: Jewish Ethics in Action*. New York: Viking Press, 1974.

Lazaroff, Allan. "Bahya's Asceticism Against its Rabbinic and Islamic Background." *Journal of Jewish Studies* 21 (1970).

Lazarus, Moritz. *The Ethics of Judaism*. 2 vols. Translated by Henrietta Szold. Philadelphia: Jewish Publication Society, 1900.

Lebendiger, Israel. "The Minor in Jewish Law." Chapter in Edward M. Gershfield, ed. *Studies in Jewish Jurisprudence*. Vol. 1. New York: Sefer Hermon Press, 1971.

Levine, Aaron. *Free Enterprise and Jewish Law*. New York: Ktav, 1980.

Lieberman, Saul. *Greek in Jewish Palestine*. New York: Feldheim, 1965.

Marcus, Ivan. *Piety and Society: The Jewish Pietists of Medieval Germany*. Leiden: E. J. Brill, 1981.

Marcus, Jacob Rader. *Early American Jewry*. Vol. 1. Philadelphia: Jewish Publication Society, 1951.

_____ . "The Handsome Young Priest in the Black Gown: The Personal World of Gershom Seixas." *Hebrew Union College Annual* 70/71 (1969/1970).

_____ , ed. *The Jew in the Medieval World*. New York: Atheneum, 1969.

Marx, Alexander. "Gabirol's Authorship of the *Choice of Pearls* and the Two Versions of Joseph Kimchi's *Shekel ha-Kodesh*." *Hebrew Union College Annual* 4 (1927).

Marx, Zvi. "Priorities in *Zedakah* and Their Implications." *Judaism* 28 (1979).

Mase-Zahav, Abraham, ed. *Tokhahat Musar*. Jerusalem, 1962.

Matt, Daniel C. "The Mystic and the *Mizwot*." Chapter in Arthur Green, ed. *Jewish Spirituality*. New York: Crossroad, 1986.

Meyer, Michael A. *Response to Modernity*. New York: Oxford University Press, 1988.

Minkin, Jacob. *The Teachings of Maimonides*. Northvale, NJ: Jason Aronson, 1987.

Mintz, Benjamin. *Sefer ha-Histalkut*. Tel Aviv: N.p., 1930.

Montefiore, C. G., and H. Loewe, eds. *A Rabbinic Anthology*. New York: Meridian, 1960.

Moore, George Foot. *Judaism: In the First Centuries of the Christian Era*. 2 vols. Cambridge, MA: Harvard University Press, 1927.

Mopsik, Charles. "The Body of Engenderment in the Hebrew Bible, the Rabbinic Tradition and the Kabbalah." Chapter in Michel Feher, ed. *Fragments for a History of the Human Body*. New York: Zone, 1989.

_____ . *Lettre sur la Saineté*. Lagrasse, France: Verdier, 1986.

Nathan of Nemirov. "The Death of Our Master." Translated by Arthur Green. *Conservative Judaism* 28:1 (1973).

Neher, Andre. *The Exile of the Word*. Translated by David Maisel. Philadelphia: Jewish Publication Society, 1981.

Neumark, David. "Jehuda Hallevi's Philosophy in its Principles." In his *Essays in Jewish Philosophy*. Cincinnati: Central Conference of American Rabbis, 1929.

Neusner, Jacob. *Tzedakah*. Chappaqua, NY: Rossel Books, 1982.

Newman, Louis E. "Ethics as Law, Law as Religion." *Shofar* 9:1 (Fall 1990).

_____ . "Woodchoppers and Respirators." *Modern Judaism* 10:1 (1989).

Newman, Louis. *The Hasidic Anthology*. New York: Schocken, 1963.

Niebuhr, Reinhold. *The Nature and Destiny of Man*. 2 vols. New York: Scribners, 1941.

Novak, David. *Law and Theology in Judaism*. New York: Ktav, 1974.

_____ . "Nahmanides' Commentary to the Torah." Chapter in Byron L. Sherwin, ed. *The Solomon Goldman Lectures*. Vol. 5. Chicago: Spertus College of Judaica Press, 1990.

Pascal, Blaise. *Pensées*. Translated by A. J. Krailsheimer. London: Penguin, 1966.

Pechter, Mordecai. "On the Citations from *Orhot Zaddikim* in the Ethical Literature of the Sages of Safed" [Hebrew]. *Kiryat Sefer* 47 (1962).

_____ . "*Orhot Zaddikim* and French Jewish Ethical Literature" [Hebrew]. *Kiryat Sefer* 47 (1972).

Pei, M. A. *The Story of Language*. Philadelphia: Lippincott, 1965.

Petuchowski, Jakob. "The Beauty of God." Chapter in Joseph Edelheit, ed. *The Life of Covenant*. Chicago: Spertus College of Judaica Press, 1986.

———. "The Concept of *Teshuvah* in the Bible and the Talmud." *Judaism* 17:2 (1968).

Pines, Shlomo. "Solomon ibn Gabirol." In *Encyclopaedia Judaica*.

Plato. *The Dialogues of Plato*. Translated by B. Jowett, 1920. Reprint. New York: Random House, 1937.

Pliskin, Z. *Guard Your Tongue*. Jerusalem: Pliskin, 1975.

Pollack, Herman. *Jewish Folkways in Germanic Lands*. Cambridge, MA: MIT Press, 1971.

Pope, Alexander. "An Essay on Criticism." In L. Kronenberger, ed. *Alexander Pope: Selected Works*. New York: Modern Library, 1948.

Preuss, Julius. *Biblical and Talmudic Medicine*. Translated by Fred Rosner. New York: Sanhedrin Press, 1978.

Rabinowitz, L. I. "Moses Maimonides." In *Encyclopaedia Judaica*.

Ravitzky, Aviezer. "Samuel Ibn Tibbon and the Esoteric Character of the *Guide of the Perplexed*." *Association for Jewish Studies Review* 6 (1981).

Reifman, Yaakov. "Some Observations About *Orhot Zaddikim*" [Hebrew]. *Ha-Karmel* 2 (1862).

Riemer, Jack, ed. *Jewish Reflections on Death*. New York: Schocken, 1974.

Riemer, Jack, and Stampfer, Nathaniel, eds. *So That Your Values Live On: Ethical Wills and How to Prepare Them*. Woodstock, VT: Jewish Lights Publishing, 1991.

Rosenzweig, Franz. *The Star of Redemption*. Translated by William H. Hallo. New York: Holt, Rinehart and Winston, 1970.

Rosin, D. "The Ethics of Solomon Ibn Gabirol." *Jewish Quarterly Review* 3 (1891).

Rosner, Fred. *Medicine and Jewish Law*. Northvale, NJ: Jason Aronson, 1990.

———. *Medicine in the Mishneh Torah of Maimonides*. New York: Ktav, 1984.

———. *Modern Medicine and Jewish Law*. New York: Yeshiva University Press, 1972.

———. *Sex Ethics in the Writings of Moses Maimonides*. New York: Bloch, 1974.

Rosner, Fred, and Bleich, J. David, eds. *Jewish Bioethics*. New York: Hebrew Publishing Co., 1969.

Rubin, Asher. "The Concept of Repentance Among the Hasidei Ashkenaz." *Journal of Jewish Studies* 16 (1965).

Samuelson, Norbert. "Gersonides." In Byron L. Sherwin, ed. *Solomon Goldman Lectures*. Vol. 5. Chicago: Spertus College of Judaica Press, 1990.

Sandmel, Samuel. *The Hebrew Scriptures*. New York: Oxford University Press, 1978.

Saperstein, Marc. *Jewish Preaching*. New Haven, CT: Yale University Press, 1989.

Schechter, Solomon. *Aspects of Rabbinic Theology*. Woodstock, VT: Jewish Lights Publishing, 1993.

———. "The Child in Jewish Literature." Chapter in his *Studies in Judaism: First Series*. Philadelphia: Jewish Publication Society, 1938.

———. "Notes of Lectures on Jewish Philanthropy." Chapter in his *Studies in Judaism. Third Series*. Philadelphia: Jewish Publication Society, 1924.

———. *Studies in Judaism*. New York: Meridian, 1958.

———. *Studies in Judaism*. Vol. 2. Philadelphia: Jewish Publication Society, 1908.

Schneid, Hayyim. *Marriage*. Philadelphia: Jewish Publication Society, 1973.

Scholem, Gershom. "Did Nahmanides Write the *Holy Letter*? [Hebrew]." *Kiryat Sefer* 21 (1944/45).

_____ . *Major Trends in Jewish Mysticism*. New York: Schocken, 1961.

_____ . *The Messianic Idea in Judaism*. New York: Schocken, 1971.

_____ . *On the Kabbalah and Its Symbolism*. New York: Schocken, 1965.

Seeskin, Kenneth. *The Message of Maimonides*. West Orange, NJ: Behrman House, 1991.

Seixas, Gershom Mendes. *A Religious Discourse: Thanksgiving Sermon*. New York: Jewish Historical Society of New York, 1977.

Sherwin, Byron L. "Fear of God." Chapter in Arthur Cohen and Paul Mendes-Flohr, eds. *Contemporary Jewish Religious Thought*. New York: Scribners, 1987.

_____ . *In Partnership with God: Contemporary Jewish Law and Ethics*. Syracuse, NY: Syracuse University Press, 1990.

_____ . "In the Shadow of Greatness: Rabbi Hayyim Ben Betsalel of Friedberg." *Jewish Social Studies* 37:1 (January 1975).

_____ . "Jewish Ethics as Theological Ethics." *Shofar* 9:1 (Fall 1990).

_____ . "Law and Love in Jewish Theology." *Anglican Theological Review* 64:4 (October 1982).

_____ . "Moses Maimonides on Perfection of the Body." *Listening* 9:1/2 (1974).

_____ . *Mystical Theology and Social Dissent: The Life and Works of Judah Loew of Prague*. London, Toronto, New York: Oxford University Press and the Littman Library of Jewish Civilization, 1982.

_____ , ed. *Solomon Goldman Lectures*. Vol. 5. Chicago: Spertus College of Judaica Press, 1990.

_____ . *Toward a Jewish Theology*. Lewiston, NY: Edwin Mellen Press, 1992.

_____ . "The U.S. Catholic Bishops' Pastoral Letter on the Economy and Jewish Tradition." Chapter in Charles R. Strain, ed. *Prophetic Views and Economic Realities*. Grand Rapids, MI: Eerdmans Publishing Co., 1989.

Sherwin, Byron L., and Dresner, Samuel H. *Judaism: The Way of Sanctification*. New York: United Synagogue of America Press, 1978.

Sherwin, Byron L., and Jegen, Carol Frances. *Thank God*. Liturgy Training Publications, 1989.

Shmeruk, Hayyim. *Sifrut Yiddish be-Polin* [Hebrew]. Jerusalem: N.p., 1971.

Shokek, Shimon. "*Sefer ha-Yashar* within the Framework of Thirteenth-Century Hebrew Ethical Literature" [Hebrew]. Ph.D. dissertation. Hebrew University, 1976.

Shrock, A. J. "The Authorship of the Ethical Treatise Entitled *Sefer ha-Yashar*." *Jewish Quarterly Review* n.s. 61:3 (January 1971).

Sills, D. L., ed. *International Encyclopedia of the Social Sciences*. New York: Macmillan, 1968–74.

Silver, Daniel Jeremy, ed. *Judaism and Ethics*. New York: Ktav, 1970.

Silverman, Morris, ed. *High Holiday Prayerbook*. Hartford, CT: Prayerbook Press, 1951.

Sinclair, Daniel. *Tradition and the Biological Revolution*. Edinburgh: Edinburgh University Press, 1989.

Singer, Irving. *The Nature of Love*. 2 Vols. Chicago: University of Chicago Press, 1984.

Sirat, Colette. *A History of Jewish Philosophy in the Middle Ages*. Cambridge, England: Cambridge University Press, 1985.

Soloveitchik, Joseph B. *On Repentance: In the Thought and Oral Discourses of Rabbi Joseph B. Soloveitchik.* Edited by Pinhas Peli. New York: Paulist Press, 1904.

Spero, Shubert. *Morality, Halakhah and the Jewish Tradition.* New York: Ktav, 1983.

Spiegel, Shalom. *Hebrew Reborn.* New York: Meridian, 1962.

Stein, S., and Loew, R., eds. *Studies in Jewish Religious and Intellectual History.* University, AL: University of Alabama Press, 1979.

Strain, Charles, ed. *Prophetic Views and Economic Realities.* Grand Rapids, MI: Eerdmans Publishing Co., 1989.

Strauss, Leo. "The Law of Reason in the Kuzari." *Proceedings of the American Academy for Jewish Research* 13 (1943).

Talmage, Frank. "Apples of Gold: The Inner Meanings of Sacred Texts in Medieval Judaism." Chapter in Arthur Green, ed. *Jewish Spirituality.* New York: Crossroads, 1986.

Tamari, Meir. *With All Your Possessions.* New York: Free Press, 1986.

Tishbi, Isaiah. *Mishnat ha-Zohar.* 2 vols. Jerusalem: Mosad Bialik, 1957–1961. Translated by David Goldstein. *The Wisdom of the Zohar.* 2 vols. London: Oxford University Press, 1988.

Tolstoy, Leo. *The Death of Ivan Ilych and Other Stories.* New York: New American Library, 1960.

Toynbee, Arnold, et al. *Man's Concern with Death.* New York: McGraw Hill, 1968.

Twersky, Isadore. *Introduction to the Code of Maimonides.* New Haven, CT: Yale University Press, 1980.

———, ed. *A Maimonides Reader.* New York: Behrman House, 1972.

———, ed. *Rabbi Moses Nahmanides.* Cambridge, MA: Harvard University Press, 1983.

———. "Some Aspects of the Jewish Attitude Toward the Welfare State." *Tradition* 5 (1963).

———, ed. *Studies in Maimonides.* Cambridge, MA: Harvard University Press, 1990.

———, ed. *Studies in Medieval Jewish History and Literature.* Vol. 2. Cambridge, MA: Harvard University Press, 1984.

Urbach, Ephraim E. "*Magamot Datiot ve-Havratiot be-Torat ha-Zedakah shel Hazal.*" *Zion* 16 (1951).

———. *The Sages.* Translated by Israel Abrahams. Cambridge, MA: Harvard University Press, 1987.

Vajda, George. "An Analysis of the *Ma'amar Yiqawwu ha-Mayim* by Samuel ben Judah Ibn Tibbon." *Journal of Jewish Studies* 10 (1959).

———. "Bahya ibn Pakudah." In *Encyclopedia Judaica.*

———. *L'Amour de Dieu dans la Theologie Juive du Moyen Age.* Paris: 1957.

Weiss, Abner. "Rabbi Loew of Prague: Theory of Human Nature and Morality." Ph.D. dissertation. Yeshiva University (1969).

Weiss, Joseph. *Studies in Eastern European Jewish Mysticism.* Edited by David Goldstein. New York: Oxford University Press, 1985.

Werblowski, R. J. Zvi. "Faith, Hope and Trust: A Study in the Concept of *Bittahon.*" Chapter in Joseph G. Weiss, ed. *Papers of The Institute of Jewish Studies.* Jerusalem: Magnes Press, 1964.

Wertheim, Aaron. *Halakhot ve-Halikhot ba-Hasidut.* Jerusalem: Mosad ha-Rav Kook, 1960.

Wineman, Aryeh. *Beyond Appearances: Stories from the Kabbalistic Ethical Writings.* Philadelphia: Jewish Publication Society, 1988.

Wittgenstein, Ludwig. *Notebooks 1914–1916.* Translated by G. E. Anscome. New York: Harper and Brothers, 1961.

Wolfson, Harry A. "Maimonides and Ha-Levi." *Jewish Quarterly Review* 2 (1911–12).

_____ . "Notes of Proofs of the Existence of God in Medieval Jewish Philosophy." *Hebrew Union College Annual* 1 (1924).

Yellin, David, and Abrahams, Israel. *Maimonides.* Philadelphia: Jewish Publication Society, 1936.

Zahavy, Zvi, ed. *Mivhar ha-Mahashavah ve-ha-Musar Ba-Yahadut.* Tel Aviv: Zioni, 1954.

Zborowsky, Mark, and Herzog, Elizabeth. *Life is with People.* New York: Schocken, 1962.

Zeitlin, Solomon. *Maimonides: A Biography.* New York: Bloch, 1955.

Zimmels, H. J. *Magicians, Theologians and Doctors.* London: Goldston, 1952.

Zinberg, Israel. *A History of Jewish Literature.* Vol. 2. Translated by Bernard Martin. Cleveland: Case Western Reserve University Press, 1972.

_____ . *A History of Jewish Literature.* Vol. 3. Translated by Bernard Martin. Philadelphia: Jewish Publication Society, 1973.

_____ . *A History of Jewish Literature.* Vol. 6. Translated by Bernard Martin. New York: Ktav, 1975.

_____ . *A History of Jewish Literature.* Vol. 7. Translated by Bernard Martin. Cincinnati: Hebrew Union College Press, 1975.

Acknowledgments

The authors gratefully acknowledge permission to quote from the following sources:

"Lord, Where Shall I Find You?" by Judah Ha-Levi. From *The Penguin Book of Hebrew Verse*, edited and translated by T. Carmi (Allen Lane, 1981), pp. 338–339. © 1981 by T. Carmi. Reprinted by permission of Penguin Books, Ltd.

From *The Gift of Life and Love* by Ben Zion Bokser, p. 118. © 1975 by Ben Zion Bokser. Reprinted by permission of Hebrew Publishing Company.

From *Zohar: The Book of Splendor,* selected and edited by Gershom Scholem, pp. 89–91, 121–122. © 1949 by Schocken Books, Inc. Reprinted by permission of Schocken Books, Inc., a division of Random House, Inc.

From *Al-Hidaya ila Fara'id Al-Qulub* (Arabic), *Sefer Hovot ha-Levavot* (Hebrew) by Bahya ibn Pakudah, translated from the Arabic by Menahem M. Mansoor, pp. 330–339, 341–343, 345–346, 349–351. © 1973 by Second Joseph Aaron Littman Foundation. Reprinted by permission of The Littman Library of Jewish Civilization.

From *Mesilat Yesharim — The Path of the Upright* by Moses Hayyim Luzzatto, translated by Mordecai Kaplan, pp. 204–212, 384–388, 408–420. © 1936 by The Jewish Publication Society of America. Reprinted by permission of The Jewish Publication Society of America.

From *Treatise on Asthma* by Moses Maimonides, translated by Fred Rosner, pp. 6, 8, 9, 24, 25, 28, 36–38, 49, 74–77, 80–85, 98–99. © 1994 by The Maimonides Research Institute, Haifa, Israel. Reprinted by permission of Dr. Fred Rosner.

From *Responsa Hikkeke Lev* (Salonika, 1840), no. 50, by Hayyim Palaggi, translated by Peter J. Haas in "Toward a Semiotic Study of Jewish Moral Discourse: The Case of Responsa," *Semeia,* vol. 34, pp. 75–82. © 1985 by Peter J. Haas. Reprinted by permission of Peter J. Haas.

"Ethical Will" by Judah ibn Tibbon. From *Hebrew Ethical Wills,* edited and translated by Israel Abrahams, pp. 56–59, 61–72, 74–76, 78–80, 83–84. © 1926 by The Jewish Publication Society of America. Reprinted by permission of The Jewish Publication Society of America.

From *Mishneh Torah—Sefer Zera'im* (The Book of Agriculture) by Moses Maimonides, translated by Isaac Klein, pp. 48, 49, 73–80, 82–86, 87–93, © 1979 by Yale University. Reprinted by permission of Yale University Press.

Index

Aaron of Karlin, 220
Aba, 61
Aboab, Isaac, 196, 218
Abraham bar Hiyya, 21
Abraham ibn Daud, xvii
Abraham Ibn Ezra, 97, 169
Abrahams, Israel, 184–191
Abravanel, 168
Action
  repentance and, 62
  Torah study and, 48
Adret, Solomon Ibn, 166–167
Afterlife
  cultural values and, 45
  death and, 138
Akiva, 114
Albo, Joseph, 61, 62, 179
Alexander the Great, 129
Altruism, Judeo-Christian ethics,
  discussion of, 214–215
Ammitai ben Shephatiah, xiv–xv
Anatoli, Jacob, 19
Anger, pride and, 84, 85
Apostasy, assimilation and, 211

Aquinas, Thomas (Saint), 101
Arba'ah Turim, 156
Aristotle, 34, 98, 120, 155
Arrogance
  ego and, 81–82
  pride and, 85
  wealth and, 127
Art, ethical literature and, xiii–xiv
Ascetics, speech and, 194–195
Assimilation, conversion and, 211
Awareness of Knowledge, The–Da'at
  Tevunah (Luzzatto), 89
Azikiri, Eliezer, 165–166

Baal Shem Tov, 38, 82, 84, 87, 156
Bahya ben Asher, 21, 59–60, 86, 88,
  125, 126, 127, 163
Bahya ibn Pakudah, xvii, xvi, 3, 5,
  17–18, 31, 48, 61–62, 67,
  68–77, 83, 84, 89, 139, 165,
  193, 201
Bar mitzvahs, thanking God, 21–22
Barukh of Medziboz, 18
Barzeloni, Judah, 97

Beauty, ethical literature and, xii–xiii
Belief in God, 3–13
Ben Sira, 100
Beriut (health). *See* Health
Birth, pride and, 83
Blaming, repentance and, 62
Blasphemy, speech and, 198
Blood, pride and, 83
Body
  health and, 108
  speech and, 199
  as tomb or Temple, 153
  wealth and, 123–124
Bokser, Ben Zion, 16
Book of Delight, The (Zabara), 111
Book of Disputation, The – Sefer ha- Vikuah (Nahmanides), 171
Book of the Commandments (Maimonides), 116, 169
Bunam of Przysucha, 88, 196

Calvinism, poverty and, 219
Camus, Albert, 4
Cardozo, Benjamin, 23
Carmi, T., 12–13
Celibacy, sexuality and, 154
Charity
  Judeo-Christian ethics, discussion of, 214–215
  levels of, 222
Chesterton, G. K., 4
Childlessness, tragedy of, 181
Child rearing. *See* Parenting
Children, parental relationships, 163–175
Choice of Pearls – Mivhar ha-Peninim (attributed to Gabirol), 81, 82–83, 100–106, 126, 195, 199
Christiani, Pablo, 171
Christianity
  God, belief in, 8

Judeo-Christian ethics, discussion of, 211–215
  loving God and, 30
  Musrei ha-Philosofim – Maxims of the Philosophers, 100
  Nahmanides and, 169, 170–171
  poverty and, 219
  pride and, 83
Circumcision, covenant and, 155
Cognition, God, belief in, 6
Cohen, A., 102–106
Cohen, Seymour J., 40–43, 130–133, 157–161, 202–209
Communications. *See* Speech
Confession, repentance and, 63–64
Conversion
  assimilation and, 211
  Nahmanides and, 171
Cordovero, Moses, 38
Covenant
  loving God and, 30
  sexual behavior and, 155
Creation
  parenting and, 177
  repentance and, 62
  sexuality and, 154
Creativity
  ego and, 86–87
  words and, 193
Cronbach, Abraham, 219
Culture, Torah study, 45–57

Da'at Tevunah – Awareness of Knowledge, The (Luzzatto), 89
Day of Atonement
  death and, 139
  repentance and, 64
Death, 135–149
Deception, speech and, 196
Deeds of Samson (Luzzatto), 89
Depression, pride and, 85

Derekh ha-Shem — Way of God, The
  (Luzzatto), 89
Destruction, speech and, 194, 195
Dietary laws, health and, 110,
  116–118
Discipline, parenting and, 179–180
Di Trani, Moses ben Joseph, 62–63
*Divine Commandments, The —
  Mitzvot ha-Shem* (Nahmanides),
  169
Duties of the Heart (Bahya), 3, 67,
  68, 69, 70–77, 201

Ebreo, Leon, 37
Economic factors
  Judeo-Christian ethics, discussion
    of, 214–215
  wealth, 123–133
Edels, Samuel, xviii, xix, 82, 125
Ego, 81–95
Eibshitz, Jonathan, 126–127
Eliezer, 61, 140
Eliezer of Metz, 167
Emancipation, Judeo-Christian
  ethics, discussion of, 211–213
Emden, Jacob, 156
Emotion
  ethical literature and, xi
  pride and, 84
Ephraim of Sudlykow, 50
Erudition, Torah study and, 48
Ethical literature
  art and, xiii–xiv
  beauty and, xii–xiii
  described, xvi–xix
  self-help manuals and, xi
Ethics, wisdom and, 98–99
Ethics of the Fathers, 83, 99, 124,
  169, 195, 199
Excretion, health and, 113
Existentialism, 4
  pride and, 83

Faith, God, belief in, 5
Faithfulness, God, belief in, 9
Falsehood, *shin* and, 197
Family, parental relationships,
  163–175
Fast of speech, 195
Financial factors. *See* Economic
  factors
Flattery, speech and, 202–203
Fountain of Life (Gabirol), 101
Franklin, Benjamin, xv, 195, 199
Freud, S., 136
Funerals, thanking God, 21–22

Gabbai, Meir ibn, 154
Gabirol, Solomon ibn, xvi, 9, 68,
  100–106, 108, 111, 112, 125
Ganz, David, 102
Gaon of Vilna, 48
Gemilut hasadim (acts of loving
  kindness), ethics and, 217, 218
Genevut da'at (theft of knowledge),
  speech and, 196
Gerondi, Jonah, 66, 82, 198, 201
Gersonides, 165, 179, 180
Giving and receiving, 211–236
Gluttony, health and, 109
God
  belief in, 3–13
  ethical literature and, xii, xiv–xv
  ethics and, 219
  health and, 110
  humility and, 86–87
  Judeo-Christian ethics, discussion
    of, 213–214
  loving God, 29–43
  parental relationships, 166
  pride and, 82
  repentance, 59–77
  sexuality and, 154, 155, 156
  speech and, 198
  thanking God, 15–28

God (*continued*)
  Torah study, 45–57
  wealth and, 123, 124
  wisdom and, 99–100
Goethe, 16–17, 136
Good deeds, wisdom and, 98–99
Government, parental relationships
    and, 165
Gratitude, thanking God, 15–28
Guide of the Perplexed, The
    (Maimonides), 34, 35, 115, 184,
    217
Guttmann, Julius, 67

Haas, Peter J., 143–149
Habits, repentance and, 62
Hahn, Joseph, 179
Halakhic authority, ethical
    literature and, xviii
Halakhot Gedolot—Great Laws
    (Karo), 169
Hasidism
  loving God and, 38
  parental relationships and, 168
  pride and, 82
  speech and, 202
  Torah study and, 50, 54
  wealth and, 123
Health, 107–121
  repentance and, 59–60
  speech and, 199
  words and, 193
Hebrew alphabet, speech and, 197
Hebrew Ethical Wills, 184–191
Heine, Heinrich, 211
Heresy, pride and, 84
Heschel, Abraham Joshua, 18,
    115–116, 141, 214
Hesed (benevolence), ethics and,
    217–218
Hikkeke Lev (Palaggi), 143–149
Hillel, xvii, 61, 140, 197–198

Hippocrates, 111
Hirschfield, Hartwig, 10–12
Hoker u-Mekubal (Luzzatto), 89
Holocaust, death and, 137
Honein ibn Ishak, 100
Horowitz, Isaiah, 62, 64
Humility
  ego and, 89–95
  pride and, 85–86
Huna, 61
Husik, Isaac, 101
Hyamson, Moses, 67
Hygiene, health and, 114, 120
Hypocrites, speech and, 196

Idolatry, pride and, 82, 84
Iggeret ha-Kodesh—The Holy Letter
    (attributed to Nahmanides),
    114, 153, 155, 157–161, 172
Improvement of the Moral Qualities
    (Gabirol), 108
Intellect
  loving God and, 34–35
  repentance and, 62–63
Interest (usury), Judeo-Christian
    ethics, discussion of, 216
Interpersonal relationships
  giving and receiving, 211–236
  parental relationships, 163–175
  parenting, 177–191
  sexual behavior, 153–161
  speech, 193–209
Islam
  God, belief in, 8
  Nahmanides and, 169
Israel of Rhyzen, 202

James I, 171
Jar of Meal, The (Bahya ben Asher),
    21, 88
Jesus, 109
Jewish law

ethical literature and, xvi
parenting and, 183
Judah Al-Harizi, 100, 101
Judah Ha-Levi, 5, 7, 8, 9–13
Judeo-Christian ethics, discussion
of, 211–215
Justice (*zedakah*), Judeo-Christian
ethics, discussion of, 211–215

Kabbalism. *See* Mysticism
Luzzatto and, 89
Nahmanides and, 171
sexual behavior and, 156
words and, 193
Kabbalists
pride and, 84, 88
repentance and, 65–66
sexuality and, 154
Torah study and, 47, 50, 54
wisdom and, 97
Kad ha-Kemah (Asher), 86
Kant, I., 212
Kaplan, Mordecai M., 90–95
Karo, Joseph, 23
Karo, Simon, 169
Kashrut, health and, 110
Kattina, 153
Keter Malkhut—Kingly Crown, The
(Gabirol), 9
Kierkegaard, S., 5
Kimchi, Joseph, 102
Kingly Crown, The (Keter Malkhut)
(Gabirol), 9
Klein, Isaac, 229–235
Knowledge. *See also* Wisdom
sexual behavior and, 158, 159
theft of, speech and, 196
wisdom and, 97–106
Kuzari, 7–9

Law
ethical literature and, xvi

parenting and, 183
Levi Yitzhak of Berditchev, 64, 123
Life-cycle occasions, thanking God,
21–22
Loew of Prague, Judah, xviii–xix,
36–37, 47, 49, 125, 128, 181,
193–194, 195, 198–199, 200
London, Jack, 195
Loving God, 29–43
Lunshitz, Ephraim, 129
Luzzatto, Moses Hayyim, 36, 67,
81, 83, 85, 88–95, 112, 128,
196–197, 199, 201

Mahler, Gustav, 211
Maimonides, Moses, xii, xvi, 3,
33–35, 47, 60, 63–64, 87,
107–108, 109, 110–121, 124,
155, 165, 167, 169, 184, 199,
217, 219
Mansoor, Menahem, 68, 70–77
Marriage
parental relationships and,
166–167, 172–173
parenting and, 180–181
Mass media, death and, 138
*Maxims of the Philosophers—Musrei
ha-Philosofim*, 100
Media. *See* Mass media
Mendel of Kotsk, xii, 49, 196, 197
Menninger, Karl, 136
Menorat ha-Ma'or (Aboab),
181–182, 218
*Mesilat Yesharim—Path of the
Upright* (Luzzatto), 81, 88–95,
99, 201
Messianism
Judeo-Christian ethics, discussion
of, 213–214
Luzzatto and, 89
Nahmanides and, 171
Midrash, Torah study and, 51

Milhemet ha-Shem — Wars of the Lord
    (Nahmanides), 169
Milton, John, 37
Mishneh Torah (Maimonides), 3,
    110, 113, 114
Mitzvot, ethics and, xvii
Mitzvot ha-Shem — Divine
    Commandments, The
    (Nahmanides), 169
Mivhar ha-Peninim — Choice of Pearls
    (attributed to Gabirol), 81,
    82–83, 100–106, 126, 195, 199
Modena, Leone da, 196
Monotheism
    ethical, Judaism definition and,
        212
    God, belief in, 3–13
Morality
    God and, xvii
    health and, 107–108
    Judeo-Christian ethics, discussion
        of, 211–215
    parenting and, 178–179
    Torah study and, 48
    wisdom and, 98
Mordecai of Chernobyl, 50
Mortality
    death, 135–149
    pride and, 83
Moses, 86, 89
    parenting and, 178
    Torah study and, 50–51
Munk, Solomon, 101
Muntner, Suessman, 116–121
Musar movement, xii, 200
Musrei ha-Philosofim — Maxims of the
    Philosophers, 100
Mysticism. See Kabbalists

Nahmanides (Ramban), xvii, 6,
    157–161, 169–172
Nahman of Bratzlav, 87, 109

Native Americans, afterlife and, 45
Nuclear war, death and, 137–138

Occupation, parenting and, 180
Orhot Zaddikim — Ways of the
    Righteous, The, 49, 84, 112–113,
    194, 195, 200, 201, 202–209

Paine, Thomas, xii
Palaggi of Izmir, Hayyim, 142,
    143–149
Parental relationships, 163–175
Parenting, 177–191
Pascal, Blaise, 135
Passover, God, belief in, 6–7
Path of the Upright, The (Luzzatto),
    36, 67
Path of the Upright — Mesilat
    Yesharim (Luzzatto), 81, 88–95
Pedagogy, parenting and, 178–179
Permissiveness, parenting and,
    179–180
Pesha, repentance and, 64–65
Philanthropy, Judeo-Christian
    ethics, discussion of, 214–215
Philosophy of Love (Ebreo), 37
Piety, ego and, 89
Pinhas ben Yair, 89–90
Pinhas of Koretz, 54
Plato, 98, 108, 153, 154, 165
Pope, Alexander, 60
Poverty
    Christianity and, 219
    ethics and, 221
    Judeo-Christian ethics, discussion
        of, 214–215
Power, words and, 193, 194
Prayer, Torah study and, 47
Pride
    ego and, 81–82
    wealth and, 127
Procreation, sexual behavior and,
    154

Punishment, repentance and, 65
Purity, sexual behavior and, 155

Rabbis
    loving God and, 32-33
    Torah study and, 46
Ramban. See Nahmanides
Rashi, 153, 181
Rebellion, repentance and, 64-65
Receiving and giving, 211-236
Reciprocity, parental relationships
    and, 167
Repentance, 59-77
Responsum, death, 142-149
Revelation, Torah study and, 47
Rosenzweig, Franz, 137
Rosh Hashanah, repentance,
    59-60

Saadya Gaon, 126, 127, 128, 201
Saladin, 115
Salanter, Israel, xii
Samuel, 61
Samuel of Uceda, 50
Sanctification, sexual behavior and,
    155
Schechter, Solomon, 87, 172
Scholem, Gershom, 55-57
Scotus, Duns, 101
Sefer ha-Kuzari (Tibbon), 9
Sefer ha-Middot. See Orhot Zaddikim
Sefer Hasidim, parental relationships
    and, 168
Sefer ha-Vikuah—Book of
    Disputation, The (Nahmanides),
    171
Sefer ha-Yashar—Book of the
    Righteous, The, 31, 39-43, 112,
    140
Sefer Histalkut ha-Nefesh—Book of
    the Departure of the Soul, The,
    141

Sefer Ma'alot ha-Middot—
    Improvement of the Moral
    Virtues (Yehiel ben Yekutiel
    ha-Rofeh), 98-99, 124, 126,
    127, 129-133, 217
Sefer Zehut—Book of Defense, The
    (Nahmanides), 169
Seixas, Gershom Mendes, 19-20,
    22-28
Self
    death, 135-149
    ego and, 81-95
    health and, 107-121
    wealth and, 123-133
    wisdom and, 97-106
Self-delusion
    humility and, 85-86
    speech and, 196
Self-help manuals, ethical literature
    and, xi
Self-knowledge, ego and, 81
Semen, pride and, 83
Senility, parental relationships and,
    167
Sexual behavior, 153-161
    health and, 108-109, 114
Sha'arey Teshuvah—Gates of
    Repentance (Gerondi), 201
Shem Tov ben Joseph ibn
    Falaquera, 114
Sherwin, Byron L., 172-175
Shin, falsehood and, 197
Shnei Luhot ha-Brit (Horowitz), 62
Shneur Zalman of Liady, 50
Sickness, repentance and, 59-60
Silence, speech and, 195
Sin
    awe of God and, 99
    pride and, 82
    repentance and, 64-67
    sexual behavior and, 159
Slander, speech and, 198
Sleep, health and, 113

Social welfare
  ethics and, 224
  Judeo-Christian ethics, discussion
    of, 214–215
Society
  parental relationships and, 165
  parenting and, 179
Solomon ben Isaac, 169
Soul
  death and, 141
  ethical literature and, xii
Speech, 193–209
  repentance and, 62
Spiritual transformation, Torah
  study and, 48
State, parental relationships and,
  165
Suicide, speech and, 198

Tarfon, 163
Tav, truth and, 197
Ten Commandments, parental
  relationships, 163
Teshuvah (repentance), 59–77
Thanking God, 15–28
Thought. See Intellect
Tibbon, Judah ibn, 9, 68, 100, 183
Tibbon, Samuel ibn, 183–184
Tolstoy, Leo, 136
Tomer Devorah (Cordovero), 38
Tongue, speech and, 194
Torah study, 45–57
Torat ha-Adam—Torah of Man, The
  (Nahmanides), 171
Tower of Strength, The (Luzzatto), 89
Toynbee, Arnold, 136–137
Treatise on Asthma (Maimonides),
  109, 110–121
Truth, tav and, 197
Twain, Mark, 15, 127

Vajda, Georges, 67
Vice, wealth and, 124

Vidas, Elijah de, 38, 65, 200
Virtue
  health and, 108–109
  wealth and, 124
  wisdom and, 98
Vital, Hayyim, 84

Wars of the Lord—Milhemet ha-Shem
  (Nahmanides), 169
Washington, George, 19
Way of God, The—Derekh ha-Shem
  (Luzzatto), 89
Ways of the Righteous, The—Orhot
  Zaddikim, 49, 84, 112–113, 194,
  195, 200, 201, 202–209
Wealth, 123–133
  ethical literature and, xiii
Weddings, thanking God, 21–22
Wholeness, health and, 107
Wilde, Oscar, 18
Will (attribute), speech and, 194
Wills (document), Hebrew Ethical
  Wills, 184–191
Wisdom, 97–106. See also
  Knowledge
  speech and, 195
  wealth and, 126
Wittgenstein, Ludwig, 5
Words, speech and, 193

Yedaya ha-Penini, 102
Yehiel ben Yekutiel ha-Rofeh,
  129–133
Yikavu ha-Mayim (Tibbon), 184

Zabara, Joseph ben Meir, 111, 114
Zeal, ego and, 89–90
Zedakah (justice), Judeo-Christian
  ethics, discussion of, 215–225
Zohar
  repentance and, 66
  Torah study and, 47, 51, 52–57
Zusia of Hanipol, 141

About JEWISH LIGHTS Publishing

People of all faiths and backgrounds yearn for books that attract, engage, educate and spiritually inspire.

Our principal goal is to stimulate thought and help all people learn about who the Jewish People are, where they come from, and what the future can be made to hold. While people of our diverse Jewish heritage are the primary audience, our books speak to people in the Christian world as well and will broaden their understanding of Judaism and the roots of their own faith.

We bring to you authors who are at the forefront of spiritual thought and experience. While each has something different to say, they all say it in a voice that you can hear.

Our books are designed to welcome you and then to engage, stimulate and inspire. We judge our success not only by whether or not our books are beautiful and commercially successful, but by whether or not they make a difference in your life.

We at Jewish Lights take great care to produce beautiful books that present meaningful spiritual content in a form that reflects the art of making high quality books. Therefore, we want to acknowledge those who contributed to the production of this book.

Stuart M. Matlins, Publisher

PRODUCTION
Marian B. Wallace & Bridgett Taylor

EDITORIAL
Sandra Korinchak, Emily Wichland,
Martha McKinney & Amanda Dupuis

COVER DESIGN
Bridgett Taylor

COVER / TEXT PRINTING & BINDING
Versa Press, East Peoria, Illinois

AVAILABLE FROM BETTER BOOKSTORES.
TRY YOUR BOOKSTORE FIRST.

Spirituality

Does the Soul Survive?
A Jewish Journey to Belief in Afterlife, Past Lives & Living with Purpose
by *Rabbi Elie Kaplan Spitz*; Foreword by *Brian L. Weiss*, M.D.

Do we have a soul that survives our earthly existence? To know the answer is to find greater understanding, comfort and purpose in our lives. Here, Spitz relates his own experiences and those shared with him by people he has worked with as a rabbi, and shows us that belief in afterlife and past lives, so often approached with reluctance, is in fact true to Jewish tradition.
6 x 9, 288 pp, HC, ISBN 1-58023-094-6 **$21.95**

The Women's Torah Commentary: *New Insights from Women Rabbis on the 54 Weekly Torah Portions* Ed. by *Rabbi Elyse Goldstein*

For the first time, women rabbis provide a commentary on the entire Torah. More than 25 years after the first woman was ordained a rabbi in America, these inspiring teachers bring their rich perspectives to bear on the biblical text. In a week-by-week format; a perfect gift for others, or for yourself. 6 x 9, 496 pp, HC, ISBN 1-58023-076-8 **$34.95**

Bringing the Psalms to Life
How to Understand and Use the Book of Psalms by *Rabbi Daniel F. Polish*

Here, the most beloved—and least understood—of the books in the Bible comes alive. This simultaneously insightful and practical guide shows how the psalms address a myriad of spiritual issues in our lives: feeling abandoned, overcoming illness, dealing with anger, and more.
6 x 9, 208 pp, HC, ISBN 1-58023-077-6 **$21.95**

Stepping Stones to Jewish Spiritual Living: *Walking the Path Morning, Noon, and Night*
by Rabbi James L. Mirel & Karen Bonnell Werth
6 x 9, 240 pp, Quality PB, ISBN 1-58023-074-1 **$16.95**

The Business Bible
10 New Commandments for Bringing Spirituality & Ethical Values into the Workplace
by Rabbi Wayne Dosick 5½ x 8½, 208 pp, Quality PB, ISBN 1-58023-101-2 **$14.95**

Moses—The Prince, the Prophet: *His Life, Legend & Message for Our Lives*
by Rabbi Levi Meier, Ph.D. 6 x 9, 224 pp, Quality PB, ISBN 1-58023-069-5 **$16.95**

Ancient Secrets: *Using the Stories of the Bible to Improve Our Everyday Lives*
by Rabbi Levi Meier, Ph.D. 5½ x 8½, 288 pp, Quality PB, ISBN 1-58023-064-4 **$16.95**

Or phone, fax, mail or e-mail to: JEWISH LIGHTS Publishing
Sunset Farm Offices, Route 4 • P.O. Box 237 • Woodstock, Vermont 05091
Tel: (802) 457-4000 • Fax: (802) 457-4004 • www.jewishlights.com
Credit card orders: (800) 962-4544 (9AM–5PM ET Monday–Friday)
Generous discounts on quantity orders. SATISFACTION GUARANTEED. Prices subject to change.

Spirituality/Jewish Meditation

Discovering Jewish Meditation
Instruction & Guidance for Learning an Ancient Spiritual Practice
by *Nan Fink Gefen*

Gives readers of any level of understanding the tools to learn the practice of Jewish meditation on your own, starting you on the path to a deep spiritual and personal connection to God and to greater insight about your life. 6 x 9, 208 pp, Quality PB, ISBN 1-58023-067-9 **$16.95**

Entering the Temple of Dreams: *Jewish Prayers, Movements, and Meditations for the End of the Day* by *Tamar Frankiel and Judy Greenfeld*

Nighttime spirituality is much more than bedtime prayers! Here, you'll uncover deeper meaning to familiar nighttime prayers—and learn to combine the prayers with movements and meditations to enhance your physical and psychological well-being.
7 x 10, 192 pp, Illus., Quality PB, ISBN 1-58023-079-2 **$16.95**

The Handbook of Jewish Meditation Practices
A Guide for Enriching the Sabbath and Other Days of Your Life
by *Rabbi David A. Cooper*

Gives us ancient and modern Jewish tools—Jewish practices and traditions, easy to use meditation exercises, and contemplative study of Jewish sacred texts—to help us quiet our minds and refresh our souls. 6 x 9, 208 pp, Quality PB, ISBN 1-58023-102-0 **$16.95**

Meditation from the Heart of Judaism
Today's Teachers Share Their Practices, Techniques, and Faith
Ed. by Avram Davis 6 x 9, 256 pp, Quality PB, ISBN 1-58023-049-0 **$16.95**;
HC, ISBN 1-879045-77-X **$21.95**

The Way of Flame: *A Guide to the Forgotten Mystical Tradition of Jewish Meditation*
by Avram Davis 4½ x 8, 176 pp, Quality PB, ISBN 1-58023-060-1 **$15.95**

Minding the Temple of the Soul: *Balancing Body, Mind, and Spirit through Traditional Jewish Prayer, Movement, and Meditation*
by Tamar Frankiel and Judy Greenfeld 7 x 10, 184 pp, Quality PB, Illus.,
ISBN 1-879045-64-8 **$16.95**; Audiotape of the Blessings and Meditations (60-min. cassette),
JN01 **$9.95**; Videotape of the Movements and Meditations (46-min.), S507 **$20.00**

The Empty Chair: *Finding Hope and Joy—*
Timeless Wisdom from a Hasidic Master, Rebbe Nachman of Breslov AWARD WINNER!
4 x 6, 128 pp, Deluxe PB, 2-color text, ISBN 1-879045-67-2 **$9.95**

The Gentle Weapon: *Prayers for Everyday and Not-So-Everyday Moments*
Adapted from the Wisdom of Rebbe Nachman of Breslov
4 x 6, 144 pp, Deluxe PB, 2-color text, ISBN 1-58023-022-9 **$9.95**

Spirituality—The Kushner Series
Books by Lawrence Kushner

The Way Into Jewish Mystical Tradition

Explains the principles of Jewish mystical thinking, their religious and spiritual significance, and how they relate to our lives. A book that allows us to experience and understand the Jewish mystical approach to our place in the world.   6 x 9, 176 pp, HC, ISBN 1-58023-029-6 **$21.95**

Eyes Remade for Wonder
The Way of Jewish Mysticism and Sacred Living
A Lawrence Kushner Reader Intro. by *Thomas Moore*

Whether you are new to Kushner or a devoted fan, you'll find inspiration here. With samplings from each of Kushner's works, and a generous amount of new material, this book is to be read and reread, each time discovering deeper layers of meaning in our lives.
6 x 9, 240 pp, Quality PB, ISBN 1-58023-042-3 **$16.95**; HC, ISBN 1-58023-014-8 **$23.95**

Because Nothing Looks Like God

by *Lawrence and Karen Kushner*; Full-color illus. by *Dawn W. Majewski*

What is God like? The first collaborative work by husband-and-wife team Lawrence and Karen Kushner introduces children to the possibilities of spiritual life with three poetic spiritual stories. Real-life examples of happiness and sadness—from goodnight stories, to the hope and fear felt the first time at bat, to the closing moments of life—invite us to explore, together with our children, the questions we all have about God, no matter what our age.
11 x 8½, 32 pp, HC, Full-color illus., ISBN 1-58023-092-X **$16.95**

Invisible Lines of Connection: *Sacred Stories of the Ordinary* AWARD WINNER!
6 x 9, 160 pp, Quality PB, ISBN 1-879045-98-2 **$15.95**; HC, ISBN 1-879045-52-4 **$21.95**

Honey from the Rock SPECIAL ANNIVERSARY EDITION
An Introduction to Jewish Mysticism 6 x 9, 176 pp, Quality PB, ISBN 1-58023-073-3 **$15.95**

The Book of Letters: *A Mystical Hebrew Alphabet* AWARD WINNER!
Popular HC Edition, 6 x 9, 80 pp, 2-color text, ISBN 1-879045-00-1 **$24.95**; *Deluxe Gift Edition,* 9 x 12, 80 pp, HC, 2-color text, ornamentation, slipcase, ISBN 1-879045-01-X **$79.95**; *Collector's Limited Edition,* 9 x 12, 80 pp, HC, gold-embossed pages, hand-assembled slipcase. With silkscreened print. Limited to 500 signed and numbered copies, ISBN 1-879045-04-4 **$349.00**

The Book of Words: *Talking Spiritual Life, Living Spiritual Talk* AWARD WINNER!
6 x 9, 160 pp, Quality PB, 2-color text, ISBN 1-58023-020-2 **$16.95**;
152 pp, HC, ISBN 1-879045-35-4 **$21.95**

God Was in This Place & I, i Did Not Know
Finding Self, Spirituality and Ultimate Meaning
6 x 9, 192 pp, Quality PB, ISBN 1-879045-33-8 **$16.95**

The River of Light: *Jewish Mystical Awareness* SPECIAL ANNIVERSARY EDITION
6 x 9, 192 pp, Quality PB, ISBN 1-58023-096-2 **$16.95**

Healing/Wellness/Recovery

Jewish Pastoral Care
A Practical Handbook from Traditional and Contemporary Sources
Ed. by *Rabbi Dayle A. Friedman*

Gives today's Jewish pastoral counselors practical guidelines based in the Jewish tradition.
6 x 9, 464 pp, HC, ISBN 1-58023-078-4 **$35.00**

Healing of Soul, Healing of Body
Spiritual Leaders Unfold the Strength & Solace in Psalms
Ed. by *Rabbi Simkha Y. Weintraub, CSW,* for The National Center for Jewish Healing

A source of solace for those who are facing illness, as well as those who care for them. Provides a wellspring of strength with inspiring introductions and commentaries by eminent spiritual leaders reflecting all Jewish movements.
6 x 9, 128 pp, Quality PB, Illus., 2-color text, ISBN 1-879045-31-1 **$14.95**

Jewish Paths toward Healing and Wholeness
A Personal Guide to Dealing with Suffering
by *Rabbi Kerry M. Olitzky*; Foreword by *Debbie Friedman*

Why me? Why do we suffer? How can we heal? Grounded in personal experience with illness and Jewish spiritual traditions, this book provides healing rituals, psalms and prayers that help readers initiate a dialogue with God, to guide them along the complicated path of healing and wholeness.
6 x 9, 192 pp, Quality PB, ISBN 1-58023-068-7 **$15.95**

Twelve Jewish Steps to Recovery: *A Personal Guide to Turning from Alcoholism & Other Addictions . . . Drugs, Food, Gambling, Sex . . .* by Rabbi Kerry M. Olitzky & Stuart A. Copans, M.D. Preface by Abraham J. Twerski, M.D.; Intro. by Rabbi Sheldon Zimmerman; "Getting Help" by JACS Foundation 6 x 9, 144 pp, Quality PB, ISBN 1-879045-09-5 **$13.95**

One Hundred Blessings Every Day: *Daily Twelve Step Recovery Affirmations, Exercises for Personal Growth & Renewal Reflecting Seasons of the Jewish Year*
by Rabbi Kerry M. Olitzky 4½ x 6½, 432 pp, Quality PB, ISBN 1-879045-30-3 **$14.95**

Recovery from Codependence: *A Jewish Twelve Steps Guide to Healing Your Soul*
by Rabbi Kerry M. Olitzky 6 x 9, 160 pp, Quality PB, ISBN 1-879045-32-X **$13.95**; HC, ISBN 1-879045-27-3 **$21.95**

Renewed Each Day: *Daily Twelve Step Recovery Meditations Based on the Bible*
by Rabbi Kerry M. Olitzky & Aaron Z. *Vol. I: Genesis & Exodus; Vol. II: Leviticus, Numbers and Deuteronomy*
Vol. I: 6 x 9, 224 pp, Quality PB, ISBN 1-879045-12-5 **$14.95**
Vol. II: 6 x 9, 280 pp, Quality PB, ISBN 1-879045-13-3 **$14.95**

Life Cycle/Grief

Moonbeams
A Hadassah Rosh Hodesh Guide
Ed. by *Carol Diament, Ph.D.*

This hands-on "idea book" focuses on *Rosh Hodesh*, the festival of the new moon, as a source of spiritual growth for Jewish women. A complete sourcebook that will initiate or rejuvenate women's study groups, it is also perfect for women preparing for *bat mitzvah*, or for anyone interested in learning more about *Rosh Hodesh* observance and what it has to offer. 8½ x 11, 240 pp, Quality PB, ISBN 1-58023-099-7 **$20.00**

Mourning & Mitzvah: *A Guided Journal for Walking the Mourner's Path through Grief to Healing, 2nd Ed.* with Over 60 Guided Exercises
by *Anne Brener, L.C.S.W.*; Foreword by *Rabbi Jack Riemer*; Intro. by *Rabbi William Cutter*

For those who mourn a death, for those who would help them, for those who face a loss of any kind, Brener teaches us the power and strength available to us in the fully experienced mourning process. 7½ x 9, 304 pp, Quality PB, ISBN 1-58023-113-6 **$19.95**

Tears of Sorrow, Seeds of Hope
A Jewish Spiritual Companion for Infertility and Pregnancy Loss
by Rabbi Nina Beth Cardin   6 x 9, 192 pp, HC, ISBN 1-58023-017-2 **$19.95**

Lifecycles
V. 1: *Jewish Women on Life Passages & Personal Milestones* AWARD WINNER!
Ed. and with Intros. by Rabbi Debra Orenstein
V. 2: *Jewish Women on Biblical Themes in Contemporary Life* AWARD WINNER!
Ed. and with Intros. by Rabbi Debra Orenstein and Rabbi Jane Rachel Litman
V. 1: 6 x 9, 480 pp, Quality PB, ISBN 1-58023-018-0 **$19.95**; HC, ISBN 1-879045-14-1 **$24.95**
V. 2: 6 x 9, 464 pp, Quality PB, ISBN 1-58023-019-9 **$19.95**; HC, ISBN 1-879045-15-X **$24.95**

A Heart of Wisdom: *Making the Jewish Journey from Midlife through the Elder Years*
Ed. by Susan Berrin; Foreword by Harold Kushner
6 x 9, 384 pp, Quality PB, ISBN 1-58023-051-2 **$18.95**; HC, ISBN 1-879045-73-7 **$24.95**

Grief in Our Seasons: *A Mourner's Kaddish Companion*
by Rabbi Kerry M. Olitzky 4½ x 6½, 448 pp, Quality PB, ISBN 1-879045-55-9 **$15.95**

Parenting As a Spiritual Journey
Deepening Ordinary & Extraordinary Events into Sacred Occasions
by Rabbi Nancy Fuchs-Kreimer 6 x 9, 224 pp, Quality PB, ISBN 1-58023-016-4 **$16.95**

A Time to Mourn, A Time to Comfort: *A Guide to Jewish Bereavement and Comfort*
by Dr. Ron Wolfson 7 x 9, 336 pp, Quality PB, ISBN 1-879045-96-6 **$16.95**

When a Grandparent Dies
A Kid's Own Remembering Workbook for Dealing with Shiva and the Year Beyond
by Nechama Liss-Levinson, Ph.D.
8 x 10, 48 pp, HC, Illus., 2-color text, ISBN 1-879045-44-3 **$15.95**

So That Your Values Live On: *Ethical Wills & How to Prepare Them*
Ed. by Rabbi Jack Riemer & Professor Nathaniel Stampfer
6 x 9, 272 pp, Quality PB, ISBN 1-879045-34-6 **$17.95**

Children's Spirituality

ENDORSED BY CATHOLIC, PROTESTANT, AND JEWISH RELIGIOUS LEADERS

Because Nothing Looks Like God

by *Lawrence and Karen Kushner*
Full-color illus. by *Dawn W. Majewski*

For ages
4 & up

MULTICULTURAL, NONDENOMINATIONAL, NONSECTARIAN

What is God like? The first collaborative work by husband-and-wife team Lawrence and Karen Kushner introduces children to the possibilities of spiritual life. Real-life examples of happiness and sadness—from goodnight stories, to the hope and fear felt the first time at bat, to the closing moments of life—invite us to explore, together with our children, the questions we all have about God, no matter what our age.

11 x 8½, 32 pp, HC, Full-color illus., ISBN 1-58023-092-X **$16.95**

Where Is God? (A Board Book)

For ages
0–4

by *Lawrence and Karen Kushner*; Full-color illus. by *Dawn W. Majewski*

Gently invites children to become aware of God's presence all around them. Abridged from *Because Nothing Looks Like God* by Lawrence and Karen Kushner.

5 x 5, 24 pp, Board, Full-color illus., ISBN 1-893361-17-9 **$7.95**

Sharing Blessings

For ages
6 & up

Children's Stories for Exploring the Spirit of the Jewish Holidays

by *Rahel Musleah* and *Rabbi Michael Klayman*
Full-color illus. by *Mary O'Keefe Young*

What is the spiritual message of each of the Jewish holidays? How do we teach it to our children? Many books tell children about the historical significance and customs of the holidays. Now, through engaging, creative stories about one family's preparation, *Sharing Blessings* explores ways to get into the *spirit* of 13 different holidays.

8½ x 11, 64 pp, HC, Full-color illus., ISBN 1-879045-71-0 **$18.95**

The Book of Miracles

For ages
9 & up

A Young Person's Guide to Jewish Spiritual Awareness

by *Lawrence Kushner*

Introduces kids to a way of everyday spiritual thinking to last a lifetime. Kushner, whose award-winning books have brought spirituality to life for countless adults, now shows young people how to use Judaism as a foundation on which to build their lives.

6 x 9, 96 pp, HC, 2-color illus., ISBN 1-879045-78-8 **$16.95**

Children's Spirituality

ENDORSED BY CATHOLIC, PROTESTANT, AND JEWISH RELIGIOUS LEADERS
MULTICULTURAL, NONDENOMINATIONAL, NONSECTARIAN

God Said Amen

by *Sandy Eisenberg Sasso*
Full-color illus. by *Avi Katz*

For ages 4 & up

A warm and inspiring tale of two kingdoms: one overflowing with water but without oil to light its lamps; the other blessed with oil but no water to grow its gardens. The kingdoms' rulers ask God for help but are too stubborn to ask each other. It takes a minstrel, a pair of royal riding-birds and their young keepers, and a simple act of kindness to show that they need only reach out to each other to find God's answer to their prayers.

9 x 12, 32 pp, HC, Full-color illus., ISBN 1-58023-080-6 **$16.95**

For Heaven's Sake

by *Sandy Eisenberg Sasso*; Full-color illus. by *Kathryn Kunz Finney*

For ages 4 & up

Everyone talked about heaven: "Thank heavens." "Heaven forbid." "For heaven's sake, Isaiah." But no one would say what heaven was or how to find it. So Isaiah decides to find out, by seeking answers from many different people.
9 x 12, 32 pp, HC, Full-color illus., ISBN 1-58023-054-7 **$16.95**

But God Remembered

Stories of Women from Creation to the Promised Land

For ages 8 & up

by *Sandy Eisenberg Sasso*; Full-color illus. by *Bethanne Andersen*

A fascinating collection of four different stories of women only briefly mentioned in biblical tradition and religious texts. Vibrantly brings to life courageous and strong women from ancient tradition; all teach important values through their actions and faith.
9 x 12, 32 pp, HC, Full-color illus., ISBN 1-879045-43-5 **$16.95**

God in Between

by *Sandy Eisenberg Sasso*; Full-color illus. by *Sally Sweetland*

For ages 4 & up

If you wanted to find God, where would you look? A magical, mythical tale that teaches that God can be found where we are: within all of us and the relationships between us.
9 x 12, 32 pp, HC, Full-color illus., ISBN 1-879045-86-9 **$16.95**

A Prayer for the Earth: The Story of Naamah, Noah's Wife   AWARD WINNER!

by *Sandy Eisenberg Sasso*; Full-color illus. by *Bethanne Andersen*

This new story, based on an ancient text, opens readers' religious imaginations to new ideas about the well-known story of the Flood. When God tells Noah to bring the animals of the world onto the ark, God also calls on Naamah, Noah's wife, to save each plant on Earth.
9 x 12, 32 pp, HC, Full-color illus., ISBN 1-879045-60-5 **$16.95**

Life Cycle & Holidays

How to Be a Perfect Stranger, In 2 Volumes
A Guide to Etiquette in Other People's Religious Ceremonies
Ed. by *Stuart M. Matlins* & *Arthur J. Magida*   AWARD WINNER!

What will happen? What do I do? What do I wear? What do I say? What are their basic beliefs? Should I bring a gift? In question-and-answer format, explains the rituals and celebrations of America's major religions/denominations, helping an interested guest to feel comfortable, participate to the fullest extent possible, and avoid violating anyone's religious principles. Not presented from the perspective of any particular faith.

Vol. 1: *America's Largest Faiths,* 6 x 9, 432 pp, HC, ISBN 1-879045-39-7 **$24.95**
Vol. 2: *Other Faiths in America,* 6 x 9, 416 pp, HC, ISBN 1-879045-63-X **$24.95**

Putting God on the Guest List, 2nd Ed.
How to Reclaim the Spiritual Meaning of Your Child's Bar or Bat Mitzvah
by *Rabbi Jeffrey K. Salkin*   AWARD WINNER!

The most influential book about finding core spiritual values in American Jewry's most misunderstood ceremony. 6 x 9, 224 pp, Quality PB, ISBN 1-879045-59-1 **$16.95**

For Kids—Putting God on Your Guest List
How to Claim the Spiritual Meaning of Your Bar or Bat Mitzvah
by Rabbi Jeffrey K. Salkin 6 x 9, 144 pp, Quality PB, ISBN 1-58023-015-6 **$14.95**

Bar/Bat Mitzvah Basics: *A Practical Family Guide to Coming of Age Together*
Ed. by Cantor Helen Leneman 6 x 9, 240 pp, Quality PB, ISBN 1-879045-54-0 **$16.95**;
HC, ISBN 1-879045-51-6 **$24.95**

The New Jewish Baby Book AWARD WINNER!
Names, Ceremonies, & Customs—A Guide for Today's Families
by Anita Diamant 6 x 9, 336 pp, Quality PB, ISBN 1-879045-28-1 **$16.95**

Hanukkah: The Art of Jewish Living
by Dr. Ron Wolfson 7 x 9, 192 pp, Quality PB, Illus., ISBN 1-879045-97-4 **$16.95**

The Shabbat Seder: The Art of Jewish Living
by Dr. Ron Wolfson 7 x 9, 272 pp, Quality PB, Illus., ISBN 1 879045-90-7 **$16.95**
Also available are these helpful companions to *The Shabbat Seder:* Booklet of the Blessings and Songs, ISBN 1-879045-91-5 **$5.00**; Audiocassette of the Blessings, DN03 **$6.00**; Teacher's Guide, ISBN 1-879045-92-3 **$4.95**

The Passover Seder: The Art of Jewish Living
by Dr. Ron Wolfson 7 x 9, 352 pp, Quality PB, Illus., ISBN 1-879045-93-1 **$16.95**
Also available are these helpful companions to *The Passover Seder:* Passover Workbook, ISBN 1-879045-94-X **$6.95**; Audiocassette of the Blessings, DN04 **$6.00**; Teacher's Guide, ISBN 1-879045-95-8 **$6.95**

The Jewish Gardening Cookbook: *Growing Plants & Cooking for Holidays & Festivals*
by Michael Brown 6 x 9, 224 pp, Illus., Quality PB, ISBN 1-58023-116-0 **$16.95**;
HC, ISBN 1-58023-004-0 **$21.95**

Spirituality & More

The Jewish Lights Spirituality Handbook
A Guide to Understanding, Exploring & Living a Spiritual Life
Ed. by *Stuart M. Matlins, Editor-in-Chief, Jewish Lights Publishing*
Rich, creative material from over 50 spiritual leaders on every aspect of Jewish spirituality today: prayer, meditation, mysticism, study, rituals, special days, the everyday, and more.
6 x 9, 304 pp, Quality PB, ISBN 1-58023-093-8 **$16.95**; HC, ISBN 1-58023-100-4 **$24.95**

Six Jewish Spiritual Paths: *A Rationalist Looks at Spirituality*
by *Rabbi Rifat Sonsino*
The quest for spirituality is universal, but which path to spirituality is right *for you*? A straightforward, objective discussion of the many ways—each valid and authentic—for seekers to gain a richer spiritual life within Judaism. 6 x 9, 208 pp, HC, ISBN 1-58023-095-4 **$21.95**

Restful Reflections: *Nighttime Inspiration to Calm the Soul,*
Based on Jewish Wisdom by *Rabbi Kerry M. Olitzky* and *Rabbi Lori Forman*
Wisdom to "sleep on." For each night of the year, an inspiring quote from a Jewish source and a personal reflection on it from an insightful spiritual leader helps you to focus on your spiritual life and the lessons your day has offered. The companion to *Sacred Intentions: Daily Inspiration to Strengthen the Spirit, Based on Jewish Wisdom* (see below).
4½ x 6½, 448 pp, Quality PB, ISBN 1-58023-091-1 **$15.95**

Sacred Intentions: *Daily Inspiration to Strengthen the Spirit, Based on Jewish Wisdom*
by Rabbi Kerry M. Olitzky and Rabbi Lori Forman
4½ x 6½, 448 pp, Quality PB, ISBN 1-58023-061-X **$15.95**

The Enneagram and Kabbalah: *Reading Your Soul*
by Rabbi Howard A. Addison 6 x 9, 176 pp, Quality PB, ISBN 1-58023-001-6 **$15.95**

Embracing the Covenant: *Converts to Judaism Talk About Why & How*
Ed. and with Intros. by Rabbi Allan L. Berkowitz and Patti Moskovitz
6 x 9, 192 pp, Quality PB, ISBN 1-879045-50-8 **$15.95**

Shared Dreams: *Martin Luther King, Jr. and the Jewish Community*
by Rabbi Marc Schneier; Preface by Martin Luther King III
6 x 9, 240 pp, HC, ISBN 1-58023-062-8 **$24.95**

Mystery Midrash: *An Anthology of Jewish Mystery & Detective Fiction*
Ed. by Lawrence W. Raphael; Preface by Joel Siegel, ABC's *Good Morning America*
6 x 9, 304 pp, Quality PB, ISBN 1-58023-055-5 **$16.95**

Wandering Stars: *An Anthology of Jewish Fantasy & Science Fiction* Ed. by Jack Dann; Intro. by Isaac Asimov 6 x 9, 272 pp, Quality PB, ISBN 1-58023-005-9 **$16.95**

More Wandering Stars
An Anthology of Outstanding Stories of Jewish Fantasy and Science Fiction
Ed. by Jack Dann; Intro. by Isaac Asimov 6 x 9, 192 pp, Quality PB, ISBN 1-58023-063-6 **$16.95**

Spirituality

My People's Prayer Book: *Traditional Prayers, Modern Commentaries*
Ed. by *Dr. Lawrence A. Hoffman*

Provides a diverse and exciting commentary to the traditional liturgy, helping modern men and women find new wisdom in Jewish prayer, and bring liturgy into their lives. Each book includes Hebrew text, modern translation, and commentaries *from all perspectives* of the Jewish world.

Vol. 1—*The Sh'ma and Its Blessings*, 7 x 10, 168 pp, HC, ISBN 1-879045-79-6 **$23.95**
Vol. 2—*The Amidah*, 7 x 10, 240 pp, HC, ISBN 1-879045-80-X **$23.95**
Vol. 3—*P'sukei D'zimrah* (Morning Psalms), 7 x 10, 240 pp, HC, ISBN 1-879045-81-8 **$23.95**
Vol. 4—*Seder K'riat Hatorah* (The Torah Service), 7 x 10, 264 pp, ISBN 1-879045-82-6 **$23.95**

Becoming a Congregation of Learners
Learning as a Key to Revitalizing Congregational Life by Isa Aron, Ph.D.; Foreword by Rabbi Lawrence A. Hoffman, Co-Developer, Synagogue 2000
6 x 9, 304 pp, Quality PB, ISBN 1-58023-089-X **$19.95**

Self, Struggle & Change
Family Conflict Stories in Genesis and Their Healing Insights for Our Lives by Dr. Norman J. Cohen 6 x 9, 224 pp, Quality PB, ISBN 1-879045-66-4 **$16.95**; HC, ISBN 1-879045-19-2 **$21.95**

Voices from Genesis: *Guiding Us through the Stages of Life*
by Dr. Norman J. Cohen 6 x 9, 192 pp, Quality PB, ISBN 1-58023-118-7 **$16.95**; HC, ISBN 1-879045-75-3 **$21.95**

God Whispers: *Stories of the Soul, Lessons of the Heart*
by Rabbi Karyn D. Kedar 6 x 9, 176 pp, Quality PB, ISBN 1-58023-088-1 **$15.95**

Being God's Partner: *How to Find the Hidden Link Between Spirituality and Your Work*
by Rabbi Jeffrey K. Salkin; Intro. by Norman Lear AWARD WINNER!
6 x 9, 192 pp, Quality PB, ISBN 1-879045-65-6 **$16.95**; HC, ISBN 1-879045-37-0 **$19.95**

ReVisions: *Seeing Torah through a Feminist Lens* AWARD WINNER!
by Rabbi Elyse Goldstein 5½ x 8½, 224 pp. Quality PB, ISBN 1-58023-117-9 **$16.95**; 208 pp, HC, ISBN 1-58023-047-4 **$19.95**

Soul Judaism: *Dancing with God into a New Era*
by Rabbi Wayne Dosick 5½ x 8½, 304 pp, Quality PB, ISBN 1-58023-053-9 **$16.95**

Finding Joy: *A Practical Spiritual Guide to Happiness* AWARD WINNER!
by Rabbi Dannel I. Schwartz with Mark Hass
6 x 9, 192 pp, Quality PB, ISBN 1-58023-009-1 **$14.95**; HC, ISBN 1-879045-53-2 **$19.95**

"Who Is a Jew?" *Conversations, Not Conclusions* by Meryl Hyman
6 x 9, 272 pp, ISBN 1-58023-052-0 **$16.95**; HC, ISBN 1-879045-76-1 **$23.95**

Ecology/Spirituality

Torah of the Earth: *Exploring 4,000 Years of Ecology in Jewish Thought*
In 2 Volumes   Ed. by *Rabbi Arthur Waskow*

Major new resource offering us an invaluable key to understanding the intersection of ecology and Judaism. Leading scholars provide us with a guided tour of ecological thought from four major Jewish viewpoints.
Vol. 1: *Biblical Israel & Rabbinic Judaism,* 6 x 9, 272 pp, Quality PB, ISBN 1-58023-086-5 **$19.95**
Vol. 2: *Zionism & Eco-Judaism,* 6 x 9, 336 pp, Quality PB, ISBN 1-58023-087-3 **$19.95**

Broken Tablets: *Restoring the Ten Commandments and Ourselves*
Ed. by *Rabbi Rachel S. Mikva*; Intro. by *Rabbi Lawrence Kushner*;
Afterword by *Rabbi Arnold Jacob Wolf*   **AWARD WINNER!**

Twelve outstanding spiritual leaders each share profound and personal thoughts about these biblical commands and why they have such a special hold on us.
6 x 9, 192 pp, HC, ISBN 1-58023-066-0 **$21.95**

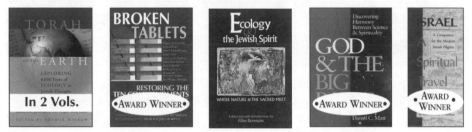

Ecology & the Jewish Spirit: *Where Nature & the Sacred Meet* Ed. and with Intros.
by Ellen Bernstein 6 x 9, 288 pp, Quality PB, ISBN 1-58023-082-2 **$16.95**;
HC, ISBN 1-879045-88-5 **$23.95**

God & the Big Bang
Discovering Harmony Between Science & Spirituality **AWARD WINNER!**
by Daniel C. Matt
6 x 9, 216 pp, Quality PB, ISBN 1-879045-89-3 **$16.95**

Israel—A Spiritual Travel Guide AWARD WINNER!
A Companion for the Modern Jewish Pilgrim
by Rabbi Lawrence A. Hoffman 4¾ x 10, 256 pp, Quality PB, ISBN 1-879045-56-7 **$18.95**

Godwrestling—Round 2: *Ancient Wisdom, Future Paths* **AWARD WINNER!**
by Rabbi Arthur Waskow
6 x 9, 352 pp, Quality PB, ISBN 1-879045-72-9 **$18.95**; HC, ISBN 1-879045-45-1 **$23.95**

The Year Mom Got Religion: *One Woman's Midlife Journey into Judaism*
by Lee Meyerhoff Hendler 6 x 9, 208 pp, Quality PB, ISBN 1-58023-070-9 **$15.95**

Israel: *An Echo of Eternity* by Abraham Joshua Heschel; New Intro. by
Dr. Susannah Heschel 5½ x 8, 272 pp, Quality PB, ISBN 1-879045-70-2 **$18.95**

The Earth Is the Lord's: *The Inner World of the Jew in Eastern Europe*
by Abraham Joshua Heschel 5½ x 8, 112 pp, Quality PB, ISBN 1-879045-42-7 **$13.95**

A Passion for Truth: *Despair and Hope in Hasidism* by Abraham Joshua Heschel
5½ x 8, 352 pp, Quality PB, ISBN 1-879045-41-9 **$18.95**

Your Word Is Fire: *The Hasidic Masters on Contemplative Prayer*
Ed. and Trans. with a New Introduction by Dr. Arthur Green and Dr. Barry W. Holtz
6 x 9, 160 pp, Quality PB, ISBN 1-879045-25-7 **$14.95**

Theology/Philosophy

A Heart of Many Rooms: *Celebrating the Many Voices within Judaism*
by *Dr. David Hartman*   AWARD WINNER!

Addresses the spiritual and theological questions that face all Jews and all people today. From the perspective of traditional Judaism, Hartman shows that commitment to both Jewish tradition and to pluralism can create understanding between people of different religious convictions. 6 x 9, 352 pp, HC, ISBN 1-58023-048-2 **$24.95**

A Living Covenant: *The Innovative Spirit in Traditional Judaism*
by *Dr. David Hartman*   AWARD WINNER!

Winner, National Jewish Book Award. Hartman reveals a Judaism grounded in covenant—a relational framework—informed by the metaphor of marital love rather than that of parent-child dependency. 6 x 9, 368 pp, Quality PB, ISBN 1-58023-011-3 **$18.95**

These Are the Words: *A Vocabulary of Jewish Spiritual Life*
by Arthur Green 6 x 9, 304 pp, Quality PB, ISBN 1-58023-107-1 **$18.95**

Evolving Halakhah: *A Progressive Approach to Traditional Jewish Law*
by Rabbi Dr. Moshe Zemer 6 x 9, 480 pp, HC, ISBN 1-58023-002-4 **$40.00**

The Death of Death: *Resurrection and Immortality in Jewish Thought* AWARD WINNER!
by Dr. Neil Gillman 6 x 9, 336 pp, Quality PB, ISBN 1-58023-081-4 **$18.95**;
HC, ISBN 1-879045-61-3 **$23.95**

Aspects of Rabbinic Theology by Solomon Schechter; New Intro. by Dr. Neil Gillman
6 x 9, 448 pp, Quality PB, ISBN 1-879045-24-9 **$19.95**

The Last Trial: *On the Legends and Lore of the Command to Abraham to Offer Isaac as a Sacrifice* by Shalom Spiegel; New Intro. by Judah Goldin
6 x 9, 208 pp, Quality PB, ISBN 1-879045-29-X **$17.95**

Judaism and Modern Man: *An Interpretation of Jewish Religion* by Will Herberg;
New Intro. by Dr. Neil Gillman 5½ x 8½, 336 pp, Quality PB, ISBN 1-879045-87-7 **$18.95**

Seeking the Path to Life AWARD WINNER!
Theological Meditations on God and the Nature of People, Love, Life and Death
by Rabbi Ira F. Stone
6 x 9, 160 pp, Quality PB, ISBN 1-879045-47-8 **$14.95**; HC, ISBN 1-879045-17-6 **$19.95**

The Spirit of Renewal: *Finding Faith after the Holocaust* AWARD WINNER!
by Rabbi Edward Feld
6 x 9, 224 pp, Quality PB, ISBN 1-879045-40-0 **$16.95**

Tormented Master: *The Life and Spiritual Quest of Rabbi Nahman of Bratslav*
by Dr. Arthur Green
6 x 9, 416 pp, Quality PB, ISBN 1-879045-11-7 **$18.95**

AVAILABLE FROM BETTER BOOKSTORES.
TRY YOUR BOOKSTORE FIRST.

The Way Into... Series

A major 14-volume series to be completed over the next several years, *The Way Into...* provides an accessible and usable "guided tour" of the Jewish faith, its people, its history and beliefs—in total, an introduction to Judaism for adults that will enable them to understand and interact with sacred texts. Each volume is written by a major modern scholar and teacher, and is organized around an important concept of Judaism.

The Way Into... will enable all readers to achieve a real sense of Jewish cultural literacy through guided study. Forthcoming volumes include:

The Way Into Torah

by *Dr. Norman J. Cohen*

What is "Torah"? What are the different approaches to studying Torah? What are the different levels of understanding Torah? For whom is the study intended? Explores the origins and development of Torah, why it should be studied and how to do it.
6 x 9, 176 pp, HC, ISBN 1-58023-028-8 **$21.95**

The Way Into Jewish Prayer

by *Dr. Lawrence A. Hoffman*

Opens the door to 3,000 years of the Jewish way to God by making available all you need to feel at home in Jewish worship. Provides basic definitions of the terms you need to know as well as thoughtful analysis of the depth that lies beneath Jewish prayer.
6 x 9, 224 pp, HC, ISBN 1-58023-027-X **$21.95**

The Way Into Jewish Mystical Tradition

by *Rabbi Lawrence Kushner*

Explains the principles of Jewish mystical thinking, their religious and spiritual significance, and how they relate to our lives. A book that allows us to experience and understand the Jewish mystical approach to our place in the world.
6 x 9, 176 pp, HC, ISBN 1-58023-029-6 **$21.95**

The Way Into Encountering God in Judaism

by *Dr. Neil Gillman*

Explains how Jews have encountered God throughout history—and today—by exploring the many metaphors for God in Jewish tradition. Explores the Jewish tradition's passionate but also conflicting ways of relating to God as Creator, relational partner, and a force in history and nature.
6 x 9, 240 pp, HC, ISBN 1-58023-025-3 **$21.95**

Or phone, fax, mail or e-mail to: JEWISH LIGHTS Publishing
Sunset Farm Offices, Route 4 • P.O. Box 237 • Woodstock, Vermont 05091
Tel: (802) 457-4000 • Fax: (802) 457-4004 • www.jewishlights.com
Credit card orders: (800) 962-4544 (9AM–5PM ET Monday–Friday)
Generous discounts on quantity orders. SATISFACTION GUARANTEED. Prices subject to change.